Marriages of

RUTHERFORD COUNTY,

NORTH CAROLINA

1779-1868

Marriages of

RUTHERFORD COUNTY,

NORTH CAROLINA

1779-1868

Compiled by

BRENT H. HOLCOMB

CLEARFIELD

Originally published by
Genealogical Publishing Co., Inc.
Baltimore, Maryland
1986

Reprinted for Clearfield Company by
Genealogical Publishing Company
Baltimore Maryland
2005, 2010

Library of Congress Catalogue Card Number 85-81711
ISBN 978-0-8063-1144-9

Made in the United States of America

INTRODUCTION

THIS VOLUME contains abstracts of all extant marriage bonds issued in Rutherford County, North Carolina, from 1779 to 1868, when marriage bonds were discontinued. The abstracts were made from a microfilm copy of the bonds and are arranged throughout in alphabetical order by the name of the groom, each entry further providing the name of the bride, the date of the bond, and the names of the bondsmen. To facilitate research, brides and bondsmen are also listed in the index. However, a few of the bonds and licenses were found in recent years still in the Rutherford County Court House, Rutherfordton, North Carolina, where they remain. The designation (C. H.) after an entry indicates that the bond or license is one remaining in the courthouse, in the office of Register of Deeds.

The reader should keep in mind that the name of the groom is spelled as the name was signed, or in the case of a person who could not write, the way it was signed for him. The name of the bride appears as it was spelled by the clerk or the person making out the bond. Since the bride did not sign, the spellings may vary widely from the way the name would properly be spelled.

Marriage bonds are the only public records of marriage prior to 1851. Although the marriage bond law was enacted in 1741 and remained in force until 1868, the clerk of the county court was required only from 1851 to keep a register of all marriages performed by license (issued with the bond). In many cases from the year 1851 (and in a few before that year), the license with return by the officiant is extant and is abstracted as well. This return usually gives the exact date of the marriage, and occasionally the place of marriage, as well as the name of the officiant.

The researcher should bear in mind that bonds alone are not proof that a marriage took place, only that a marriage was intended. Also, not everyone who married in Rutherford County between 1779 and 1868 is identified in this work, for some marriages were performed after publication of banns and no bond, license, or other public record of marriage was required.

BRENT HOWARD HOLCOMB, C. G.
Columbia, South Carolina

Abram, John & Lydia Parish, 14 Aug 1810; Andrew Miller, bm.

Abram, W. P. & Mary Miller, 1 Aug 1842.

Abrams, Dennis M. & Eliza A. Greenway, 27 Feb 1852; R. S. Abrams, bm; m 27 Feb 1852 by Luke Waldrop, J. P.

Adair, James Henderson & Armentey Koon, 11 Oct 1837; James Hensley, bm.

Adams, Aza & Mary Runyan, 18 Aug 1833; Jeremiah Runyan.

Adams, Francis & Elasebeth Hamrick, 23 Sept 1802; Abednego Adams, bm.

Adams, James W. & Sarah L. Keeter, 3 Feb 1855; Osborne Stacy, bm.

Adams, M. L. N. & Sarah A. L. Bennick, 12 May 1853; George E. M. Bennick, bm; m 12 May 1853 by H. Harrill, J. P.

Adams, Samuel & Mrs. Elizabeth Liles, 24 Dec 1805; Birgis Liles, Nathan Earls, bm.

Adare, William & Anney Tyler, 12 Sept 1813; John Whitaker, bm.

Adkins, Thomas & Jane Hawkins, 17 Jan 1831; George C. Camp, bm.

Agle, David & Sarah A. McEntire, 7 May 1856; C. Burnett, bm; m 8 May 1856 by Paul F. Kistler, Methodist Preacher.

Albright, Elias & Margaret Finley, 5 Jan 1860; H. M. Miller, bm; m 5 Jan 1860 by H. M. Miller.

Albright, William & Frances Cruise, 5 Dec 1840; J. Hampton, Jr., bm.

Aldrig, Frances & Margaret Cole, 19 Oct 1789; David Cole, bm.

Alen, Danl. & Mary Smart, 3 Nov 1786; Jno. Lewis, bm.

Alexander, Abram & Mary Been, 4 June 1803; Marten Beem, bm.

Alexander, Adam & M. A. Logan, 7 May 1850; J. C. Wilson, bm.

Alexander E. A. & Manerva M. Goode, 11 Dec 1856; Jos H. Harris, bm; m 11 Dec 1856 by O. C. Green, J. P.

Alexander, Gabriel & Caroline Campbell, 14 July 1834; Martin Quin, bm.

Alexander, Gabriel & Sarah Hambright, 9 Dec 1840.

Alexander, Isaac & Susaah McIntire (no date); John Alexander, Alaxander McIntire, bm.

Alexander, Lawson & Viney Mayhue, 24 Sept 1826; Wm. Mayhute, bm.

Alexander, M. R. & Charlotte Hill, 17 Jan 1855; A. A. Lynch, bm; m 17 Jan 1855 by A. Hamby, L. E. of M. E. Church South.

Alexander, William & Mary Ann Gosea, 22 Oct 1846; David Beam, bm.

Alford, Francis Asbury H. (or Halford, Francis Asbury) & E. Clementine, 2 Nov 1842; John N. Scoggin, bm.

Alford, John & Dinsey Lunsford, 12 Jan 1826; Jones Bradley, bm.

Alford, Killes & Elizabeth Jones, 14 Nov 1795; John Alford, bm.

Alford, Noah & Martha Hunter, 4 Aug 1854; Jas. Earley, bm; m 10 Aug 1854 by Bailey Bruce, M. G.

Alford, Thomas H. & Sally Hill, 27 Jan 1824; Elijah Dalton, bm.

Allan, A. G. & Nancy Bradley, 19 Jul 1847; Thornton Bradley, bm.

Allan, Carter & Jincy Groves, 5 Mar 1820; William Allan, bm.

Allan, John & M. Bauldrige, 14 Jan 1807; John Allan Sr., bm.

Allan, Paschal & Mary Koone, _____ 18__; Noah Koone, bm; m 15 Jan 1861 by M. Wilkerson, J. P.

Allen -- see also Alen, Allin.

Allen, Anderson G. & Lucy Newman, 19 Sept 1839; James L. Wilkins, bm.

Allen, Daniel C. & Mira Logan, 7 Apr 1855; A. L. Logan, m 19 Apr 1855 by H. W. Patterson.

Allen, David & Polley Johnston, 1 Apr 1817; J. H. Alley, bm.

Allen, David & Ricksy Early, 16 Sept 1866; Thomas Weaver, bm.

Allen, Drury D. & Rebecca Allen, 21 Jul 1839; John Logan, bm.

Allen, E. P. & S. J. Flack, 22 Oct 1858; Jos B. Carrier, bm; m 11 Nov 1858 by James M. Spratt.

Allen, J. P. & Mary E. Watson, 9 Mar 1862; Martin Walker, bm; m 12 Mar 1862 by Jas. M. Spratt.

Allen, James & Miss ___ Braden, 12 Apr 1810; John W. Allen, bm.

Allen, James & Phebe Johnston, 1 Nov 1810, Elisha Wheekes, bm.

Allen, James & Nancy Blankinship, 19 Jan 1821; John Blankinship, bm.

Allen, James & Jane Melton, 23 Jan 1860; Jere Webb, bm; m 26 Jan 1860 by D. Ponnel.

Allen, James B. & Nancy Mills, 9. Jul 1850; Wm. Rucker, bm.

Allen, James T. & Leathy Wilkins, 10 Nov 1836; Thomas Wilkins, bm.

Allen, James W. & Jane Camp, 19 Jan 1861; J. H. Bradly, bm; m 20 Jan 1861 by J. L. Taylor, J. P.

Allen, Joel R. & Katharine Gray, 4 Feb 1834; John W. Gray, bm.

RUTHERFORD COUNTY MARRIAGES 1779-1868

Allen, John & Sarah Ann Yelton, 22 Oct 1833; Jonathan Walker, bm.

Allen, Joseph & Polly McGaughy, __ Nov 1806; Richard Fortune, bm.

Allen, Larkin & Drusilla Sprulin, 8 Aug 1825; Isaac Spurlin, bm.

Allen, Lemuel & Barbary Edwards, 10 Nov 1804; William Allen, bm.

Allen, Robt. J. & Mary J. Carson, 22 Oct 1845; Robert W. Clark, bm.

Allen, W. L. & Lucy E. Bradley, 24 Aug 1857; F. D. Wood, bm; m 25 Aug 1857 by T. B. Justice.

Allen, William & Nancy Baldridge, 10 Nov 1804; Leml. Allen, bm.

Allen, William & Nancy Covel, 29 Dec 1819; Stephen Camp, bm.

Alley, Frederick F. & Susanna Hampton, 21 Jan 1815; J. H. Alley, bm.

Alley, John & Nancy Clemmons, 14 Mar 1835; Jonathan Hampton, Jr., bm.

Alley, John H. & Urcilla Hampton, 21 Nov 1810.

Alley, M. N. B. J. H. & Nancy E. Camp, 23 Mar 1842; Jas. L. Taylor, bm.

Allin, James & Matthew Dickey, 29 Sept 1816; N. Hampton, bm.

Ally, John Jr. & Sarrah Guffy, 11 Mar 1849; Cornelius Clements, bm.

Alphard, John & Sally Dolton, 27 Oct 1789; Thomas Morriss, bm.

Anderson, Robert & Jean Walters, 8 June 1782; William Maxwell, bm.

Anderson, Robert & Cathrine Culbreath, 23 Dec 1822; Samuel Anderson, bm.

Anderson, Wm. & Mary F. Bowan, 4 Sept 1846; C. Burnett, bm.

Anderson, Wm H. & Ella E. Brockman, 22 Feb 1866; J. W. Harris, bm; m 22 Feb 1866 by N. Shotwell, Pastor of Presbn. Church of Rutherford, Ruthd. Co., N. C.

Andrews, Benjamin & Polly Robinson, 30 Oct 1804; Hugh Watson, bm.

Andrews, Benjamin & Elizabeth Watson, 5 Jun 1821; Robert Huggins, bm.

Andrews, Benjamin W. & Martha Fortune, 27 Apr 1850; J. M. Andrews, bm.

Andrews, J. M. & Lucy M. Melton, 1 Dec 1857; Jos. Reid, bm; m ___ by T. E. Davis.

Andrews, James & Nancy Swafford, _____ ; Thos. White, Joseph W. Renolds, bm.

Andrews, John m. & Nancey E. Moss, 9 Aug 1840; A. L. Patten, bm; m 10 ___ Aug 1840 by Hugh Watson, J. P.

Andrews, Samuel & Mira M. Groves, 6 Jan 1835; Andrew B. Long, bm.

Angel, John & Patsy Harris, 3 Jan 1811; Absalom Coxsey, bm.

Anthony, William & Hannah Clark, 8 Apr 1785; William Hall, bm.

Arawood, John H. & Trisa Boheelar, m 12 Sept 1858 by E. M. Carpenter.

- 3 -

Arledge, G. Bery & Rebeca Waldrop, 11 Feb 1855; T. D. Waldrop, bm; m 11 Feb 1855 by J. M. Hamilton, J. P.

Arledge, Samuel & Polley Russell, 1 Sept 1806; Isaac Arledg, bm.

Armstrong, Martin & Catharine Armstrong, 12 Sept 1843; John Mellan, bm.

Armstrong, Thomas H. & Anna Covington, 13 Jul 1826; Hazzael Hicks, bm.

Arnett, Thomas & Betsey Morrow, 18 Jan 1814; Charles Richardson, bm.

Arnold, Robert & Temperance Wadkins, 6 Feb 1841; Roas Ray, bm.

Arowood, Chism & Elisa Perkins, 1 Jun 1843; J. E. Perkins, bm.

Arrowood, James Sr. & Rachel Davis, 1 Apr 1802; James Arrowood, bm.

Arrowood, John H. & Trissa Bohelar, 12 Sept 1858; James McMahan, bm.

Arther, Robert D. & Pheby Padgett, 6 Nov 1845; G. B. Padgett, bm.

Arthur, William & Providence Montague, 11 Jan 1820; George Jones, bm.

Arwood, Benson & Malinda Harvel, 3 Jun 1844; Cheson Erawood, bm.

Ashby, James & Betsey Whitesides, 21 Feb 1818; Isaac Hill, bm.

Askew, Elisha & Jane F. Gray, 8 Feb 1827.

Aspey, Samuel & Druciller Webb, 29 Jul 1819; Jacob Magnes, bm.

Atkin, W. B. & N. E. Shemwell, 1 Feb 1866; T. J. Downey, bm.

Autrey, Hiram & Polly Fox, 17 Jun 1806; Absalom Autrey, bm.

Baber, Achilles & Martha Logan, 3 Feb 1834; George W. Baber, bm.

Baber, B. W. & Leanan Price, 27 May 1843; B. W. Andrews, bm.

Baber, Barnabas & Matilda Baber, 18 Jul 1825; George Baber, bm.

Baber, Barnabas A. & Nancy Miller, 15 Feb 1842; W. D. Harris, bm.

Baber, James & Sarah Hudlow, 12 Nov 1845; Edward Toms, bm.

Baber, James Jr. & Catharine B. Bell, 29 Oct 1817; John Martin, bm.

Baber, John & Nancy Daniel, 1 May 1820; Issac Craton, bm.

Baber, John T. & Catharine Daniel, 23 Apr 1849; J. A. Carpenter, bm.

Baber, Jos H. & Eliz. Morrow, 7 Aug 1857; J. H. Blanton, bm.

Baber, Robert & Polly Daniel, 27 Sept 1816.

Baber, S. D. & Harriet Earley, 10 Oct 1864; J. A. Hays, bm; m 16 Oct 1864 by T. P. Sorrels, J. P.

Baber, William & Polly Burge, 1 Oct 1808; Kinchin Carpenter, bm.

Baber, William A. & Rachel Goode, 14 Jan 1835; Edward Toms, bm.

Baber, Wm. O. & Nancy L. Freeman, 22 Oct 1866; W. A. Baber, bm; m 23 Oct 1866 by G. W. Rollins.

Bagwell, Drury & Nancy Goodbread, 20 May 1809; Benjm. Hyde, bm.

Bagwell, John H. & Susannah McFaddin, 5 Sept 182-; Arthur Erwin, bm.

Bagwell, S. H. & Tempy Malinda Ledbetter, 14 Nov 1859; H. Padgett, bm; m 20 Nov 1859 by W. H. Logan, Baptist Minister.

Bagwell, William O. & Polly Ballard, 25 Jun 1836; John H. Wilkins, bm.

Bailey, Agustus & Elizeh. Cloud, 27 Oct 1808; Andrew Hamilton, bm.

Bailey, Brien & Rachal Lee, dau Robert Lee, 17 Oct 1854; L. D. Haynes, bm.

Bailey, Hiram & Malinda Dye, 2 Feb 1839; William Dicas Jr., bm.

Bailey, John & Ruth Wray, 13 Mar 1827; Samuel Baily, bm.

Bailey, John & Arminty Harper, 18 Aug 1857; John Burgess, bm; m 19 Aug 1857 by Wm. Bostick, J. P.

Bailey, Samuel S. & Julyann Thompson, 5 Jan 1836; John Bailey, bm.

Bails, Eldrige & Sarah Burnitt, 14 Nov 1791; Claybon Burnett, bm.

Baily, Johnathan & Mary Wilson, 28 Nov 1829; S. C. Gold, bm.

Baily, Levi & Eliza McClain, 25 Dec 1847; Isaac V. Davis, bm.

Bainard, John & Jane Nanney, 18 Jun 1860; W. H. Miller, bm; m 18 Jun 1860 by T. J. Hawkins, J. P.

Bainard, Martin & Polly Griffin, 7 May 1829; Lemman Bradley, bm.

Baits, James & Elisabeth Tubbs, 19 Jul 1782; William Tomson, bm.

Baity, Thomas M. & Mary Adalade Jones, 27 Dec 1853; J. B. Smawley, bm; m 27 Dec 1853 by Williamson Fortune, J. P.

Baldridge, Alexander & Jane McMurry, 8 Nov 1819; William Allen, bm.

Baldridge, John & Nancy Tylor, 19 Sept 1810.

Baldridge, John Sr. & Sarah Long, 6 Jan 1829; John Baldridge Jr., bm.

Baldridge, Joseph & Elizabeth Janes, 15 Nov 1819; William Baldridge, bm.

Baldridge, Samuel & Susannah Logan, 26 Jan 1831; John Baldridge, bm.

Bales, David & Polly Dunham, 15 Sept 1794; Richard Yielding, bm.

Baley, Amous & Margret Harmon, 17 Aug 1865; Jonathan Baly, bm.

Ballard, Perry & Nancy A. Bagwell, 26 May 1856; Franklin Taylor, bm.

Ballard, Perry & Mary Flyn, 10 Nov 1860; S. H. Bagwell, bm; m 10 Nov 1860 by Wm. Devenport, J. P.

Ballard, Thomas & Elisebeth Dalton, 26 May 1801; John Dalton, bm.

Bandy, Absalom & Sally Walker, 6 Mar 1832; Thomas Walker, bm.

Bandy, William & Dicy Green, 24 Oct 1836; Cornelius Green, bm.

Bankston, Andrew & _____, 3 Nov 1819; John Harrill, A. Bankston, bm.

Banther, Sharod & Mary Queen, 29 Sept 1855; John Hall, bm; m 1 Oct 1856 by M. Wilkerson, J. P.

Barber, Robert & Sarah Shroud, 25 Feb 1840; Benja. D. Durham, bm.

Barclay, A. & Katharin Nelson, 20 Jan 1842; Joa. Hallert, bm.

Barclay, James & Mary Corruth, 17 Jun 1789; Alexander Carruth, bm.

Barfield, James & Elizabeth Carpenter, 30 Mar 1837; John Logan Jr., bm.

Barnard, Wm. T. & Eveline Lynch, 4 Apr 1850; William Walker, bm.

Barnes, Charles A. & Sarah Starkes, 30 Jun 1834; Dr. Jno. McFarland, bm.

Barnett, Levi W. & Mary Jinkins, 27 Aug 1858; Wm. Barnett, bm; m 27 Aug 1858 by J. H. Carpenter, J. P.

Barr, Silas & Sarah Huddlestone, 17 Oct 1803; William Watson, bm.

Barr, William & Elizabeth Chidlers, 12 Oct 1843; Ambrose Thompson, bm.

Barrott, John & Mary Goldman, 19 Aug 1779; Joseph Underwood, John Walker, bm.

Bartlet, John & Rebecca Sorrells, 12 Nov 1832; Thomas Green, bm.

Barlett, Orris & Sarah E. Michal, 1 Nov 1848; G. W. Baxter, bm.

Barton, Elijah Jr. & Nancy Jones, 11 Mar 1824; Eliga Barton Sr., Jones Bradley, bm.

Bates, E. M. & Cynthia Hunter, 20 Nov 1844.

Bates, Humphrey & Rachael Mitchall, 29 Sept 1788; Gavin Erwin, bm.

Bates, John & Elizabeth Williams, 12 Nov 1785; George Mitchy, bm.

Bates, Richard & Jane Mitchel, 29 Aug 1795; Humphrey Bates, bm.

Bates, William & Frances T. Stokes, 3 Jan 1837; William Stokes, bm.

Battle, William & Polly Moore, 5 Apr 1796; John Moore, William Kannon, bm.

Baxter, Andru & Sarah Horton, 15 Feb 1818; John Short, bm.

Baxter, Elisha & Harriet Patton, 16 Aug 1849; G. W. Baxter, bm.

Baxter, John & Mahala H. Hines, 17 Oct 1836; James Young Jr., bm.

Baxter, John Jr. & Henryetta White, 1 Aug 1839; John Gilkey, bm.

Baxter Joseph & Mrs. Mary Baber, 30 Dec 1812; James Baxter, bm.

Baxter, Joseph & sarah Justice, 25 Nov 1847; S. Eaves, bm.

Baxter, Taylor A. & Charity E. Patten, 29 Dec 1851; M. O. Dickerson, bm.

Baxter, Thos. & Aroazena Hayns, 31 Oct 1842; Joseph Baxter, bm.

Baxter, Thos. & Jane Phillips, 12 Jan 1846; B. H. Padgett, bm.

Baxter, Wm. & Margaret M. Patton, 3 Apr 1843; H. A. Miller, bm.

Baxter, William Jr. & Nancy Suttle, 16 Oct 1821; Thomas Baxter, bm.

Baxter, William Jr. & Martha Young, 18 Nov 1833; James Young, bm.

Bayle, John & Betsay Simmons, 3 Feb 1814; Squire Simmons, bm.

Bayley, Benjamin B. & Lucinday Brady, 9 Dec 1846; Wm. Green, bm.

Beam, Abel C. & Lucy O. Camp, 3 Apr 1835; John G. Estridge, bm.

Beam, David & Rebeckah Harrill, 2 Sept 1822; Samuel Harrill Jr., bm.

Beam, Marten & Elizabeth Alexander, 18 Oct 1803; John Mc___, bm.

Beam, William C. L. & Priscilla Grose, 15 Mar 1859; W. M. Culbreath, bm.

Bear, Peeler & Barbra Horse, ____ 1806; William Newton, Christian Bear, bm.

Beard, John R. & Selena Burnett, 17 May 1819; Clay Burnett, bm.

Beatey, Francis & Rebakah McBrayer, 2 Dec 1807; Wallace Beatey, bm.

Beaver, James & Elizabeth Bolton, 8 Jan 1832; John Bolton, bm.

Beaver, John & Salley Seffus, 17 Jan 1810; Benj. Willis, David Willis, bm.

Bechtler, Charles & Katharine Dater, 10 Jan 1839; Daniel Michal, bm.

Bedford, James & Anna Pool, 26 Sept 1805; Jesse Richardson, bm.

Bedford, James & Elizabeth Byars, 10 Dec 1833; James Byars, bm.

Bedford, Janes M. & Catharine Mooney, 8 Apr 1833; Jno. McFarland, bm.

Bedford, John H. & Sarah Waters, 8 Dec 1824; Jesse Sullins, bm.

Bedford, John H. & Elizabeth Wallis, 29 Oct 1835; F. W. Lee, bm.

Bedford, Jonas & Margaret Sweezy, 14 Mar 1837; John Crowder, bm.

Bedford, Joseph & ____ Taylor, 24 Nov 1820; George Towry, bm.

Bedford, Joseph & Nancy Elliott, 28 Aug 1829; Abraham Byar, bm.

Bedford, Peter R. & Hazy Sweezy, 12 Feb 1839; Paton Horton, bm.

Bedford, Seth & Mary Francis, 10 Oct 1796; William Hunt, bm.

Bedford, Seth B. & Martha L. Spurlin, 22 Sept 1862; B. B. Byers, bm.

Been, John & Polly Tyler, 26 Feb 1821; Stephen Jones, bm.

Belk, William & Martha Moore, 15 Nov 1839; Robert McClain, bm.

Bell, Andrew & Nancy Horton, 29 Dec 1812; Wm. Edgerton, bm.

Bell, Bynum W. & Mary King, 8 Dec 1823; Thoe F. Birchett, bm.

Bell, Hartwell & Betsey Fortune, 25 Jul 1818; Lindsey Fortune, bm.

Bell, James & Nancy Denton, 17 Oct 1822; Jesse Hogus, bm.

Bell, L. W. & N. E. Nanny, 21 Dec 1866; Martin Benard, bm.

Bennard, Charles & Susan Conner, 4 Apr 1857; Geo W. Conner, bm; m 7 Apr 1857 by M. Wilkerson.

Bennet, John N. & Catharine Baxter, 24 Jun 1850; Joseph Baxter, bm.

Bennett, Hugh & Nancy C. Baxton, 17 Jul 1860; Joseph Baxter, bm.

Bennick, George E. M. & C. E. Shitle, 19 Jul 1854; A. B. Long, bm; m 13 (sic) Jul 1854 by John C. Carson, M. G.

Bennick, George J. & Nancey A. Pentuff, 20 Aug 1860; H. L. Stephens, bm; m 20 Aug 1860 by E. M. Carpenter, J. P.

Bennick, Henry J. & Elmina Pintuff, __ Jan 1867; H. Padgett, bm.

Benson, Christopher & Mary Hughlen, 23 Sept 1779; Alexander McFadin, bm.

Benson, Christopher & Bathia George, 10 Aug 1784; John Miller, bm.

Bently, Edmond & Treecy Baker, 17 May 1783; Timo. Riggs, bm.

Berry, Simpson & Kissy Stinnit, 18 Jan 1807; Samuel Crawford, bm.

Bias, George & Patsy Doggett, 22 Feb 1850; Barney King, bm.

Bias, Thomas & Mary Kilbern, 15 Jun 1845; Michael McGuin, bm.

Bigerstaff, Aron Jr. & Margaret Gold, 25 Oct 1830; Thomas Walker, bm.

Bigerstaff, Samuel P. & Nancy Toney, 2 Nov 1842; Thos. Walker, bm.

Biggerstaf, Samuel & Sarah Eakins, 12 Feb ___; Aron Bigerstaf, bm.

Biggerstaff, A. W. & M. S. Early, 17 Feb 1866; Jefferson Toney, bm; m 22 Feb 1866 by G. W. Rollins.

Biggerstaff, Aaron & Jane Carter, 5 Jul 1800; Daniel McGaukey, bm.

Biggerstaff, Aaron Jr. & Milley Ann Baber, 16 Oct 1838; Isaiah Green, bm.

Biggerstaff, Benjamin & Jane Goforth, 28 Oct 1833; William C. Goforth, bm.

Biggerstaff, Benjamin & Mary Mooney, 16 Feb 1843; Joseph Biggerstaff, bm.

Biggerstaff, Benjamin & Louisa Vickers, 13 Jan 1854; M. O. Dickerson, bm.

Biggerstaff, Elijah & Marthy J. Baber, 14 Dec 1859; T. W. Hawkins, bm; m 20 Dec 1859 by John Freeman.

Biggerstaff, J. N. & Sousan Cowan, 21 Feb 1866; John W. Biggerstaff, bm; m 26 Feb 1866 by G. W. Rollins.

Biggerstaff, Joseph W. & Rebecca Lockadoo, 21 Feb 1849; Ransom P. Biggerstaff, bm.

Biggerstaff, Kincheon & Marilla Denton, 3 Jul 1824; James Bell, bm.

Biggerstaff, Noah & Letty Price, 14 Feb 1831; Thomas Walker, bm.

Bigham, Jacob & Jane Willis, 9 Sept 1839; Burrel Grigg, bm.

Bigham, James & Matilda Sutton, 28 Jun 1840; Wm. Herndon, bm.

Bigham, John & Dicy King, 13 Jan 1807; Robt. Goode, bm.

Bigum, William & Nancy Colbert, 3 Mar 1859; L. C. Pope, bm; m 3 Mar 1859 by W. A. Tanner, J. P.

Bilingham, John & Sefia Clak, 2 Dec 1794; Robert Orr, bm.

Bingham, Drury & Mary Dawson, 31 Jan 1837; Joseph C. Dawson, bm.

Birchett, Thoe F. & Ann Elizabeth Miller, 16 Nov 1836; W. H. Miller, bm.

Bird, Charles & Margarett Cheatwood, 2 Jan 1837; John H. Carpenter, bm.

Bird, Jno. & Nancy Mills, 8 Nov 1797; John McKinney Jr., bm.

Bird, William & Nancey Canipe, 13 Dec 1857; Jo. Mooney, bm; m 13 Dec 1857 by B. E. Rollins, M. G.

Bird, Wilson R. & Nancy B. Teal, 23 Apr 1833; Charles Bird, bm.

Bivings, James D. & Mary M. Morris, 3 Nov 1841; John Baxter Jr., bm.

Blacburn, James & Rosannar Scrugs, 8 Aug 1802; Wm. Blanton, bm.

Black, Hugh & Margart Smart, 7 Nov 1799; William Flack, bm.

Black, Jas. H. & Sarah A. Sims, 4 Nov 1854; Elijah Melton, bm; m 15 Nov 1854 by B. E. Rollins, M. G.

Black, James M. & Elizabeth Daniel, 21 Dec 1829; Joseph Walker, bm.

Black, John & Polly Harris, 4 Feb 1795; Alexander Porter, bm.

Black, John R. & Isabella C. Carson, 19 May 1847; William Carson, bm.

Black, Joseph M. & Sarah Miller, __ Sept 1805; Joseph B. Miller, bm.

Black, Moses & Nancy Willis, 25 Sept 1838; Jesse R. Black, bm.

Black, William & Katharine Tailor, 27 May 1792; Thomas Heslep, bm.

Black, William & Sindney Olliver, 14 Dec 1819; Samuel Willis, bm.

Black, William S. & Lydia Pope, 9 Aug 1833; William P. Carson, bm; m 9 Aug 1833 by Hugh Watson, J. P.

Black, Wm W. & Rachel Sims, 6 Dec 1853; Joseph McK. Baldridge, bm; m 7 Dec 1853 by Williamson Fortune, J. P.

Blackburn, Samuel & Marget Patterson, 21 Dec 1797; Robert Patterson, bm.

Blackwell, J. W. & Mary Williams, 26 Feb 1854; Johnson S. King, bm; m 26 Jan 1854 by J. W. McBrayer.

Blackwell, James & Polly Blackwell, 30 Nov 1819; M. Hawkins, Thos. ____, bm.

Blackwell, James & Sealah Whirly, 3 May 1821; Thomas Worly, bm.

Blackwell, James & Polly Scott, 7 Apr 1826; Moses Scott, bm.

Blackwell, Joel & Demarias Musick, 17 Nov 1819; Thomas Worley, bm.

Blackwell, Jonathan & Susanna Littlejohn, 15 Nov 1831; Francis A. Littlejohn, bm.

Blackwell, Joseph & Adaline Lyles, 28 Feb 1842; Thomas Liles, bm.

Blackwood, Thomas & Mary J. Walker, 8 Apr 1850; Wiley S. Walker, bm.

Blalock, John & Margaret Neal, 26 Nov 1832; Philip Fulks, bm.

Blalock, Joseph B. & Sarah L. Cochran, 21 Jan 1851; Joseph Cochrun, bm.

Blalock, Nelson G. & P. A. Durham, 31 Jul 1858; S. C. Vance, bm; m 1 Aug 1858 by S. M. Collis, M. G.

Bland, Jacob C. & Malicy Rollins, 24 Jul 1848; Miles Padgett, bm.

Bland, William & Vienah Padgett, 15 Apr 1847; Jonathan Gillespie, bm.

Blankcenship, Archibald & Patsey Keeter, 31 Mar 1830; Caleb A. Moore, bm.

Blankenship, Barhanabus & Ruth Coone, 30 Aug 1832; Thomas Green, bm.

Blankenship, Drury & Martha Adair, 27 Nov 1866; M. L. Blankenship, bm; m 29 Nov 1866 by T. P. Sorrels, J. P.

Blankenship, Elijah & Naley Proctor, 11 Dec 1823; Ruben Proctor, bm.

Blankenship, Isham & Delilah Earley, 31 Dec 1827; George Mooney, bm.

Blankenship, John & Rebecah Houge, 15 Jan 1813; John Moore, bm.

Blankenship, Joseph & Susan R. Norrel, 21 Jul 1859; A. Hunt, bm; m 21 Jul 1859 by B. E. Rollins, M. G.

Blankenship, Spencer & Meriah Scoggin, 2 Oct 1832; Alford Burton Dycus, bm.

Blankenship, William & Eliza Hunt, 8 Feb 1847; H. H. Hower, bm.

Blankinship, Archibold & Tabithy Nancy, 16 Dec 1846; Charles Hill, bm.

Blankinship, Elisha & Mary Roberson, 8 Aug 1831; Capt. William Long, bm.

Blankinship, Gillbert & Fanny Deane, 25 Jul 1832; John J. Williams, bm.

Blankinship, Hampton & Sarah Taylor, 10 May 1847; H. H. Hower, bm.

Blankinship, Hesekiah & Susannah Long, 8 Oct 1857; K. J. McCrow, bm; m 8 Oct 1857 by B. E. Rollins.

Blankinship, Isam & Polley Chambers, 27 Mar 1799; John Chambers, bm.

Blankinship, James & Patsy Marloe, 15 Jan 1820; William Hunter, bm.

Blankinship, James & Lucinda Hunt, 12 Jan 1854; Daniel T. Melton, bm; m 12 Jan 1854 by Williamson Fortune, J. P.

Blankinship, John & Nancy J. Long, 20 Dec 1819; Gloud F. Long, bm.

Blankinship, Micajah & Melley Marlow, 2 Aug 1813; W. Hunter, bm.

Blankinship, Stephen & Betsey Patterson, 22 Feb 1822; William Patterson, bm.

Blanton, A. J. & Jain Padgett, 16 Feb 1836; Thos J. Blanton, bm.

Blanton, Alfred B. & Mirrah G. Melton, 19 Nov 1840; James Randol, bm.

Blanton, Andrew & Elizabeth Jolley, 1 Mar 1838; James D. Butler, bm.

Blanton, Benjamin & Margaret Feagins, 21 Dec 1835; Joab Wilkie, bm.

Blanton, Daniel & Frances Wilkins, 15 Aug 1804; Charles Wilkins, bm.

Blanton, Daniel Jr. & Uninas Doss, 17 Dec 1835; George Blanton, Bryson Humphrey, bm.

Blanton, Edward & Lucinda Hughs, 19 Dec 1833; Sandford Hughs, bm.

Blanton, Franklin & Sarah Chitwood, 14 Jan 1860; Arthur Blanton, bm; m 17 Jan 1860 by G. W. Rollins.

Blanton, George & Priscilla Harrill, 17 Sept 1821; Samuel Harrill, James Blanton, bm.

Blanton, James & Nancy Edwards, _____ 1809; Abner Wesson, bm.

Blanton, James & Sarah Burns, 28 Jan 1845; S. F. Blanton, bm.

Blanton, James & Clarissa Bigham, 24 Jan 1835; Josiah Blanton, bm.

Blanton, John & Rachel Brooks, 21 Jan 1835; Larkin Bryan, bm.

Blanton, Joseph R. & Mary E. Dimsdale, 21 Apr 1851; Preston Lewis, bm; m 29 Apr 1851 by Bailey Bruce, M. G.

Blanton, Josiah & Elizabeth Davis, 19 Feb 1815; Jas. Sheaves, bm.

Blanton, Josiah & Mary Bridges, 18 Jan 1831; Royley Blanton, bm.

Blanton, Josiah & Lucy Westbrook, 12 Feb 1833; John Simmons, bm.

Blanton, K. C. & Roseanah Hamrick, 22 Jan 1866; John Harrill, bm; m 8 Feb 1866 by D. Ponnell.

Blanton, Melvin C. & Sousen Wilkie, 31 Mar 1866; E. Hamrick, bm.

Blanton, Obediah & Judy Wardin, 21 Dec 1823; Marvel Melton, bm.

Blanton, Pinckney & Catherin C. McMory, 7 Feb 1841; John McMory, bm.

Blanton, Ransom & Anna Painter, 16 Jan 1841; Riley Blanton, bm.

Blanton, Reuben & Mary Dunn, 21 Jan 1836; James Dunn, bm.

Blanton, Riley & Nancy Burns, 5 Apr 1838; James Harrill, bm.

Blanton, Royley & Dolley Mase, 25 Jan 1821; Stith Mayes, Jeremiah Blanton, bm.

Blanton, S. F. & Sarah McDaniel, 28 Jan 1845; Jas. Blanton, bm.

Blanton, Thomas J. & Elizabeth Johnston, 19 Nov 1838; A. J. Blanton, bm.

Blanton, William & Martha Clarey, 7 Jul 1855; George Blanton, Bryson Humphrey, bm.

Blanton, William C. & Eliza Wilkey, 29 Dec 1826; William Blanton Sr., bm.

Blanton, William J. & Denica L. Whiteker, 10 Aug 1839; Josiah Blanton, bm.

Blanton, William Jay & Cynthia E. Coward, 24 Jan 1844; James Blanton, bm.

Blasingame, William & Mary B. Prince, 1 Dec 1828; William Twitty, bm.

Boheler, Jacob & Polly Downey, 10 Feb 1834; Achilles Durham, bm.

Boheler, John T. & Margrett Tate, 20 Dec 1857; S. A. Webb, bm; m 20 Dec 1857 by J. H. Carpenter, J. P.

Bohelo, Jacob & Eliza Bolton, 3 Apr 1853; Henry Bradley, bm; m 3 Apr 1853 by J. H. Carpenter, J. P.

Bohelor, David & Terrissa Downey, 5 Nov 1841; A. Durham, bm.

Bolton, William & Drusy McEntire, 28 Aug 1821; Samuel McEntire, bm.

Bolton, Wm. S. & Rebecker Boheler, 16 Sept 1851; C. H. Haynes, bm; m 16 Sept 1852 by J. H. Carpenter, J. P.

Bomar, Elisha & Amarillis Earle, 7 Mar 1823; John Bomar, bm.

Boon, Thomas & Margaret Clements, 16 Mar 1840; Cornelius Clements, bm.

Bostick, Chesley & Susanah Webber, 23 Dec 1806; Reubin Bostick, bm.

Bostick, George T. & Margaret Goode, 8 Jan 1856; Francis Moore, bm; m 8 Jan 1856 by Wm. Harrill.

Bostick, John & Cynthia Harrell, 5 Dec 1827; Martin Beam, bm.

Bostick, McByer & Kathrine Long, 20 Dec 1865; S. Harrrill, bm; m 21 Dec 1865 by G. W. Rollins.

Bostick, Rubin & Marget Davidson, 12 Sept 1797; Richard Bostick, bm.

Bostick, Samuel & Jane Suttle, 15 Oct 1850.

Bowdon, Simon & Olivine M. Price, 24 May 1841; William Thompson, bm.

Bowen, Berry (or Odam, Berry) & Susannah Odum, 30 Jan 1841; Wm Cooper, bm.

Bowen, Greef & Polley Hamrick, 14 Jan 1831; Hosea Hraden, bm.

Bowen, Joseph & Mildred Twitty, 15 Nov 1821; Theodorick F. Birchett, bm.

Bowen, William & Caroline Christmas, 22 Jun 1836; Achilles Durham, bm.

Bowers, John A. & Mary M. Walker, 21 May 1857; Jonathan Waters, bm; m 21 May 1857 by J. N. Biggerstaff, J. P.

Bowlen, Jerrymah & Elisabeth Brooks, 23 Dec 1849; J. B. Jones, bm.

Bowman, Eli & Catharine McHan, 10 Nov 1828; William Richardson, bm.

Bowman, John & Mary L. Wilkin, 9 Jun 1856; Joab Wilkin, bm; m 12 Jun 1856 by John Koone, Clm.

Bowman, John R. & Olive Sorrels, 17 May 1855; Wm. W. Sorrels, bm; m 17 May 1855 by T. B. Justice, M. G.

Bowman, William & Mary E. Killpartrick, 28 Aug 1847; L. C. Richardson, bm.

Bowman, Wm. C. & Sallie N. Wilkie, 28 Apr 1866; C. Burnett, bm; m 6 May 1866 by T. B. Justice.

Boyd, Henry & Theresa Holland, 14 Nov 1850; Alston McMury, bm.

Boyd, Robert & Sary Roper, 18 Sept 1795; Jesse McGlamry, bm.

Boyd, Thomas & Elizabeth Anderson, 21 Oct 1791; David Roper, bm.

Boyd, Thomas & Elisabeth Roper, 23 Oct 1794; John Keyel, bm.

Boys, John C. & Mary Milligan, _____ ; John Alexander, James Wray, bm.

Brack, Robert F. & Catharine Suttle, 23 May 1857; Shoemake Allen, bm.

Bracket, Bengamin & Elizabeth Apton (or Upton), 1 Aug 1793; Robert Orr, Joseph Carpenter (signed Joseph Zimmerman), bm.

Bracket, Burrel & Rebecah Wood, 23 Feb 1792; William Quin, _____, bm.

Bracket, Thomas & Elizabeth Downs, 9 May 1824; Robert Hall, bm.

Brackett, Joseph A. & Elizabeth Martail, 2 Nov 1848; Jos. Taylor, bm.

Brackett, Jofres & Nancy Sursey, 23 Apr 1862; Jasock Miles, bm; m 23 Apr 1862 by Wm. Devenport, J. P.

Braddy, Alfred & Eliz. Lovelis, 22 Nov 1855; Jesse Rogers, bm; m 22 Nov 1855 by A. Harrill, J. P.

Braddy, Jos. & Sarah Robertson, 3 Feb 1848; Philip H. Grose, bm.

Bradley, Augustin & Linnay Gilliam, 9 Jun 1836; John Bradley, bm.

Bradley, Augustus & Marthean Green, 28 Dec 1854; L. Chefus Bias, bm; m 28 Dec 1854 by H. Culbreath.

Bradley, Calvin & Sarah Largent, 15 Sept 1852; L. L. Deck, bm; m 15 Sept 1852 by J. Gilkey, J. P.

Bradley, Drury & Jain Ledbetter, 26 Aug 1834; Norman Williams, bm.

Bradley, Edward & Nancy Flin, 29 Sept 1829; Isaac Ledbetter Jr., bm.

Bradley, G. W. & Nancy Bradley, 30 Mar 1845; George Bradley, bm.

Bradley, George W. & Sarah Bradley, 25 Dec 1840; Samuel Wilkins, bm.

Bradley, Holland & Patsy Grant, 20 Feb 1827; James More, bm.

Bradley, Hugh & Nancy Fouch, 28 Sept 1804; Peter Fargason, bm.

Bradley, Isaac & Sarah Coxey, 10 Jun 1814; Geo. Flack, bm.

Bradley, Isaac & Middy Ledbetter, 5 Jan 1828; James Holland Bradley, bm.

Bradley, Isaac M. Jr. & Belinda Vess, 30 Aug 1860; N. H. P. Whiteside, bm; m 30 Aug 1860 by James H. Whiteside, J. P.

Bradley, J. H. & Nancy C. Jordan, 5 Sept 1854; L. C. Byas, bm; m 5 Sept 1854 by Henry Culbreath, M. G.

Bradley, J. J. & Martha Harris, 23 Dec 1858; J. Shitle, bm; m 23 Dec 1858 by Wm. H. Logan, M. G.

Bradley, James & Elizabeth Banther, 18 Apr 1839; Alfred B. Callahan, bm.

Bradley, James M. & Amanda Bradley, 20 Aug 1863; W. Bradley, bm; m 20 Aug 1863 by J. W. Morgan, J. P.

Bradley, John & Sarah Reed, 4 Jun 1840; A. B. Callahan, bm.

Bradley, John M. & Malinda Humphreys, 17 Mar 1836; James Humphrys, bm.

Bradley, John N. & Mary McHann, 11 Feb 1851; Nathaniel Nodine, bm.

Bradley, Ledbetter & Jane Ledbetter, _____ ; John Elms, bm.

Bradley, Ledbetter & Mary(?) Allen, 8 Aug 1799; Edward Bradley, John Allen, bm.

Bradley, Milleton P. & Peggy Griffin, 27 Jun 1833; Coalman Bradley, bm.

Bradley, Richard & Minty Bradley, 9 Apr 1823; Philip Head, bm.

Bradley, Simmons & Winney Walker, 11 Jun 1822; John Bradley, bm.

Bradley, Terry & Cloy Elliot, 13 Apr 1810; Moses Whiteside, bm.

Bradley, Thomas & Elizabeth Williams, 6 Feb 1827; Jones Bradley, bm.

Bradley, Thornton & Angelina Aldridge, 10 Mar 1845; G. W. Bradley, bm.

Bradley, William & Cynthia Metcalfe, 11 Jan 1837; W. Barton Metcalf, bm.

Bradley, Wm. & Eve Banther, 1 Jul 1841; Georg J. Banther, bm.

Bradley, Williams & Mary Haynes, 20 Jan 1831; Harvy Carrier, bm.

Bradley, Willis & Elizabeth McKinney, 2 Dec 1826; James J. Hampton, bm.

Bradley, Wilson & Jane Bright, 21 Jan 1833; M. P. Bradley, bm.

Bradley, Wilson Jr. & Sarah Harris, 9 Aug 1860; J. J. Bradley, bm; m 9 Aug 1860 by J. W. Morgan, J. P.

Bradly, Anselm & Polly Hampton, 25 Oct 1797; Harris Reavis, bm.

Bradly, Isaac & Elizabeth Flinn, 26 Sept 1853; Jas H. Bradly, bm; m 10 Nov 1853 by J. W. Morgan, J. P.

Bradly, James & Elizabeth Burgess, 4 Apr 1858; James L. Cogan, bm; m 4 Apr 1858 by J. W. Morgan, J. P.

Bradly, John & Nancy Hampton, 10 Mar 1790; Benja Hampton, bm.

Bradly, John & Margarett McFadden, 19 Dec 1833; Wm. Bradley, bm.

Bradly, Walton & Sarah Goodbread, 12 Jan 1791; John Goodbread, bm.

Bradly, William A. & Elizabeth Arrowood, 8 Sept 1859; M. Wilkerson, bm; m 8 Sept 1859 by M. Wilkerson, J. P.

Bradly, Willis & Elizabeth Vaughn, 9 Sept 1791; Andw. Hampton, bm.

Brady, Benjamin & _____, _____ ; D. McBrayer, bm.

Brady, Jesse & Easter Tanner, 13 Sept 1816; Allen Rogers, bm.

Brandel, Aaron & Harriet Carbo, 17 Apr 1862; Wm. D. Hutchins, bm; m 17 Apr 1862 by Wm. G. Mode, J. P.

Breedlove, James & Nancey Simmons, 13 Nov 1800; Z. Sullins, bm.

Brian, J. M. & Sarah Mooney, 22 Jan 1848; T.; G. Henson, bm.

Bridgers, Samuel & Eliza Hambrick, _____ ; Drury Dobbins, Jonathan Dobbins, bm.

Bridges -- see also Bridgis, Briges, Brigis.

Bridges, A. W. & Susanah Write, 20 Dec 1847; Woody Burge, bm.

Bridges, Aaron & Elizabeth Smith, 24 Sept 1801; Aron Bridges, James Bridgis, bm.

Bridges, Aaron Jr. & Sarah Hamrick, 4 Oct 1804; Jas Hamrick, Aaron Bridges Sr., bm.

Bridges, Alexander D. & Hetty Davis, 19 Dec 1833; Terrel Horton, bm.

Bridges, Anderson & Nancy Moss, 16 Apr 1840; John Bordes, bm.

Bridges, Anderson & Nancy Bedford, 16 Jan 1853; S. Burel Byers, bm; m 16 Jan 1853 by Wm. Harrill.

Bridges, Berrymon & Sarah Mays, 2 Dec 1828; John Bridges, bm.

Bridges, Caleb & Nancy Young, 30 Jan 1827; Samuel Bridges, bm.

Bridges, David & Margaret Horton, 24 Aug 1859; J. J. Bridges, bm; m 25 Aug 1859 by J. M. Chitwood, J. P.

Bridges, Dial & Deademia Scrugs, 11 Apr 1834; Jesse Scruggs, bm.

Bridges, Drury & Sarah Weeks, 24 Feb 1841; Samuel Harrill, bm.

Bridges, Drury S. & Elizabeth Robertson, 31 ___ 1836; Richard Robertson, bm.

Bridges, Ephraim & Sally Dobbins, 25 Nov 1832; William Dobbins, bm.

Bridges, F. M. & M. C. McDaniel, 19 Feb 1866; D. D. McDaniel, bm; m 22 Feb 1866 by M. Ponnell, M. G.

Bridges, G. B. & Martha Bedford, 27 Jul 1854; John S. Bridges, bm; m 27 Jul 1854 by Wm. Harrill, J. P.

Bridges, Henderson H. & Lydia McDaniel, 15 Mar 1838; Aaron Bridges, bm.

Bridges, Isah & Jenny Bridges, 3 Sept 1867. (statement acknowledging their cohabitation since 25 Dec 1842 signed by J. W. Beam, J. P.)

Bridges, James & Elizebeth Adams, 21 Dec 1795; Wm. Blanton, bm.

Bridges, James & Biddy A. S. Johnston, 19 May 1842; Willis Johnson, bm.

Bridges, Jesse & Adaline, m by B. B. Byers, J. P., in the month of April 1864. (affidavit by B. B. Byers, 9 June 1866). (C. H.)

Bridges, John & Mary Morehaed, 18 Feb 1841; Samuel Harrill, bm.

Bridges, Lawson & Patsey Warren, 2 Feb 1826; Richard Bridges, bm.

Bridges, Minor & Martha Smart, 6 Sept 1832; Joseph Smart, bm.

Bridges, Moses & Peggy Bridges, 3 Aug 1809; Isaac Bridges, Aaron Bridges, bm.

Bridges, S. & Maryan Green, 15 Mar 1866; J. S. Lovelace, bm (C. H.); m 15 Mar 1866 by G. W. Rollins.

Bridges, Washington & Atemessa Hamrick, 31 Mar 1836; Caleb Bridges, bm.

Bridges, Wiley & Elizabeth Bedford, 22 Nov 1858; G. B. Bridges, bm.

Bridges, William & Peggy Haws, 7 Apr 1809; John Bridges, bm.

Bridges, William & Nancy Mays, 1 Dec 1827; Stephen Mayes, bm.

Bridges, William J. & Fanny Winn, 15 Mar 1845; John Wilson, bm.

Bridgis, Jesse & Betey Harrell, 17 Jan 1821; Jno. Harrill, Saml. Bridges, bm.

Bridgis, John & Fanney Jones, 24 Jun 1801; John Jones, Mosis Bridgis, bm.

Bridgis, John & Cynthia Jones, 30 Sept 1834; Edmund Jones, bm.

Bridgis, William Jr. & Mary McSwain, 10 Sept 1839; George McSwain, bm.

Briges, Wiley & Lavina Huckaby, 17 Jan 1849; William A. Bridges, bm.

Briggs, Jesse & Esther Miller, 7 Dec 1787; Gray Briggs, bm.

Bright, Aaron & Mary Grant, 21 Feb 1842; J. A. Grant, bm.

Bright, French & Jinney Stumon, 17 Oct 1825; William Hogan, bm.

Brigis, James & _____, 26 Nov 1800; Aron Brigis, bm.

Brindal, Henry & Sarah Bigerstaff, 26 Oct 1831; Noah Biggerstaff, bm.

Brisco, Wm. & Susan A. Camp, 8 Mar 1852; J. W. Morgan, bm.

Britain, Saml. & Sarah W. Harris, 27 Mar 1855; G. L. Harris, bm; m 27 Mar 1855 by Wm. Hicks, M. G.

Britt, John & Mary Henson, 28 Dec 1787; Philip Henson, bm.

Brock, Moses & Caroline Johnson, 12 Oct 1865; D. T. Searcy, bm; m 23 Oct 1865 by T. H. Whiteside, J. P.

Brooks, Benjamin & Margaret Smart, 24 Nov 1842; Elisha Howlett, bm.

Brooks, D. M. & Mrs. L. J. Walker, 17 Jan 1867; A. C. Wall, bm.

Brooks, David & Betsey Smart, 8 Feb 1808; William Brooks, bm.

Brooks, Isaac & Nancy Logan, 26 Oct 1815; Jos. Smart, bm.

Brooks, Jacob & Mrs. Elizabeth Goode, 4 Oct 1863; Joseph Harmon, bm; m 4 Oct 1863 by B. McMahan, J. P.

Brooks, James G. & Mary A. Johnson, 20 Feb 1845; Minor Bridges, bm.

Brooks, Joseph & Catharine Cristmas, 29 Jan 1833; Jesse Right, bm.

Brooks, Samuel & Rebecca McKinney, 16 Dec 1863; A. Harrill, bm; m 17 Dec 1863 by R. Depriest.

Brooks, Thomas R. & Rhody Green, 23 Nov 1837; Isaac Brooks, bm.

Brooks, Thomas R. & Lucinda Blanton, 27 Dec 1842; Minor Bridges, bm.

Brooks, William H. & Rachel Green, 14 Feb 1838; Drury D. Harrill, bm.

Brown, Claton & Lucinday Reavis, 13 Oct 1817; Morgan Reavis, bm.

Brown, D. C. & S. M. Frady, 25 Aug 1866; William Gibbs, bm; m 4 Sept 1866 by W. H. Logan.

Brown, Daniel & Nancy Reavis, 9 Aug 1818; Morgan Reavis, bm.

Brown, Evan & Sarah M. Dickerson, 3 Jan 1826; Thoe F. Brichett, bm.

Brown, Felding R. & Frances Bradley, 30 Jan 1863; J. J. Bradley, bm; m 30 Jan 1862 (sic) by Wm. Devenport, J. P.

Brown, Fielding G. & Sarah M. McGwinn, 30 Sept 1847; John Gibbs, bm.

Brown, Gideon & Catreen Wilson, 10 Aug 1791; James Byrd, bm.

Brown, Hobson & Elisabeth Brown, 3 Apr 1801; Saml. Young, bm.

Brown, Jacob & Betsy Toney, 29 Jan 1820; James Smith, bm.

Brown, John & Marget McGaughy, 30 Nov 1798; Jos. M'Gahey, bm.

Brown, Samuel & L. H. Wall, 17 Apr 1865; A. C. Wall, bm.

Brown, Thomas & Betcy Abernathy, 6 Nov 1815; John Parker, bm.

Brown, Thornton & Elizabeth Ravis, 1 Jun 1816; John Case, bm.

Brown, William & Caroline Tony, 21 Nov 1852; Joseph C. Waldrop, bm; m 21 Nov 1852 by Luke Waldrop, J. P.

Brown, Wilson & Elizabeth Dimsdale, 12 Sept 1860; James Brown, bm.

Bruce, S. J. & Sarah E. Hemphill, 20 Aug 1860; T. P. Hemphill, bm; m 20 Aug 1860 by J. C. Grayson, M. G.

Bryan, Edmund & Urcilla Hampton, 30 Jul 1822; James Graham, bm.

Bryan, Joseph & Elizabeth Clarke, 6 Nov 1834; George W. Clarke, bm.

Bryant, John & Polly Morris, 26 Dec 1797; Thomas Grant, bm.

Bryson, William & Patsey Fisher, 19 Jan 1805.

Buchanan, Joseph & Sally Jones, 22 Feb 1792; James Buchanan, bm.

Buckhanon, William & Elizabeth Jones, 8 Apr 1793; John Irvine, bm.

Bullington, F. F. & Lorinda Collins, 17 Feb 1853; John H. Pricne, bm; m 17 Feb 1853 by J. M. Hamilton.

Bumgarner, John & Jamimah Prewett, 15 Aug 1838; John H. Swafford, bm.

Burge, John & Polly Green, _____ ; F. D. Burges, bm.

Burge, John & Leah Green, 17 Nov 1817; James Green, Joseph Green, bm.

Burge, John & Priscilla Blanton, 31 Dec 1853; Robert L. Gilkey, bm; m 4 Jan 1854 by Hansen Harrill, J. P.

Burge, John & Hester A. Cabines, 21 Nov 1859; Wm. P. Burge, bm; m 21 Nov 1859 by T. B. Justice, Baptist minister.

Burge, Nathaniel & Nann Green, 10 Nov 1814; F. D. Burge, bm.

Burge, William P. & Nancy T. Smith, 18 Dec 1861; J. C. Burge, bm; m 24 Dec 1861 by J. C. Grayson, M. G.

Burge, Woody & Elizebeth Thomas, 7 Apr 1821; John Burge, Wm. Baber, bm.

Burge, Wuooty & Dulcena McEntire, 7 Jan 1834; Peter Mooney, bm.

Burges, Azar & Nancy Brathey, 28 Jan 1824; Jas. More, bm.

Burgess, Albert & Elicabeth McDaniel, 6 Jan 1861; James Webb, bm; m 6 Jan 1861 by M. Wilkerson, J. P.

Burgess, Henry & Adra Harden, 8 Feb 1825; James Young, bm.

Burgess, J. P. & S. A. Dobbins, 1 Dec 1865; J. J. Padgett, bm.

Burgess, James & Malvina Smith, 17 Nov 1827; Henry Burgess, bm.

Burgess, John & Matilda L. Edney, 26 Feb 1860; Jones O. Williams, bm; m Feb 1860 by M. Wilkerson, J. P.

Burgin, J. D. W. & Marthy M. Allin, 17 Mar 1851; J. W. Allen, bm.

Burgin, Robert H. & Zilla Williams, 26 Aug 1849; Whitenton Williams, bm.

Burleson, Simeon & Mary Ledford, 10 Apr 1805; James CHitwood, bm.

Burlingson, James & Elizabeth Shipman, 24 Dec 1791; Jacob Shipman, bm.

Burn, Christopher & Margret Gordon, __ Dec 1809; John Gordon, bm.

Burnes, Benjamin & Susannah Smith, 7 Apr 1803; Charles Darbey, Henry Guin, bm.

Burnes, James & Sally Green, 22 Feb 1823; John Burnes, bm.

Burnes, John & Mary Hamblin, 1 Dec 1829; James Burnes, bm.

Burnet, Eldridge & Fanny Cisme, 4 Jun 1800; Starling Price, bm.

Burnet, Roland & Polly Hurt, 14 Jul 1783; Joseph Hurtt, bm.

Burnett, Benjamin M. & Pheobe Carpenter, 6 Dec 1827; John Logan Jr., bm.

Burnett, Carter & Sarah Depriest, 14 Mar 1836; Andrew Tanner, bm.

Burnett, Claybon & Urcilla Dicus, 18 Dec 1821; Henry Burnett, bm.

Burnett, Claybon & Mary Melone, 2 Nov 1791; David Geer, bm.

Burnett, Clayborn & Sally Lewis, 20 Feb 1819; Robert Baber, bm.

Burnett, Dugger & Rebekah Freeman, 19 Sept 1815; James Keeter, bm.

Burnett, Eldridge & Sarah Harrison, 29 Feb 1832; Edward Harrison, bm.

Burnett, Federick & Peggy Neill, 14 Apr 1795; John Gweltenney, bm.

Burnett, Henry & Rachel Moris, 5 Apr 1820; Micajay Moris, bm.

Burnett, John & Caroline Wilson, 13 Feb 1845; John W. Burnett, bm.

Burnett, John C. & Susanna Eliot, 21 Feb 1817; James Moore, bm.

Burnett, Joseph & Rachel Mucdannel, 25 Mar 1779; Saroon Egerton, David Hadelston, bm.

Burnett, Landrun & Marian Harrell, 19 Sept 1865; Drury Bridges, bm; m 19 Sept 1865 by G. W. Rollins.

Burnett, Robert & Rachel Black, 6 May 1819; Hugh B. Cook, bm.

Burnett, Thomas & Margaret Porter, 11 Oct 1830; Hugh W. Long, bm.

Burnett, Valentine & Mildred Upchurch, 22 Feb 1823; Adam Upchurch, bm.

Burnett, William & Elizabeth Baker, 1 Apr 1802; John Melton, bm.

Burnett, Wm. & Manerva Brown, 22 Dec 1850; J. E. Graham, bm.

Burns, John & Deide Smart, 23 Jul 1817; Levy Burns, THomas Smart, bm.

Burns, Levi & Drusy Green, 19 Dec 1842; Jesse Rogers, bm.

Burris, Aaron & Susannah Green, 14 Aug 1821; David Miller, bm.

Butler, George & Francis R. Good, 2 Nov 1849; John Watkins, bm.

Butler, James H. & Mary Dogett, 25 Mar 1862; Reuben McDaniel, bm; m 25 Mar 1862 by W. H. Bertie, J. P.

Butler, John & Sarah Colbert, m 1 Mar 1857 by W. A. Tanner.

Butler, John & Charlotte Bigham, 4 Jan 1863; Joseph B. Huntley, bm; m 5 Jan 1863 by Wm. J. Willkie.

Butler, Martain D. & Matilda Morrow, 20 Mar 1847; Newton Cole, bm.

Butler, Othneal & Martha Anne Doggett, 21 Dec 1824; George Doggett, bm.

Butler, Richard & Elizabeth McDaniel, 8 Apr 1829; Rueben McDaniel, bm.

Butler, Thomas & Betsy McClure, 2 Jan 1826; James Gray, bm.

Butler, William & Jane McClure, 31 Dec 1827; Thomas Butler, bm.

Butler, Wm. & Elizabeth Morrow, 11 Oct 1863; William Morrow, bm; m 11 Oct 1863 by B. McMahan, J. P.

Buttler, Marvil & Margaret Minor, 19 Apr 1854; Drury Dobbins, bm; m 19 Apr 1854 by D. D. Allen, J. P.

Byars, William & Andess McOme, 27 Jul 1826; John Padgett, bm.

Byas, Vedo & Jane Bradley, 18 May 1854; A. Bradley, bm; m 18 May 1854 by Henry Culbreath, M. G.

Byers, David & Rebekah McClain, 30 Dec 1800; E. McClain, bm.

Byrd, R. J. & Mary Koon, 12 Nov 1866; M. A. Wilkerson, bm; m 13 Dec 1866 by J. N. Somers.

Cabiniss, George & Patey Martin, 23 Mar 1820; John Martin, bm.

Cabaniss, James W. & Elizabeth D. Elliott, 26 ___ 1835; Thomas Good, bm.

Cabaniss, John & Susannah Hord, 15 Dec 1825; John Cornwiell, bm.

Cabaniss, William H. & Caroline J. Smith, 15 Jan 1839; Geo. Herndon, bm.

Cagdell, Eligah & Mary Proctor, 24 Nov 1796; Fredrick Cagdill, bm.

Cagle, John & Evaline Mills, 1 Mar 1850; Wm. S. Mills, bm.

Calahan, John H. & Sarah Hilles, 22 Aug 1844; J. Gilkey, bm.

Calahan, Saml. W. & Mariann Keeter, 23 Sept 1847; Wm. Keeter, bm.

Calaway, Thos. & Morning Nanney, 1 Apr 1847; Samuel King, bm.

Callahan, Alfred B. & E. L. Wallis, 13 Dec 1841; John H. Callahan, bm.

Callahan, James A. & Anna Hale, 26 Aug 1822; William Hale, bm.

Callahan, James C. & Rachel Keeter, 9 Oct 1851; William Hayle, bm; m 9 Oct 1851 by J. Gilkey, J. P.

Callahan, R. E. & M. C. Keeter, 4 Nov 1860; Wm M. Keeter, bm; m 4 Nov 1860 by T. G. Hawkins, J. P.

Callahan, R. S. & A. E. Geer, 27 Dec 1865; Wm. B. Dobbins, bm.

Callahan, Robert & Cyntha Baits, 8 Nov 1811.

Callihan, Drury & Rebecca Gillaspie, 13 Oct 1828; John Callihan, bm.

Callihan, William & Hanna Harrill, 24 Mar 1842; Drury Callihan, bm.

Calloway, Berry & Esther Grice, 8 June 1837; Absalom Bradley, bm.

Caloway, James & Nancy Guffey, 16 Oct 1834; Nimrod T. Stafford, bm; m by Hugh Watson, J. P.

Calton, John W. & Jane Baber, 18 Sept 1852; Jas H. Sweezy, bm.

Calton(?), Wm. & Hanah Smith, 21 Jul 1818; Vallintine C. ____, Eliah Self, bm.

Calvin, William & Anna Roberson, 9 Sept 1833; Townsend Roberson, bm.

Cambell, T. J. & E. J. Simmons, 2 Dec 1857; M. W. Simmons, bm.

Camele, Alfred B. & Elisabeth Erley, .___ 1841(?); Enoch C. Moorhead, bm.

Cammel, Samuel & Polly McGain, 4 Nov 1812; Thomas McGain, bm.

Camp, Aaron & Frances Terrell, 25 Jul 1803; Geo. Camp, bm.

Camp, Capt. J. C. & Margaret A. Twitty, 7 Oct 1862; Wm. L. Twitty, bm; m 7 Oct 1862 by N. Shotwell, M. G.

Camp, J. H. & Elizebeth Sorrels, 9 Dec 1865; J. Hampton, bm.

Camp, John & Polly Gear, 11 Aug 1835; William Flack Jr., William Black, bm.

Camp, Joseph T. & Harriet Mills, 1 Aug 1826; Stephen Camp, bm.

Camp, Joshua & Salley Mosley, 6 Aug 1817; Jos. Green, bm.

Camp, Joshua & Edy Smith, 15 Aug 1846; Wm Camp, bm.

Camp, Lewis & Elizabeth McKinney, m 21 Jan 1851 by C. Smith, M. G.

Camp, Lewis & Sarah Wilkerson, 20 May 1856; L. C. Pope, bm.

Camp, Madison & Adaline Fagans, 5 Aug 1850; Obadiah Cockerhan, bm.

Camp, Oliver G. & Narcissa Hamrick, 15 Aug 1828; David K. Fisher, bm.

Camp, Saul & Mrs. Polley Willis, 16 Mar 1810; Bedneygo Adens, bm.

Camp, Terrell L. & Mary Ann T. Hord, 10 Jan 1825; John Hord, bm.

Camp, Thomas & Jane Ford, 12 Jan 1825; Terrell L. Camp, bm.

Camp, William & Nancy Whitlock, 14 Feb 1828; Jonathan Dyer, bm.

Campbell, James & Polly Guffey, 30 Sept 1819; John Guffey, bm.

Campbell, James R. & Emily Marshall, 17 Jul 1834; Janes W. Carson, bm.

Campbell, John & Elizabeth Kits, 14 Apr 1807; Robt. Campbell, bm.

Campbell, John B. & Rosanneh B. Murray, 31 Dec 1844; W. D. Murray, bm.

Campbell, T. R. & Nancy M. Guffey, 18 Aug 1858; Wm. S. Robertson, bm; m 18 Aug 1858 by John Freeman, J. P.

Campbell, William & Jane Huddleton, ___ Jan 1794; James Hudleston, bm.

Campbell, Wm. & Amanda Vickers, 16 Mar 1856; E. P. Allen, bm; m 26 Mar 1856 by James M. Spratt, J. P.

Campbell, William M. & Mary J. Guffey, 12 Feb 1848.

Campell, James P. & Sarah Crowder, 1 May 1852; John Crowder, bm.

Canada, John & Narcissa Webb, 12 Jan 1843; J. H. Bedford, bm.

Cancellor, Phillip & Mary Johnston, 10 Oct 1818; John Cancellor, bm.

Cannon, Noah & Elvira M. Kilpatrick, 3 Sept 1852; J. W. Kilpatrick, bm.

Cantrell, Wesley E. & Sally Callihan, 10 Jan 1839; John Callihan, bm.

Cantrell, Wm. H. & Elizabeth Lewis, 10 Mar 1862; C. Burnett, bm.

Capshaw, David & Ruth Luallen, 20 Dec 1800.

Carborough, John & Nancy Land, 25 Oct 1838; Jacob Knipe, bm.

Carel, John & Nancy Janes, 7 Mar 1843; William Bates, bm.

Carell, Dennis & Nancy Waggoner, 23 Dec 1814; Jason Johnson, bm.

Carpenter, David & Mrs. _____ Jonston, 1 May 1802; Danel Jonston, bm.

Carpenter, E. M. & Janie Derreberry, 13 Jul 1844.

Carpenter, J. Beattie & Marthia Jane Carpenter, 1 Mar 1860; H. D. Lee, bm; m 1 Mar 1860 by A. Hamby, Elder.

Carpenter, Jacob & Susannah Achor, 11 Apr 1786; Joseph Carpenter (signed Zimmerman), Joseph Walker, bm.

Carpenter, Jacob & Anna Mooney, 20 Oct 1825; Solomon Young, bm.

Carpenter, Jacob D. & Sarah Johnston, 2 Oct 1837; George W. Tanner, bm.

Carpenter, James & Martha Johnson, 8 Feb 1832; E. M. Carpenter, bm.

Carpenter, James & Nancy Edwards, 2 Apr 1844; Benson Edwards, bm.

Carpenter, James H. & Cyntha D. Wilson, 25 Apr 1835; William Baxter Junr, bm.

Carpenter, John & Polly McGhey, 8 Feb 1855; James McGahhey, bm.

Carpenter, John C. & Letetia A. Haynes, 17 Aug 1866; Wm. M. Webster, bm; m 19 Aug 1866 by J. D. Carpenter, M. G.

Carpenter, Jonithan & Masse Lee, 24 Feb 1835; Barnbas King, bm.

Carpenter, K. T. & Judieth Suttle, 27 Feb 1848; Wm. Carpenter, bm.

Carpenter, Kinchin & Anna Baber, 5 Mar 1808; Andr. Crooks, bm.

Carpenter, Samuel & Amanda Hamilton, 8 Jun 1867; Wiley Lookadoo, bm. (C.H.)

Carpenter, William & Nancy Suttelles, 4 Dec 1849; Joseph R. McDaniel, bm.

Carrell, John & Jane Janes, 22 Sept 1815; Thos. Janes, bm.

Carrell, Wm. H. & Susannah Bostick, 2 Jul 1856; Geo T. Bostick, bm.

Carrier, Elias & Elisebeth Jane Oliphant, 29 Apr 1857; Jos. C. White, bm; m 29 Apr 1857 by T. E. Davis, M. G.

Carrier, Harvy & Julia A. Dickerson, 14 Jun 1832; James W. Cabaniss, bm.

Carrock, John & Elizabeth Edwards, 16 Mar 1793; Ezekiel Enloe, bm.

Carroll, John & Mrs. Elisabeth Pruett, 27 Jan 1807; Thomas Davis, Abram Irvine, bm.

Carroll, Thomas & P. Bostick, 8 Dec 1865; Andrew McDaniel, bm.

Carruth, Alexander & Sarah Logan, 12 Mar 1792; Jas. Logan, bm.

Carruth, Alexander & Letty Scott, 12 Apr 1818; John Lankford, bm.

Carruth, Ephraim & Susanna Lankford, 31 May 1810; Alexander Carruth, bm.

Carruth, James & Mary Logan, 7 Dec 1802; Alexander Carruth, bm.

Carruth, Leeroy & Sibey Lankford, 15 Dec 1816; Nathan Lankford, bm.

Carson, A. B. & Martha R. McFarland, 5 Oct 1858; P. L. Carson, bm; m 6 Oct 1858 by John C. Carson, M. G.

Carson, A. B. & Edith E. Lawrence, 11 Mar 1861; E. Carrier, bm; m 12 Mar 1861 by Elder G. W. Rollins.

Carson, Charles & Margaret Wilson, 22 Apr 1812; Jason Carson, bm.

Carson, Daniel & Mary Watson, 7 Nov 1798; William Carson, bm.

Carson, Felix Wolson & Polly J. Carson, 10 Dec 1818; Wm. Carson, bm.

Carson, George W. & Matilda Moore, 20 Mar 1819; Jno. Carson, bm.

Carson, James M. C. F. & Rebecca McFarland, 9 Mar 1835; James McFarland Jr., bm.

Carson, James W., son of Jno Carson, & Cay Canceller, 11 Feb 1814; Jno. Carson, bm.

Carson, Jason H. & Jane Moore, 20 Mar 1843; Walter Duffy, bm.

Carson, John & Mary Withrow, 2 Feb 1789; George Watson, bm.

Carson, Jno. & Betsey Thompson, 10 Jun 1813; R. K. Wilson, bm.

Carson, John C. & Martha M. Guffy, 19 Dec 1850; H. K. Smart, bm.

Carson, Joseph McD. & Margaret C. Mills, 6 Nov 1862; Franklin Coxe, bm; m 6 Nov 1862 by Joseph Hunter.

Carson, Oliver P. & Nancy W. Dickerson, 10 Jun 1840; John J. Herndon, bm.

Carson, Patrick W. & Eliza Graves, 15 Feb 1823; Hugh Watson, bm.

Carson, Dr. Philip L. & Mary A. Moore, m 13 Nov 1851 by Solomon W. Davis, Minister of the Methodist Episcopal Church South.

Carson, Samuel P. & Sarah Catharine Wilson, 10 MAr 1831; Thomas Dews Jr., bm.

Carson, Thomas L., son of Jas. W. Carson, & Delila Harrell, dau. of H. Harrell, m 11 Jul 1867 by G. M. Webb.

Carson, William & Jane Carson, 1 Feb 1817; Felix Carson, bm.

Carson, William & Mary McFarland, 27 Nov 1850; James W. Allen, bm.

Carson, William P. & Sarah Flemming, 9 Nov 1829; Jno. Carson, bm.

Carson, Wm. P. & Margaret R. Witherow, 17 Jan 1849; J. H. Depriest, bm.

Carter, Jiles & Selah Queen, 14 Jan 1806; John Queen, bm.

Carter, Joel & Mary Morehead, 5 Nov 1840; Ransom Proctor, bm.

Carter, William & Mary Price, 25 Sept 1799; John Carter, bm.

Carter, William & Amy Hasten, 18 Oct 1831; Samuel Thompson, bm.

Cartright, James & Jane Thomason, 13 Sept 1800; Samuel Thomasson, bm.

Carver, Benjamin & Delilah Robinson, 11 Apr 1810; John Moore, bm.

Causner, Joseph & Barbary Gipson, 14 Feb 1832; John Fronaleargey, bm.

Cawlis, James & Mary Bomgartner, 11 Sept 1795; David Cline, bm.

Chaffers, Burrel, & Rachel Robbertson, 11 Jun 1809; Teary Bradley, bm.

Chaffin, Elijah & Anna Jackson, 18 Nov 1820; Amos Jackson, bm.

Chambers, Alexander & Ann Monroe, 17 Sept 1789; Thomas Whiteside, Thomas Lattimore, bm.

Champion, Henry & Elizabeth Moore, 22 Oct 1834; Thomas Green Jr., son of Isaac Green, bm.

Champion, Robert C. & Salinda Ledbetter, 27 Apr 1835; George Champion, bm.

Champion, William & Judy H. Owins, 14 Dec 1864; William Green, bm; m 14 Dec 1864 by Nathan Scoggin, J. P.

Champion, William Jr. & Margaret Champion, 6 Jan 1836; Henry Champion, bm.

Chapman, Nicholas & Sarah Selah, 17 Dec 1787; James Swafford, bm.

Cheek, William B; & Ann O. Roberts, 13 Jan 1846; E. Carrier, bm.

Cherry, John T. & Sarah Nix, 8 Apr 1829; Allexander W. Allen, bm.

Cherry, John T. & Sarah Goforth, 16 May 1836; William Flack, bm.

Childers, Tench & Nelly K. Colbirt, 9 Nov 1854; Jonathan Walker, bm; m 9 Nov 1854 by H. Padgett, J. P.

Childress, John & Elizabeth Walker, m 8 June 1851 by Samuel Stone, J. P.

Chilton, James A. & Sarah King, 14 Aug 1866; R. L. Taylor, bm; m 14 Aug 1866 by J. R. Bowman, M. G.

Chissom, David & Mary Ragsdall, 1 Feb 1812; Henry Franklin, bm.

Chitwood, Amos & Mrs. Prudence Lademor, 1 Oct 1793; Francis Lattimore, bm.

Chitwood, John & Sarah Dicus, 18 Dec 1849; Jas. Daniels, bm.

Christopher, Wm. & Nancy Taylor, 8 Feb 1806; Robert Taylor, bm.

Cimwrig(?), Fredrick D. & Peggy Conner, 1 Mar 1833; George W. Conner, bm.

Claghorn, John & Abigal Scott, 15 Jan 1800; Arthur McCluer, bm.

Clane, Robert & Jane Ramse, 1 Oct 1791; Peter Lohler(?), bm.

Clark, Benjamin B. & Mary Ann Moorhead, 14 Jan 1830; Elijah Patton, bm.

Clark, Hiram & Sally Moore, 17 Aug 1820; Jno. Clarke, James W. Carson, bm.

Clark, John & Agness Gorden, 13 Mar 1802; Gloud Long, bm.

Clark, Capt. John W. & Mary Twitty, m 21 Mar 1865 by N. Shotwell, Pastor of the Preb'n Church, Rutherfordton, N. C.

Clark, Robert W. & Millisa Allen, 13 Oct 1843; Wm. Rucker, bm.

Clarke, Oliver & Sarah Edwards, 5 Dec 1831; Otis P. Mills, bm.

Clements, Cornelias & Susanna Goforth, 18 Jan 1783; Andrew Goforth, Miles Goforth, bm.

Clements, Cornelius & Mira M. Guffey, 13 Dec 1838; George M. Reid, bm.

Clements, Cornelius & Mary Henseley 5 Aug 1853; A. K. Wallace, bm; m 7 Aug 1853 by G. Gilkey, J. P.

Clemments, John & Elizebeth Cross, 16 May 1841; Isaac K. Freeman,bm.

Clemonds, Andrew & Sarah Sellers, 25 Dec 1810; Permenter Morgan Jr., Cornelious Clemonds, bm.

Clinton, Abram & Lively Usery, 1 Jan 1784; Robert Clinton, bm.

Cloninger, George & Elizabeth Sims, 9 Feb 1830; Littleton Sims, bm.

Cloud, Calvin & Elmirey Robison, 22 Apr 1861; S H. Bagwell, bm; m 22 Apr 1861 by Wm. Devenport, J. P.

Cocherhan, H. Deator & Mary Scoggin, 15 Oct 1849; Jesse Scoggins, bm.

Cochran, John & Sally Johnston, 16 Jan 1819; Robt. Johnson, bm.

Cockerham, David & Nancy Allen, 24 Nov 1831; Sanders D. Allen, bm.

Cockerham, Jephtha & Elisabeth Bradly, 10 Nov 1844; Levi Arledge, bm.

Cockerham, Henry & Martha Searcy, 29 Dec 1861; J. R. Mecom, bm; m __ Dec 1861 by Wm. Devenport.

Cockram, David & Sarah Coward, 13 Jan 1802; James Coward, bm.

Cockram, Henry & Polly Richarson, 3 Oct 1805; William Richardson, bm.

Cockran, Jos. & Elizabeth Alonzo, 31 Dec 1811; Thomas Cokram, bm.

Cockran, Obadiah & Elizabeth Padgett, 29 Oct 1834; Martin Walker, bm.

Cockran, Robert Jr. & Pamela Norvill, 14 Jan 1824; Wyley J. Norvill, bm.

Coday, Richard & Polly Smith, 26 Sept 1816.

Cohran, Reed & Polly D. Allen, 7 Sept 1826; Wyley J. Norvill, bm.

Cohran, William & Jane Allen, 22 Jun 1829; Robert G. Twitty, bm.

Cokcrum, Charles R. & Margreat Webb, 12 Nov 1828; William K. Kerr, bm.

Cokley, Z. D. & Maryan Hyder, 7 Oct 1866; Amos L. Hyder, bm; m 7 Oct 1866 by J. R. Bowman, M. G.

Colbert, Alexander & Mary Sutton, 27 May 1834; John Colbert, bm.

Colbreth, Mathy C. & Druciler H. Long, 23 Aug 1860; Barnabas Melton, bm; m 23 Aug 1860 by John Freeman, J. P.

Coldwell, Edward & Sally Griple, 26 Aug 1816; Henry Culbreath, bm.

Cole, Jason F. & Nancy M. Blanton, 26 Nov 1860; H. M. Corbet, bm.

Cole, Joseph & Elizabeth Putnam, 18 Mar 1839; Newton Cole, bm.

Cole, Newton & Martha Butler, 22 Mar 1851; George B. Ford, bm; m 23 Mar 1851 by Edward Toms, J. P.

Coleman, Geo. S. & Ellen Douglass, 12 Jan 1841; W. Twitty, bm.

Colins, Russel & Eliza Wilkie, 8 Feb 1853; W. A. E. Roberts, bm; m 8 Feb 1853 by Merit Richman.

Collins, Abraham & Dicey Moore, 18 Nov 1824; John Proctor, bm.

Collins, D. B. & Amelia B. Edwards, 15 Jun 1860; L. D. Hamrick, bm; m 4 Oct 1860 by J. B. McDaniel, J. P.

Collins, Daniel & Seliny A. Brooks, 4 Jan 1838; Isaac Brooks, bm.

Collins, Jacob & Mrs. Ginna Hardin, 17 Mar 1807; David Hardin Jr., bm.

Collins, James & Caty Cool, 4 Nov 1808; Josiah Womack, bm.

Collins, James & Elizebeth Wilmon, 14 Feb 1836; William Weathers, bm.

Collins, John & Catherine McMurry, 2 Apr 1809; John McMory, Josiah Davis, bm.

Collins, John & Deliah Eaves, 19 Aug 1814; William Smat, bm.

Collins, John & Adaline Owens, 22 Dec 1853; Robert McClan, bm; m 22 Dec 1853 by J. M. Hamilton, J. P.

Collins, Joseph & Kesiah Gibbs, 9 Jan 1795; Jesse Gibbs, bm.

Collins, Paschal E. & Emeline Borders, 7 Mar 1833; John Borders, bm.

Collins, Sabert & Jane Farmer, 31 May 1797; Edmon Smith, bm.

Collins, Samuel & Sarah Griggs, 28 Dec 1803; Robert Harden, bm.

Collis, John & Hanner Buckhanan, 24 Nov 1796; William Buckhanan, bm.

Collis, William & Fanny Ross, 24 Oct 1826; James Ross, bm.

Condrey, James & Lilly Ann Loin, _____ ; C. Condrey, bm.

Conner, Calvin & Malinda Dalton, m 27 Dec 1866; by W. H. Logan, M. G.

Conner, Georg W. & Nancey A. Radford, 5 Sept 1844; John Carrell, bm.

Conner, George & Susen Dalton, 22 Mar 1851; Gilbert Conner, bm.

Conner, Gilbert & Mary Frady, 29 May 1858; R. H. Robertson, bm; m 1 Jun 1858 by Wm. O. Bagwell, J. P.

Conner, J. W. & Cintha Flinn, 18 May 1865; Martin Banard, bm; m 25 May 1865 by W. H. Logan.

Conners, Noah & Mary Davis, 29 Jan 1857; Silas Davis, bm; m 29 Jan 1857 by J. A. Grant, J. P.

Connor, Allen & Polly Crawford, 17 Feb 1830; Isaac Connor, bm.

Connor, George & Jinsy Smith, 12 Jan 1829; James Edwards, bm.

Connor, Gilbert & Susannah Robertson, 7 Mar 1827; William Adair, bm.

Connor, Isaac & Rosy Earley, 17 Nov 1824; William Fleming, bm.

Constant, Eligah & Jean Haulkens, 2 Jul 1804; Edward Constant, bm.

Cook, Aaron & Martha White, 25 Apr 1865; Ephraim Ledford, bm; m 25 Apr 1865 by A. Hunt, Minister.

Cook, Ephram & Jane Watkins, 28 Oct 1812; Isaiah Watkins, bm.

Cook, Humphry & Elizabeth Black, 26 Aug 1843; John Black, bm.

Cook, James & Salley Collis, 20 Jan 1815; Benj. (Beaver?), bm.

Cook, James & Pegga Hanman, 29 Sept 1826; Isam Cook, bm.

Cook, John & Nancy Keeter, 27 Dec 1811; G. Walton, bm.

Cook, John & Mary A. McEntire, 26 May 1857; John Haynes, bm; m 5 Jun 1857 by T. B. Justice.

Cook, Jonathan & Francis Harris, 25 Dec 1811; William Cook, bm.

Cook, Lana F. & Francis Johnston, 5 Jul 1825; Eli Harris, bm.

Cook, William & Susanna Hill, 27 Dec 1806; Eli Hanes, bm.

Cooper, James & Susanah Webb, 23 Nov 1813; J. McEntire, bm.

Cooper, James A. & Biddy C. Edwards, 5 Aug 1859; Plato Durham, bm; m 30 Sept 1859 by J. B. McDaniel, J. P.

Cooper, Joseph & Elizabeth Cole, 12 Oct 1854; John Cole, bm; m 12 Oct 1854 by Henry Culbreath.

Cooper, N. C. & Lucinda Bohela, 10 Mar 1860; Wm. Butler, bm; m 13 Mar 1860 by M. R. Moore, J. P.

Cooper, Osama & Sally Hardin, 26 Jan 1850; Wm. Harrill, bm.

Cooper, William D. & Elizebeth C. Bland, 30 May 1839; William Bland, bm.

Copeland, Charles & Hulda Williams, 22 Sept 1845; John Giles, bm.

Copeland, William & Diannah Hopper, 23 Mar 1835; John Weber, bm.

Corbet, Henry & Tempy Roberts, 7 Dec 1848; C. E. Green, bm.

Corbet, William & Elizabeth Roberts, 15 Mar 1849; R. A. Wallis, bm.

Corbitt, Lewis & Mrs. Nancy Elliott, 23 Oct 1833; William Slade, bm.

Cornelius, ____ & Polly Gadds, ____; Jonathan King, bm.

Cornwell, Abner & Susey London, 23 Mar 1826; James Singletary, bm.

Coston, John & Margaret Baxter, 4 Sept 1809; James Baxter, bm.

Coston, John & Catharine Kerr, 28 Nov 1855; Joseph Baxter, bm; m 28 Nov 1855 by Bailey Bruce, M. G.

Coston, William & Sarah C. Baxter, 24 Nov 1838; Solomon W. Davis, bm.

Coulter, James & Catherine Tunnel, 6 Jul 1792; David Dickey, bm.

Covington, Andrew J. & Olivia Ellis, 4 Jan 1838; Abel H. Roberts, bm.

Covington, David & Rachel McIntire, 11 Jan 1821; Wm. McEntire, William Covington, bm.

Covington, J. M. & Eveline Johnson, 15 Nov 1844; J. B. Sloan, bm.

Covington, John & Sussana Covington, 16 Feb 1796; Aaron McEntire, bm.

Covington, Josiah or Walker, John & Mary Morgan, 21 Feb 1785; John Walker, Sam. Moore, bm.

Covington, Josiah & Unity Fondren, 5 Feb 1828; James Love, bm.

Covington, Thomas & Patsey Coventon, _____ 180-; Wm. McEntire, bm.

Covington, Thomas & Betsy Grizzle, 14 Jun 1824; Richard Covington, bm.

Covington, William & Roda McEntire, 16 Apr 1795; Thomas Clark, bm.

Cowan, Joseph & Margaret Street, 4 Jul 1862; D. F. Melton, bm; m 4 Jul 1862 by W. H. Atkin, J. P.

Coward, Elihu & Charlotte Bird, 27 Jan 1823; Jacob Michal, bm.

Coward, James Jr. & Mary Worley, 8 Nov 1812; Thomas Worley, Thomas Ward, bm.

Coward, Lewis & Ozella Bradley, 10 Dec 1842; Jesse T. Lewis, bm.

Coward, Peter & Nancy Dimsdil, 13 Jan 1801; James Coward, bm.

Coward, Peter C. & Olive Clifton, 19 Dec 1838; Eli F. Littlejohn, bm.

Coward, Stephen & Milly Rogers, 29 Nov 1815; Elihue Coward, bm.

Cowen, Alfred & Nancy L. Fortune, 5 Jan 1854; Willia N. Long, bm; m 5 Jan 1854 by Williamson Fortune, J. P.

Cowen, James & Aveline Warren, 27 Feb 1858; E. J. McCrow, bm.

Cowen, Joseph & Mary M. Long, 9 Dec 1845; W. F. Bright, m.

Coxe, Francis Sidney, of Philadelphia, Pa., & Jane McBee Alexander, 24 Apr 1823; Leonard Daniel, bm; Jos. Gooden, Elizabeth B. Craton, wit.

Coxey, Richard & Marey C. Burlett, 8 Jul 1860; Osborn Coxsay, bm; m 8 Jul 1860 by J. Gilkey, J. P.

Coxey, William & Elizabeth Sorrels, 28 Aug 1810; John Johnson, bm.

Coxsay, William & Winney Bradley, 21 Jul 1824; James Edwards, bm.

Coxsey, Absalom & Elizabeth Haile, 12 Oct 1815; James Keeter, bm.

Coxy, John & Mary Whiside, 3 Mar 1840; N. H. Ledbetter, bm.

Crain, Demcye & Grace Ross, 25 Apr 1792; Jas. Ross, Mofield Crain, bm.

Crain, William & Elisebeth Collens, 11 Jan 1808; Allick Mctire, bm.

Craton, Isaac & Elizabeth B. Miller, 31 Jan 1822; Edmon Bryan, bm.

Craven, Thomas W. & Mrs. Phalby Lewis, 9 Sept 1821; David Dickey, bm.

Crawford, A. W. & Tempy E. Wilkerson, 11 Jun 1860; W. H. Wilkerson, bm; m 14 Jun 1860 by M. Wilkerson, bm.

Crawford, Aaron & Sarah Luntesford, 19 Jul 1827; H. Harris, bm.

Crawford, David W. & Mary Walker, 5 Jun 1852; James A. Webster, bm.

Crawford, Dillard L. & Arminta Holford, 11 May 1865; J. L. Williams, bm; m 11 May 1865 by W. H. Logan, M. G.

Crawford, Francis & Elizabeth Harriss, 16 Sept 1806; Samuel Crawford, bm.

Crawford, James & Cynthia Suttin, 2 Aug 1817; John Crawford, bm.

Crawford, John & Charlote Hunter, 19 May 1803; Saml. Hunter, bm.

Crawford, Marcus & Martha Conner, 16 May 1849; Robert Davis, bm.

Crawford, Silvester & Martha Jolly, 6 Dec 1853; Wm. Conner, bm; m 8 Dec 1853 by M. Wilkerson, J. P.

Crawford, Washington & Polly Hunter, 29 Oct 1804; Sam. Hunter, bm.

Crofird, Dillard & Susannah Robeson, 4 Jan 1844; Azariah Frady, bm.

Crook, William & Susanna Keeter, 20 May 18201 Gray Crow, bm.

Cross, J. S. & Mary Fisher, 12 Dec 1842; James Sumner, bm.

Cross, Joseph & Ann Cogdill, 20 Oct 1797; William Cogdill, bm.

Crow, Abraham & Patsy McCurry, 20 Aug 1818; Danl. Carson, bm.

Crow, Abraham & Sinthy Hunt, 14 Jan 1841; J. B. Jones, bm.

Crow, Green & Jinsy Street, 17 Dec 1816; Sampson Price, bm.

Crow, James & Letty Milton, 5 Feb 1812; J. H. Alley, bm.

Crow, James O. & Susan Melton, 14 Aug 1843; K. J. McCrow, bm.

Crowder, A. P. & Martha Walker, 15 Feb 1864; J. B. Walker, bm; m 18 Feb 1864 by D. Ponnell.

Crowder, Allin & Febee Grigg, 10 Oct 1811; Burell Grigg, bm.

Crowder, Bartlet & Mary Brown, 24 Mar 1825; Jesse Grigg, bm.

Crowder, James & Biddy Beam, 9 Aug 1836; Martin Beam, bm.

Crowder, Jarel & _____, 9 Aug 1807; David Nowlin, Wm. Crowder, bm.

Crowder, Jarrell J. & Ann Whisnant, 24 Feb 1840; Jarrel CRowder, bm.

Crowder, John & Unicey Bedford, 6 Sept 1818; Jas. Jones, bm.

Crowder, John D. & Eliza Price, 13 Mar 1848; John M. Sweezy, bm.

Crowder, Matthew & Milly Wells, 17 Nov 1858; William Y. Green, bm; m 21 Nov 1858 by G. W. Rollins, Baptist Minister.

Crowder, Richard & Mitchel Dimsdale, 20 Dec 1849; Wms. Odum, bm.

Crowder, William & _____, 9 Dec 1812; Robert Wells, bm.

Crowder, William & Lucy Thompson, 15 Sept 1825; Thomas Martin, bm.

Cruse, Thomas & Polly Patterson, 19 Agu 1821; Robert McAfee, bm.

Culbrath, James & Julyan Grisle, 9 Apr 1850; Daniel Culbreath, bm.

Culbreath, Daniel & Elizabeth Green, 23 Dec 1847; James Culbreath, bm.

Culbreath, Henry & Edda Bowan, 21 Oct 1818; Henry Feagins, bm.

Culbreath, Henry J. & Nancy M. Bradley, 12 Feb 1852; William M. Culbreath, bm; m 12 Feb 1851 by H. Culbreath.

Culbreath, Jno. & Rachel Green, 16 Jul 1815; Henry Feagins, bm.

Culbreath, Lorenzo D. & Ursula E. Dobbins, 8 Feb 1860; D. Caloway Dobbins, bm; m 14 Feb 1860 by H. Culbreath, M. G.

Culbreath, William M. & Araminsa Wells, 18 Jul 1852; Henry Culbreath, bm; m 18 Jul 1852 by Wm. Harrill.

Cuningham, Alexander & Ruth Carouth, 31 May 1791; Alexander Carruth, bm.

Curry, John & Frances Ellener Jane, 9 Oct 1819; Thom Jane, bm.

Dailey, John & Susannah Walker, 26 Dec 1820; Moses McDaniel, bm.

Dale, Alkenay & Elisabeth Francis, 2 Oct 1792; Edwerd Francis, bm.

Dale, William & Maryan York, 25 Dec 1823; Andrew York, bm.

Dalton, Benj. W. & Nancy Dalton, 25 May 1845; R. O. Ledbetter, bm.

Dalton, Bradley & Mary Hills, 25 Dec 1827; John Hills, bm.

Dalton, Bradley & Narcissa Heyden, 12 Nov 1840; William Richardson, bm.

Dalton, Elijah & P. Grant, 4 Jan 1809; James Morris, bm.

Dalton, Jackson & Adaline Smith, 2 Jan 1853; M. D. Carn, bm; m 2 Jan 1853 by J. M. Hamilton, J. P.

Dalton, James & Sarah Wilson, 21 Jan 1831; Thomas Dalton, bm.

Dalton, John & Milley Metcalfe, 5 Mar 1828; Harvy Carrer, bm.

Dalton, Jonathan & Martha Wilson, 20 May 1844; M. Wilkerson, bm.

Dalton, Joseph G. & Martha Ann Thompson, 13 ___ 1860; James P. Dalton, bm.

Dalton, Noah W. & Sarah A. Conner, 15 Nov 1853; James A. Dalton, bm; m 17 Nov 1853 by Wm. O. Bagwell, J. P.

Dalton, Thomas & Elizabeth Morriss, 25 Feb 1789; William Ballard, bm.

Dalton, William & Elizabeth Young, 25 Jun 1832; Micajah Durham, bm.

Daniel, Joseph & Matilda Griffin, m 30 May 1854 by Campbell Smith.

Daniel, Walter K. & Mary S. Alexander, 10 Feb 1820; Isaac Craton, bm.

Darbey, Charles & Nancy Biddey, 22 May 1819; Micheal Hawkins, bm.

Dartey, Chrestien & Nancy Blankenship, 11 Apr 1839; Daniel Michal, bm.

Daugherty, Andrew & Seley Mode, 22 Mar 1796; James Moade, Joseph Bradley, bm.

Daughtry, Martin & Catharine Harris, 12 Apr 1840; Hardin Nowlin, bm.

Daves, Green & Margaret Rudisel, 6 Oct 1826; Jesse H. Benton, bm.

Daves, James & Nancy Justice, 25 Feb 1856; J. M. Chitwood, bm; m 6 Mar 1856 by G. W. Rollins.

Daves, L. D. & Emilia Taylor, 2 Aug 1844; James Davis, bm.

Daves, Thomas & Rachel Grayson, 5 Dec 1831; Elijah Parker, bm.

Daves, Thomas & Mary M. Hamric, 31 Aug 1865; W. S. McCurry, bm.

Daves, W. S. & Elizabeth Blankinship, 11 May 1859; J. S. Melton, bm; m 11 May 1859 by B. E. Rollins, M. G.

Daves, Wm. & Caroline Daves, 11 Sept 1857; C. B. Walker, bm; m 13 Sept 1857 by A. Harrill, J. P.

Daves, Wm. J. & Fanny Ann Gosa, 5 Jan 1850; Jas. Davis, bm

Davidson, Hezekiah & Lettice Isbell, 15 Oct 1795; Alxr. Davison, bm.

Davis, A. Benson & Hannah Beann, 16 Apr 1841; Carter Tanner, bm.

Davis, Anderson & Mira Luquire, 22 Jan 1843; James Crowder, bm.

Davis, B. W. & C. J. Edwards, 6 Oct 1855; Jos P. Green, bm; m 11 Oct 1855 by H. Harrill, J. P.

Davis, Barclay & Polly Wray, 10 Aug 1789; James Miller, bm.

Davis, Benjamin Jr. & Rebeca Haney, 4 Sept 1815; Benjamin Davis Sr., bm.

Davis, Binjamin P. & Nersisa Hamrick, 23 Aug 1840; Moses Hamrick, bm.

Davis, C. T. N. & Mirah McDowel, 27 Nov 1850; W. M. Shipp, bm.

Davis, David & Sally Price, 10 Jun 1797; Bartlet Eves, bm.

Davis, David & Kitty Daves, 12 Apr 1823; William Davis, bm.

Davis, Eli & Nercissa Blanton, 25 May 1848; James White, bm.

Davis, Elijah & Elizabeth Bowman, 23 Oct 1828; Ephraim Davis, bm.

Davis, Elknah & Drusilla Owens, 20 Nov 1850; Larkin Deyard, bm.

Davis, Ephraim & Casea McHann, 1 Dec 1804; William Davis, bm.

Davis, George & Lucinda Wamack, 30 Jun 1832; William Davis, bm.

Davis, Gilford (col.) & Clarsa Hamilton, 28 Apr 1866; Jock Eaves, bm; m 28 Apr 1866 by Toliver Hamilton.

Davis, Isaac V. & Adaline Deck, 21 Apr 1840; Jacob Yelton, bm.

Davis, Isah & Eunice Willson, 3 Sept 1805; John Willson, Josiah Davis, bm.

Davis, J. W. & S. Jennie Eaves, 18 Feb 1867; J. B. Eaves, bm.

Davis, Jacob & Betsey Biggerstaff, 15 Mar 1815; Benjamin Davis, bm.

Davis, Jacob & Mary A. Sparks, 2 Aug 1863; Wm. M. Harrill, bm; m 2 Aug 1863 by J. B. McDaniel, J. P.

Davis, James & Mary Watkins, 5 May 1841; Moses Simmons, bm.

Davis, James & Vianah Davis, 15 Nov 1848; Wm. Davis, bm.

Davis, Jesse & Milley Mullins, 22 Aug 1807; D. C. Mullins, bm.

Davis, John & Polly Philbeck, 13 Jul 1832; Richard Philbeck, bm.

Davis, John & Rachel Jolly, 13 Nov 1833; William Davis, bm.

Davis, John & Sarah Westbrook, 31 May 1836; James M. Tate, bm.

Davis, John & Anna Womack, 20 Feb 1837; Gassaway Womack, bm.

Davis, John & Margaret J. Galbreath, 30 Oct 1850; J. A. Carpenter, bm.

Davis, John & Sina Davis, 17 Sept 1856; Albert L. Davis, bm; m 18 Sept 1856 by A. Harrill, J. P.

Davis, John & Sally Price, 4 Jan 1860; Ransom Hollifield, bm; m 5 Jan 1860 by G. W. Rollins.

Davis, John H. & Araazenn Scoggins, 24 Jan 1840; Isaac V. Davis, bm.

Davis, John Wesley & Rhodey Dalton, 6 Dec 1856; John C. Dalton, bm; m 6 Dec 1856 by J. A. Grant, J. P.

Davis, Logan C. & E. M. Davis, 5 Jun 1859; A. D. Whitlock, bm.

Davis, M. C. & Susan Dalton, 22 May 1865; A. A. Dalton, bm.

Davis, Micajah & Mrs. Elisabeth Bridges, 9 Feb 1811; Thomas Reynolds, bm.

Davis, Nathan & Minerva Daves, 28 Feb 1854; Siman Davis, bm.

Davis, Robert & Anna Davis, 14 Apr 1827; Patrick Eaves, bm.

Davis, Robert & Lucilla Taylor, 27 Mar 1843; Joseph Crews, bm.

Davis, Robert & Eliz. Yelten, 28 Dec 1855; Jos P. Green, bm.

Davis, Robert B. & Sabry Gage, 14 Aug 1829; John M. Hall, bm.

Davis, Samuel & Malinda Levins, 13 Sept 1824; Henry Norvell, bm.

Davis, Samuel & Lucinda Davis, 12 Jul 1826; Lewis Johnston, bm.

Davis, Samuel Jr. & Alisa Morriss, 16 Sept 1824; Wm. Morries, bm.

Davis, Simon & Nancy Womack, 15 Aug 1828; John Teal, bm.

Davis, Toliver & Caty Logan, 6 Jun 1830.

Davis, William & Sally Womack, _____; Anderson Womack, Robt. Randal, bm.

Davis, William & Sarah Callahan, 22 Aug 1781; James Cook, bm.

Davis, Wm. & Sarah Walker, 13 Dec 1847; J. Young Jr., bm.

Davis, William J. & Mary Malinda Blanton, 19 Oct 1841; William F. Davis, bm.

Davis, Wm. L. & M. A. Moore, 6 Feb 1854; Andrew Hudlow, bm; m 8 Feb 1854 by A. Hamby, Elder.

Davison, Alexander & Mary Ellis, 28 Apr 1783; Mosses Bridges, bm.

Dawdle, Charles & Sally Janes, 8 Dec 1826; Thomas Janes, bm.

Dawson, Isaac B. & Malinda Allen, 23 Nov 1826; John Wilkins, bm.

Dawson, Manus & Denady Nolin, 31 Aug 1826; W. D. Metcalf, bm.

Dawson, Thomas J. & Isabelah Cockerham, 5 Apr 1832 ; Churchwil Moris, bm.

Dean, Drury & Mary M. McHann, 28 Oct 1852; John W. Dean, bm.

Dean, Hosea J. & Elizabeth Mills, 13 Oct 1834; William E. Mills, bm.

Dean, John William & Mary Michal, 18 Jan 1850; Drury Deen, bm.

Dean, Robert & Jane Collins, 23 Dec 1818; Jeremiah Dean, bm.

Debord, Edward & Rebecca Bates, 6 Mar 1832; Hiram Searcy, bm.

Deck, G. W. & L. M. Long, 24 Nov 1857; J. Deck, bm; m 24 Nov 1857 by B. E. Rollins.

Deck, Henry & Polly Long, 25 Nov 1822; James W. Carson, bm.

Deck, Jacob & Eave Ponter, 6 Mar 1812; George Ponter, bm.

Deck, L. L. & Jane Reid, 6 May 1856; Wm. K. Reid, bm; m 6 May 1856 by Thomas E. Davis.

Dedman, Thomas & Mary Linkhorn, _____ ; Mark Dedmon, bm.

Dedman, William & Elizabeth Shean, 3 Dec 1844; G. H. Wilkins, bm.

Dedmon, John L. & Nancey Singeltary, 6 Mar 1832; Thomas Dedmon, bm.

Denton, John & Pheby Freeman, 5 Apr 1806; William Picket, bm.

Denton, John & Christian Williams, 28 Dec 1844; M. R. Waldrop, bm.

Denton, Joseph & Nelly Martindale, 6 Apr 1829; Harvy Carrier, bm.

Denton, Thomas & Pressy Denton or Wesson, 12 Aug 1806; Stephen Philips, bm.

Depreast, Benjamin F. & Jane Brooks, 2 Nov 1853; Adam Weaver, bm.

Depriest, James B. & Margaret Depriest, m 20 Feb 1856 James Baber.

Depriest, John H. & Mary J. Hamilton, 15 Nov 1854; Andrew Hamilton, bm; m 15 Nov 1854 by Wm. G. Mode, J. P.

Depriest, John O. & Cynthia Crowder, 23 Jul 1842; Jesse Chitwood, bm.

Depriest, Randolph & Eliza Harmon, 8 Feb 1834; William H. Walton, bm.

Depriest, William Jr. & Julee Cansiler, 30 Dec 1809; John Early, bm.

Deprist, John & Elizabeth Owens, 3 Nov 1813; Thomas Owens, bm.

Derryberry, Barny & Sarah Hase, 7 Feb 1853; Thomas Hase, bm; m 13 Feb 1853 by J. Gilkey, J. P.

Devenport, John & Sarah Jones, 21 Oct 1848; W. M. Lynch, bm.

Devenport, Mathew & Susanah Littlejohn, 26 Jan 1819; Elias Linch, bm.

Devenport, Mathew & Margaret Littlejohn, 15 Feb 1842; Ely Littlejohn, bm.

Devenport, William & Elizabeth Lynch, 25 May 1853; T. H. W. Whiteside, bm; m 25 May 1853 by Wm. Rucker, J. P.

Deveny, Felix W. & Elizabeth Taylor, 20 Sept 1830; Joseph G. Deveny, bm.

Deveny, Jinkins & Sally Grayson, 28 Aug 1831; Robert Deveny, bm.

Deveny, Joseph G. & Cathrine Hunt, 13 May 1829; Lewis Payne, bm.

Deveny, Robert & Nancy Derreberry, 15 Nov 1831; Richard Bowers, bm.

Deviney, Aaron & Sarah Hunt, 15 Mar 1864; J. T. Mode, bm; m 15 Mar 1864 by G. Mode, J. P.

Deviney, W. G. & Margret Richard, 6 Aug 1866; John Deviny, bm; m 6 Aug 1866 by A. Hunt, M. G.

Devinney, Aron J. & Rachael McFarland, 28 Oct 1839; John McFarland, bm.

Dickerson, Garland & Elizabeth Reavis, 10 Sept 1804; Richard Lewis, bm.

Dickerson, Marcus O. & Mary M. Patten, 16 Jul 1839; Francis A. Littlejohn, bm.

Dickerson, Terry & Martha McTyre, 29 Nov 1828; T. F. Birchett, bm.

Dickey, G. W. H. L. & Polly Moore, 19 Oct 1814.

Dickey, George W. & Jane A. Kilpatrick, 15 Feb 1836; Madison H. Kilpatrick, bm.

Dickey, Jerry, colored, son of Phelix Dickey, & Clorsa Whitesides, dau. of A. Whitesides, m 1 Aug 1867 by W. B. McEntire.

Dickey, John B. & Katharine W. Kilpatrick, 14 Oct 1839; James L. Taylor, bm.

Dickson, Andrew & Mrs. Jain Wray, 10 Sept 1816; James Wray, bm.

Dickson, John & Elizabeth Nowlin, 12 Nov 1816; David Nowlin, bm.

Dickson, Thomas & Olive Nowlin, 4 Mar 1824; David Nowlin, bm.

Dickson, William & Hanah Hughey, _____; Felix Walker, C. C., wit.

Dicky, Moses & Susanah Ballard, 14 Oct 1802; William Ballard, bm.

Dicus, Elijah & Viney Green, 1 Nov 1826; Elijah Walker, bm.

Dicus, William & Usely Walker, 12 Apr 1803; Thd. Walker, bm.

RUTHERFORD COUNTY MARRIAGES 1779-1868

Dicus, William Jr. & Emsey Bailey, 2 Feb 1839; Hiram Bailey, bm.

Dilback, Jacob & _____, 25 Jul 1799; David Blackwell, bm.

Dillingham, Benjn Clarke & Cynthia H. Hannon, 18 Jan 1817; Ezekiel Graham, bm.

Dillingham, Archabd. & Mary Blanton, 24 Jun 1802; Arthur Grahm, bm.

Dills, Thomas & Nancy Fowler, 2 Apr 1798; Philip Henson, bm.

Dimsdale, Joseph & Elizabeth Elizer Jackson, 2 Sept 1849; Jacob Jackson, bm.

Dimsdale, Nasbut & Elizabeth Gibbs, 15 Jan 1834; William Dimsdale, bm.

Dimsdale, Riley & Elmina Jons, 13 Aug 1846; D. W. Brown, bm.

Divinny, J. J. & Rebecca McGahey, 4 Dec 1858; E. M. Carpenter, bm; m 6 Jan 1858 (sic) by E. M. Carpenter.

Dobbines, George R. & Nancy C. Walker, 19 Feb 1857; Joel J. Dobbins, bm; m 19 Feb 1857 by W. A. Tanner, J. P.

Dobbins, A. J. & M. A. Wallace, 27 Dec 1865; W. B. Dobbins, bm; m 28 Dec 1865 by Wm. J. Willkie, M. G.

Dobbins, C. C. & Martha King, 18 Oct 1866; J. T. Culbreath, bm; m 25 Oct 1866 by Wm. J. Willkie, M. G.

Dobbins, Daniel & Luncinda Hawkins, 4 Jul 1861; Daniel Hawkins, bm.

Dobbins, J. J. & Harriet Vickers, 14 Apr 1859; John M. Freeman, bm; m 14 Apr 1859 by John Freeman, J. P.

Dobbins, J. M. & A. F. Wilson, 4 Nov 1865; W. B. Dobbins, bm.

Dobbins, James B. & Polly Hawkins, 6 Feb 1840; Thomas Hawkins, bm.

Dobbins, John & Elizabeth Webb, 8 Oct 1832; Joel Smith, bm.

Dobbins, Lewis & Lethe Bowen, 13 Jan 1830; Lewis Bowen Jr., bm.

Dobbins, Nehemiah & Druzilla Wall, 18 Mar 1841; Joel Smith, bm.

Dobbins, W. B. & Mary J. McClure, 28 Dec 1865; Wm. J. Wilkie, bm.

Dobbins, William & Elizabeth Scrugs, 3 Sept 1789; John Byrns, bm.

Dobson, Jno. & Nancy Parks, 19 Nov 1803; Benjamin Parker, bm.

Dodd, John & Charlotte Earle, 16 Sept 1825; Aspasio Earle, Harvy Carrier, bm.

Dogget, J. L. & Cemantha Tanner, 5 Mar 1857; J. P. Eaves, bm; m 8 Mar 1857 by A. Hamby, M. G.

Doggett, Bushrod R. & Frances Bridges, 19 Oct 1843; Richard Doggitt, bm.

Doggett, Charles Y. & Mrs. Mary Roberts, 10 Feb 1810; George Doggett, bm.

Doggett, Coalman & Mary A. Smith, 24 Apr 1833; John T. Cherry, bm.

Doggett, G. W. & Mary McDaniel, 10 Jun 1863; M. O. Dickerson, bm.

Doggett, George & Milly Carpenter, 24 Apr 1812; Andrew Eaves, bm.

Doggett, Micajah H. & Narcissa Hardin, 14 Feb 1856; L. N. McBrayer, bm; m 14 Feb 1856 by Wm. Harrill.

Doggett, Richard & Jane Goode, 6 Dec 1821; William Green, bm.

Doggett, W. D. & Elizebeth Buttler, 17 Dec 1865; R. P. Doggett, bm.

Doggitt, George W. & Elizabeth Wadkins, 11 Mar 1830; Marvel Sutton, bm.

Dogwood, George & Angaline Alexander, 7 Jan 1850; R. Scoggin, bm.

Donaldson, Saml. & Mary Adams, 17 Aug 1788; Thomas Donaldson, bm.

Donner, Michael & Polly Wikle, 3 Nov 1800; Michl. Donner, bm.

Dorten, William & Chalot Johnson, 17 Nov 1783; William Ballard, bm.

Doss, William & Nancy Flin, 14 Oct 1803.

Dotey, John & Elizabeth McMillin, 1 Dec 1797; Robt. McMillin, bm.

Dougherty, James & Mary Standford, 29 Jan 1783; Drewry Logan, bm.

Dowdel, John & Sally Enloe, 16 Jul 1804; Am. Enloe, bm.

Downey, Burton & Mary Covington, 21 Aug 1856; E. M. Carpenter, bm; m 21 Aug 1856 by E. M. Carpenter.

Downey, Ez & Templa Scruggs, 12 Oct 1857; D. S. Goode, bm; m 12 Oct 1857 by J. H. Carpenter, J. P.

Downey, Jeffeson T. & Mary Padgett, 23 Sept 1860; Berry P. Hardin, bm; m 23 Sept 1860 by B. McMahan, J. P.

Downey, Samuel & Mrs. Sally Murroon, 16 Aug 1810; John Murroon, John McMory, bm.

Downy, T. J. & Marthey Padgett, 24 Sept 1854; S. A. Webb, bm; m 24 Sept 1854 by J. H. Carpenter, J. P.

Doyle, Allen & Mary Reavis, 8 Jan 1800; John Doyle, bm.

Doyle, Allen & Rosey Horton, 24 Jun 1806.

Doyle, James Jr. & Elizabeth Horton, __ Nov 1806; Ansel Bradly, bm.

Doyle, James O. & Betsy Russel, 21 Mar 1818; William Bradley, bm.

Draper, James & Peggy Osborne, 17 Dec 1788; Landy Shuemaker, bm.

Driskel, William & Sarah Scott, 11 Dec 1788; John McCluer, bm.

Driskill, John & Polly Kilpatrick, 18 Dec 1797; Arthur McCluer, bm.

Drisll, William & Betsy Mitcalf, 10 Dec 1813; William D. Metcalf, bm.

Drury, Michael & Sucky (Susanna) Guffy, 26 Jun 1799; J. Miller, Noble Hamlton, bm.

Duck, Charon & Polly Mullins, 26 Jul 1814; Arthur McCluer, bm.

Duck, Leeroy & Margery Walker, 27 May 1814; George Feagin, bm.

Duck, Leroy & Nancy Eaves, 22 Jun 1818; G. Dickerson, bm.

Duck, Robert & Margt. McClure, 23 Jan 1815; Arthur McCluer, bm.

Duck, Thaddeus & Sely Mullins, 8 Sept 1813; G. Dickerson, bm.

Dudley, John W. & Christy Moore, 11 Dec 1837; William Taber, bm.

Dudley, Logan C. & E. M. Darden(?), m 5 Jun 1859 by J. A. Grant, J. P.

Duett, R. T. & Carla R. Allen, 10 Jun 1865; J. A. Fagg, bm.

Duffy, Thomas S. & Catharine Carson, 21 Jan 1846.

Dulin, William & Nancy Russell, 29 May 1795; Martin Russell, bm.

Dun, John B. & Susan Edwards, 23 Nov 1845; Wm. Ricahrdson, bm.

Dun, Samuel M. & Julian Blanton, 26 Dec 1839; Joseph Byars, bm.

Dunbar, Henry & Mary Bracket, 19 MAr 1792; James M'Callon, bm; Francis Guthrie, wit.

Dunkin, Charles & Sally Whitesides, 19 Jan 1837; Henry Gibbs, bm.

Dunkin, William & _____, 1 Jan 1814; Hiram Dunkin, Joseph Hunter, bm.

Dunlop, Ephraim, of Lincoln Co., & Sally B. Deveny, 21 Feb 1811; Aaron Deveny, bm.

Dunlop, Gilbert & Elizabeth McDow, 28 Jan 1800; Lewis Bailey, bm.

Dunn, Charles N. & Laury Foster, 1 Feb 1841; Fendale Foster, bm.

Dunn, James & Catharine Dunn, 6 Nov 1850; A. R. Bryan, bm.

Dunnaway, Clemment, Susannah Condry, 12 Sept 1831; James Condry, bm.

Dupriest, John G. & rebecca Harrison, 23 Feb 1861; B. F. Dupriest, bm; m 24 Feb 1861 by R. Depriest, J. P.

Durham, Akillis & Mrs. Edith Hicks, 31 Mar 1808; Bery Hicks, Abraham Cantrell, bm.

Durham, Benjamin D. & Sarah J. Horn, 13 Oct 1859; Alpha Sparks, bm; m 13 Oct 1859 by H. Culbreath, M. G.

Durham, Charles Crawford & Unicea J. Evans, 8 Apr 1835; Vincent B. Rollins, Cameron A. Durham, bm.

Durham, David D. & Malinda Hughes, 14 Feb 1831; Minor W. Smith, bm.

Durham, Edmond & Polly Lee, 22 Sept 1829; David D. Durham, bm.

Durham, Edmond & Nancy Dogwood, 22 Aug 1849; Barnabas King, bm.

Durham, Micajah & Esther Baxter, 9 Apr 1835; Matthew Yong, bm.

Durham, R. Achiles & Amelia R. Beam, 1 May 1854; Martin Beam, bm; m 4 May 1854 by H. Harrill, J. P.

Durham, Richard & Jane Davis, 29 Jan 1798; Thomas Harden, William Bridges, bm.

Duval, Alexander & Malinda C. Perkson, 16 Feb 1846; A. G. McEntire, bm.

Dycus, Alfred B. & Rebecca Moore, 21 Dec 1834; Oliver Scoggins, bm.

Dycus, Edward & Martha Mullens, 9 Jan 1833; Golsbery Dycus, bm.

Dycus, Golsbery & Peggy Blankenship, 17 Jan 1828; Davis Stockton, bm.

Dycus, James & Polly Edwards, 15 Dec 1814; William Dycus, Jeremiah Blanton, bm.

Dycus, Wm. & Elizabeth Thompson, 3 Aug 1848; B. Washburn, bm.

Dye, Whitson & Jane Yarbeory, 2 Jan 1840; Edward P. Jones, bm.

Dyer, Absalum & Rebecca Scruggs, 31 Aug 1828; John Dyer, bm.

Dyer, Jasper & Polly Waller, 22 Dec 1824; Jonathan Dyer, bm.

Dyer, John & Mary Trollender, 1 Nov 1819; Jonathan Dyer, bm.

Dyer, John & Mirah Sutton, 22 Dec 1851; William Sutton, bm; m 24 Dec 1851 by James Sutton, J. P.

Dyer, Jonathan & Susan Green, 16 May 1840; J. Sullins, bm.

Dyer, Thomas & Fanny Waller, 13 nov 1827; Jonathan Dyer, bm.

Dykes, James & Sarah Wilson, 4 Mar 1817; William Johnson, bm.

Dyre, Archibald & Barbary E. Emery, 13 Jan 1846.

Dysart, James & Jennet Woods, 23 Feb 1791; Robert Woods, bm.

Eadney, Easea & Sarah Miler, 31 Dec 1797; Thomas Cochram, bm.

Eakin, George & Sally Melton, 14 Jan 1810; Thos. Morris, bm.

Eakins, John & Sally Walker, 16 Aug 1808; J. Hamilton, bm

Eakins, Samuel & Polly Hix, 19 Feb 1803; Thomas Eakins, bm.

Eakins, Thomas & Jane Daves, 3 May 1798; Richd. Lewis, bm.

Earl, Perry & Catharine Davis, 9 Jun 1858; James W. Davis, bm.

Earle, Joshua & Elizabeth Yelton, 8 Feb 1828; James Yelton, bm.

Earle, Pleasant & Nancy Webb, 17 Oct 1801; Haburd Hawkins, bm.

Earles, Noah & Patsy Hutchins, 28 Jan 1839; John Earles, bm.

Earles, W. M. & Leonra S. D. Smith, 30 May 1852; William Smith, bm.

Earley, A. B. & Nancy Davis, 3 Feb 1866; J. M. Allen, bm; m 18 Feb 1866 by D. Ponnell.

Earley, Drewry & Huldah Taylor, 10 May 1856; John H. Taylor, bm; m 22 May 1856 by J. A. Grant, J. P.

Earley, Georg & Sarah Hutchens, 13 Feb 1854; James Gettys, bm.

Earley, James & Amanda Olford, 4 Oct 1853; Josiah Vess, bm; m 14 Oct 1853 by H. W. Patterson.

Earley, John P. & Rutha Hill, 28 Nov 1859; D. B. Earley, bm;

Earley, Ransom & Betsey Cherry, 11 Oct 1859; J. H. Bradly, bm.

Earley, Thos. & Sinthey Earley, 30 Mar 1842; A. B. Campbell, bm.

Earley, William & Caroline Black, 28 Dec 1848; Eli Guffey, bm.

Earls, John & Marguet Melton, 3 Oct 1861; David Melton, bm; m 3 Oct 1861 by B. E. Rollins, Baptist minister.

Earls, Joshua & Elizabeth Melton, 30 Jun 1858; Joshua Toney, bm; m 4 Jul 1858 by John Freeman, J. P.

Earls, Pleasant & Sarah Horton, 9 Nov 1859; Henry Yelton, bm.

Earls, Zachariah & Jamima Harden, 18 Oct 1812; William Earls, Able Harden, bm.

Early, Edward & Margaret Hill, 6 Jul 1830; John Hall, bm.

Early, George & Nancy Liles, 20 Feb 1814; David Liels, bm.

Early, John & Lettice Fortune, 14 Apr 1829; Lindsey F. Melton, bm.

Early John & Margart Black, 31 Oct 1838; A. F. Huddelston, bm.

Early Lauson & Minerva Melton, 22 Nov 1841; J. Melton Burton, bm.

Early, Thomas & Patsey Proctor, 18 Mar 1812; Reuben Proctor, bm.

Early Wm. & Elisa Shitles, 8 Apr 1861; John Halford, bm; m 25 Apr 1861 by Wm. Devenport, J. P.

Earwood, Edmund & Polly Adams, 15 Jul 1806; Major James Smith, bm.

Eaves, Andw. & Polly Carpenter, 18 Nov 1799.

Eaves, Andrew & M. A. Logan, 1 Oct 1860; L. D. Hamrick, bm; m 2 Oct 1860 by Jas. S. Ervin.

Eaves, Guilfed & Levina Mooney, 28 Feb 1833; Jesse Sullins, bm.

Eaves, J. B. & A. J. Logan, 19 Feb 1866; Daniel May, bm; m 20 Feb 1866 by Daniel May.

Eaves, Jonathan & Nancy Womack, 10 Oct 1809; Abr. Womack, bm.

Eaves, N. Spencer & Ursilla Wallace, 22 Jul 1846; John M. Scoggin, bm.

Eaves, Spencer & Jane Baxtger, 12 Sept 1821; James J. Hampton, bm.

Ederington, John & Margert Gilmour, 26 Dec 1781; David Heddlestone, bm.

Edgerton, John & Eliz. Jones, 19 Mar 1804; Thomas Capel, bm.

Edgerton, Ransom & Mimy Logan, 10 Mar 1808; Am. Enloe, bm.

Edgerton, Scroop & H. E. Stott, 3 Feb 1842; George Tomberlin, bm.

Edney, Asa & Harrit Ruth Freeman, 1 Sept 1844; D. B. Freeman, bm.

Edwards, Alexander & Anna Waters, 8 Nov 1851; Barnabas King, bm; m 12 Dec 1851 by J. Young, J. P.

Edwards, Amos & Bedy Crowder, 12 Mar 1851; J. O. Beam, bm; m 12 Mar 1851 by Martin Beam, J. P.

Edwards, Benjamin & Susannah Edwards, 13 Jul 1814; John W. Allen, bm.

Edwards, George & Tempy Blanton, 24 Apr 1821; John Edwards, Jeremiah Blanton, bm.

Edwards, George M. & Jane Lewis, 30 Oct 1848; Peter Mooney, bm.

Edwards, James L. & Susanah McDaniel, 12 Dec 1844; A. Edwards, bm.

Edwards, James M. & Mary Ann Bedford, 4 Jan 1860; John L. McDaniel, bm; m 5 Jan 1860 by J. B. McDaniel, J. P.

Edwards, James M. C. & Mildred M. Lewis, 22 Nov 1820; John Moore, bm.

Edwards, James W. & Ann Prator, 12 Nov 1814; Thomas Prator, bm.

Edwards, Jesse & Liddy Crawford, 12 Jan 1802; William Harris, bm.

Edwards, John & Jane Littlejohn, 27 Dec 1840; Jas. Morris, bm.

Edwards, Joseph M. & Priscilla C. Beam, 9 Jul 1849; A. S. Harrell, bm.

Edwards, Malcome M. & Alvira Fagans, 6 Mar 1854; Wm. Edwards, bm; m 7 Mar 1854 by A. Padgett, M. G.

Edwards, Thomas & Jency Flack, 6 Nov 1804; George Flack, bm.

Edwards, Thomas F. & Nancy Bowman, 12 Apr 1847; _____, bm.

Edwards, William & Elizabeth Dunn, 1 May 1836; Samuel Pack, bm.

Edwards, William & Elizabeth Bates, 18 Sept 1865; Samuel Wilkins, bm; m 18 Sept 1865 by C. L. Harris, J. P.

Edwards, Z. A. & M. A. Beam, 28 Feb 1866; J. L. Edwards, bm; m 15 Mar 1866 by Wm. Harrill.

Egerton, James N. & Ursilla Walker, 9 Feb ___; Wm. Edgerton, bm.

Egerton, T. R. & Sarah Logan, 17 Jan 1856; James H. Whiteside, bm; m 17 Jan 1856 by T. B. Justice, M. G.

Egerton, Thomas & Mrs. E. L. Whitesides, 19 May 1842; Joseph U. Whiteside, bm.

Ekins, John & Lettuce W. Melton, 8 Sept 1809.

Elam, Alexander & Betsey _____, __ Sept 1815; ____ Burnett, bm.

Elerson, John & Elmira Pack, 27 Dec 1854; Wm. Spawn, bm; m 17 Dec 1854 by J. M. Hamilton, J. P.

Elexandra, James & Frances Brackett, 18 May 1850; William C. Hamrick, bm.

Eliott, Henry & Nanney Moore, 19 Sept 1827; Caleb A. Moore, bm.

Elison, William & Alvira Thompson, 2 Sept 1846; John Walker, bm.

Ellison, William Jr. & Elizabeth Collins, 19 Jan 1854; William A. Elison Sr., bm; m 19 Jan 1854 by J. M. Hamilton, J. P.

Elkins, Wm. & Jane Johnson, 14 Feb 1867; J. H. Suttles, bm.

Ellett, A. H. F. & Verzilla Green, 24 Mar 1832; John T. Goode, bm.

Elliot, Andrew & Zilphy Kelley, 5 Oct 1813; William Elliot, bm.

Elliot, James F. & Elisabeth Doggett, dau. of George Doggett, request for license by George Doggett, 22 Feb 1807.

Elliot, John & _____, 1799; Merrel Elliot, bm.

Elliot, Jonathan & Sarah Bates, 16 Jun 1842; D. J. Twitty, bm.

Elliot, William & Lavinia Harris, 26 Dec 1820; Henry Elliot, bm.

Elliott, Albirty T. & Amelia McBrayer, 24 Oct 1839; J. H. Alley Jr., bm.

Elliott, James L. & Jane Burges, 25 Sept 1849.

Elliott, Jesse & Winney (Winifred) Bradley, 7 May 1828; William Wells, bm.

Elliott, John W. H. & Ellen Whiteside, 4 Nov 1850; Wm. Elliott, bm.

Elliott, Johnson & Martha Whiteside, 24 Jun 1856; John Ledbetter, bm; m 26 Jun 1856 by Wm. O. Bagwell, J. P.

Elliott, Jonathan & Sally Harris, 19 Jan 1822; William Elliot, bm.

Elliott, Martha Sr. & Mrs. Betsey McCombs, 15 Sept 1826; Major McCombs, Thomas Good___, bm.

Elliott, Noah & Elizabeth Taylor, 28 Feb 1844.

Elliott, Thomas & Delinsey Elms, 5 May 1832; James McEntire, bm.

Elliott, Thomas F. & Maria L. Smith, 5 Feb 1834; William H. Cabaniss, bm.

Elliott, W. H. & Mary E. Lancaster, 17 Dec 1866; N. E. Walker, bm; m 3 Jan 1867 by J. W. Morgan, J. P.

Elliott, Wm. M. & Barbary Carson, 6 Apr 1844; Spencer Eaves, bm.

Ellis, Absolom & Hannah Weber, 30 Jul 1809; William Hoppor, bm.

Ellis, Caleb & _____, 13 Mar 1827; Samuel Baily, bm.

Ellis, Francis & Sarah Breedlove, 21 Oct 1800; Charles Breedlove, bm.

Ellis, James W. & Rachel Hill, 13 Mar 1815; Daniel Smith, bm.

Ellis, Jesse & Malindey Gipson, 30 Sept 1846; C. L. Harris, bm.

Ellison, Benjamin & Anny Bradley, 14 Mar 1826; James Humphries, bm.

Ellison, John & Rebecca Newman, 27 Aug 1815; William Newman Jr., bm.

Ellison, Posey & Levina Alford, 7 Oct 1817; Sims Harris, bm.

Ellmore, James & Ann Newton, 8 Nov 1827; Ebenezer Newton, bm.

Elmore, Mastan & Elizebeth Stice, 15 Dec 1796; Edward Rippey, bm.

Elms, John & Sally Williams, 26 Aug 1824; John Ellis, bm.

Elms, Jonathan & Siddy Bradley, 5 Jan 1828; Jones Bradley, bm.

Endsley, James & Nancy A. Jackson, 13 Dec 1832; Benjamin Hoyle, bm.

England, Joseph & Polly Dolton, 29 Feb 1820; Thomas Dolton, bm.

Enloe, Abraham & Sally Edgerton, 9 Jan 1795; James Morris, bm.

Enloe, Anthony & Patsey Burnett, 4 Oct 1791; Jos. Burnett, bm.

Enloe, David & Jane Ross, 26 Sept 1792; James Ross, bm.

Enloe, Ezekiel & Sally Porter, 20 Feb 1795; James Miller, bm.

Ensly, William L. & Jane Morrison, 1 Sept 1859; John P. Flack, bm; m 1 Sept 1859 by Jas. M. Spratt, J. P.

Eplee, A. J. & Lusindey Thomson, 19 Aug 1865; Paul F. Searcy, bm; m 19 Aug 1865 by T. H. W. Whiteside, J. P.

Epps, James & Rebecca Ledbetter, 16 Dec 1834; Wm. Smith, bm.

Erawod, Levy & Martha J. Erawod, 24 Dec 1846; Wm. Hufstedler, bm.

Errowood, James & Lisey Crowder, 11 Jun 1805; Henry Peeler, bm.

Ervin, Jas. & Levinia Liles, 18 Sept 1815; Wm. Carson, bm.

Erwin, Arthur & Evaline A. Terrell, 15 Jan 1825; Thoe F. Birchett, bm.

Erwin, James S. & U. H. Williams, 5 Sept 1864; B. R. Morrison, bm.

Erwin, John C. & Martha Ann King, 15 Dec 1826; Noah Sullins, bm.

Erwin (Capt.) L. P. & E. R. Carrier, 14 __ 1863; L. B. Bryan, bm; m 14 May 1863 by Nl. Shotwell, Pastor of the Presb'n Church, Ruth'n, N. C.

Erwin, William & Cynthia Groves, 2 Aug 1825; Ben F. Logan, bm.

Erwood, Edmon & Sary Jaen, 21 Jul 1796; William Yong, bm.

Erwood, John & Elizabeth Alexander, 18 Jun 1831; William A. Wilson, bm.

Eskridge, Elijah & Harriet P. Wilkins, 4 Dec 1834; Hezekiah Wilkins, bm.

Eskridge, John G. & Elizabeth Thompson, 12 Oct 1827; Hambleton Eskridg, bm.

Eskridge, William F. & Intha Louisa Reed, 21 Dec 1865; Williamson F. Gold, Nl. Shotwell, bm; m 21 Dec 1865 by Nl. Shotwell, Pastor of the Presb'n Church.

Eskrig, Hamilton & Mary Irwin, 5 Apr 1831; Abram C. Irvin, bm.

Evans, David & Anna Beam, 15 Jan 1828; Benjamin D. Durham, bm.

Fagans, George & Elizabeth Lyles, 26 May 1832; Daniel Feagans, bm.

Faihair, Adam & Elizabeth Miller, 10 Jan 1849; Davis Hambree, bm.

Falkner, Thomas & Catherine Timens, 3 Sept 1793; Jes MGlamry, bm.

Falls, James & Nancy Fisher, __ Nov 1806; Richard Lewis, bm.

Farnsworth, Alexander D. & Mary E. Long, 21 Sept 1855; J. H. Wilkins, bm; m by T. E. Davis, M. G.

Feagaines, Edman G. & Artildia Green, 8 Sept 1849; Calvin J. Sparks, bm.

Feagans, John Henry & Martha Edwards, 23 Jan 1854; G. Decater Morris, bm; m 25 Jan 1854 by A. Hamby, D. D.

Feagins, Edmund G. & Nancy Wilson, 27 Feb 1837; Henry Feagins, bm.

Feagins, George & Rachel Johns, 2 Aug 1814; Zachariah Johnson, bm.

Feagins, Henry & Temperance Wilson, 14 Aug 1835; Charles Wilson, bm.

Feagins, John & Christina Fortuneberry, 1 Mar 1813; A. M. Dickey, bm.

Feagins, Williams & Jane Johns, 29 Oct 1816; Jas. Johns, bm.

Featherston, Mn. & Milly Mills, 5 Nov 1799; Ambrose Mills, bm.

Fergus, John & Ann Battle, 7 Jan 1783.

Figgins, Silas & Mary Lequir, 11 Feb 1808; John Loqure, Wm. Maghe, bm.

Fike, George A. & D. E. Hicks, 23 Mar 1844; M. F. Simmons, bm.

Files, John & Ann Eddy, 10 Nov 1781; William Walker, bm.

Fillbeck, George & Marias Randol, 30 Apr 1821; George Fillbeck, bm.

Finley, James & Hannah Allen, 2 May 1820; Thomas Prater, bm.

Finley, Robit W. & S. A. Melton, 8 Dec 1857; John B. Martin, bm; m 8 Dec 1857 by G. K. Andrews.

Finly, Robert & Sarah Scott, 19 Oct 1791; James Scott, bm.

Fisher, David K. & Julia B. Camp, 10 May 1791; James Scott, bm.

Fisher, Jacob & Martha B. Alexander, 31 Jan 1815 (consent signed by Elias Alexander).

Fisher, Wm. & Evaline Hip, 29 Nov 1842; T. D. Morgan, bm.

Fittsgarrel, John & Poley Joans, 5 May 1808; Danl. Reinhardt, bm.

Flack, Andrew & Polly Porter, 11 Apr 1796; William Spann, bm.

Flack, Andrew & Delilah Moore, 2 Jan 1844; Daniel Michal, bm.

Flack, George & Prisilla Edwards, 2 Jun 1806; Thomas Edwards, bm.

Flack, George Jr. & Elizabeth Urcula Elliott, 25 Mar 1858; Wm. Harrill, bm; m 25 Mar 1858 by William Harrill, O. P. M.

Flack, J. P. & S. M. Clements, 26 Dec 1859; G. P. Watson, bm; m 27 Dec 1859 by Jas. M. Spratt, bm.

Flack, John & Martha Boman, 28 Dec 1846; W. Bowman, bm.

Flack, John & Mary Bowman, dau. of Eli Bowman, 17 Mar 1853; Thos. F. Edwards, bm; m 20 Mar 1853 by Wm. Rucker, J. P.

Flack, John J. & Mary Bryson, 9 Jun 1832; John Moore, bm.

Flack, John P. & I. J. Watson, 17 Jan 1866; C. C. Hawkins, bm; m 18 Jan 1866 by Jas. M. Spratt, J. P.

Flack, Lewis B. & Nancy Morgan, 18 Aug 1860; A. D. Flack, bm; m 21 Aug 1860 by D. Koone.

Flack, Mills H. & Margaret A. Hemphill, 9 Nov 1859; H. P. Whiteside, bm; m 9 Nov 1859 by T. B. Justice.

Flack, William & Jane Nix, 16 Jun 1812; John Nix, bm.

Flack, William Jr. & Mary Gofotth, 12 Dec 1836; John T. Cherry, bm; m 15 Dec 1836 by Hugh Watson, J. P.

Fleming, Isaac & Jane R. Guffy, 7 Aug 1815; John Guffy, bm.

Fleming, John & Jane Lago, 10 Mar 1782; James Gray, bm.

Flin, G. L. & Sarah Ann Livingston, 14 Apr 1860; J. J. Bradley, bm; m 15 Apr 1860 by M. Wilkerson.

Flin, Hazael & Sousan M. Bates, 2 May 1848; John D. Searcy, bm.

Flin, William H. & Martha J. Levenston, 5 Aug 1860; S. H. Bagwell, bm; m 5 Aug 1860 by Wm. Devenport, J. P.

Flinn, G. H. & N. M. Harris, 19 Mar 1866; P. Wilkerson, bm; m 21 Mar 1866 by W. H. Logan.

Flinn, Jackson & Emily Crawford, 27 Apr 1854; Russel Collins, bm.

Flinn, John Jr. & U. Odine, 2 Jan 1843; John Flin, bm.

Flinn, John B. & Mary Malinda Williams, 28 Nov 1866; J. M. Allen, bm; m 30 Nov 1866 by W. H. Logan, Elder.

Flinn, Miles & Isabella Robbins, 19 Feb 1845; Samuel Wilkins, bm.

Flinn, William & Catharine Bagwell, 22 Sept 1838; Ephraim Padgett, bm.

Flowers, James & Sarah Ann Thogmorton, 25 Oct 1838; Geo W. Clarke, bm.

Floyd, Henry & Fanny Janes, _____ 1815; John Glass, bm.

Floyd, John & Chany Brummit, 17 Sept 1822; Samuel Laughter, bm.

Floyd, John & Nancy White, 19 Jan 1831; Abraham Emery, bm.

Floyd, Nathan M. & Mary Deck, 26 Feb 1838; Jacob Deck, bm.

Fondren, John & Kezia Roberts, 26 Apr 1803; Morris Roberts, bm.

Fondren, Samuel & Susanah Winbrown, 10 Dec 1809; John Winbrown, James V. Harper, bm.

Fondren, Whitmon H. & Malissa Powel of Lincoln Co., 10 May 1835; Martin Roberts, bm.

Forbess, James & Rachel Street, 7 Jan 1826; Anthony Street, Wm. Murry, bm.

Forgus, David R. & Prisciler Hardin, 1 Jul 1858; J. R. Walker, Jr., bm; m 1 Jul 1858 by John Freeman, J. P.

Forbush, Francis & Drucilla Ann Johnson, 1 Oct 1861; James T. McDaniel, bm; m 3 Oct 1861 by W. J. Norvill, J. P.

Ford, Betlon & Juda Berry, 9 Feb 1817; Thaddeus Deck, bm.

Ford, George B. & E. C. Carrier, 3 Jul 1856; W. L. Twitty, bm; m 3 Jul 1856 by C. T. Bland, M. G.

Ford, James & Judith Prince, 17 Oct 1781; Robt. Prince, bm.

Ford, John S. & Jane McClure, 5 Jan 1816; David Gray bm.

Ford, John S. & Sophia W. Camp, 17 Aug 1826; Young Brizendine, bm.

Ford, M. L. & Nancy L. Oliphant, 22 Apr 1857; E. Carrier, bm; m by T. E. Davis, M. G.

Ford, S. K. & M. E. Alexander, 28 Apr 1863; R. L. Gilkey, bm; m 28 Apr 1863 by A. Hamby, L. E. of M. E. Church, South.

Forman, Bold A. & Mrs. Cynthy Jones, 21 Feb 1832; Peter Summy, bm.

Forney, A. G. & Elizabeth W. Logan, 6 Apr 1844; Jos. W. Calloway, bm.

Forney, J. H. & E. M. Logan, 11 Nov 1844.

Fortenbury, James & Polly Seratt, 12 Jul 1813; D. Lyles, bm.

Fortinberry, Demcey & Elizabeth Allen, 27 Mar 1827; Danniel King, bm.

Fortner, Ezekel & Mary Watts, 6 Jan 1791; Samuel Carpenter, bm.

Fortun, William & Clary Smelly, 15 Sept 1816; Hugh Watson, bm.

Fortune, Joseph G. & Sarah L. Melton, 8 Sept 1851; Jerrel Melton, bm; m 11 Sept 1851 by Lewis McCurry.

Fortune, Joseph G. & Mary D. Long, 30 Oct 1855; G. W. Deck, bm; m 30 Oct 1855 by B. E. Rollins.

Fortune, Lindsey & Rebecca Bill, 14 Jul 1816; William Fortune, bm.

Fortune, Pleasant & Elizabeth Melton, 19 Feb 1839; Silas R. Melton, bm.

Fortune, Pleasant & M. E. Suttles, 26 Aug 1849; Dugger Freeman, bm.

Fortune, Thomas & Jane Depriest, 7 Apr 1832; David Morehead, bm.

Fortune, William & Elizabeth Deck, 17 Jul 1827; Williamson Fortune, bm.

Fortune, Wm. P. & Lurena J. Long, 15 Jan 1867; J. O. Waters, bm.

Fortune, Williamson & Elizabeth Grayson, 24 Dec 1827; Lindsey F. Melton, bm.

Foster, Alfred & Cinthia Street, 26 Oct 1865; M. O. Dickerson, bm; m 26 Oct 1865 by G. Eaves, J. P.

Foster, Daniel & Patsey Lankford, 17 Jan 1816; Edmond Foster, bm.

Foster, Edmund & Mary Edwards, 29 Oct 1850; E. Carrier, bm.

Foster, Elkin & Mary Justice, 6 May 1800; John Foster, bm.

Foster, H. F. & Mary Green, 19 Sept 1844; Geo. W. Jones, Tolliver Smith, bm.

Foster, James L. & Nancy Smith, 31 May 1859; E. D. Hawkins, bm; m 12 Jun 1859 by Robt. G. Twitty, J. P.

Foster, James P. & Jane A. Prince, 5 Oct 1841; Geo. W. Logan, bm.

Foster, John & Mildred Tailor, 9 Jun 1789; John Foster Sr., bm.

Foster, William & Nancy Hughes, 4 Feb 1802; Lewis Taylor, bm.

Foster, William & Cimmon Kerr, 1 Jan 1846; Milton McWhirter, bm.

Foster, William H. & Fanny Green, 22 May 1845; Robert McClain, bm.

Foster, Wm. W. & Mary Nodine, 20 Oct 1853; J. M. Nodine, bm; m 20 Oct 1853 by J. M. Hamilton, J. P.

Fowler, Lawson & Mary Coxey, 21 Dec 1812; Wm. Rollins, bm.

Fowler, Leonard & Jane L. Hinson, 9 Mar 1858; D. W. Fowler, bm.

Fowler, Zechariah & Sarah Sheehen, 22 Aug 1850; Elias Carrier, bm.

Frachur, David & Lina Hall, 11 Nov 1845; M. Hall, bm.

Fradey, John & Milley Searcy, 23 Apr 1831; Alson M. Edney, bm.

Frady, Azariah & Sarah Roberson, 31 Aug 1840; John W. Robertson, bm.

Frady, George W. & Sally Dalton, 31 Oct 1842.

Frady, Henry & Nancy M. Wheler, 12 Aug 1848; James J. Smith, bm.

Frady, Isaac M. & Mary Wilkerson, 2 Mar 1846; Moses Wilkerson Jr., bm.

Frady, Joel M. & Ann Coxey, 10 Apr 1845; William Coxsy, bm.

Frady, L. R. & Matilda Bartlett, 8 Oct 1864; A. M. Robertson, bm; m 9 Oct 1864 by T. P. Sorrels, J. P.

Francis, Joseph & Susana Whorlek, 18 Apr 1793; James Wilson, bm.

Franklin, Henry & Ann Gibbs, 24 Jan 1797; John Franklin, bm.

Franklin, Henry & Nancy Sism, 8 Jan 1805; Lewis Franklin, bm.

Franklin, John P. & Nercissee J. Proctor, 14 Feb 1853; Robert Price, bm; m 14 Feb 1853 by R. T. Price, J. P.

Franklin, Lewis & Meriah Daves, 18 May 1823; Joseph Geer, George Franklin, bm.

Frasear, William & Salley Richards Turpin, 5 Feb 1807; Thomas Turpin, bm.

Fraser, John & Betsey Vermilion, 16 Sept 1809; Joshua Faser, bm.

Fraser, Thomas & Polly H. Wilson, 20 Aug 1807; Alexander Fraser, bm.

Freasure, James & Agegy Austin, 8 Aug 1799; Isaac Morrow, bm.

Freeman, Albert G. & Drucilla Morehead, 6 Jan 1845; Enoch B. Morten, bm.

Freeman, Andrew B. & Catharine Murrow, 17 Mar 1842; B. W. Andrews, bm.

Freeman, B. W. & Nancy Jane Robertson, 2 Feb 1854; J. G. Freeman, bm; m 2 Feb 1854 by John Freeman, J. P.

Freeman, Benjamin & Nancy Pope, 19 Aug 1819; Adin Keeter, bm.

Freeman, Dobson B. & Elzira Wadkins, 8 Nov 1826; Jas. Marlow, bm.

Freeman, Dugger, & Sally Prince, 18 Sept 1789; Wm. Eaves ,bm.

Freeman, Dugger & Nancy Shamwell, 3 Sept 1834; George W. Logan, bm.

Freeman, E. B. & E. C. Hunter, 26 Jan 1860; J. L. Wallace, bm; m 26 Jan 1860 by John Freeman, J. P.

Freeman, Ephraim & Jane Walker, 19 Jan 1847.

Freeman, George & Polly Carpenter, 11 Aug 1827; Emanuel M. Carpenter, bm.

Freeman, George & Lucy Fortune, 5 Feb 1836; John Freeman, bm.

Freeman, James & Lucy Vanhoose, 2 Mar 1813; Joel Freeman, bm.

Freeman, James & Elizabeth Hill, 25 Jul 1839; Thomas Bracket, bm.

Freeman, James G. & Nancy Jane Long, 1 Oct 1856; W. N. Long, bm; m 1 Oct 1856 by Rev. B. E. Rollins.

Freeman, Jarret & Ann Porter, 3 Jun 1827; Robertson Freeman, bm.

Freeman, Jay W. & Patsey Watkins, 3 Nov 1824; James Marlow, bm.

Freeman, Joel & Polly Haney, _____; Robert Wilson, Timothy Haney, bm.

Freeman, John & Barbery Painter, 12 Jul 1804; Starling Prince, bm.

Freeman, Michael B. & Mary Shamwell, 25 Nov 1835; Edward Freeman, bm.

Freeman, Michael B. & Dicy R. Calton, 14 Apr 1858; John M. Freeman, bm; m 14 Apr 1858 by John Freeman, J. P.

Freeman, Moten F. & Mira Bagwell, 12 Mar 1838; A. W. Whiteside, bm.

Freeman, Nathaniel Robinson & Caty Seward, 7 Oct 1801; Robert Newton, bm.

Freeman, Pberry T. & Jan Edney, 23 Feb 1840; John J. Nix, bm.

Freeman, Peter & Betsey Truelove, 12 Oct 1807; Robert Freeman, bm.

Freeman, Peter & Artimincy Dicus, 24 Oct 1824; Marvill Melton, bm.

Freeman, Robert & Manda C. Carpenter, 27 Dec 1866; Jerry Michal, bm (C. H.); m 27 Dec 1866 by C. C. Goforth, J. P.

Freeman, W. B. & Lucilla M. Wallis, 11 Oct 1847; John Freeman, bm.

Freeman, William & Elizabeth Campbell, 22 Apr 1806; Dugger Freeman, bm.

Freeman, William & Cinthia G. Kilpatrick, 1 Sept 1814; James Kilpatrick, bm.

Friday, A. S. & Mary Jane Depriest, 24 Sept 1866; D. L. Depriest, bm.

Fuller, David & Jane Seward, 15 Dec 1815; Robt. Newton, bm.

Gad, James & Rhoday Taylor, 13 Jan 1806; Jesse Taylor, bm.

Gage, Mosses & Sarah Wood, 15 Oct 1783; Timothy Riggs, bm.

Gaither, Wm. E. & Martha A. McEntire, 26 May 1853; W. H. Miller, bm; m 26 May 1853 by Wm. C. Sheets, M. G.

Gamble, J. L. & Eliz. Fortune, 30 Oct 1865; R. L. Gilkey, bm; m 16 Nov 1865 by B. E. Rollins, M. G.

Gamble, John R. & Rebecca C. Hunt, 25 Aug 1864; Jasper L. Crow, bm; m 25 Aug 1864 by K. J. McCrow, J. P.

Gamble, William & Mirah Davis, 25 Oct 1841; Alfred B. Moony, bm.

Gamewell, U. A. & M. A. McDowell, 23 Nov 1839; Campbell Smith, bm.

Gardner, Martin & Lydda Horn, __ May 1832; John Cornwall, bm.

Gardner, O. P. & Margaret Young, 12 May 1858; G. E. Blanton, bm; m 19 May 1858 by G. W. Rollins.

Gardner, William & Rebekah Beam, 4 Sept 1827; Jeremiah Gardner, bm.

Garner, Daniel & Celia Heslep, 20 Apr 1797; Thomas Garner, bm.

Garner, Jeremiah & Jain Huston Alexander, 20 Oct 1812; John Alexander, bm.

Garner, Martin & Nancy Glasscock, 16 Aug 1821; Thos. Glasscok, bm.

Garner, Thomas & Alice Martin, 25 Nov 1792; Bengemen Wilkeson, bm.

Garner, Thomas & Cathrine Haslep, 4 Jun 1795; Thomas Heslep, bm.

Garner, William & Polly Butner, ____ 1807; John Barber, Isaac White, bm.

Garret, Edmond & Margeret Sorrels, 18 Mar 1801; Walter Sorrels, bm.

Garretson, Robert & Rachel Wassom, 5 Jan 1815; Joab Johnson, bm.

Garrett, William & Sally Hawkins, 25 Jan 1819; Martin Thompson, bm.

Garrison, Alfred & Sally Hutchins, 11 Feb 1830; Moses Hutchins, bm.

Garrison, George & Sally Foxe, 23 Sept 1808; James Jackson, bm.

Garrison, John & Betsey Wadkins, 25 Nov 1819; John Yelton, bm.

Garrison, William & Catharine Roberts, 2 May 1837; John H. Alley Jr., bm.

Garrot, William & Nancy Spicer, 16 Jan 1830; Ambrose Mills, bm.

Gasperson, John & Elizabeth Burnet, 8 Jan 1782; Wm. Mittchleford, Robt. Prince, bm.

Gattis, Wm. Costen & Margaret Hambree, 30 Oct 1852; James Hanbree, bm.

Gaulteny, John & Alley Cism, 23 May 1806; John Kelley, bm.

Gay, John & Elizabeth Watson, 9 Dec 1793; John Andrews, bm.

Gee, Jackson & Saphirona Cooper, 18 Dec 1851; J. R. McDanil, bm; m 18 Dec 1851 by J. H. Carpenter, J. P.

Gee, Walton L. & Francis E. Jenkins, 28 Oct 1847; John Gee, bm.

Geer, John & Matsy Harris, 11 Jan 1815; James Justis, bm.

Geer, John Jr. & Jane Bradley, 14 Mar 1849; Robt. A. Wallis, bm.

Geer, R. Pinkney & D. C. Edwards, 30 Sept 1866; J. F. Edwards, bm; m 30 Sept 1866 by J. R. Bowman, Elder.

Geer, Solomon & Sarah Harriss, 17 Mar 1842; John Harris, Adin Keeter, bm.

Geer, William M. & Elizabeth Harris, 13 Jun 1840; Solomon Geer, bm.

George, Aaron P. & Elizabeth Cross, 7 Dec 1857; R. L. Gilkey, bm; m 7 Dec 1857 by Randolph Depriest, J. P.

George, Jesse & Pheby George, 12 Jan 1796; Solomon George, bm.

Gettys, Alexander & Elizabeth Chitwood, 2 Jan 1840; James A. Gettys, bm.

Gettys, James & Eliz. C. Watson, 16 Oct 1816; Geor. Watson, bm.

Gettys, James & Elizabeth R. Goins, 14 Sept 1864; G. W. Toney, bm; m 14 Sept 1864 by H. A. Toney, J. P.

Gettys, James A. & Martha A. Mode, 24 Oct 1861; John A. McFarland, bm; m 24 Oct 1861 by J. M. Chitwood, J. P.

Gettys, John & Alpha A. Toney, 5 Feb 1863; G. W. Toney, bm; m 5 Feb 1863 by James W. Murray, J. P.

Gettys, Jno. C. & Eliza E. McFarland, 12 Dec 1844; W. M. Gettys, bm.

Gettys, R. L. & Catharine Crowder, 6 Dec 1865; Wm. G. Price, bm.

Gettys, Robert & Sarah P. Toney, 19 Sept 1860; G. W. Toney, bm; m 17 Sept 1860 by J. M. Chitwood.

Gettys, Samuel & Nelly Gordon, 7 Feb 1803; Wm. Carson, bm.

Gettys, W. Smith & Sarah Bedford, 20 Oct 1866; R. Depriest, bm; m 25 Oct 1866 by Wm. McSwain, J. P.

Gettys, William & Tabitha Price, 14 Dec 1835; John Price Jr., bm.

Gettys, William M. C. & Maryann Carson, 19 Sept 1831; James W. Carson, bm.

Gibbines, Jessey & Eliza Runyan, 25 Feb 1836; Jeremiah Runyan, bm.

Gibbs, Andrew J. & Sarah Dimsdale, 13 Dec 1841; Henry Gibbs, bm.

Gibbs, Henry & Elmina Metcalf, 13 Feb 1845; Martin Walker, bm.

Gibbs, James & Polly Smart, __ Feb 1799; Jos. Smart, bm.

Gibbs, John & Acky Moore, 24 Feb 1814; Henry Gibbs, bm.

Gibbs, Thomas & Sarah Byas, 18 Jan 1845; Robt. Allen, bm;

Gibson, J. L. & J. C. Livingston, 25 Oct 1863; J. W. Johnson, bm; m 25 Oct 1863 by J. W. Morgan, J. P.

Gibson, Solomon & Mary Todd, 30 Jan 1842; B. W. Andrews, bm.

Gibson, W. H. & Sarah Wilkerson, 14 Nov 1859; Andrew Wilkerson, bm; m 1 Dec 1859 by J. W. Morgan, J. P.

Gidney, Saml. S. & Cynthia Wells, 24 Jul 1828; Robert Wells, bm.

Gidneys, Cornelus & Phebe Bailey, 15 Nov 1835; John Borders, bm.

Giles, Jeremiah & Milly Dove, 14 Sept 1784; Leonard Sceylor, bm.

Gilkey, John & Cinthy Logan, 31 May 1821; James Cherry, bm.

Gill, Wm. & Ann McReynolds, ____; Thos. White, Jos. Renolds, bm.

Gillaspie, J. R. & M. E. Brown, 18 __ ___; L. O. Jolley, bm.

Gillespie, James A. & Jane M. Ramsay, 17 Jan 1836; James L. Cowan, bm.

Gillespie, James B. & Mary J. Scoggin, 12 Feb 1859; C. Burnett, bm; m 20 Feb 1859 by G. W. Rollins, M. G.

Gillespie, John & Sarah Bridges, 15 Nov 1831; Jonathan Gillespie, bm.

Gillespie, Jonathan & Nancy Bland, 15 Aug 1840; Wm. D. Cooper, bm.

Gilliam, Calvin W. & Mary E. Withrow, 25 Feb 1850; Thos. L. Parkes, bm.

Gilliam, William & Sally Souther, 20 Mar 1811; Harriss Gilliam, bm.

Ginkins, Charles & Pricilla Farmer, 13 Jan 178-; F. Walker, C. C., wit.

Ginnings, John Pryer & Miranna Moore, 16 Feb 1821; Richard Shagog, bm.

Given, Robert & Patty Wilson, ____; Joseph Dawson, Joseph McRenolds, bm.

Gladen, John L. & Patience Hardin, 26 May 1819; John Jinkins, bm.

Glenn, James & Marry Clarke, ____; John Clark, Joseph McReynolds, bm.

Glover, Samuel & Channy Petters, ____; James McReynolds, Robert McReynolds, bm.

Goans, Robard & Pegah Newton, 3 Mar 1808; Wm. Hunt, bm.

Goforth, John & Mary Moore, 25 May 1837; Wm. Goforth, Tolliver Smith, bm.

Goforth, John H. & Sarah Ann Davis, 20 Mar 1860; Elbert Davis, bm; m 27 Mar 1860 by D. Ponnell.

Goforth, Preston & Parthena B. Mitchell, 24 Dec 1827; John Guffey, bm.

Goforth, T. J., son of W. C. Goforth, & M. L. McArthur, dau. of Walter McArthur, m 11 Dec 1867 by D. Ponnell.

Goforth, Thomas B. & Lavina Stafford, 12 Oct 1842; C. C. Goforth, bm.

Goforth, William & Rosannah Harvill, 27 Nov 1829; Nathan Right, bm.

Goin, Edward & Salley Goin, 11 Nov 1817; Joel Johnson, bm.

Going, William Jr. & Polly Griffin, 14 Jul 1785; William Goinges, bm.

Gold, Daniel P. & Margaret M. Jinkins, 15 Nov 1838; William M. Gold, bm.

Gold, Milton & Martha Fortune, 6 Dec 1830; Thomas Fortune, bm.

Gold, Sterling C. & Cynthia Hainey, 12 Aug 1816; Daniel Gold, John Haney, bm.

Gold, William M. & Thane Wilson, 24 Aug 1820; Thomas Wilson, Daniel Gold, bm.

Gold, William M. & Catherine Wasburn, 9 Oct 1838; Milton Gold, bm.

Gooch, Nathan & Elizabeth Williams, 20 Sept 1785; David Dickey, bm.

Good, James & Martha Kenady, 19 Feb 1851; H. H. Hopper, bm.

Good, John & Elizabeth Webb, ____ 1807; Ambros Christopher, Richard Harrold, bm.

Good, Napoleon & Susanna Snowden, 24 Apr 1840; Adam Hunsinger, bm.

Good, Richard & Pheby Webb, 19 Sept ____ (during term of Gov. Benjamin Williams, 1800-1802 or 1807-08); Ambrose Brittone, Wm. Wall, bm.

Good, Wm. & Permelia Webb, 2 Aug 1850; Noah Hopper, bm.

Goodbread, John & Mary Bradly, 28 Apr 1779; Jonathan Hampton, bm.

Goodbread, John & Nancy Elmes, 13 Aug 1821; John Bradley, bm.

Goodbread, Thomas & Nancy Hider, 26 Oct 1804; Benjamin Hyder Jr., bm.

Goode, Abraham & Barbary Hudlow, 9 Feb 1830; Joseph Head, bm.

Goode, Benjamin F. & Sarah Magness, 14 Nov 1831; Milton Gold, bm.

Goode, David S. & Sarah Downey, 7 Oct 1852; Barnard McMahan, bm; m 7 Oct 1852 by J. H. Carpenter, J. P.

Goode, E. A. & Rossley Durham, 16 Dec 1847; K. T. Carpenter, bm.

Goode, Edward & Fanny Rowland, 22 Nov 1808; Moses Smart[?], bm.

Goode, Edward & Lydia J. Scoggin, 11 Mar 1864; J. M. Goode, bm; m 11 Mar 1864 by Nathan Scoggin, J. P.

Goode, Francis & Martha Jane Philips, 1 Jul 1862; Wm. E. Walker, bm; m 10 Jul 1862 by T. B. Justice.

Goode, G. W. & Harriet Callihan, 27 Sept 1864; H. H. Mitchell, bm; m 26 ____ 1864 by W. H. Logan, M. G.

Goode, George & Nancy Waters, 1 Jan 1818; Alfred McKinney, bm.

Goode, George & Rebecca Webb, 23 May 1855; J. W. Goode, bm.

Goode, James & Mary Toms, 1 Dec 1830; Abraham Goode, bm.

Goode, John & Patsy Goode or Gill, 28 Jan 1789; James Camp, bm.

RUTHERFORD COUNTY MARRIAGES 1779-1868

Goode, John & Janie Hawkins, 14 Jul 1795; Wm. Johnson, bm.

Goode, John W. & Mary Hopper, 8 Apr 1843; James M. Tate, bm.

Goode, Martin E. & Malinda Walker, 29 Oct 1830; Paschal T. Grigg, bm.

Goode, Noah S. & Sarah Willkie, 23 Dec 1865; J. M. Goode, bm; m 23 Dec 1866 by G. M. Webb.

Goode, Robert & Martha Hawkins, 4 Jan 1788; Thos. Goode, bm.

Goode, Robert & Elizabeth Hawkins, 23 Mar 1806; Wm. Hawkins, bm.

Goode, Thomas & Jamimah Jones, 27 Aug 1836; William Robbins, bm.

Goode, Tolliver & Martha Bland, 16 Jul 1831; William H. Green, bm.

Goode, W. T. & J. M. Webb, 23 Dec 1865; J. L. Eaves, bm; m ___ 1865 by J. C. Burge.

Goode, William & Sarah Green, 24 Aug 1821; Garland Dickerson, bm.

Goode, Wm. & Feriba Hopper, 27 Oct 1854; Walter Gee, bm; m 17 Oct 1854 by J. H. Carpenter, J. P.

Gooden, Joseph & Elmina Graham, 12 May 1830; Robert G. Twitty, bm.

Goodlett, Jesse & Betsey H. Johnson, 8 Sept 1802.

Goodman, John & Mary Robertson, 9 Dec 1802; St. Jno. Camp, William Goodman, bm.

Goodman, John & Poley Thomas, 5 Sept 1808; Ebenezer Newton, bm.

Goodman, John & Martha Reavis, 16 Jul 179-; Isham REavis, bm.

Gordon, Benjamin & Nancy Laughter, 23 Apr 1832; Wiley Laughter, bm.

Gosea, Moses & Salley Beam, 13 Feb 1821; Aaron Gosea, David Bea, bm.

Goudelock, John B. & Sarah M. Doggett, 3 Feb 1832.

Gragg, William & Elise Wats, 18 May 1797; Robert Orr, bm.

Graham, Andrew Jr. & Thaney Mitchel, 22 Jan 1824; Isral Graham Jr., Andrew Graha, bm.

Graham, Arthur H. & Elizabeth D. S. Ray, 15 Jan 1834; Wm J. T. Miller, bm.

Graham, Elisha & Lenora Harris, 17 Oct 1820; John Gradley, bm.

Graham, Henary & Cathrin Mitchel, 12 Feb 1824; Isaac Graham, Benjamin Harris, bm.

Graham, Levi S. & Mary Searcy, 21 Nov 1850; John E. Graham, bm.

Graham, William & Susanna Twitty, 29 Dec 1806; John Lewis, bm.

Grainger, H. H. & Amanda Caroline Rhodes, 9 Dec 1857; J. W. Morgan, bm; m 9 Dec 1857 by J. W. Morgan, J. P.

Grainger, William James & Prissilla Edwards, 9 Sept 1830; Sims Harris, bm.

Grant, Andrew & Mashew McGee, 18 Dec 1788; Robt. Young, bm.

Grant, Andrew & Sally Decker, 30 Oct 1823; James Keeter, bm.

Grant, B. F. & Mary Jinkins, 19 Oct 1859; J. L. Carpenter, bm; m 19 Oct 1859 by J. H. Carpenter, J. P.

Grant, Benjamin & Tilatha Dyer, 8 Jun 1834; Robert Goode, bm.

Grant, Charles & Polly Morris, 8 Feb 1821; Andr. Grant Jr., bm.

Grant, James & Nancy Tomerlin, 13 Oct 1818; William Grant, bm.

Grant, James & Sally Eliott, 16 Dec 1825; Jese Elliott, bm.

Grant, James & Molinda Grant, 19 Sept 1844; Thomas Grant, bm.

Grant, John A. & Mintey M. Bruce, 13 Sept 1841; John Gibbs, bm.

Grant, Morris & Almira M. Marlow, 23 Dec 1837; James Marlow, bm.

Grant, Thomas & Amy Coxey, 5 Aug 1801; Andrew Grant, bm.

Grant, W. L. & Emily Matilda Crawford, 15 Nov 1858; A. W. Crawford, bm; m 25 Nov 1858 by J. W. Morgan, J. P.

Grant, William & Sally Elms, __ Feb or Mar 1813.

Grant, Wm. E. & Sarah L. Amanda Noblet, 30 Dec 1860; M. C. Noblitt, bm; m 30 Dec 1860 by M. Wilkerson, J. P.

Grason, Joseph & Lettice J. Melton, 19 Mar 1807; Daniel Melton, bm.

Gray, D. J. & S. C. Wilkins, 26 Oct 1854; G. B. Ford, bm; m 26 Oct 1854 by A. Hamby, Elder.

Gray, Hampton & Susana Griffin, 24 Feb 1828; John Bradley, bm.

Gray, Joseph & Elizabeth Williams, 22 Dec 1802; James Gray, bm.

Gray, Samuel & Frankey Moore, 22 Dec 1802; James Gray, bm.

Grayson, Benj. G. & Sarah Houser, 8 Aug 1844; H. H. Howser, bm.

Grayson, Isaac & Polly Melton, 20 Aug 1807; John Fortune, bm.

Grayson, John M. & Polly Melton, 8 Jan 1829; Lewis Vansant, bm.

Grayson, John M. & Rebecca Hunt, 25 Jun 1836; Thomas Daves, bm.

Grayson, Joseph & Rachel Vanzant, 17 Dec 1807; James Vanzant, bm.

Grayson, Joseph C. & Eliza R. Wilson, 23 Jan 1827; Jonathan B. Wilson, bm.

Grayson, K. J. Mc & Mary L. Melton, 11 Nov 1860; W. A. McCurry, bm; m 11 Nov 1860 by J. M. M. Price, J. P.

Grayson, Wm. & Susanna Login, 17 Oct 1807; Joseph Login, bm.

Grayson, William G. & Christina McCurry, 28 Apr 1835; Joseph C. Grayson, bm.

Green, A. J. & J. A. Wilson, 3 Nov 1865; S. D. Green, bm.

Green, Abner & Elizebeth Wilson, 26 Jul 1832; Shadrach Green, bm.

Green, Abner & Marian Matilda Chrsitmas, 5 Apr 1836; Elias Upchurch, bm.

Green, Abraham B. M. & Elizabeth Young, 20 Dec 1832; Robert Magness, bm.

Green, Amos J. & Rebecca Culbreath, 11 Feb 1845; James Culbreath, bm.

Green, Anscel & Frances Champion, 3 Aug 1817; John Lewis, bm.

Green, Anselm & Elizebeth Philbeck, 11 Feb 1822; Shadrach Green, George Philbeck, bm.

Green, Archibald & Susanna Nix, 16 Feb 1817; John Colbreath, bm.

Green, Asa & Milly Green, 17 Jul 1864; Wm. Green, bm; m 17 Jul 1864 by Nathan Scoggin, J. P.

Green, Benjamin & Harriat Green, 12 Aug 1866; D. Lovelace, bm; m 12 Aug 1866 by Nathan Scoggin, J. P. (C. H.)

Green, Berry & Jane Owens, 17 Nov 1864; Wm. Green, bm.

Green, Berrymon & Rhoda Melton, 1 Dec 1828; Henry Green, bm.

Green, C. O. & Hannah M. Briscoe, 19 Jan 1839; William Goode, bm.

Green, Charles E. & Mary Morris, 9 Apr 1850; D. J. Gray, bm.

Green, Cornelius & Martha Harrill, 30 Jan 1838; Shadrach Green, bm.

Green, Drury & Nancy Tesenyear, 30 Dec 1834; Nicholas Tesenyear, bm.

Green, Drury & Elizabeth A. Bridges, 15 Feb 1859; B. B. Byers, bm; m 17 Feb 1859 by G. W. Rollins.

Green, Drury & Elendor Toney, 23 Sept 1866; Thomas Toney, bm.

Green, Drury D. & Priscilla J. Balton, 24 Nov 1864; Bary Green, bm.

Green, E. Govan & Ann Daniel, 1 Mar 1858; Andrew Hudlow, bm; m 4 Mar 1858 by J. N. Covington, J. P.

Green, Edwin & Nancy Smith, 30 Mar 1839; Thomas L. McEntire, bm.

Green, Elias & Rebecca Hamrick, 22 Dec 1827; Richard Champion, bm.

Green, George & Lucy Jones, 13 Mar 1784; Kusiah Johnson, bm.

Green, George M. & Rody McDade, 15 Aug 1854; H. B. Green, bm; m 15 Aug 1854 by J. M. Hamilton, J. P.

Green, Gilbert & Ca:Rah Ledford, 6 Feb 1840; Thomas Ledford, bm.

Green, Green L. & Sally Moore, 27 Feb 1830; Thomas Green, bm.

Green, Henry & Veannah Owens, 21 Nov 1842; William Lovles, bm.

Green, Henry L. & Eliza H. Colbreath, 22 Dec 1846; Alanson Padgett, bm.

Green, Isaack & Nanney Wilson, _____ ; Henrey Green, Levens Burns, bm.

Green, Isaiah & Sally Melton, 10 Aug 1829; Henry Green, bm.

Green, J. L. & Sarah M. Hamrick, 1 Sept 1864; W. J. Hardin, bm.

Green, J. W. & Catharine Harrill, 9 Aug 1855; John Burg Jr., bm; 9 Aug 1855 by G. W. Rollins, M. G.

Green, James & Saley Ellis, 1 Sept 1808; William Covington, Aaron McEntire, bm.

Green, James A. & Rebeckey Green, 17 Jul 1864; Benjamin Green, bm; m 17 Jul 1864 by Nathan Scoggin, J. P.

Green, James M. & Maryan Griffin, 18 Nov 1857; S. C. Harrill, bm; m 19 Nov 1857 by A. Hamby, Elder.

Green, James M. & Sarah R. Beam, m 13 May 1866 by B. B. Byers, J. P.

Green, James M. & Hanah Hawkins, 25 Feb 1867; George M. Moore, bm.

Green, John & Leathy McKinney, 20 Dec 1819; William Green, bm.

Green, John & Leathea Sofronia Culbreath, 12 Jul 1847; William M. Culbrath, bm.

Green, John P. & Mary Green, 12 Sept 1859; D. Loveless, bm.

Green, Joseph & Bellanah Twitty, 2 Jun 1791; A. W. Irvine, bm.

Green, Joseph & Polly Ellis, __ Sept 1800; Abram Enloe, bm.

Green, Joseph & Nancy Horton, 16 Feb 1823; William Green, bm.

Green, Joseph P. & Sarah Edwards, 1 Mar 1856; George Green, bm; m 6 Mar 1856 by G. W. Rollins.

Green, Joseph P. & Nancy Clarindon, 9 Feb 1859; Green Loveles, bm; m 11 Feb 1859 by H. Harrill, J. P.

Green, Joseph P. & Sarah M. McDaniel, 1 Oct 1860; Franklin Blanton, bm; m 10 Oct 1860 by J. M. Chitwood, J. P.

Green, L. M. & Nancy Bridges, 23 Oct 1860; George Green, bm.

Green, Lewis & Elizabeth Loweless, 12 Oct 1842; Thomas Green, bm.

Green, Loyd E. & Margaret S. Green, 5 Jun 1864; Wesley S. Spurlin, bm; m 5 Jun 1864 by J. B. McDaniel, J. P.

Green, Martin & Phebe Ledford, 22 Dec 1837; Richard Covington Sr., bm.

Green, Marvel & Elizebeth Dicus, 1 Aug 1833; Shadrach Green, bm.

Green, Michal & Jane C. Lansing, 2 Mar 1848; Jonas Green, bm.

Green, Oliver & Nancy E. Lee, 29 Nov 1854; Geo W. Dupriest, bm; m 30 Nov 1854 by A. Padgett, M. G.

Green, Peter & Sarah Brisco, 23 Jan 1855; Joseph N. Goode, bm; m 23 Jan 1855 by Alanson Padgett.

Green, Peter H. & Eliza Camp, 3 Sept 1827; James M. Erwin, bm.

Green, Richard & Sarah Spicer, 30 Sept 1826; Hiram Searcy, bm.

Green, Robert & Polly Bridges, 17 Jul 1834; Noah Davis, bm.

Green, Ruben & Polly Bradley, 6 Feb 1832; John Flinn, bm.

Green, S. D. & N. E. Blanton, 22 Dec 1865; G. T. Bostick, bm.

Green, S. J. & Margaret S. Young, 3 Feb 1865; E. M. Sweezy, bm.

Green, Samuel & Scicely Padgett, 1 Oct 1857; A. J. Scoggins, bm; m 1 Oct 1857 by G. W. Rollins, Baptist minister.

Green, Shad. & Mary Gage, 20 Dec 1782; Timothy Riggs, bm.

Green, Stephen & Judith Moore, 6 Apr 1833; Lewis Green, bm.

Green, Thomas & Nancy Singleton, 4 Aug 1820; William Champion, bm.

Green, Thomas & Ama Sorrels, 8 Feb 1821; John Kilbreath, bm.

Green, Thomas Jr. & Peggy Moore, 9 Sept 1836; Lewis Green, bm.

Green, Thomas M. & Elizabeth Hullet, 2 Aug 1844; E. M. Carpenter, bm.

Green, Thomas M. & Elmira Hamright, 10 Aug 1844; J. H. Callahan, bm.

Green, William & Polly Moore, 1 Oct 1812.

Green, William & Jane Baber, 9 Mar 1815; Harbert Wallace, bm.

Green, William & Elizabeth Melton, 25 Oct 1831; William Davis, bm.

Green, William & Catharin Rodgers, 7 Nov 1841; John Freeman, bm.

Green, William & Malena Lovelace, 17 May 1862; William Loveless, bm; m 18 May 1862 by P. G. Washburn, J. P.

Green, William & Nancy Bridges, 20 Aug 1865; Wm Champion, bm; m 10 Aug 1865 by N. Scoggins, J. P.

Green, William & Rachel Davis, 11 Sept 1865l; John Davis, bm; m 17 Sept 1865 by John McFarland, J. P.

Green, William H. & Unicy Durham, 25 Dec 1832; Charles Durham, bm.

Green, Wm. H. & Matilda Dobbins, 30 Oct 1859; Wm. Wilson, bm; m 30 Oct 1859 by J. B. McDaniel, J. P.

Green, William T. & Elvira Murrow, 16 Jan 1830; William H. Green, bm.

Green, Willis & Polly Smart, 24 Mar 1828; Lewis Green, bm.

Green, Willis & Patsy Green, 16 Apr 1839; Green L. Green, bm.

Green, Willis & Priscellah Bridges, 23 Dec 1851; Richard Covington, bm.

Green, Willis & Sarah E. Scoggins, 25 Nov 1859; Carter Burnett, bm; m 25 Nov 18569 by T. B. Justice, Bapt. Min'r.

Green, Zachariah & Rebeca Dobbins, 17 Apr 1860; Wm. H. Green, bm; m 22 Apr 1860 by J. B. McDaniel, J. P.

Greenlea, James & Mary Bolton, ____ 1808; John McEntire, bm.

Greenlee, James M. & Eliza A. Morriss, 15 Nov 1836; James H. Greenle, bm.

Greenlee, Samuel & Minerva Lackett, 4 Jun 1822; William Koone, bm.

Greenway, G. A. & Nancy Jane Watson, 18 Sept 1854; John T. Petty, bm; m 18 Sept 1854 by Alanson Padgett, M. G.

Greenway, Gideon A. & Eliza Ballard, 24 Jan 1841; William L. Petty, bm.

Greenwood, William & Mary George, 21 Oct 1795; Hugh Greenwood, bm.

Gregory, Jackson & Susan M. McAfee, 19 Sept 1822; Joshua Camp, bm.

Grenway, Franklin & Elizabeth Madison, 29 May 1854; Thomas Hunsinger, bm; m 6 Jul 1854 by H. Padgett, J. P.

Greyor, James & Franky Tailor, 18 Jan 1796; Patrick Scott, bm.

Grayson, W. G. & Julian Melton, 11 Feb 1867; Jno. M. Grayson, bm.

Griffes, George & Salley Patterson, 19 Mar 1796; John Woodburn, bm.

Griffin, Chislom & Frances Terrel, 31 Mar 1790; A. Logan, bm.

Griffin, Greenberry & Faithey Halbert, 7 Dec 1830; Baylis W. Lewis, bm.

Griffin, John G. & Nancy Martin, 15 Oct 1827; William M. Gold, bm.

Griffin, William L. & Elizabeth Sutton, 22 Feb 1821; Greenberry Griffin, bm.

Grigg, Banister & Rebekah Randele, _____; Joseph Willis, David Willis, bm.

Grigg, Bolin & Susannah Stogden, 11 Sept 1817; Joseph Willson, bm.

Grigg, Federick & Polly Crowder, 18 Dec 1800.

Grigg, Joel & Eunice Patterson, 17 Aug 1811; Robert Patterson, bm.

Grigg, Paschal T. & Nancy Elliott, 3 Dec 1830; David W. Schenck, bm.

Grise, Lawson & Jane Banther, 30 Sept 1856; R. F. Marlow, bm; m 30 Sept 1856 by J. Gilkey, J. P.

Grizel, John & Sally Taylor, 15 Apr 1813; Jesse Taylor, bm.

Grizzle, Elias & Betsy Jane or Mary Milliard, 12 Dec 1859l; Lorenzo D. Culbreath, bm; m 15 Dec 1859 by H. Culbreath, M. G.

Grizzle, James & Rachel King, 19 Dec 1826; Barney King, bm.

Grose, Joseph & Nancy Brandal, 29 Oct 1840; Joseph McCurry.

Gross, Cain & Mary Wiley, 8 Oct 1866; Jack Eaves, bm (C. H.); m 10 Oct 1866 by Toliver Hameton.

Gross, Hoyle U. & Susan Harrill, 10 Jul 1845; A. W. Haril, bm.

Gross, Leander & Mary Tanner, 19 Dec 1833; William Tanner, bm.

Gross, P. H. & Margaret Daniel, 22 Nov 1863; Thomas Toms, bm; m 22 Nov 1863 by A. Hamby, Elder.

Groves, J. B. & M. N. Wells, 12 Jan 1859; Wm. L. Ensley, bm; m 13 Jan 1859 by Jas. M. Spratt.

Groves, Jesse U. & Margaret Long, 17 Sept 1822; William Long, bm.

Groves, William H. & Jane A. Wallis, 9 Jan 1839; Jesse M. Groves, bm.

Groves, Wm. H. & Malinda Groves, 13 Sept 1858; Wm. O. Wallace, bm; m 14 Sept 1858 by Jas. M. Spratt.

Guffay, Thomas & Rhue Marshall, 18 Dec 1798; Benjamin Martias, bm.

Guffey, David & Nancy Campbell, 13 Nov 1866; Wm J. Toney, bm. (C. H.)

Guffey, E. P. & Lucinda Franklin, 4 Nov 1866; S. D. Price, bm; m 4 Nov 1866 by Mijamin Price, J. P.

Guffey, Eli & Lucinda Elliott, 6 Nov 1856; G. W. Deck, bm; m 6 Nov 1856 by Wm. Harrill.

Guffey, George W. & Sarah Clemmons, 14 Dec 1836; William Menteeth Jr., bm.

Guffey, George W. & Terrissa Vickers, 29 Sept 1841; Geo. M. Reid, bm.

Guffey, George W. & Jane Menteith, 24 Jul 1851; C. Clements, bm; m 24 Jul 1851 by John Freeman, J. P.

Guffey, Isaac & Margaret A. Prope, 23 May 1855; P. N. Long, bm; m 27 May 1855 by John Freeman, J. P.

Guffey, James & Martha Anderson, 28 Nov 1791; George Watson, bm.

Guffey, James & Anny Freman, 27 Apr 1819; Hamblen Freeman, bm.

Guffey, James & Fanny Guffey, 1 Dec 1819; Glowd Finly Long, bm.

Guffey, James & Ridley Freeman, 2 Oct 1824; John Freeman, bm.

Guffey, James F. & Mary Cochran, 2 May 1838; Cornelius Clements, bm.

Guffey, James M. & Mary E. Hutchins, 12 Feb 1865; James Caloway, bm; m 12 Feb 1865 by D. L. McCurry, J. P.

Guffey, John & Elizabeth Mitchel, 1 Oct 1814; Jas. Mitchel, bm.

Guffey, John & Margaret Guffey, 18 Dec 1859; A. W. Lookadoo, bm; m 18 Dec 1859 by John Freeman.

Guffey, John Alason & Elasebeth Bradly, 4 Mar 1841; A. B. Callahan, bm.

Guffey, John S. & Matilda Freeman, 14 Jul 1819; John Guffey, bm.

Guffey, John S. & Eliza Moorehead, 15 Nov 1820; William Long, bm.

Guffey, Josire & Eliza Franklin, 15 Jan 1855; James G. Freeman, bm; m 17 Jan 1855 by John Freeman, J. P.

Guffey, R. E. & Julian Ensley, 27 Aug 1863; C. P. Carson, bm; m 27 Aug 1863 by Jas. M. Spratt, J. P.

Guffey, Robert & Jenny Clemmons, 30 Sept 1831; William Smart, bm.

Guffey, Robert E. & Mary Cochran, 13 Dec 1843; Robert Cochran, bm.

Guffey, S. R. & Martha A. Webbe, 30 Oct 1856; H. K. Smart, bm; m 30 Oct 1856 by John Freeman, J. P.

Guffey, Thomas & Nancy Clements, 8 Dec 1826; William Smart, bm.

Guffey, Thomas Sr. & Polly Griggs, 30 Sept 1819; John Guffy, Joab Johnson, bm.

Guffey, William & Izabella Smart, 2 Feb 1793; James Smart, bm.

Guffey, William & Delila Philbeck, 6 May 1830; George Philbeck, bm.

Guffie, Jas. & Jane Fleming, 11 Dec 1815; John Guffey, bm.

Guffy, Archable R. & Patsey Cochram, 7 Aug 1815; John Guffy, bm.

Guffy, Archibald & Inthy Haynes, 19 Dec 1854; E. M. Bates, bm; m 21 Dec 1854 by John Koone.

Guffy, E. P. & Rachel Luckydoo, m 13 Aug 1865 by Wm. G. Mode, J. P.

Guffy, Eli & Anna Walker, 1 Mar 1851; John R. Guffy, bm.

Guffy, Eli & Mary P. Long, 13 Dec 1853; Wm. K. Reid, bm; m 15 Dec 1853 by Thomas E. Davis, M. G.

Guffy, Isaac & Mary Jarrell, 19 Aug 1863; Adam Jarrell, bm; m 20 Aug 1863 by Adam Hunt, M. G.

Guffy, James W. & Lercresa Poap, 18 Jul 1861; John Guffy, bm; m 18 Jul 1861 by Jas. M. Spratt.

Guffy, John A. & Mary Wilson, 28 Feb 1850; James W. Allen, bm.

Guffy, John R. & Mary Huchins, 12 Nov 1855; George W. Guffey, bm; m 13 Nov 1855 by Jas. M. Spratt, J. P.

Guffy, Monroe & Jane Early, 17 Jan 1844; Thomas Early, bm.

Guitis, Robert & Sarah Toney, 6 Oct 1862; H. A. Toney, bm; m 7 Oct 1862 by James W. Murray, J. P.

Gutery, James & Sally Stone, 4 Feb 1808; Andy Hamilton, bm.

Guttrey, Reubin & Susannah Holland, 29 Aug 1805; John Guttry, bm.

Haile, Benjamin & Elizabeth Ketter, 6 Mar 1824; James Justis, bm.

Haines, John & Celia Webb, 24 Aug 1819; Daniel Haines, Jesse Dobbins, bm.

Hains, Wilkerson & Elizabeth Keeter, 30 Jan 1826; Eli Hains, bm.

Hairs, Samuel & Mary Donaldson, 30 Mar 1792; Richard Daugherty, bm.

Halbet, Joseph & Lucy Aleson, 25 Jun 1812; John Aleson, bm.

Halford, Andy & Elizabeth Harris, 15 Jan 1812; Jos. Halford, bm.

Halford, or Alford, Francis Asbury & E. Clementine, 2 Nov 1842; John N. Scoggin, bm.

Halford, J. W. & Nancy Taylor, 20 Jun 1861; J. C. Taylor, bm; m 20 Jun 1861 by Wm. Devenport.

Halford, J. W. & Louisa Hill, 7 Dec 1866; D. L. Crawford, bm; m 11 Dec 1866 by W. H. Logan, Elder.

Halford, Jones & Polly Earley, 16 Sept 1820; Andrew Earley, bm.

Halford, Surrel & Mary Young, 3 Jan 1803; Jesse Halford, bm.

Hall, Alfred & Mary Parker, 16 Jul 1859; Jethro Parker, bm; m 21 Jul 1859 by J. W. Morgan, J. P.

Hall, David & Polly Queen, 11 Mar 1827; James Queen, bm.

Hall, Elijah & Marey Stot, 23 Sept 1847; David Fracheur, bm.

Hall, G. W. & Intha Hutchins, 15 Aug 1866; D. M. Justice, bm; m 18 Aug 1866 by A. K. Wallace, J. P.

Hall, J. J. & Eliza M. Deal, 2 Mar 1853; Hampton Queen, bm.

Hall, James & Rachel Hill, 22 Nov 1830; John Hall, bm.

Hall, James & Vincy Head, 5 Jan 1838; Laben Smith, bm.

Hall, Jesse & Hanah Kelley, 16 Aug 1785; Thos. Hall, bm.

Hall, John & Eliza Young, 16 Apr 1828; William Hall, bm.

Hall, John & Barbary U. F. Banther, 10 Mar 1847; David Fracheur, bm.

Hall, Jno. A. & Martha J. Kilpatrick, 8 Feb 1843; Jas. L. Taylor, bm.

Hall, John M. & Elenor Davis, 21 Dec 1822; Jacob Davis, bm.

Hall, Joseph & Jane Deviney, 23 Sept 1855; Felix W. Deviney, bm.

Hall, Joshua & Jane Queen, 5 Nov 1807; William L. Queen, bm.

Hall, Joshua & Adaline Flack, 5 Sept 1851; Jonathan Ledbetter, bm; 11 Sept 1851 by Bailey Bruce, M. G.

Hall, Lightner & Nancy Cole, 5 Jan 1866; Wm. Morton, bm.

Hall, Micajah & Polly Sellers, 26 Sept 1796; Isaac Sellers, bm.

Hall, Moses & Nancy E. Panther, 3 Oct 1854; Shered Panther, bm; m 19 Oct 1854 by M. Wilkerson, J. P.

Hall, William & Elizabeth Morgan, 28 Dec 1831; Jonathan Morgan, bm.

Hambelton, Andrew & Sally Giffen, 14 Sept 1799; William Giffen, bm.

Hamblin, Leonard & Rebeccah Harthorn, 6 Oct 1821; Andrew Bell, bm.

Hambrick, James & Mary McSwaine, 1 Jan 1832; Wm. McSwain, bm.

Hambrick, Travis & Faney Tankesley, 19 Sept 1797; Henrey Hambrick, bm.

Hambrick, William & Mary Ann Morrow, 22 Feb 1829; Stith Mayes, bm.

Hames, Edmund & Louisa Amos, 11 Oct 1847; David Amos, bm.

Hames, Wm. R. & Sarah J. Scruggs, 15 Nov 1866; Danial A. Scruggs, bm; m 15 Nov 1866 by G. M. Webb, M. G.

Hamilton, Benjamin & Nancy Whitesides, 30 Apr 1835; Marcus O. Dickerson, bm.

Hamilton, Benjamin & Mary M. Morrison, 5 Feb 1857; E. P. Morrison, bm; m 5 Feb 1857 by Paul F. Kistler, M. G.

Hamilton, James A. A. & Catharine E. Metcalf, 31 Mar 1847; Alexander Jones, bm.

Hamilton, Jesse & Margaret McMellion, 12 Mar 1806; Andrew Hamilton, bm.

Hamilton, S. G. & Mrs. Eliza Eaves, 26 Mar 1844; Wm. A. Mooney, bm.

Hampton, Adam & Lucy Bradley, 7 Jan 1821; Sherrod Upchurch, bm.

Hampton, Andw. & Esther Price, 2 Dec 1789; Willis Bradly, bm.

Hampton, Benjamin & Ruth Devault, 6 Jul 1790; George Gray Junr., bm.

Hampton, J. L. & Catharine P. Long, 19 Jun 1861; H. D. Carrier, bm; m 20 Jun 1861 by Nl. Shotwell, M. G.

Hampton, James J. & Elizabeth White, 8 Feb 1843; John McHan, bm.

Hampton, Jonathan & Nancy Walker, 14 Jul 1779; Andw. Hampton, bm.

Hampton, John W. & Mary Hunter, 18 Jul 1844; J. H. Wilkins, bm.

Hampton, Noah & Ann Love, 23 Jan 1807; Chrysly Mooney, bm.

Hampton, Noah H. & C. S. Walker, 6 Dec 1860; D. Dobbins, bm.

Hampton, Samuel D. & Margaret E. Logan, 6 Sept 1848; C. J. Webb, bm.

Hampton, T. Jefferson & Jane Long, 17 Dec 1857; H. D. Currier, bm; m 17 Dec 1857 by A. Hamby, Elder.

Hampton, W. & Margret Vickers, 5 Feb 1817; Gm. Hampton, F. F. Alley, bm.

Hamrick, Allen & Susannah McSwain, 12 Jul 1835; Richard McSwain, bm.

Hamrick, Asa & Drucinda Bridges, 28 Feb 1839; William Hamrick, bm.

Hamrick, Berryman & Catherine M. Hamrick, 2 Jun 1839; William Hamrick, bm.

Hamrick, Chesley & Metildy Rollins, 20 Jul 1837; Edmond Hamrick, bm.

Hamrick, David Jur. & Sarah Hamrick, 14 Jan 1836; David Hamrick Sr., bm.

Hamrick, Drury D. & Sarah Harden, 19 Dec 1857; David Harrell, bm; m 22 Dec 1857 by G. W. Rollins, M. G.

Hamrick, Edmund & Mary Scoggin, 28 May 1851; James M. McDaniel, bm; m 29 May 1851 by J. M. Bryan, M. G.

Hamrick, Elijah & Hannah Hamrick, 14 Jan 1836; David Hamrick Sr., bm.

Hamrick, George & Rebekah Hamrick, 11 Jul 1839; David Hamrick, bm.

Hamrick, James Y. & Katharine Hardin, 17 Jul 1829; Charles Blanton, bm.

Hamrick, Jehu & Elizabeth Green, 21 Oct 1865; J. Y. McEntire, bm; m 22 Oct 1865 by D. Ponnell.

Hamrick, Jonathan M. & Elizebeth Hamrick, 11 Jun 1840; Berryman Hamrick, bm.

Hamrick, Martin H. & Betsy Harmon, 16 Apr 1831; Joel J. Harriss, bm.

Hamrick, Nathan & Elizabeth Elliott, 17 Feb 1827; William Green, bm.

Hamrick, Samuel & Susanah Adams, 13 Dec 1807; James Bridges, bm.

Hamrick, Wm. & Mary Bridgess, 8 Feb 1816; Andeson Willy, J. Roberts, bm.

Hamrick, William B. & Jane Hamrick, 17 Nov 1839; Edmond Hamrick, bm.

Hanby, John & Phebe West, 14 Apr 1807; John West, bm.

Hanby, John & Cecil Murray, 12 Jun 1819; Iby Murray, bm.

Hanes, Eli & Elizabeth Cook, 26 MAr 1802; Phillip Stice, bm.

Hanes, Hugh H. & Talatha McLure, 29 Jan 1841; John McLure, bm.

Hanes, Robert & Nancy Webb, 28 Dec 1821; Johnathan Webb, bm.

Hanes, Robert & Melinda Smith, 30 Jul 1827; Joel Smith, bm.

Hanes, Timothy & Nancy Dobbins, 30 Aug 1840; Jacob Smith, bm.

Hannon, Edwin & Carline Earle, 5 Jan 1793.

Hannon, William & Elizabeth Briggs, 2 Mar 1797; Saml. Young, bm.

Hannon, William & Phebe Dickarson or Disharoon, 23 Mar 1810; Geo. M. Logan, bm.

Hannon, William & Elizabeth Carruth, 12 Jan 1825; Terrell L. Camp, bm.

Hardcastle, Elisha G. & Nancy Brooks, 25 Oct 1831; John Hardcastel, bm.

Hardcastle, James & Milly Dufonton, 29 Mar 1798; Thos Cufonton, bm.

Hardcastle, John & Nancy Cowder, 22 Jun 1830; Luke Mullins, bm.

Hardcastle, Robert & Susana Whilkerson, 23 Sept 1794; Elisch Hardcarsel, Thomas Garner, bm.

Harden Ancel J. & Eliza A. Gordon, 12 Dec 1837; Wright H. Wilson, bm.

Harden, George & Polly Harrell, 15 Dec 1830; D. Dobbins, bm.

Harden, Jesse & Nercissa Holland, 10 Mar 1836; James Y. Hamrick, bm.

Harden, John S. & Nancy Lee, 3 May 1821; John Lee, bm.

Harden, Thompson & Vianna Brooks, 2 Feb 1833; Richard Harrill, bm.

Harden, William L. & Elizabeth L. Lee, 11 Nov 1834; John L. Hardin, bm.

Harder, William & Rachel Cole, 1 Jul 1789; William Cole, bm.

Hardin, Asa A. & Mary Wilson, 28 Dec 1846; Wm. H. Green, bm.

Hardin, Benjamin & Elizabeth Scott, 31 Dec 1782; John Scott, James Scott, bm.

Hardin, Berryman & Jane McDonel, 1 Apr 1852; Joseph Harmon, bm; m 1 Apr 1852 by Wm. Harrill, M. G.

Hardin, Davis & Temperance Amos, 17 Apr 1842; J. E. Rollins, bm.

Hardin, Hardy & Tabitha Roberts, 4 Jul 1805; Morris Roberts, Josiah Roberts, bm.

Hardin, James & _____, 1 Feb 1798; Martin Roberts, bm.

Hardin, James B. & Frances Butler, 6 Jan 1853; James McMahan, bm; m 6 Jan 1853 by Wm. Harrill, M. G.

Hardin, Jesse & Hanner Irvine, 15 Feb 1836; Isaac J. Irvine, bm.

Hardin, Jesse N. & Caroline McClure, 15 Nov 1858; D. D. Phillips, bm; m 20 Nov 1858 by Wm. Harrill, M. G.

Hardin, John E. & Nancy Upchurch, 3 Aug 1861; Henry M. Miller, bm; m 8 Aug 1861 by L. G. Hawkins, J. P.

Hardin, Johnston & Elizabeth Queen, 27 Apr 1835; Thomas Martin, bm.

Hardin, Joseph & Elisabeth Putman, 19 Nov 1828; Roberts P. Putman, bm.

Hardin, Martin & Rebeck Evans, 13 Dec 1832; Ancel J. Hardin, bm.

Hardin, R. A. & Susan Butler, 9 Mar 1848; M. R. Alexander, bm.

Hardin, Young John & Mary Collins, 14 Feb 1808; Abel Harden, bm.

Hargrave, Hezkiah & Ann McMubry, 30 Dec 1785; James Harrel, bm.

Harison, Starling C. & Jensey Nanny, 10 Aug 1832; Davis Stockton, bm.

Harlike, Absolum & Sally Crowder, _____; William Crowder, William White, bm.

Harmon, Alfred & Elizabeth Hardin, 26 Jan 1850; Wm. Harrill, bm.

Harmon, Andrew & Dolly Braddy, 29 Oct 1825; Jesse Braddy, bm.

Harmon, Anthony & Lucresy Wills, 11 Nov 1816; Thos. Wells, bm.

Harmon, Benskin & Elizabeth Doyle, 19 Jun 1794; Jas. Doyle, bm.

Harmon, D. G. & Margaret C. Carpenter, 21 Nov 1857; M. O. Dickerson, bm; m 11 Nov 1857 by B. E. Rollins.

Harmon, Joseph & _____ Donner, __ Nov 1797; Daniel Donner, bm.

Harmon, Joseph & Patsey Geer, 25 May 1822; William Wood, bm.

Harmon, Joseph & Cindrilla Hardin, 1 Jan 1851; Ross A. Hardin, bm.

Harper, Franklin & Elizabeth Moore, 4 Jun 1849; J. H. Wilkins, bm.

Harper, John & Sussanna Edwards, 29 May 1828; Jones Bradley, bm.

Harrell, David R. & Amelia Harrill, 2 May 1867; Wm. H. Harrell, bm; m 2 May 1867 by G. M. Webb.

Harrell, Drury & Nancy Hawkins, 2 Dec 1828; Drury Dobbins, bm.

Harrell, Gilbert & Sally Jones, 4 Feb 1831; Hausen Harrell, bm.

Harrell, Housen & Abi Beam, 12 Feb 1826; Jno. Harrell, bm.

Harrell, James & Susanna Blanton, 19 Nov 1829; Wm. Harrell, bm.

Harrell, Martin & Vina Webb, 18 Dec 1849; C. J. Webb, bm.

Harrell, Street & Sarah McCombs, 2 Oct 1831; Abraham Washburn, bm.

Harril, A. H. & Urcillah Suttle, 5 Jan 1847; R. H. Gilkey, bm.

Harrill, A. S. & Hanah McDaniel, 16 Feb 1850.

Harrill, Albert & L. Elizabeth McArthur, 29 Aug 1859; H. Harrill, bm; m 1 Sept 1859 by Wm. Harrill.

Harrill, David & Sarah Ann Lynch, 21 Nov 1859; A. W. Harill, bm; m 24 Nov 1859 by G. W. Rollins.

Harrill, H. D. & Martha B. King, 21 Apr 1866; W. G. Blanton, bm; m 22 Apr 1866 by A. W. Harill.

Harrill, Housen & Levisa McBrayar, 19 Sept 1820; Garland Dickerson, bm.

Harrill, James A. & Angelina Philps, 3 Mar 1842; John H. Harrill, bm.

Harrill, James A. & Sarah L. Price, 16 Jul 1863; J. T. Mode, bm; m 16 Jul 1863 by Wm. G. Mode.

Harrill, John & Nancy Bostick, 31 Jul 1797; Howsen Harrill, bm.

Harrill, John & Sarah Suttle, 26 Dec 1854; J. H. Blanton, bm; m 28 Dec 1854 by Jos. Suttle.

Harrill, Robert M. & Catharine M. Suttle, 30 Jan 1860; James W. Suttle, bm; m 2 Feb 1860 by H. Harrill, J. P.

Harrill, Samuel & Leaher McBrier, 9 Mar 1846; A. W. Harill, bm.

Harrill, William & Easther Suttle, 13 Aug 1850.

Harris, Benjamin & Fanny Michel, 15 Jan 1818; Sims Harris, bm.

Harris, C. L. & Susan L. Logan, 11 Nov 1846; G. W. Baxter, bm.

Harris, Colemon & Tempy Ledbetter, 3 Mar 1861; G. W. Harris, bm; m 3 Mar 1861 by M. Wilkerson, J. P.

Harris, George W. & Charity Vassey, 5 Nov 1851; Noah Hopper, bm; m 5 Nov 1851 by Jas. H. Carpenter, J. P.

Harris, Harbert & Nancy M. Wilkerson, 7 Apr 1861; James Thomas, bm; m 7 Apr 1861 by M. Wilkerson, bm.

Harris, Isaac & Rachel Goodbread, 27 Mar 1821; Philip Humphreys, bm.

Harris, James A. & Mary L. Gilkey, 16 Oct 1851; George B. Ford, bm; m 16 Oct 1851 by Paul F. Kistler, M. G.

Harris, Joel J. & Mary M. Moore, 4 Feb 1829; Caleb A. Moore, bm.

Harris, John & Charity Harden, 13 Jul 1807; Phillip Henson, bm.

Harris, Martin & Anny Keeter, 1 Apr 1840; James A. Keeter, bm.

Harris, R. B. & E. R. Upton, 15 Mar 1860; J. E. Greanhill, bm; m 15 Mar 1860 by B. E. Rollins.

Harris, Sims & Nancy Hall, 24 Feb 1859; M. Wilkerson, bm; m 24 Feb 1859 by M. Wilkerson, J. P.

Harris, Thomas & Mira Keeter, 19 Jul 1831; John Geer, bm.

Harris, Washington & Sally Whitesides, 16 Mar 1818; Jacob Michal, bm.

Harris, William & Reachell Boyle, 28 Sept 1795; Benjamin Hampton, bm.

Harris, Wm. W. & Caroline Elizabeth Houser, 28 Jan 1858; D. S. Melton, bm; m 28 Jan 1858 by B. E. Rollins, M. G.

Harris, Zadock & Polly Ledbetter, 14 Jul 1813; Johnston Ledbetter, bm.

Harrison, Edward & Cynthia McCurry, 14 Apr 1830; Leonard Deck, bm.

Harrison, James & Mary Lands, 16 Nov 1838; Jesse Smiley, bm.

Harrison, James & Mary Yelton, 23 Feb 1862; R. R. Gettys, bm; m 23 Feb 1862 by B. E. Rollins.

Harrison, Joseph & Margret Hill, 16 Jan 1787; Thomas Harisson, bm.

Harriss, Daniel & Precilla Humphreys, 2 Jan 1816; Thos. Mason, bm.

Harriss, Hurbert & Esther Dornbuch, 9 Jan 1818; Sims Harris, bm.

Harriss, John & Rebecca Green, 16 Mar 1843; Jere D. Harriss, bm.

Harriss, Martin & Polly Blankinship, 7 Feb 1844; T. Edwards[?], bm.

Harriss, Robt. H. & M. Smith, 25 Jan 1843; G. W. Nix, bm.

Harriss, Starlin & Elizabeth Dolton, 11 Jan 1840; James Naney, bm.

Harriss, William & Martha Nanny, 22 Sept 1807; Absalom Coxsey, bm.

Harriss, William & Sarah Wilkerson, 29 Sept 1851; Andrew Ledbetter, bm; m 2 Oct 1851 by Bailey Bruce, M. G.

Harrold, Richard & Artumincee Dobbins, 14 Feb 1807; John Harrill, bm.

Hart, George & Delila Wadlington, 22 Jan 1793; Allen Twitty, bm.

Harton, A. M. & A. G. Baber, 14 Mar 1843; John M. Harton, bm.

Harton, Harbert & Elizabeth Baber, 14 Feb 1818; N. Hampton, bm.

Harton, James & Julia Smith, 18 Mar 1861; A. C. Weber, bm; m 21 Mar 1861 by A. Hamby.

Harton, Robert H. & Jane B. Good, 6 Apr 1848; D. D. Lollua, bm.

Harton, Thos. J. & Martha Ann Blan, 5 Nov 1855; J. M. Harton, bm; m 10 Nov 1855 by Bailey Bruce, M. G.

Harvey, John & Robitha Burnes or Burnet, 4 Oct 1779; Geo. Winters, Abram Clark, bm.

Harvil, Govan & Louesa Radford, 11 Nov 1860; J. H. Nanney, bm; m 11 Nov 1860 by D. Koone.

Harvil, James & Elizabeth Callahan, 5 Apr 1848; J. G. Early, bm.

Harvil, Jepsa A. & Martha Naney, m 4 Sept 1851 by T. B. Justice.

Harvill, Daniel & Emaline Lee, 21 Sept 1865; P. A. Carpenter, bm; m 21 Sept 1865 by A. W. Harill.

Harvill, William & Hanner Jewell, 11 Dec 1817; Elijah Morris, bm.

Harvill, Wm. & Sarah Nanny, 28 May 1848; John Nanny, bm.

Haskew, William & Katherine Breedlove, 29 Feb 1796; Zachariah Sullins, bm.

Hastin, William & Nancy Moore, 29 Aug 1815; William Hastin, Phillip Moore, bm.

Hause, John & Elizabeth Whisnant, 16 Jan 1822; Adam Whisnant, bm.

Hauser, William H. & Mary A. Noell, 1 Nov 1845; E. Hauser, bm.

Hawkins, Daniel & Peggy Dobbins, 27 Nov 1832; William Dobbins, bm.

Hawkins, Edward & Polly Rollins, 25 Jun 1801; Jesse Reardson, bm.

Hawkins, Edward D. & Sally Scruggs, 26 Nov 1840; Thomas Hawkins, bm.

Hawkins, James F. & Nancy Hensley, 2 Feb 1841; J. H. Alley Jr., bm.

Hawkins, Martin & Delila Robbins, 30 Dec 1846; D. D. Rollins, bm.

Hawkins, Michael & Elizabeth Bradon, __ Nov 1806; James Green, bm.

Hawkins, Michael Junr. & Joannah Musick, 15 Dec 1794; Jonathan Musick, bm.

Hawkins, Ransom & Patsy Williams or Wilson, 26 Dec 1833; David Williams, bm.

Hawkins, Ransom N. & Julia A. Winn, 16 Sept 1856; Jackson Robbins, bm; m 18 Sept 1856 by G. W. Rollins, M. G.

Hawkins, Samuel & Elizabeth Shanon, 5 Jul 1803; William McDannil, bm.

Hawkins, Samuel & Jinny Webb, 29 Jun 1820; Edward Hawkins, John Goode, bm.

Hawkins, Terel G. & Betsy Cherry, 22 Oct 1859; L. A. Mills, bm; m 23 Oct 1859 by J. Gilkey, J. P.

Hawkins, William Jr. & _____ Walton, 20 Mar 1802.

Haws, Thomas & Sally Bridges, 29 Mar 1809; Drury Dobbins, Daniel Webb, bm.

Hay, George & Mary Purdon, 5 Mar 1793; David Willcockson, bm.

Hay, George Purdy & Drusilla Covington, 24 Jun 1828; George Suttle, bm.

Hayden, Thomas A. & Matilda C. Alexander, 3 Nov 1841; William Wilkins, bm.

Haydon, Thomas A. & Mrs. Nancy Mc. Walker, 3 Dec 1836; Francis A. Littlejohn, bm.

Hayes, Jno. S. & Caldona A. Mitchell, 1 Mar 1866; Alexander Kelley, bm; m 1 Mar 1866 by Daniel May.

Hayle, Bengamin & Mary Vickers, 15 Aug 1844; Thomas J. Moris, bm.

Haynes, A. W. & Martha E. Searcy, 13 Feb 1860; B. G. Haynes, bm; m 22 Feb 1860 by James H. Whiteside.

Haynes, Edward A. & Nancy E. Hunter, 11 Nov 1865; W. P. Moffitt, bm; m 16 Nov 1865 by Washington Haynes, M. G.

Haynes, Francis M. & Catharine Littlejohn, 27 Aug 1862; Washington Haynes, bm; m 25 Sept 1862 by Washington Haynes, M. G.

Haynes, Henry C. & S. R. Panthy Leroy, 16 Nov 1865; Augustus B. Haynes, bm; m 23 Nov 1865 by Washington Haynes, M. G.

Haynes, Jacob & Nancy Wilky, 16 Oct 1817; Wm. Willkie, bm.

Haynes, Robert & Milley A. C. Crooks, 26 Mar 1825; George Baber, bm.

Haynesworth, Jas. & Mary Franks, 24 Dec 1798; Jacob Franks, bm.

Hayns, Augustis B. & Martha Jane McEntire, 20 Nov 1866; Francis M. Haynes, bm; m 20 Nov 1866 by Washington Haynes, M. G.

Hayns, Hilliard & Sarah C. Lee, 25 May 1845; B. H. Padgett, bm.

Hays, Albert & Cassey Padget, 25 Feb 1851; Thos. Hayse, bm; m 27 Feb 1851 by Wm. Rucker, J. P.

Hays, John A. & Cyntha Head, 27 May 1861; Thomas Hays, bm; m 30 May 1861 by T. P. Sorrels.

Hays, Thos. & Vina Head, 17 Sept 1847; Henderson Hays, bm.

Head, Elbert & Susannah Keeter, 7 Jan 1858; John A. White, bm; m 7 Jan 1858 by Wm. Rucker, J. P.

Head, Isham & Sarah McGuire, 27 Sept 1837; John H. Wilkins, bm.

Head, James & Lurany Keeter, 13 Sept 1855; Andrew Tomberlin, bm; m 13 Sept 1855 by J. Gilkey, J. P.

Head, John & Mira Grant, 19 Apr 1822; James Grant, bm.

Head, Joseph & Elizabeth Nix, 26 Jan 1832; Isham Wood, bm.

Heart, Ephraim & Lucy Greeman, 20 Feb 1813; R. K. Wilson, bm.

Hedcoock, Thomas & Catty Cooper, _____; John McCurry, bm.

Hedloe, Mikael & Sally Goode, 24 aug 1808; Jno. McEntire, bm.

Hembree, Abram & Levina Floyd, 25 Aug 1830; John Floyd, bm.

Hembree, Isaac & Elizabeth White, 4 Jan 1830; Abraham Hembree, bm.

Hembree, James & Delilah Hembree, 22 Jul 1852; Davis Hembree, bm.

Hembrick, George & Febey Right, 23 Sept 1801; Richard Wright, Owen Lee, bm.

Hembrick, John & Elizebeth Robertson, 12 Jan 1808; Moses Bridges, James Bridges, bm.

Hemphill, Robert & Mary Queen, 15 Nov 1812; Edward Jones, bm.

Hemphill, T. P. & Mary A. Flack, 7 Apr 1857; A. L. Logan, bm; m 16 Apr 1857 by J. W. Morgan, J. P.

Hemphill, William & Jane McKown, 4 Feb 1809; James McKeown, bm.

Hemrick, Jeremiah & Sealey Hemrick, 12 Dec 1801; Arom Bridges, Samuel Bridges, bm.

Henderson, Allen & Temp. Grizzle, 17 Jun 1836; Barnabas A. Baber, bm.

Henderson, Andrew & Sebary Splaun, 16 Mar 1826; Middleton Sutton, bm.

Henderson, Irvine & Elizabeth Doggett, 17 Dec 1830; Jeffferson Henderson, bm.

Henderson, Wm. & Sarah Dalton, 25 Jan 1855; John Denton, bm; m 25 Jan 1855 by J. M. Hamilton, J. P.

Hendrick, James & Elizebeth Glasscock, 27 Sept 1838; George Hendrick, bm.

Hendrick, William & Charity Love, 10 May 18211 Charles Love, J. Roberts[?], bm.

Hendrick, William G. & Dicy Pool, 10 May 1821; James E. Elam, Samuel Bailey, bm.

Henry, William & Mary Allin, 3 Apr 1784; Fendall Whitworth, bm.

Hensley, Buttler P. & Margaret Potiet, 5 Feb 1866; James A. Hensley, bm; m 8 Feb 1866 by Washington Haynes, M. G.

Hensley, James A. & Sarah Morgan, 12 Apr 1831; Jno. Morgan, bm.

Henson, Benjamin F. & Decdamia Camp, 7 Apr 1824; Phillip Henson Sr., bm.

Henson, E. J. & Nansey Robbins, 11 Mar 1854; Moterson Panter, bm; m 11 Mar 1854 by J. H. Carpenter, J. P.

Henson, Elias & Lettice Findley, 19 Jan 1820; James Findley, bm.

Henson, J. C. & Margret Robbins, 10 Dec 1857; James Henson, bm; m 10 Dec 1857 by J. H. Carpenter, J. P.

Henson, J. G. & Jane Robins, 6 Dec 1856; Elias R. Sutton, bm; m 6 Dec 1856 by J. H. Carpenter, J. P.

Henson, James & Sarah Corson, 18 Jan 1837; Westley McGuire, bm.

Henson, John & Margaret Harriss, 2 Aug 1844.

Henson, Joseph & Mary McMahan, 26 Mar 1861; B. McMahan, bm; m 26 Mar 1861 by W. H. Bostic.

Henson, Phillip & Leah Amons, __ Mar 1866; J. C. Henson, bm; m 11 Mar 1856 by Wm. J. Willkie.

Henson, Reuben & Eliza Sutton, 21 Nov 1838; Middleton Sutton, bm.

Henson, Thos. G. & Nancy C. Abrams, 29 Jan 1851; George B. Ford, bm.

Henson, Wm. & M. J. Stricling, 6 Mar 1866; J. A. Ledford, bm; m 6 Mar 1866 by Wm. J. Willkie.

Henson, William D. & Isabella Cole, 14 Nov 1839; Joseph Cole, bm.

Herndon, John J. & J. M. Field, 10 May 1841; Joseph W. Calloway, bm.

Herroll, Levy & Mrs. Sary Foutch, 3 Dec 1807; Jesse Spurlin, bm.

Heslep, Andr. & P. Littlejohn, 6 Sept 1808; Thos. Littlejohn, bm.

Hester, Abraham & Margaret Everton, 3 Dec 1833; Jonathan Blackwell, bm.

Hester, John & Sally Green, 17 Sept 1825; John Culbreath, bm.

Hester, William & Elizabeth Blackwell, 1 Oct 1841; James Hester, bm.

Hicks, J. W. & C. A. Parker, 13 Dec 1866; A. Smith, bm; m 13 Dec 1866 by A. Hunt.

Hicks, Dr. Oliver & Laura McEntire, 27 Feb 1865; P. L. Gilkey, bm; m 28 Feb 1865 by Joseph Hunter.

Hicks, R. H. & M. L. Simmons, 5 Nov 1844.

Hicks, William G. & Elizabeth Eakins, 20 Aug 1816; W. Hill, bm.

Hider, Alfred & Sarah Kizer, m 30 Jun 1859 by J. L. Taylor, J. P.

Higdon, John & Martha Rope, ____ 1789; Samuel Carbenter, bm.

Higgins, J. S. & Janie Justice, 25 Jul 1864; L. P. Erwin, bm; m 27 Jul 1864 by B. E. Rollins, M. G.

Higgins, Mills & Mary Elliott, 24 Mar 1854; William Higgins, bm; m 24 May 1854 by T. B. Justice, M. G.

Higgins, William L. & Minervia Flack, 2 Feb 1854; John Flack, bm.

Higton, Lenert & Susannah Harris, 30 Mar 1791; Samuel Carpenter, bm.

Hildebrand, Cunnor & Caty Young, 1 Jun 1809; Daniel Hall, bm;

Hill, Aaron & Elizabeth Wilson, 29 Nov 1832; Thomas J. Halford, bm.

Hill, Abel & Drusilla Mooney, 30 Aug 1825; David Hill, bm.

Hill, Alexander & Leviney Street, 24 Jan 1821; Henry Pettit, bm.

Hill, Anonymous & Drusey Philbeck, 28 Aug 1847; William Walker, bm.

Hill, Asaph & ____ Headlow, 7 Jan 1830; Zachariah Wilkins, bm.

Hill, Avington & Elizabeth Read, 11 Mar 1843; A. G. Forney, bm.

Hill, Barnet & Narcissa Nanny, 29 Mar 1848; Cornelius Clements, bm.

Hill, Buryl & Rachel Hill, 2 Oct 1788; Reubin Hill, Adam Whiteside, bm.

Hill, C. C. & Elizabeth Tomberlin, 22 May 1865; Jonathan Hunter, bm; m 28 May 1865 by Washington Haynes, M. G.

Hill, Carson & Mary Arledge, 10 May 1848; Franklin Harper, bm.

Hill, Charles & Frances Blankinship, 29 Aug 1821; Joseph Hunter, bm.

Hill, Clinton & Dicey McDaniel, 17 Sept 1836; Stanhope Hill, bm.

Hill, Ellick & Martha Coopper, 22 Oct 1843; Starling C. Harrison, bm.

Hill, Ephram & Nancy Ownsbey, 2 Oct 1803; Porter Ownbey, bm.

Hill, George W. & Sarah A. Green, 6 Mar 1832; Pinckney Reed, bm.

Hill, George W. & Grizey Nanney, 31 Oct 1860; Cebern Nanney, bm; m 1 Nov 1860 by D. Koone.

Hill, Green & Milly Harriss, 7 Apr 1806; James Harris, bm.

Hill, Harbard & Jarusha McKay, 24 Jun 1818; Rob. Hills, bm.

Hill, James & Charity Williams, 28 Apr 1807; Robt. H. Taylor, bm.

Hill, James & Elizabeth Eaves, 25 Apr 1822; Andrew Eaves, bm.

Hill, James & Bitha McCraw, 11 Sept 1860; William Hill, bm; m 11 Sept 1860 by James H. Whiteside.

Hill, James B. & Louisa E. Stott, 17 May 1852; James Hills, bm; m 30 May 1852 by T. B. Justice, M. G.

Hill, Jeremiah & Mary Upton, 3 Sept 1806; Thomas Upton, bm.

Hill, Jeremiah & Sally Hutchins, 5 Oct 1828; Alexander Hill, bm.

Hill, John & Nicy Eaves, 23 Jun 1848; A. G. McEntire, bm.

Hill, John & Mary Hill, 28 Dec 1865; John N. Scoggin, bm.

Hill, Micajah & Jensey Pryor, 8 Mar 1825; Lewis Lively, bm.

Hill, Noah & Eliza Hannon, 17 Oct 1843; James Carpenter, bm.

Hill, Reuben & Margaret McBrayer, 4 Aug 1829; Asaph Hill, bm.

Hill, Reubin & Margaret Brien, 9 Feb 1791; Thos Camp, bm.

Hill, Rial & Karon Hapoch Gear, 24 Jun 1815; J. Gilkey, bm.

Hill, Richard & Margaret Irvine, 17 Jan 1794; Thomas Camp, bm.

Hill, Robertson & Ailsey Nanny, 20 May 1825; John Hill, bm.

Hill, Stanhop & Celia Edwards, 26 Feb 1838; A. J. Covington, bm.

Hill, W. S. & Mary Bostick, 3 Mar 1857; M. R. Alexander, bm; m 5 Mar 1857 by Wm. Harrill.

Hill, William & Caroline Baxter, 28 Oct 1819; David Hill, bm.

Hill, William A. & Temperance Philips, 23 Jan 1840; Sampson Philips, bm.

Hill, Wm. A. & Polly Weathers, 15 Dec 1853; T. J. Dalton, bm; m 15 Dec 1853 by John Koone, M. G.

Hill, Zadock & Rebekah Harvey, 1 Feb 1800; Charles Hill, bm.

Hills, Hennery & Susanna Rich, 1 Dec 1801; William Ritch, bm.

Hills, James & Delpha Marlow, 16 Jan 1826; Jacob Michal, bm.

Hills, James & Susanah Clemens, 25 Sept 1849; Cornelius Clements, bm.

Hills, John or Robert & Sarah Wheeler, 27 Sept 1808; Robert Hills, bm.

Hills, Johnathan & Jane Almara Mitchel, 22 Oct 1858; James Hills, bm; m 24 Oct 1858 by Wm. Rucker, J. P.

Hills, Robt. & Polly Robinson, 18 Dec 1802; Zadock Hills, bm.

Hills, Robert or John & Sarah Wheeler, 27 Sept 1808; John Hills, bm.

Hills, William & Patsy Deboard, 10 Feb 1819; Hiram Dunkin, bm.

Hines, J. L. B. & Elizabeth H. Wilson, 1 May 1851; Kindred Hines, bm; m 1 May 1851 by Alanson Padgett, M. G.

Hines, Kinand N. & Sarah A. Wilson, 9 Dec 1850; W. A. Bishop, bm.

Hinenhart, Henry & _____, 22 Aug 1789; Saml. Carbender, bm.

Hix, Jeremiah & Suckey Liveret, 11 Apr 1804; Wm. Levret & Wm Hicks, bm.

Hix, Jesse & _____, 17 Aug 1801; Saml. Dileny, bm.

Hix, Martin & Lavinia Murrey, 13 Aug 1829; John Hix, bm.

Hix, Thomas A. & Anna Smith, 1 Dec 1804; Jo. Smith, bm.

Hobbs, Benedict H. & Elizabeth Scott, 11 Sept 1834; William Twitty, bm.

Hodge, Stephen D. & Cassa Teage, 17 Apr 1864; David Mosely Jr., bm; m 17 Apr 1864 by Wm. J. Willkie.

Hofner, Wm. L. & Dora C. Killpatrick, 22 Jan 1866; F. D. Wood, bm; m 25 Jan 1866 by A. Hamby, Elder.

Hogue, Jesse & Milly Powell, 2 Feb 1824; James W. Carson, bm.

Hogue, Stephen & Judith Burge, 17 Jun 1845; John Burge, bm.

Hoil, Hiram & Elzira E. Blankenship, 14 Dec 1863; E. Carrier, bm; m 17 Dec 1863 by T. P. Sorrels, J. P.

Holifield, Daniel & Minimia Smith, 4 Jul 1831; John Smith, bm.

Holifield, Daniel & Margaret Scruggs, 19 Oct 1844; Nolon Holifield, bm.

Holifield, Jacob & Minima Dobbins, 10 Nov 1837; Sampson Philips, bm.

Holifield, Jacob & Easter Wall, 22 Dec 1856; Jno. W. Wiley, bm.

Holifield, James & Nancy C. McDaniel, 7 Dec 1856; Jason McDaniel, bm; m 7 Dec 1856 by J. H. Carpenter, J. P.

Holifield, Nolen & Jain Smith, 25 Jul 1835; William Whitaker, bm.

Holifield, Nolin & Hannah Padget, 9 Dec 1844; William Smith, bm.

Holland, G. W. & J. E. S. Hames, 22 Feb 1864; B. T. Hopper, bm; m 23 Feb 1864 by D. Ponnell.

Holland, James & Sarah Gilbert, 12 Jan 1780; James Miller, Jno Moore, bm.

Holland, Pheneas & Abbegail Rollins, 6 Jun 1819; Francis Young, George Rollins, bm.

Holland, William & Jane Biggerstaff, 16 Oct 1852; Leander Jolley, bm.

Hollifield, N. J. & S. A. Walker, 14 May 1857; A. P. Hollifield, bm; m 14 May 1857 by B. E. Rollins.

Hollifield, Ransom & Sabra Price, 9 Dec 1839; Hampton Padgett, bm.

Holmes, Joseph C. & Nancy C. Dysart, 29 Mar 1857; A. W. Burton, bm.

Holyfield, H. C. & C. M. Long, 18 Feb 1866; F. W. Biggerstaff, bm; m 18 Feb 1866 by H. A. Toney, J. P. (C. H.)

Honeycut, Rowland & Patsey Taylor, 20 Dec 1797; John Taylor, bm.

Hood, John & Maryan Barr, 18 Jan 1797; Adam Watson, bm.

Hood, William & Fanny Reed, 9 Dec 1807; James Grifes, bm.

Hooper, James & Mary Matthews, 18 Dec 1798; Thomas Lits, bm.

Hopkins, Elkana & Rhoda Dunaway, 3 Aug 1835; John H. Wilkins, bm.

Hopper, H. H. & Mary Goode, 3 Dec 1842; John W. Goode, bm.

Hopper, John A. M. & Nancy Gantt, 5 Sept 1845; John B. Neal, bm.

Hopper, Noah L. B. & Catharine Kenady, 11 Feb 1851; J. O. Jones[?], bm.

Hoppers, Jacop & Diadamy Pool, 8 Mar 1819; James Bedford, bm.

Hopson, Henry & A. Goode, dau. of Richard Goode, 21 Mar 1805.

Hopson, John & Aggy Goode, 22 Jan 1802; Richard Lewis, bm.

Hord, James W. & Elizabeth Reynolds, 21 Jun 1832; Richd. T. Hord, bm.

Hord, Richard T. & Margaret H. Thompson, 5 Mar 1839; J. G. Gilkey, bm.

Horl, S. Hiram & Mirey Parten, 7 Aug 1859; James Floid, bm; m 7 Aug 1859 by J. J. Gilkey, J. P.

Horn, Daniel & Amey Jones, 21 Jul 1834; William H. McKinney, bm.

Horn, John & Polley Wolf, 7 Dec 1820; Abel Beaty, bm.

Horn, Joseph & Mary Gorden, 16 Aug 1798; John Gordon, bm.

Horton, Anthony & Christina Moore, 7 Dec 1805; Edwin Horton, bm.

Horton, David & Alce Chitwood, 29 Jan 1823; William Horton, bm.

Horton, G. J. & Martha J. Randol, 23 Jan 1862; Drury Green, bm; m 23 Jan 1862 by James W. Murray, J. P.

Horton, George & Barbary Depriest, 29 Jan 1833; Jesse Chitwood, bm.

Horton, Terrell & Cynthia Davis, 11 Jan 1832; William Horton, bm.

Horton, William & Margaret Moore, 23 Feb 1797; William Barnett, bm.

Horton, William & Drusilla Melton, 27 Dec 1828; Joseph Green, bm.

Horton, William T. & Malinda J. Murray, 24 Jan 1860; John W. Murray, bm; m 25 Jan 1860 by James W. Murray.

Houser, Jackson & Nancy Boheler, 13 Jan 1835; David Williams, bm.

Howard, Nathan & Ann Collins, 9 Jan 1813; Wm. Franklin, bm.

Howel, William & Eddie Eddins, 26 Sept 1822; Thomas Howel, bm.

Howell, James & Mrs. Salley Whitworth, 23 Dec 1824; Jacob Wolf, bm.

Howell, Joseph & Mary M. L. Simmons, 13 Jan 1835; Moses Simmons, bm.

Howell, Joshua & Bettsey Horn, __ Jul 1809; Jesy Horn, bm.

Howell, William & Francis Michael, & Aug 1866; John V. Wilkinson, bm.

Howser, Absalum & Sarah Howser, 3 Mar 1846; H. H. Howser, bm.

Howser, David & Mira Yelton, 2 Mar 1867; W. T. Robertson, bm.

Howser, H. H. & P. C. Grason, 7 Apr 1858; Wm. W. Horney, bm; m 78 Apr 1858 by B. E. Rollins, M. G.

Hoswer, Henry H. & Elizabeth Blankenship, 20 Nov 1839; Joseph McCurry, bm.

Howser, Henry H. & Louisa Grayson, 4 Aug 1854; Wm. Gamble, bm; m 6 Aug 1854 by Wm. G. Mode, J. P.

Hoyl, David & Betsey Willis, 4 Jan 1816; Henry Hoyles, bm.

Hoyl, John & Rachel Lattamore, 9 Jan 1798; John Lattimore, bm.

Hoyles, Henry & Marget Maneth, 6 Aug 1807; Joseph Carkews, bm.

Hoysed, Walter & Rebekah Kuikendall, 11 Oct 1787; Samuel Carbender, bm.

Huchins, Isaa & Lucinda Collins, 26 Aug 1849; Wm. D. Hutchins, bm.

Huchins, Isaac & Martha Walker, 7 Apr 1859; M. S. McCurry, bm; m 7 Apr 1859 by Wm. G. Mode, J. P.

Huchins, Jonathan & Delila Franklin, 3 Nov 1859; John F. Franklin, bm; m 3 Nov 1859 by Wm. G. Mode, J. P.

Huckeby, Berrymon & Sarah J. Melton, 4 Nov 1841; John Huckabay, bm.

Huddelston, Archibald F. & Mahala Early, 31 Oct 1838; John Early, bm.

Huddelston(e), David & Littice Huddlestone, 16 Apr 1793; John Huddleston, bm.

Huddleston, Charles & Martha Lollar, 5 Aug 1803; Thomas Lollar, bm.

Huddleston, James & Sarah Mantieth, 26 Feb 1839; John Black, bm.

Huddleston, John & Jean Huddlestone, 12 Aug 1793; David Huddleston, bm.

Huddleston, William & Agnis Huddleston, 14 May 1793; William Long, bm.

Huddleston, William & Tabitha South, 17 Nov 1798; Arthur McCluer, bm.

Hudgins, Josiah & Susanah Ownsby, 23 Mar 1836; John H. Wilkins, bm.

Hudgins, Nimrod P. & Lusinda Searcy, 7 Mar 1836; John H. Wilkins, bm.

Hudgins, Robert & Polley M. Watson, 28 Dec 1814; John Logan, bm.

Hudgins, Silas & Malinda Searsey, 11 Oct 1840; Wm. Hudging, bm.

Hudgins, W. Miles & Lucinda Searcy, 6 Feb 1847; N. P. Hudgins, bm.

Hudgins, William & Melinda Early, 8 Mar 1852; N. P. Hudgins, bm; m 15 Mar 1852 by Wm. O. Bagwell, J. P.

Hudgins, William D. & Sary Surcey, 1 Aug 1841; Nimrod P. Hudgs, bm.

Hudleson, James M. & Issabella Clemmons, 29 Aug 1857; Wm. L. Ensley, bm; m 30 Aug 1857 by James M. Spratt, J. P.

Hudloe, Andrew & Martha Goode, 18 Mar 1858; J. A. Goode, bm; m 18 Mar 1858 by W. A. Tanner.

Hufstutler, Ryel A. & Jane Johnson, 12 Oct 1851; Alfred B. Moore, bm; m 12 Oct 1851 by J. Gilkey, J. P.

Huggeons, William & Nancy Walkins, 25 Jul 1839; William W. Nix, bm.

Huggins, John & Sophia Porter, 9 Feb 1808; Jno. Carson, bm.

Hughes, Oen & Elizabeth Lashley, 8 Jan 1800; John Doyle, bm.

Hughs, John & Martha Ross, 20 Mar 1800; James Ross, bm.

Hughs, Young & Sally Blanton, 22 Mar 1809; Drury Dobbins, Benjamin Hughs, bm.

Hullet, John & Sarah Dalton, 23 Jun 1841; Ellet Mitchell, bm.

Hullit, William & Rachael Rice, 26 Oct 1796; Benjaman Rice, bm.

Humphres, David & Polley McCraw, 9 Jan 1836; John Humphres, bm.

Humphres, Jesse & Mirey Doss, 7 Mar 1836; George Planton, bm.

Humphres, Jesse & Nancy Daverson, 15 Oct 1836; Moses Davidson, bm.

Humphreys, Philip & Sally Morris, 23 Oct 1819; Henry Morris, bm.

Humphris, David & Acmy Moore, 12 Oct 1808; James Humphris, bm.

Humphris, Robt. & Eliza Wren, 24 Aug 1794; Britain Lile, bm.

Humphrys, Phillip & Betsy Bradley, 6 Sept 1821; Richard Bradley, bm.

Hunsinger, Adam & Dosey Goode, 7 Oct 1844; Jas. Madeson, bm.

Hunt, A. W. & Elizebeth Grason, 2 Sept 1858; A. Jones, bm.

Hunt, Absalom & Sarah Teel, 12 Nov 1862; Wm. Gamble, bm; m 12 Nov 1862 by Wm. G. Mode, J. P.

Hunt, Bedford & Margret Carbo, 17 Jul 1864; W. A. Hunt, bm; m 17 Jul 1864 by A. Hunt, M. G.

Hunt, Elijah & Catherine Grose, 27 Apr 1843; James O. Crow, bm.

Hunt, Elisha & Martha Taylor, 18 Oct 1848; B. G. Grayson, bm.

Hunt, John & Rachel Latimore, 2 Apr 1839; William Hunt, bm.

Hunt, Thomas & Elizabeth Lowrey 25 Jul 1830; Jos. G. Deveny, bm.

Hunt, W. & Polley Grayson, 4 Sept 1862; W. W. Black, bm; m 4 Sept 1862 by B. E. Rollins.

Hunt, Wagstaff, & Francess Elam, 9 Apr 1817; William Elam, bm.

Hunt, William & Ruthe Carpenter, 7 Feb 1839; Joseph C. Lettimore, bm.

Hunt, William Jr. & Ruth Johnson, 24 Jul 1825; Robert Hall, bm.

Hunt, William H. & Susan Jarrel, 16 Feb 1865; Joseph W. Powell, bm; m 16 Feb 1865 by Wm. G. Mode, J. P.

Hunter, Elijah & Jane Harwell, 22 Oct 1829; William Richardson, bm.

Hunter, Francis & Nelly Johnson, 12 Sept 1796; Moses Hutson, bm.

Hunter, John & Polly Edwards, 29 Aug 1803; Saml. Hunter, bm.

Hunter, John & Mary Harriss, 13 Oct 1813; B. Jones, bm.

Hunter, Jonathan & Susan Early, 16 Feb 1842; James Sorrels, bm.

Hunter, Joseph & Patsey Jackson, 19 Nov 1831; Caleb A. Moore, bm.

Hunter, Mark & Mary Largen, 10 Mar 1853; George D. Largent, bm; m 10 Mar 1853 by T. B. Justice.

Hunter, Robert & P. Dyar, 22 Aug 1792; Chas. Lewis, bm.

Hunter, Robert & Susanah Stice, 14 Jan 1807; Samuel Hunter, bm.

Hunter, Thomas & Sally Gillkey, 23 Apr 1802; James Love, bm.

Hunter, William & Lucy Marlow, 6 Apr 1804; John Marlow, bm.

Huntley, David & Mary A. Shehan, 22 Dec 1851; James Shehan, bm.

Huntley, James & Esther Liverett, 12 May 1865; Miles W. Huntley, J. C. Willkie, bm; m 14 May 1865 by Wm. J. Willkie, bm.

Huntly, William & Sarah Collins, 23 Oct 1839; Joab Willky, bm.

Huntsinger, Demires & Francenen Nodine, 4 Apr 1847; John M. Nodine, bm.

Huntsinger, Noah & Malinda Bradley, 5 Aug 1866; A. W. Haynes, bm; m 5 Aug 1866 by J. J. Bradley.

Huntsinger, Thomas & Nancy Covington, 10 Dec 1857; Shefus Bias, bm; m 10 Dec 1857 by Henry Culbreath, M. G.

Huntsinger, W. D. & Hulda Daves, 17 Nov 1864; John Huntsinger, bm; m 17 Nov 1864 by Wm. G. Mode, J. P.

Huntsinger, William & Sarah Upchurch, 26 Oct 1860; John A. Murray, bm; m 28 Oct 1860 by T. G. Hawkins, J. P.

Husky, Thomas & Sally Champain, 22 Jan 1818; Richard Harris, bm.

Hutchens, John & Luranah Biggerstaff, 16 Oct 1823; Thos. Hutchens, bm.

Hutchins, A. B. & M. Smiley, 5 Feb 1857; Elijah M. Hutchins, bm; m 5 Feb 1857 by Jas. M. Spratt, J. P.

Hutchins, John & Sarey M. Grayson, 2 Feb 1841; Is. Hutchins, bm.

Hutchins, John & Mary Jane Parker, 27 Oct 1859; Ransom P. Biggerstaff, bm.

Hutchins, John C. & Susanah Yelton, 25 Oct 1859; Leonard Yelton, bm; m 25 Oct 1859 by John Freeman, J. P.

Hutchins, Moses & Jerusia Norvill, 11 Feb 1830; Alford Garison, bm.

Hutchins, Thomas & Elizabeth Smart, 2 Mar 1853; Cornelius C. Smart, bm; m 3 Mar 1853 by John Freeman, J. P.

Hutchins, William & Polly Weaver, 6 Apr 1815; Reuben Proctor, bm.

Hutchins, William & Mary Yelton, 15 Dec 1840; Aaron Biggerstaff, bm.

Hutchins, Wm. G. & Biddy Biggerstaff, 23 Oct 1849; Y. F. Beatey, bm.

Hutchins, Wright & Martha Ann Smiley, 25 Oct 1847; John Hutchins, bm.

Hutchins, Young & Jane Waters, _____; Jonathan Waters, bm.

Hutchinson, John & Winifred Hilton, 6 Nov 1835; Ambrose Mills, bm.

Hutson, Isaac & Nelly Baker, 16 Sept 1795; Baxter Baker, bm.

Hutson, Noah & Mary Ann Johnson, 18 Dec 1856; A. Mooney, bm; m 18 Dec 1856 by J. N. Biggerstaff, J. P.

Hyder, Alfred & Sarah Kizer, 30 Jun 1859; J. S. Queene, bm.

Hyder, Andrew H. & Mary Jane Metcalf, 24 Dec 1861; R. L. Gilkey, bm; m 24 Dec 1861 by J. L. Taylor, J. P.

Hyder, Andrew K. W. & Louisa A. Metcalf, 15 Jul 1850; Thos. A. Allen, bm.

Hyder, B. W. & Martha M. Metcalf, 23 Feb 1860; Lewis Preston, bm; m 23 Feb 1860 by J. L. Taylor.

Hyder, Benj. & Isabella Metcalf, 12 Dec 1808; Wm. Metcalf, bm.

Hyder, Benjamin D. & Jane C. Walton, 9 Jul 1836; James V. Jay, bm.

Hyder, John Wallis, son of Benjamin, & Lucy Mullins, 29 Mar 1811; James Allin, bm.

Hyder, Robert & Elizabeth Padgett, 15 Aug 1852; Jas. L. Rucker, bm; m 15 Aug 1852 by A. Hamby.

Hyder, Warner J. & Mildred M. Simmons, 24 Nov 1838; Benjn D. Hyder, bm.

Hydor, John & Nelly Prather, 11 Sept 1834; Charles Lewis, bm.

Irvin, Abram C. & Louisa Beam, 16 Mar' 1830; Martin Irvine, bm.

Irvin, Ancil J. & Elizebeth Beam, 17 Dec 1837; A. C. Irvin, bm.

Irvin, Thomas & Betsy Blanton, 24 Jun 1835; Burwell Blanton, bm.

Irvine, Abram & Sarah Graham, 22 Mar 1795; James Kuykendall, bm.

Irvine, Gavin & Agnis McGaughy, 10 Aug 1792; Robt. Finley, bm.

Irvine, Isaac J. & Esther M. Ray, 2 Jun 1836; John Baily, bm.

Ivester, Jacob & Margarett Cline, 24 Dec 1812; George Ivester, bm.

Ivins, William & Tabitha Ledbetter, 22 Aug 1809; Able Harden, bm.

Jackson, Ambrose & Hannah Byers, 4 Nov 1840; John Gibbs, bm.

Jackson, Andrew & Catharine Gray, 19 Feb 1836; David Gray, bm.

Jackson, Ephrem & Intha Camp, 27 Apr 1845; Calvin Keeter, bm.

Jackson, J. F. B. & M. C. Morris, 11 Oct 1858; Samuel Wilkins, bm; m 12 Oct 1858 by A. Hamby, Elder.

Jackson, James & Isabella Gray, 22 Dec 1838; James L. Gray, bm.

Jackson, Jerry & Luvina Cagle, 1 Aug 1839; Samuel McMurry, bm.

Jackson, John & Eave Still, 16 Apr 1808; John Allen, bm.

Jackson, John & Susanna Edwards, 22 Dec 1814; Daniel Edwards, bm.

Jackson, John & Alzira McMurry, 20 May 1849; C. C. McMurry, bm.

Jackson, John & Eliz. D. Coward, 26 Oct 1854; David Cockerham, bm; m 26 Oct 1854 by H. W. Patterson.

Jackson, Lemuel & Nassy Suttles, 9 Oct 1840; Hiram Dunkin, bm.

Jackson, Lewis & Susanna Gear, 26 Oct 1804; Ranson Egerton, bm.

Jackson, Lewis & Rachel McGaughy, 25 Jan 1811; John Vickers, bm.

Jackson, Moses & Mira McWilliams, 9 Nov 1837; Ephraim Lils, bm.

Jackson, Samson & Susannah Crook, 16 Dec 1823; Amos Jackson, bm.

Jackson, Tandy & Eliz. Smith, 12 Apr 1804; Marvel Mills, bm.

Jackson, William & Nancy Stanley, 23 Dec 1814; Arthur Ownby, bm.

Jackson, William & Lucinda Jackson, 30 Mar 1851; John Consten, bm; m 30 Mar 1851 by Thomas Egerton, J. P.

Jackson, Wm. R. & Susen Dimsdale, 26 Sept 1853; Joseph Dimsdal, bm.

James, Robert & Martha Edwards, 13 Sept 1860; L. D. Hamrick, bm; m 13 Sept 1860 by J. B. McDaniel, bm.

Janes, Davis & Polly McCollom, 6 Sept 1816; James Edwards, bm.

Janes, Thomas & Algey Mitchel, 27 Feb 1832; Jacob Michal, bm.

Jarrel, Milton & Mary Ann Burnett, 30 Sept 1827; Joseph Denton, bm.

Jarrel, Doctor Jones & Margaret Nancy Black, 11 Mar 1862; Milton Jarrell, bm; m 13 Mar 1862 by B. E. Rollins, M. G.

Jarrell, Milton & Elizabeth Mooney, 25 Sept 1851; John E. McFarland, bm; m 16 Oct 1851 by Lewis McCurry.

Jaxtson, James & Anna Early, 16 Feb ____; Soloman Jackson, bm.

Jay, Edwards Ga. & Jain Grigg, 21 Feb 1824; Joseph Scoggin, bm.

Jay, James V. & Catharine W. Hyder, 18 Dec 1832; John W. Ervin, bm.

Jay, Joseph & Patsey Goode, 24 Jul 1799; Richard Lewis, bm.

Jay, Joseph McD. & Martha Jane Geer, 24 Feb 1863; W. H. M. Jay, bm; m 24 Feb 1863 by T. B. Justice.

Jay, W. H. M. & Nancy E. Lewis, 27 Sept 1860 by Carter Burnett, bm; m 27 Sept 1860 by J. L. Taylor, J. P.

Jefferson, Thomas & Nancy Ann Patton, 3 Sept 1834; George Flack, bm.

Jefferson, Thomas E. & Mary F. Foster, 10 Sept 1844; Bozzel Jefferson, bm.

Jeffrey, Samuel & Jenney Johnson, 26 Mar 1811; George Ives, Jno. Jeffers, bm.

Jenkins, Benjamin & Sophiah Stogdon, 29 Nov 1855; John J. Morehead, bm; m 29 Nov 1855 by A. Harrill.

Jenkins, Benjamin A. & Nancy Chitwood, 17 Sept 1851; Calvin J. webb, bm.

Jenkins, Samuel & Mary Vassy, 4 Jul 1848; J. H. Carpenter, bm.

Jenkins, Thomas & Prusia Vassey, 24 Aug 1844; J. D. Goode, bm.

Jenkins, William & Elvira Wood, 9 Apr 1854; Marke Wood, bm; m 9 Apr 1854 by J. H. Carpenter, J. P.

Jennings, Edmund & Lucy M. Birchett, 25 Oct 1825; Thoe. F. Birchett, bm.

Jennings, Jacob & Jane Harris, 31 May 1854; M. O. Mooney, bm; m 31 Mar 1854 by B. H. Padgett, J. P.

Jinkins, Alfred & Delilah Harris, 5 Nov 1851; C. Gee Walton, bm; m 6 Nov 1851 by J. H. Carpenter, J. P.

Jinkins, Henry & Vina A. Wood, 18 Jul 1850; Miles Padgett, bm.

Jinkins, Henry & Mary A. Simmons, 19 Jan 1864; C. Burnett, bm; m 19 Jan 1864 by J. H. Carpenter, J. P.

Johns, John & Lucinda Smith, 27 Sept 1824; James Johns, bm.

Johns, William & Elizabeth Easter, 23 Mar 1813; Robert Hunter, bm.

Johnson, Abel & Marthew Emmens, 3 Dec 1804; Daniel McDaniel, bm.

Johnson, Andrew J. & Jane Harden, 23 Jan 1866; H. M. Warren, bm; m 30 Jan 1866 by G. M. Webb.

Johnson, Daniel & Patty Jackson, 19 Nov 1796; Patrick Scott, bm.

Johnson, Rev. Daniel & E. Jane Daniel, 13 Dec 1848; Thos. A. Hayden, bm.

Johnson, Denerson & Sarah Moore, 24 Oct 1850; Avington Hill, bm.

Johnson, Edward & Mary McMinn, 14 Jul 1791; William Johnson, bm.

Johnson, Enoch & Jane Holyfield, 23 Feb 1827; George Bird, bm.

Johnson, F. F. & Mary E. Deal, 22 May 1853; D. P. Johnson, bm.

Johnson, George & Newfany A. Callihan, 31 Jan 1843; John Harris, bm.

Johnson, George & Margaret Sprouce, 12 Feb 1854; Wm. Sprouce, bm; m 12 Feb 1854 by Thos. Egerton, J. P.

Johnson, Gerrard & Mary Callihan, 24 Oct 1843; Spencer Eaves, bm.

Johnson, Isaac & Nancy Moore, 2 Dec 1818; James Morris, bm.

Johnson, Jacob & Lucrecy Walker, 29 Oct 1838; Benjamin Pope, bm.

Johnson, James & Mrs. Mary Earwood, 26 Dec 1820; John Johnson, bm.

Johnson, Joab & Maryann Blankinship, 13 Jun 1807; John Blankinship, bm.

Johnson, John & Milly Nanny, 23 Sept 1794; Uriah Nany, bm.

Johnson, John & Mary Reavis, 17 Feb 1800; John Doyle, bm.

Johnson, John & Prissy Grigg, 18 Dec 1800; Federick Grigg, bm.

Johnson, John & Hanney Cook, 26 Mar 1812; Edward Cook, bm.

Johnson, Leonard D. & Mary M. Dalton, 5 Sept 1839; James L. Wilkin, bm.

Johnson, Lewis & Anna Blanton, 2 Aug 1812; Jason Johnson, bm.

Johnson, Madison & Martha Taylor, 27 Aug 1843; Jas. Sutton, bm.

Johnson, Nathaniel & Lucinda Long, 19 Dec 1833; James L. Walker, bm.

Johnson, Nathaniel & Nancy Pullum, 26 Sept 1838; William Pullam, bm.

Johnson, Orsborn & Mereney Henderson, 19 Aug 1828; Daniel Upton, bm.

Johnson, Robt. & _____, 10 Mar ___; A. Bowman, bm.

Johnson, Robert & Mary Jones, 4 Oct 1849; Edmund Johnson, bm.

Johnson, Samuel & Polly Bradley, 3 Nov 1808; Philip Goodbread, bm.

Johnson, Thomas & Martha Bostick, 3 Jan 1827; Emanuel M. Carpenter, bm.

Johnson, William & Margrett Hawkins, 2 Aug 1785; Elias Alexander, Thos. Goode, bm.

Johnson, William & Elizabeth Justice, 22 Jun 1804.

Johnson, William & Jenney Brown, 17 Sept 1818; Joel Johnson, bm.

Johnson, William & Elizabeth Bates, 19 May 1838; John Camp, bm.

Johnson, William F. & Nancy Wilson, 9 Jan 1838; Benjamin Pope, bm.

Johnson, William Faten & Eden Johnston, 3 Nov 1841; Jacob Johnson, bm.

Johnston, Benjamin & Nancy Allin, 18 May 1819; Robt. Johnson, bm.

Johnston, Daniel & Elisabeth Cansler, ____; James Bell, John Cochran, Ross F. Johnson, bm.

Johnston, David & Clarissia Williams, ____; Samuel Bailey, William White, bm.

Johnston, Elisha & Caroline Pope, 31 May 1842; Benjamin Pope, bm.

Johnston, William & Barbary Garrison, 10 Nov 1809; Robert Smith, bm.

Johnston, William & Sarah Bailey, 21 Jan 1818; William Hambleton, bm.

Johnston, Willis & Sarah White, 25 Apr 1843; Thos Geer, bm.

Johnston, Wyley & Rebecca Keeter, 31 Dec 1825; William Johnson, bm.

Jolley, Joseph & Mary Crafford, 25 Sept 1860; A. B. Bradley, bm; m 25 Sept 1860 by Wm. Devenport, J. P.

Jolley, M. & Marey A. White, 4 Feb 1867; L. O. Jolley, bm.

Jolley, Peter & Rachel Rogers, 15 Apr 1831; John Blanton, bm.

Jolly, Fetherston & Dalilah Write, 7 Sept 1834; William W. Right, bm.

Jolly, John & Rosa Malinda Roberson, 16 Feb 1832; Larkin Bryan, bm.

Jolly, M. M. & H. E. Good, 26 Feb 1867; B. Green, bm.

Jolly, Noah & Nancy J. Roberson, 31 May 1858; R. H. Robertson, bm; m 1 Jun 1858 by Wm. O. Bagwell, J. P.

Jones, Alexander & Susanah Spurlin, 7 Jun 1851; Joshua F. Davis, bm.

Jones, Alfred & Rebecca Waters, 12 Mar 1861; W. W. Blankenship, bm.

Jones, Andrew J. & Rhoda Callihan, 23 Dec 1835; John Callihan, bm.

Jones, Andrew Jackson & Sally Gage, 10 Sept 1833; Robert Jones, bm.

Jones, Benjamin & Susanna Gibbs, 21 Jul 1803; Moses Huton, bm.

Jones, Benjamin & Mary Gibbs, 3 May 1832; Neeasbete Dimsdale, bm.

Jones, Benjamin & Anna Ownsby, 25 Jun 1841; John Gibbs, bm.

Jones, Berry & Mary Harrriss, 4 Jul 1808; Francis Crawford, bm.

Jones, Drury & Elizabeth Scruggs, 12 Nov 1835; Lewis Webb, bm.

Jones, Edmund & Susanah McKinney, 17 Jan 1808; William McKinney, John Jones, bm.

Jones, Edward P. & Carlotte Bridges, _____ 183-; Caleb Bridgs, bm.

Jones, Ephraim & Olive Hills, 15 Dec 1795; Darling Jones, bm.

Jones, Freeman & Christian Paris, 7 Nov 1785; James Green, bm.

Jones, James & Salley Bridges, 27 Aug 1821; Wm. Bridges, Thomas Moreland, bm.

Jones, James & Marthy C. Moore, 1 Jul 1851; P. A. Carpenter, bm.

Jones, Jeremiah H. & Delila Harton, 22 Oct 1817; John Logan, bm.

Jones, John & Mary More, 26 Mar 1789; Alexander Coulter, bm.

Jones, John & Mary A. Scrugs, 28 Dec 1848; Jesse Tate, bm.

Jones, Dr. John & Mary J. Taylor, 17 Oct 1853; Allen Hamby, bm; m 20 Sept (sic) 1853 by A. Hamby.

Jones, Jonas B. & Elizabeth Melton, 8 Oct 1834; Jno. M. Grayson, bm.

Jones, Jonathan H. & Polly Hunt, 29 Mar 1832; James Queen, bm.

Jones, Joseph & Rachel Runnels, 25 Mar 1799; Samuel Carbender, bm.

Jones, Josiah & Catharine Queen, 13 Feb 1806; Meredith Queene, bm.

Jones, Kezer & Rebekah Hall, 24 Jan 1805; Alex. Frisson, bm.

Jones, Lewis & Molley Bridges, 27 Jul 1797; John Jones, bm.

Jones, Moses & Sidney Silvers, 9 May 1784; John Jones, bm.

Jones, Robert & Polly McKinny, _____ 1807; John Jones, bm.

Jones, Standerford & S. Stice, 7 Apr 1810; Benj. Jones, bm.

Jones, Stantipher Jr. & Malinda Porter, 31 Mar 1838; Cabert Keeter, bm.

Jones, Stephen & Cintha Moore, _____ ; David Burge, John Jones, bm.

Jones, Thomas & Jemima Latimore, 27 Mar 1806; Amos Chitwood, bm.

Jones, William & Sally Collens, 23 Dec 1813; Joseph Colens, bm.

Jones, William & Sally McDaniel, 17 Apr 1820; John McDaniel, bm.

Jones, Wm D. & Mary Bryan, 18 Jun 1861; A. R. Bryan, bm; m 18 Jun 1861 by Nl. Shotwell, M. G.

Jones, Wm. L. & Minerva Hughes, 22 Aug 1842; Geo. W. Logan, bm.

Jones, Wm. W. & Margaret Howard, 30 Dec 1854; J. H. Jones, bm; m 30 Dec 1854 by Wm. G. Mode, J. P.

Jones, Willis M. & Nancy Horne, 21 Sept 1834; Edmund Jones, bm.

Jones, Wilson & ____ Gold, 4 Oct 1832; Milton Gold, bm.

Jonson, John & Elisebeth A. Callahan, 26 Aug 1843; A. B. Callahan, bm.

Johnsone, M. R. & Sarah Upton, 24 Oct 1858; F. F. Johnson, bm.

Jordan, Media & Sarah M. Rhea, 28 Aug 1829; Richard McCluer, bm.

Jordan, Samuel & Mary Staten, 18 Apr 1807; Elijah Dalton, bm.

Julin, Isom & Betsey Patterson, 15 Aug 1811; George Julin, Robert Patterson, bm.

Julin, Samuel & Bettsey Bailey, __ Feb 1809; Samuel Bailey, George Gulin, bm.

Justes, Thomas & Fanny Grist, 31 Aug 1833; William Camp, bm.

Justice, Amos & Mary McBrayor, 20 Jun 1785; David Dickey, bm.

Justice, Berrymon & Mary Sisk, 13 Jan 1837; L. D. Hamrick, bm.

Justice, Buckner & Elizabeth Nanny, 4 Feb 1806.

Justice, Frances & Nancey Carpenter, 28 Jul 1842; James Cherrey, bm.

Justice, James D. & Anna Cud, 20 Jul 1852; James Jackson, bm; m 20 Jul 1852 by Luke Waldrop, J. P.

Justice, James D. & Quintina A. Wallace, 15 Sept 1859; C. B. Justice, bm; m 15 Sept 1859 by J. C. Grayson, M. G.

Justice, John & _____, _____ 1799; Thos. Garner, bm.

Justice, John & Sarah Keeter, 9 Feb 1835; Elbert Keeter, bm.

Justice, John & Mary Rogers, 1 Mar 1858; J. M. Chitwood, bm; m 2 Mar 1858 by J. M. Chitwood, J. P.

Justice, Jno. Jr. & Aimy Neel, 14 Jul 1783; John Justice Sr., John Price, bm.

Justice, R. B. & Lusinda Sorrels, 11 Aug 1850; Samuel Wilkins, bm.

Justis, J. A. & Prisilla Hill, 29 Jan 1866; W. P. Porter, bm; m 30 Jan 1866 by T. P. Sorrels, M. G.

Justis, James & Rachel Gear, 12 Apr 1809; Thos. Edwards, bm.

Justis, James & Sarah Keeter, 18 Sept 1823; James Smith, bm.

Justis, John A. & Sarah Anne Wallace, 30 Oct 1845; David W. Geer, bm.

Justus, Lowranse Dow & Deliah Spicer, 28 Jun 1832; Amos Green, bm.

Kanadey, Thomas & Mary M. Webb, 21 Sept 1854; S. A. Webb, bm; m 21 Sept 1854 by J. H. Carpenter, J. P.

Keeter, Adin & Rachel Smith, 21 Oct 1832; John Logan Jr., bm.

Keeter, Adin & Elizabeth Smith, 7 Apr 1842; James L. Wilkins, bm.

Keeter, Benjn. & Patty Johnson, 22 Dec 1808; Joshua Keeter, bm.

Keeter, Cabert & Syntha Jackson, 29 Sept 1836; Elbert Keeter, bm.

Keeter, Elbert & Nancey Geere, 16 Feb 1838; John Baxter, bm.

Keeter, Fred & Mattie Bradly, 10 Nov 1866; J. K. Deck, bm; m 13 Nov 1866 by Daniel May.

Keeter, G. Johnson & Malinda Sorrels, 10 Sept 1859; Wm. White, bm; m 11 Sept 1859 by J. Gilkey, J. P.

Keeter, George J. & Darcus Allen, 24 Jan 1838; Ames Protre, bm.

Keeter, H. D. & Laura Earley, 6 Aug 1864; J. Adam Justis, bm; m 7 Aug 1864 by T. P. Sorrels, J. P.

Keeter, Henry & Elizabeth Cooksey, 14 Aug 1789; John Flack, bm.

Keeter, Henry & Mira Pell, 7 Aug 1824; William Pell, bm.

Keeter, Ichabod & Patsey Keeter, 7 Feb 1827; Adin Keeter, bm.

Keeter, J. A. W. & Cintha Cherry, 21 Nov 1859; James C. Keeter, bm; m 21 Nov 1859 by D. Koone, J. P.

Keeter, J. M. & S. E. Williams, 17 Dec 1866; J. H. Bradley, bm; m 18 Dec 1866 by W. H. Logan, Elder.

Keeter, James & Eliza Flack, 16 Dec 1817; James Keeter, bm.

Keeter, James & Elizabeth Justice, 4 Feb 1829; Samuel White, bm.

Keeter, James & Sarah Keeter, 2 Aug 1837; Thomas Harris, bm.

Keeter, James & Elasebeth Porter, 5 Aug 1849; A. B. Callahan, bm.

Keeter, James A. W. & Mary E. Moore, 23 Oct 1856; John M. Keeter, bm; m 23 Oct 1856 by J. Gilkey, J. P.

Keeter, James C. Jr. & Susannah Reed, 24 Oct 1850; Rufus J. Williams, bm.

Keeter, James H. & Elizabeth White, 16 Mar 1859; Henry White, bm; m 17 Mar 1859 by Wm. Rucker, J. P.

Keeter, John & Susannah Justice, 25 Oct 1828; Henry Keeter, bm.

Keeter, John H. & Luciller Callahan, 6 Nov 1853; A. B. Callahan, bm; m 6 Nov 1853 by J. Gilkey, J. P.

Keeter, John M. & A. C. Hale, 23 Nov 1858; Henry Nanny, bm; m 23 Nov 1858 by J. Gilkey, J. P.

Keeter, Joshua Jr. & Abigail Coxsey, 21 Dec 1837; Elbert Keeter, bm.

Keeter, Joshua Jr. & Elizabeth Wadkins, 27 Feb 1849; Joel Wadkins, bm.

Keeter, R. D. & N. S. Smith, 14 Dec 1866; M. J. Isaacs, bm; m 14 Dec 1866 by T. P. Sorrels, J. P.

Keeter, Samuel C. & Emeline Elliott, 13 Aug 1866; Henry White, b; m 16 Aug 1866 by J. J. Bradley.

Kelleay, William & Susan Suttles, 27 Sept 1823; John Kelleay, bm.

Kellee, John & Patsey Gualtney, 18 Jun 1805; John Gualtney, bm.

Kelley, Alexander & Rebecca J. Hayes, 11 Jan 1866; J. C. L. Harris, bm; m 11 Jan 1866 by Daniel May.

Kelley, Elijah & Esther Cook, 2 Dec 1815; Henry Kelley, bm.

Kelley, James & Salley Sullings, 2 Jul 1807; Za. Sullins, bm.

Kelley, John & Margit Waldrope, 23 Oct 1821; Jechonias Waldrop, bm.

Kelley, John & Dulcena Walker, 3 Oct 1866; A. J. Kelly, bm; m 4 Oct 1866 by B. W. Andrews, J. P.

Kelly, John & Eliz. Byars, 29 May 1795; Jonas Bedford, bm.

Kelly, William & Dicy Alfred, 3 Sept 1795; Henry Kelly, bm.

Kennedy, James & Elizabeth Cooper, 29 Oct 1842; Wm. Cooper, bm.

Kennedy, Levi & Pruddy Scruggs, 4 Dec 1832; Robert Scruggs, bm.

Kerr, Andrew & Huldah Koone, 17 Dec 1837; Daniel D. Koone, bm.

Kerr, D. D. D. & Jemima Laughter, 7 Feb 1841; Eli F. Littlejohn, bm.

Kerr, Hugh M. & Elizabeth Morgan, 7 Oct 1832; Martin Rippy, bm.

Keter, James & Katy Springfield, 17 Dec 1799; William Pell, bm.

Keter, James & ____ Johnson, 22 Jan 1800; James Keeter, bm.

Kilgore, Wm. C. & Louisa Haris, 14 Dec 1848; Wm. J. Hoke, bm.

Kilpatrick, Benj. & Marey Logan, 27 May 1843; Julis Logan, bm.

Kilpatrick, J. J. & Catharine Staten, 31 Mar 1851; Joseph C. Waldrop, bm.

Kilpatrick, James & Fanny Henson, 14 Jul 1799; Berryman Jones, bm.

Kilpatrick, James & Elizabeth Watson, 10 Nov 1803; Isaac Lollar, bm.

Kilpatrick, James & Polly Metcalf, 7 Jan 1809; William Metcalf, bm.

Kilpatrick, Joseph & Martha Harrison, 24 Aug 1789; Hugh Kilpatrick, bm.

Kilpatrick, Madison & Martha M. Lynch, 6 Jan 1841; Samuel Wilkins, bm.

Kilpatrick, N. M. & Nancey J. Scoggins, 17 Feb 1842; J. N. Scoggin, bm.

Kilpatrick, William & Jane Whary, 23 Nov 1808; Arthur McCluer, bm.

Kincaid, Robert & Sally Webb, 28 Nov 1822; Alfred Webb, bm.

Kindrick, Larkin H. & Carey J. Martin, 3 Jan 1833; Samuel Bailey, bm.

King, Barnabas & Susan Doggett, 13 Dec 1830; John Baber, bm.

King, Daniel & Malena Lynch, 1 Mar 1834; Edison Lynch, bm.

King, Drury & Piny Panter, 14 Apr 1809; Joseph Petty, bm.

King, George Jr. & Elizabeth Butler, 22 Dec 1836; Barnabas A. Baber, bm.

King, Henry & Drusilla Covington, 22 Sept 1846; William Maraw, bm.

King, James & Jane Henderson, 6 Apr 1818; Bushrod Suttle, bm.

King, John J. & Rebecker Stepp, 26 Jul 1841; H. K. Jones, bm.

King, Johnson & Sarah Suttles, 7 Dec 1847; William SUtton, bm.

King, Jonas & Jane Mills, 10 Jul 1828; Noah King, bm.

King, Jonathan & Sarah Taylor, 5 Dec 1798; John Taylor, bm.

King, Joseph & Mrs. ____ Morgan, 18 Oct 1793; Elias Morgan, bm.

King, Joseph & Mary Amanda Lynch, 31 Oct 1838; Laxton Lynch, bm.

King, Lewis & _____, 21 Apr 1822; John _____, bm.

King, Lewis & Sousen Egerton, 23 Oct 1842; Thos. Egerton, bm.

King, Lewis & Clarissa Milliard, 23 Dec 1859; Henry King, bm; m 12 Jan 1860 by H. Culbreath, M. G.

King, Noah & Rebecca Linch, 8 Dec 1831; Jonas King, bm.

King, Samuel & Evelina Lynch, 25 Apr 1834; Ambrose Mills, bm.

King, Samuel Junr. & Polly Kelly, 20 Sept 1792; Samuel King Senr., bm.

King, Spencer & Mary Canterell, 8 Dec 1829; Dunlap Scott, bm.

King, William & Nancy King, 20 Sept 1827; Robert Sutton, bm.

Kinipe, John & Thisba N. Napier, 6 Aug 1840; Jos. McCury, bm.

Kirkland, William & Polly Kirtlen, 4 MAr 1824; Bradley Simmons, bm.

Kirkpatrick, Abraham & Talitha Bird, 6 May 1822; Balding Bird, bm.

Kirkpatrick, William & _____, 15 Jul 1819; Charles Hill, bm.

Kistler, Leeplus & Sarah Kistler, 16 Mar 1843; B. W. Andrews, bm.

Kitchens, William & Lurana Harrell, 12 Jan 1831; Alexander Ramsey, bm.

Kizer, A. W. & Catharine L. Hyder, 8 Jan 1862; C. Burnett, bm; m 9 Jan 1862 by J. L. Taylor, J. P.

Kizer, D. D. & Eliz. Cockerham, 25 Jun 1856; M. M. Roberson, bm; m 25 Jun 1856 by John Koone, M. G.

Kizer, Frederick A. & Narcissa Bagwell, 10 Nov 1828; Jno. M. Whiteside, bm.

Kizer, J. B. & Nancy Wheler, 14 Apr 1857; G. W. Koone, bm.

Knipe, John & Mary W. Arriwood, 2 May 1861; W. A. Bradley, bm; m 2 May 1861 by A.R. Bennick, M. G.

Knipe, Noah & Jane Rooker, 2 May 1837; Alfred B. Mooney, bm.

Koon, Calvin & Elizabeth J. Hensley, 8 Aug 1859; J. B. Eaves, bm; m 9 Aug 1859 by B. E. Rollins.

Koon, George & Annaster Ownby, 7 Nov 1804; Porter Ownby, bm.

Koon, John & Louisa Bowman, 19 Jul 1855; John Bowman, bm; m 19 Jul 1855 by James Raines, M. G.

Koon, Spencer & Ciley Cawson, 13 Aug 1866; James Hamilton(?), bm; m 16 Aug 1866 by Vinson Micheal. (C. H.)

Koone, Aaron & Leah M. Bedix, 3 May 1857; John Haynes, bm; m 30 May 1857 by John Koone, M. G.

Koone, Daniel D. & Rebecca Morgan, 26 Mar 1836; John Koone, bm.

Koone, Dewalt & Sarah Flack, 15 Jan 1851; O. Bartell, bm.

Koone, Elisha & Rebecca Parker, 19 Aug 1866; P. Wilkerson, bm; m 19 Aug 1866 by J. W. Morgan, J. P.

Koone, John & Eveline Kerr, 30 Aug 1834; John M. Richardson, bm.

Koone, Madison & Mourning Blankenship, 26 Oct 1833; Barnett Blankinship, bm.

Koone, Marion & Elizabeth Allen, 25 Feb 1840; Thomas Nanney, bm.

Koone, Noah & Susan L. Hunter, 5 Sept 1854; Andrew Eaves, bm; m 6 Sept 1854 by John Koone.

Koone, Peter & Susanna Owenby, 19 Oct 1811; James Ownbey, bm;

Krause, Charles F. & Nancey Bradly, 22 Jun 1841; John Guffey, bm.

Kraws, Hiram & Prisila Hills, 29 Mar 1846; Randol Nanney, bm.

Lackey, Alexander & Pegah Ray, 9 Nov 1819; James Wray, bm.

Lackey, Samuel & Salley Cline, 7 Oct 1820; James Lackey, bm.

Lafferty, Alexander & Maryann Phillips, 20 May 1789; John Meggs, Henry Murry, bm.

Lain, Archabald & Betsey Hurt, 10 Dec 1822; Jeremiah Hase, bm.

Lain, David & Elizabeth Price, 25 Apr 1863; Francis Yelton, bm; m 26 Apr 1863 by H. A. Toney, bm.

Lancaster, L. R. & Jane Padgett, 10 Aug 1849; James M. Tate, bm.

Lancaster, William D. & R. C. Padgett, 11 Apr 1850; B. H. Padgett, bm.

Lance, Samuel & Eliza Perkins, 18 Jan 1843; John E. Perkins, bm.

Land, Thomas H. & Chatherine Allen, 27 Dec 1841; John Allen, bm.

Lane, David & Mary Earles, 27 Apr 1848; A. B. Long, bm.

Lane, Edward H. & Sarah E. Davis, 20 Jan 1848; C. L. Harris, bm.

Lane, Elijah & Nancy Marshe, 12 Jan 1858; Peter Lane, bm; m 12 Jan 1858 by Jas. M. Spratt, J. P.

Lane, Jesse & Mary Allen, 28 Nov 1853; Wm. Wilson, bm; m 30 Nov 1853 by Jas. M. Spratt, J. P.

Lane, Peter & Isabella Guffey, 15 Sept 1857; Jesse Lane, bm; m 15 Sept 1857 by John Freeman, J. P.

Lanes, William & Mary E. Smart, 16 May 1848; James M. Spratt, bm.

Lankford, Braxton & Susanah Dalton, 16 Jan 1817; Jos. Cloud, bm.

Lankford, Curtis & Catharine Caruth, __ Jan 1834; William Scott, bm.

Lankford, John & Mina Caruth, 7 Dec 1816; Wm. Henderson, bm.

Largant, Hugh & Aimy Jones, 21 May 1828; James Edwards, bm.

Largant, John & Elizabeth Janes, 23 Oct 1830; James Nany Jr., bm.

Largant, James & Elizabeth Still, 28 Jul 1807; Hugh Black, bm.

Largent, Georg D. & Anthro T. Davis, 21 Apr 1853; Noah Largant, bm.

Largent, Noah & Mary Humphreys, 30 Jan 1822; Adin Keeter, bm.

Largent, Noah Jr. & Polly Kinley, 10 Sept 1836; Alfred Owens, Hardy Flowers, bm.

Lassly, James & Margrett Nelson, 21 Aug 1779; Andrew Nelson, bm.

Lasswell, William & Salley Hoge, 12 Sept 1808; William Queen Sr., bm.

Latimore, Daniel & Sary Carpenter, 3 Nov 1796; Samuel Carpenter, bm.

Lattimore, John & Isabell C. Carson, 8 Jun 1830; William M. C. Gettys, bm.

Lattimore, Samuel & Lucinda Evans, 27 Jan 1831; James Waters, bm.

Lattimore, W. C. & R. C. Harris, 18 May 1865; J. T. Mode, bm; m 18 May 1865 by B. E. Rollins, M. G.

Laugheter, Riley & Mary Spicer, 17 Jun 1843; Wm. Dimsdale, bm.

Laughter, Anthony & Sarah Wharey, 9 Feb 1787; Thos. Randall, bm.

Laughter, Hix & Sarah Doyle, 27 Mar 1789; Samul Ballard, bm.

Laughter, James Hicks & Nancy Hill, 19 Oct 1830; Samel Laughter, bm.

Laughter, John & Polly Crooks, 1 Sept 1819; William Bradley, bm.

Laughter, John Jr. & Elizira Hills, 1 Aug 1837; Asa E. Young, bm.

Laughter, Wiley & Jenny Ried, 1 Jul 1829; James Bedford, bm.

Laughter, Wm & Mary Ann Jackson, 2 Jan 1854; Thos. Dias, bm; m 8 Jan 1854 by Wm. Dimsdale, J. P.

Laughter, Wyley & Anne Shelton, 23 Feb 1796; Joel Shelton, bm.

Laurence, John B. & Patsy Morris, 1 Aug 1820; John Morris, bm.

Lawing, Isreal & Esy Malinda Harris, 15 Aug 1837; Isaac Harriss, bm.

Lawing, James & Sarah Watkins, 27 Nov 1833; Isaac Harriss, bm.

Lawing, William & Elizabeth Hogin, 23 Nov 1819; Nathaniel Hogin, bm.

Lawrence, Martin & Jenny Gardner, 11 Sept 1800; Lewis Martin, bm.

Laws, Isaiah & Margaret Washburn, 3 Jan 1808; Gilberd Harell, bm.

Layton, Washington & Elizabeth Hoges, 24 Oct 1838; Irvin Henderson, bm.

Lea, Henry & Elizabeth Cox Maddox, 10 Sept 1807; Saml. Luckett, Joseph Lea, bm.

Lea, Larken & Polly Wadkins, 15 Nov 1823; John Flinn, bm.

Ledbetter, A. B. & Arminty Bradley, 17 Jan 1861; G. W. Harris, bm; m 17 Jan 1861 by J. W. Morgan, J. P.

Ledbetter, A. M. & E. J. Melton, 1 Jun 1858; James H. Whitesides, bm; m 1 Jun 1858 by B. E. Rollins, M. G.

Ledbetter, Andrew & Malinda Wilkerson, 26 Mar 1857; A. R. Bryan, bm; m 26 Mar 1857 by J. W. Morgan, J. P.

Ledbetter, Barzillai & Sarah Eliott, 12 Dec 1824; Jonson Ledbetter, bm.

Ledbetter, George & Lizer Murphey, 8 Sept 1841; F. Ward, bm.

Ledbetter, Grandison & Polly Wilkerson, m 5 Jan 1857 by C. Livingston, Elder.

Ledbetter, Isaac & Ursilla Bradley, 13 Jun 1806; Coalman Bradley, bm.

Ledbetter, John & B. Whitesides, 11 Aug 1804; Richard Ledbetter, bm.

Ledbetter, John W. & Martha Sursey, 20 Nov 1862; G. H. Bagwell, bm; m 20 Nov 1862 by Wm. Devenport.

Ledbetter, Johnston & Nancy Whitesides, __ Jan 1810; Jo. Ledbetter, bm.

Ledbetter, Jonathan & Nancy Wells, 25 Nov 1822; John Goodbread, bm.

Ledbetter, Jonathan & Amanda Rucker, 18 Sept 1856; James W. Morgan, bm; m 18 Sept 1856 by J. W. Morgan, J. P.

Ledbetter, Noah & Zilphia Hill, 7 Jan 1828; Jones Bradley, bm.

Ledbetter, R. O. & M. U. Ledbetter, 28 Mar 1867; B. Ledbetter, bm; m 28 Mar 1867 by J. B. Bowman, M. G.

Ledbetter, Richard & Mary Whiteside, 17 Jul 1800; John Elms, bm.

Ledbetter, Richard Sr. & Elizabeth Berry, 18 Apr 1822; James Ward Sr, bm.

Ledbetter, Richard O. & Elizabeth Harriss, 15 Dec 1831; Robert Searcy Jr., bm.

Ledbetter, William & Melinda Williams, 7 Feb 1834; William Elliott, bm.

Ledbetter, William H. & Ruth Lewallen, 2 Jun 1826; Shadrach Lewlin, bm.

Ledbetter, William R. & Julia A. Lookadoo, 11 Nov 1866; J. B. McDaniel, bm; m 11 Nov 1866 by B. B. Byers, J. P.

Ledford, Alexander H. & Sarah M. Bradley, 5 May 1859; Lawson H. Ledford, bm; m 5 May 1859 by H. Culbreath, M. G.

Ledford, Jesse & Mareny McCurry, 11 Jan 1846; Jas. M. McCurry, bm.

Ledford, John W. & Nancy Hendrick, 26 Jul 1863; J. T. Mode, bm; m 16 Jul 1863 by Wm. G. Mode.

Ledford, Lawson H. & Elizabeth Bradley, 29 Mar 1859; Daniel H. Ledford, bm; m 31 Mar 1859 by Henry Culbreath.

Ledford, Lewis & Dorcas Ellis, 19 Jul 1812; John White, bm.

Ledford, Lewis & Fanney Pool, 8 May 1825; James Wray, bm.

Ledford, McFalls & Nancy Morriss, 7 May 1832; George W. Miller, bm.

Ledford, Thomas & Rebeckka Crowder, 18 Aug 1812; Robert Wells, bm.

Lee, George & Priscilla Bridges, 28 Feb 1833; John S. Hardin, bm.

Lee, James Q. & Mary Harrill, 3 May 1850; C. J. Webb, bm.

Lee, James R. & Pricilla Flinn, 19 Feb 1835; Reuben McDanniel, bm.

Lee, Matthias & Sarah Lucket, 4 Feb 1808; Saml. Lucket, Joseph Lee, bm.

Lee, Osbon & Rosanna Bridges, 10 Oct 1839; George Lee, bm.

Lee, Vincent W. & Elizabeth Grigg, 12 Nov 1835; William Lee, bm.

Lee, William & Nancy Bedford, 9 Jan 1806; Jesse Richardson, bm.

Lee, William O. & Harriett Adaline Bridges, 10 Dec 1835; Aaron Bridges Junr, bm.

Lequire, Miner & Irene Womack, 15 Feb 1842; John H. Harrill, bm.

Leventhorpe, Collett & Louisa L. Bryan, 1 Apr 1849; L. B. Bryan, bm.

Lewis, Charles & Elizabeth Russel, 25 Oct 1785; Richd. Lewis, bm.

Lewis, Charles & Jincey Flack, 21 Nov 1825; George Flack, bm.

Lewis, George M. & Narcissa Ray, 16 Oct 1835; James Lewis, bm.

Lewis, H. G. & Mourning Mills, 17 Dec 1791; James Miller, bm.

Lewis, Henry R. & Nancy Goodbread, 17 Dec 1839; R. O. Ledbetter, bm.

Lewis, J. W. & M. C. Benit, m 16 Dec 1866 by W. H. Logan, Elder.

Lewis, Jesse T. & Susanah Cowan, 20 Dec 1842; Preston Lewis, bm.

Lewis, John & Annah Earl, 21 Dec 178-; John Crawford, bm.

Lewis, Peter & _____, 18 Nov 1817; Eber. Newton, bm.

Lewis, Pitman & Intha Dalton, 30 May 1837; William Dalton, bm.

Liles, Abner & Elizabeth Randal, 23 Jan 1812; Silas Randal, bm.

Liles, John & Ann Copely, 4 Aug 1846; Joseph Blackwel, bm.

Liles, Jonal & Lavina Mullins, 7 May 1805; Jesse Richardson, bm.

Linch, Laxton & Elizabeth Richardson, _____ ; John Morgan, bm.

Linder, W. L. & N. R. Tanner, 29 Mar 1866; J. B. Carpenter, bm; m 19 Apr 1866 by Daniel May.

Liney, William C. & Patsey Baxter, 11 Feb 1841; Moormer White, bm.

Linsey, James & Fanney Logan, 15 Mar 1813; Thomas Morelang, bm.

Linsford, Edwin & Elizabeth Dalton, 4 Apr 1800; Jno. Thompson, bm.

Lipscombe, Miner & Nancy Patterson, 7 Jul 1818; David Patterson, bm.

Little, Danil A. & Elizabeth Wilmoth, 4 Nov 1840; R. O. Ledbetter, bm.

Little, William & Elizabeth Guffey, 31 May 1830; John S. Guffey, bm.

Littlefield, A. & Martha Roberts, 20 Mar 1865; G. W. Bradley, bm; m 20 Mar 1865 by C. Burnett, J. P.

Littlejohn, Abraham & Sarah Richardson, 9 Dec 1816; Josiah Sullins, bm.

Littlejohn, Eli F. & A. Lavina Kerr, 11 Sept 1841; Francis A. Littlejohn, bm.

Littlejohn, Francis A. & Lavinia Gray, 1 Jun 1829; John Wilekins, bm.

Littlejohn, James & Mary Amanda Ooens, 29 Nov 1843; John Littlejohn, bm.

Littlejohn, John & Catharine Kerr, 27 Dec 1837; Francis A. Littlejohn, bm.

Littlejohn, Thomas & Minerva Wilkins, 10 Dec 1832; James T. Wilkins, bm.

Lively, John C. & Pheby Milton, 21 Apr 1825; Frederick F. Price, bm.

Lively, William & _____, 3 Dec 1792.

Liverett, Jona. & Barbary Tanner, 22 Nov 1842; W. A. Tanner, bm.

Liverett, Robert & Polly Tomberlinson, 13 Oct 1807.

Liverett, Thomas & Nancy Winsor, 17 Apr 1808; Charles Hill, bm.

Logan, Albert G. & Nancy T. Logan, 1 Jan 1838; Marcus O. Dickerson, bm.

Logan, Andrew & Polly Hider, 9 May 1791; Robert Finly, bm.

Logan, Benjamin & Phebe Simmons, 12 Feb 1818; Wm. Grayson, bm.

Logan, Bengamin & Mary Fortune, 7 Aug 1829; John Withrow, bm.

Logan, Felix & Cinthia Bagwell, 25 Oct 1821; J. Gilkey, bm.

Logan, Francis & Huldah Powell, 12 Aug 1825; William Wallis, bm.

Logan, Green & Pamela Blanton, 14 May 1853; Meredith Jolley, bm.

Logan, J. C. & M. E. Long, 8 Mar 1867; F. A. Shotwell, bm; m 14 Mar 1866 by G. W. Rollins.

Logan, James & Nancy Egerton, __ Mar 1801.

Logan, James & Sally Lankford, 2 Dec 1813; John Lankford, bm.

Logan, James & Margaret Hill, 8 Aug 1831; Lawson H. Logan, bm.

Logan, James & Elisabeth Hill, 18 Jan 1844; Avington Hills, bm.

Logan, James Jefferson & Mary Ann Weatherow, 28 Nov 1827; William Jefferson Withrow, bm.

Logan, John & Patsey Harton, 29 Oct 1811; Jas. Humphreys, bm.

Logan, John & Catharine Hampton, 3 Jan 1852; M. O. Dickerson, bm; m 6 Jan 1852 by Allen Hamby, M. G.

Logan, John & Elizabeth Williams, 30 Mar 1854; M. O. Dickerson, bm; m 2 Apr 1854 by T. B. Justice, M. G.

Logan, Julius & Polly Jones, 21 Jun 1821; Isam Wood, bm.

Logan, Lawson H. & Lurana Young, 28 May 1834; Lorin Walker, bm.

Logan, Moses & Susanna Hider, 22 Oct 1799; Jo. Alexander, bm.

Logan, Reuben F. & Isabella F. Long, 16 Feb 1857; M. O. Dickerson, bm; m by T. E. Davis, M. G.

Logan, Reubin & Rachel Moore, 26 Mar 1794; Elisha Moore, bm.

Logan, W. H. & Mary Bagwell, 31 Jan 1862; W. H. Flinn, bm; m 31 Jan 1862 by T. B. Justice.

Lollar, Archibal & Meria Dicky, 30 Aug 1813.

Lollar, Isaac & Jane Kilpatrick, 12 Nov 1794; Hugh Kilpatrick, bm.

Lollar, Isaac C. & Jane Morris, 1 Feb 1847; Isaac D. McCluer, bm.

Lollar, L. D. & L. M. Littlejohn, 4 Jan 1867; J. Jones, bm.

Lollar, Thomas & Jane Owens, 9 Jun 1807.

Lomucks, Thomas & Susanah Murroor, 16 Oct 1810; Elijah Fatthy, bm.

London, Edward & Maryan Peeler, 30 Sept 1824; Andrew Peeler, bm.

London, James & Maria J. Bennett, 18 Dec 1838; John Bennett, bm.

London, John & Elizabeth Peeler, 21 Jul 1825; Andrew Peeler, bm.

Long, A. B. Jr. & Sarah Long, 29 Jan 1857; J. L. Wallace, bm; m 29 Jan 1857 by John Freeman, J. P.

Long, Andrew B. & Sarah A. Andrews, 26 Feb 1822; Samuel Andrews, bm.

Long, Andrew B. & Nancy Long, 29 Jan 1844; P. W. Watson, bm.

Long, Andrew Mos. & Catharine Edwards, 23 Jan 1833; James Findley Long, bm; m 24 Jan 1833 by Hugh Watson, J. P.

Long, Cisero, son of C. M. Long, & Cinda Bostick, m 8 Mar 1868 by J. W. Mode, J. P.

Long, Claudius & Sarah Long, 3 Dec 1792; Jas. Cooke, bm.

Long, Elisha W. & Sinthy Baber, 17 Jan 1854; Jas G. Freeman, bm; m 19 Jan 1854 by John Freeman, J. P.

Long, Francis Marion & Henrietta L. Stacy, 23 Oct 1860; James B. Vickers, bm; m 25 Oct 1860 by A. Hamby, Elder.

Long, Gloud F. & Elizabeth Wells, 1 Feb 1821; William Long, bm.

Long, Gloud M. & Nancy Deck, 27 Jan 1835; Jacob Deck Jr., bm.

Long, Hugh Watson & Martha Burnett, 25 Feb 1819; John Oliver, Leroy Burnett, bm.

Long, James & Susanna Parcks, 4 May 1803; Benjn. Parks, bm.

Long, James & Sally Whitesides, 17 Nov 1822; Joseph G. Whiteside, bm.

Long, James Findley & Margaret Robertson, 18 Feb 1828; James Robertson, bm.

Long, James Findley & Mary M. Long, 29 Aug 1832; Andrew M. Long, bm; m 30 Aug 1832 by Hugh Watson, J. P.

Long, James T. & Belinda Stafford, 18 Aug 1836; Stephen L. Stafford, bm.

Long, Jerry, son of Benj. Good and Eliza Young, colored, & Jushur Logan, 17 Dec 1867.

Long, John & Izebella Long, 15 Aug 1791; William Long, bm.

Long, John A. & Sarah Clemmons, 6 Aug 1834; Andrew Clemts, bm; m 7 Aug 1834 by Hugh Watson, J. P.

Long, John S. & Dicey Johnston, 19 Mar 1823; William Long, bm.

Long, Thomas J. & Amandah R. Wallis, 3 Feb 1851; James W. Allen, bm.

Long, Thomas S. & Dicey Shamwell, 9 Feb 1829; Pinckney Reid, bm.

Long, William & Jane Smart, 17 Dec 1793; John Long, bm.

Long, William & Becky Corthron, 12 Jan 1815; Hugh Watson, bm.

Long, William & Sarah Robertson, 16 Sept 1829; Henry M. Kerr, bm.

Long, William J. & Mary Morrison, 28 Dec 1829; Joseph Reed, bm.

Long, Wm. L. & Susan C. Sims, 2 Jan 1862; H. Cowen, bm.

Long, Wm. N. & Clara O. Melton, 12 Feb 1866; J. G. Freeman, bm.

Lonon, John & Saraw A. Devina, 18 Mar 1861; B. C. Fortun, bm; m 18 Mar 1861 by B. E. Rollins.

Loocdoo, John & Sarah R. Mitchell, 14 Nov 1826; Gorge Lookadoo, bm.

Lookado, James & Mary Ann Moorehead, 15 Dec 1832; John Moorehead, bm.

Lookadoo, Alfred W. & Rachel Swezey, 1 Apr 1856; Jesse Lookadoo, bm; m 9 Apr 1856 by John Freeman, J. P.

Lookadoo, George & Eliza Smiley, 8 Apr 1829; Henry Lookadoo, bm.

Lookadoo, Geo W. & Julia Ann McDaniel, 4 Oct 1860; W. A. McKinney, bm; m 4 Oct 1860 by D. Ponnell.

Lookadoo, Henry & Mary Smiley, 14 Nov 1837; George Lookado, bm.

Lookadoo, James W. & Parozade Huntsinger, 6 Oct 1857; Jesse J. Lookadoo, bm; m 15 Oct 1857 by John Freeman, J. P.

Lookadoo, Jesse & Elizabeth Earls, 2 Jun 1858 ; John Lookadoo, bm; m 10 Jun 1858 by John Freeman, J. P.

Lorance, William R. & Lamira Weeks, 12 Dec 1838; William Pullam, bm.

Lorance, Wm. R. & Jemima Moore, 21 Mar 1843; B. W. Andrews, bm.

Lourey, Samuel & Anne Waters, 10 May 1817; Isaac Craton, bm.

Love, James & Anna Whipple, 28 Jan 1779; Richard Lewis, bm.

Love, Osborn & Jane Fondren, 15 Aug 1825; Charles Love, John Fondren, bm.

Love, Robert & Jane Palley, 27 Nov 1806; Aron Deveny, bm.

Lovelace, Asa & Susanah Harden, 23 Jul 1806; Abraham Cantrill, Thomas Davis, bm.

Lovelace, Benjamin & Nicy Green, 2 Mar 1858; James Lovelace, bm; m 4 Mar 1858 by John Freeman, J. P.

Lovelace, G. L. & Sarah P. Williams, 8 Apr 1866; J. P. Franklin, bm; m 8 Apr 1866 by Mijamin Price, J. P. (C. H.)

Lovelace, John & Silla Wood, 13 Feb 1837; John Teal, bm.

Loveland, Lewis Green & Margaret Lovelace, 10 Oct 1866; D. William Scoggin, D. D. McSwain, bm; m 20 Oct 1866 by John Davis, J. P.

Lovelace, M. R. & Unicy J. Wright, 8 Jan 1867; G. L. Lovelace, bm.

Loveless, Asa & Polly Green, 11 Mar 1840; Lewis Green, bm.

Loveless, Green & Marthy Nichols, 14 Sept 1840; Lewis Green, bm.

Loveless, James & Judith Hamrick, 12 Jan 1821.

Loveless, James & Sarah Tessenmir, 11 Dec 1846; Lewis Green, bm.

Loveless, John & Elizabeth Wiggins, 1 Nov 1831; John Teal, bm.

Loveless, William & Cynthia Holifield, 15 Feb 1839; Lewis Green, bm.

Lovells, Danl. & Elizabeth Green, 29 Jan 1856; Reuben Melton, bm; m 31 Jan 1856 by A. Harrill, J. P.

Lovlace, G. L. & Mary J. Green, 8 Feb 1866; H. C. Hollifield, bm; m 8 Feb 1866 by A. P. Hollifield, J. P.

Lovlas, Albert & Margaret Braddy, ____ 1860; A. D. Rollins, bm; m 14 May 1860 by R. Depriest, J. P.

Lovles, Wm. & Sarah Birdges, 26 Oct 1854; James Lovles, bm.

Lowrance, J. L. & Sarah Harrill, 2 Apr 1857; Andrew Eaves, E. Jennings, bm; m 2 Apr 1857 by P. F. Kistler, M. G.

Lowrance, J. Moten & Jane Reece, 16 Sept 1847; M. S. Lowrance, bm.

Lowry, Samuel & Susan Miller, 17 Nov 1810; Robt. McAfee, bm.

Lucas, James & Marey Davis, 13 May 1813; John Lucas, bm.

Lucas, Jno & Barbara Aker, 5 Aug 1813; Henry Hoyle, Soln. Hoyl, bm.

Lukquire, John S. & Polly Flinn, 20 Oct 1846; Jackson Moore, bm.

Lumpkin, John K. & Ann Hopson, 14 Dec 1807; Nevill Hobson, bm.

Luquier, Joseph & Martha Wamack, 11 Oct 1852; Daniel Melton, bm.

Lyman, William & Maria Ward, 5 Feb 1845; Richard Morris, bm.

Lynch, A. O. & Easther Leadbetter, 25 Jul 1861; Jesse Hilliard, bm; m 29 Jul 1861 by J. C. Grayson, M. G.

Lynch, Adin A. & Margaret Hill, 8 Nov 1848; B. Smith, bm.

Lynch, Ahijah O. & Nelly Green, 12 Jan 1835; John Richardson, bm.

Lynch, Columbus & Adline Moore, 26 Nov 1866; Toliver Twitty, bm; m by 23 Nov 1866, by Vincen Micheal. (C. H.)

Lynch, Edison & Mary Frady, 9 Dec 1833; Norman Lynch, bm.

Lynch, Elias & Fany Devenport, 3 Dec 1807; John Devenport, bm.

Lynch, Elias M. & Sarah E. Whitesides, 9 Oct 1843; J. W. Morgan, bm.

Lynch, H. P. & Margarett E. Harrill, 21 Nov 1859; A. W. Harrill, bm; m 23 Nov 1859 by Wm. Rucker, J. P.

Lynch, John & Henrietta Augusta Huffmaster, 30 Jul 1865; E. M. Lynch, bm; m 31 Jul 1865 by E. L. Taylor, M. G.

Lynch, L. M. & S. U. Searcy, 22 Jul 1859; William Y. Green, bm; m 28 Jul 1859 by Wm. Rucker.

Lynch, Norman & Mary J. L. Kerr, 5 May 1828; William Rucker, bm.

Lynch, Tolifarro Devenport, & Nancy C. Whitesides, 12 May 1829; Edmond Sebastian, bm.

Lynch, Toliver D. & Nercissa Edwards, 17 MAr 1831; James L. Taylor, bm.

Lynch, Wm. A. & Martha J. Metcalf, ____ 185-; M. O. Dickerson, bm; __ Apr 1858 by J. Morgan, J. P.

McAbee, Elisha & Mary Sprouce, 1 Sept 1849; S. M. Coward, bm.

McAfee, James T. & Rebecca G. Dickerson, 23 Mar 1829; Robert G. Twitty, bm.

McAlister, Samuel & Jane King, 26 Oct 1853; J. K. Lynch, bm; m 27 Oct 1853 by Jas. L. Taylor, J. P.

McArther, James & Sally Crooks, 3 Sept 1818; Wm. Baber, bm.

McArthur, David & Drusilla Cochran, 22 Nov 1851; M. O. Dickerson, bm.

McArthur, David T. & Elizebeth Medcalf, 22 Oct 1866; J. R. Padgett, bm; m 28 Oct 1866 by G. M. Webb.

McArthur, E. & Mary A. Walker, 9 Sept 1860; N. E. Walker, bm; m 9 Sept 1850 by Wm. Harrill, M. G.

McArthur, John G. & Julia Good, 14 Aug 1866; Joseph Wilson, bm; m 14 Aug 1866 by Wm. Harrill, Elder.

McArthur, William G. & Eliza Magness, 10 Nov 1840; Walter S. McArthur, bm.

McBrayer, Adolpus & Nercissy Gillam, 5 Nov 1839; James McBrayer, bm.

McBrayer, David & Elizabeth Durham, 2 Mar 1843; Benja. D. Durham, bm.

McBrayer, James & Fanny Doggett, 11 Jul 1820; Francis Beatey, George Doggett, bm.

McBrayer, Jason & Amelia Julin, 10 Jan 1831; Housen Harrill, bm.

McBrayer, L. N. & Catharine King, 6 Jan 1856; Joseph C. Wllkie, bm; m 10 Jan 1856 by Wm. Harrill.

McBrayer, Martin & Nancy Purkins, 17 Sept 1846; Thos. Parkes, bm.

McBrayer, N. B. & MAry E. Sparks, 8 Aug 1865; J. B. Eaves, bm; m 12 Sept 1865 by A. W. Harill, J. P.

McBrayer, Robert & Frances Harrell, 10 Mar 1831; Wm. McBrayer, bm.

McBrayer, Samuel & Rhoda McEntire, 29 Oct 1811; Wm. McEntire, Wm. McBrayer, bm.

McBrayer, Wm. & Drusilla McEntire, 24 Jun 1824; Housen Harrill, bm.

McBrayer, William & Sarah Dye, 11 Jan 1841; Peter Jolly, bm.

McBryar, Tilman W. & Almeda Bridges, 30 Oct 1839; Samuel McBryar, bm.

McCachun, W. H. & Narcissus L. Mitchell, 4 Sept 1866; J. S. Hayes, bm; m 4 Sept 1866 by Daniel May.

McCallahan, Andrew & Anna Keeter, 20 Dec 1824; James Keeter, bm.

McCann, James & Nancy Dearing, 5 May 1803; John McCann, John Dalton, bm.

McCarthie, Thos. R. & Mary Ann Guffy, 26 Dec 1843; Thos. Moore, bm.

McClean, Charles & Elizabeth Hughes, 16 May 1797; Joil Terrell, bm.

McClendon, William & Peggy Garrett, 6 Nov 1809; Elijah Thompson, bm.

McCluer, Alexander & Elizabeth Nix, 8 Dec 1796; William Nix, bm.

McCluer, Isaac D. & Marthar Ann Loller, 6 Apr 1836; Larkin B. Bryan, bm.

McCluer, John Jr. & Nancy Young, 24 Jan 1798; Arthur McClure, bm.

McCluer, John Jr. & Permealia Kilpatrick, 26 Sept 1811; Arthur McEntire, bm.

McCluer, Richard & Ann Gray, 7 Feb 1782; John McCluer, bm.

McClure, John & Mary Ann Norrell, 29 Feb 1808; Henry Norrell, bm.

McClure, Levi & Milly McClure, 14 Jan 1836; John Baber, bm.

McClure, Richard & Rebecca Wilkerson, 18 Jan 1849; J. S. Upchurch, bm.

McClure, Richard Jr. & Sarah Jordan, 29 Dec 1829; MEdia Jordan, bm.

McClure, Samuel & Sarah Norville, 10 Sept 1842; Wm. Dedman, bm.

McCosh, J. J. & S. O. Long, 25 Sept 1859; C. Gregg, bm; m 25 Sept 1859 by E. M. Carpenter, J. P.

McCown, _____ & _____, 16 Feb 1812; Archd. Lollar, bm.

McCraw, Abner B. & Mary Davis, 1 Sept 1836; James M. Tate, bm.

McCraw, Cabret & Mary Tate, 6 Jan 1805; Jessey Tate, bm.

McCraw, Josiah & Rebecca Pearson, 2 Oct 1831; Herod Blanton, bm.

McCraw, Josiah & Polly Jolley, 27 Aug 1840; Richard Champion, bm.

McCraw, Peter W. & Faney Tate, 21 Aug 1855; Hilmon Philips, bm; m 21 Aug 1855 by J. H. Carpenter, J. P.

McCraw, Robert & Synthy Wood, 31 Oct 1839; William Wood, bm.

McCraw, Sheaderok & Arrana Humphris, 5 Mar 1840; Bannon Humphrys, bm.

McCraws, Cabret & Polly McGowin, 28 Dec 1817; Samuel ___, Beyard McCraws, bm.

McCray, H. & _____, 9 Mar 1806; Saml. Young, bm.

McCray, Robt. & Elizabeth Johns, 10 Apr 1799; Zachariah Johns, bm.

McCurry, Amos & Rachel Webb, 26 Dec 1820; Silas McCurry(?), bm.

McCurry, D. S. & Jane Norrel, 3 Aug 1852; Rochig Block, bm.

McCurry, H. & Martha Parker, 27 Mar 1845; Jas. M. McCurry, bm.

McCurry, Jacob & Betsey Wellman, _____; William Wellman, John McCurry, bm.

McCurry, James M. & Rebecca Upton, 4 May 1842; J. B. Jones, bm.

McCurry, John R. & Jane Jones, 28 Feb 1858; J. H. Melton, bm; m 28 Feb 1858 by Wm. G. Mode, J. P.

McCurry, Joseph & Huldah L. Crow, 15 Jan 1841; Benjn. Taylor, bm.

McCurry, Lewis & Dorias Carson, 21 Apr 1822.

McCurry, Randal & Mary Green, 4 Oct 1840; Squire Melton, bm.

McCurry, Simeon & Easther Gardner, 15 Oct 1829; Smith McCurry, bm.

McCurry, W. A. & M. J. Watters, 12 Jan 1862; K. J. M. Grayson, bm; m 12 Jan 1862 by B. E. Rollins.

McCurry, William & Mareny A. Harrison, 28 Feb 1855; James M. Harrison, bm; m 28 Feb 1855 by John Freeman, J. P.

McCurry, Wm. B. & Frances Mooney, 25 Feb 1847; Geo. Mooney, bm.

McDade, Thomas & Catharine Metcalf, 10 Oct 1854; George W. Ponder, bm.

McDanel, Andy & Tempy Bostick, 15 Aug 1865; Noah W. Womack, bm; m 22 Aug 1865 by H. Harrill, J. P.

McDanel, James & Maryann Edwards, 22 Aug 1853; Wm. J. Blanton, bm; m 25 Aug 1853 by Joseph Suttle.

McDaniel, Colemon & Sarah McDaniel, 20 Jan 1832; Reuben McDaniel, bm.

McDaniel, Drury & C. E. Hughes, 17 Oct 1842; B. W. Andrews, bm.

McDaniel, George & Fanny Carpenter, 5 Feb 1822; Samson McDaniel, bm.

McDaniel, Godfrey & Alvira Guffy, 20 Aug 1856; John P. Eaves, bm; m 20 Aug 1856 by W. A. Tanner, J. P.

McDaniel, Guilford & Rachel Depriest, 31 Jan 1855; Alfred W. Baxter, bm; m 6 Feb 1855 by J. H. Carpenter, J. P.

McDaniel, J. A. & Elizabeth Johnson, 28 Aug 1863; M. V. Johnson, bm; m 28 Aug 1863 by W. H. Atkin, J. P.

McDaniel, James & Catey Hanes, 21 Oct 1802; Daniel McDaniel, bm.

McDaniel, James T. & Nancy N. Forbus, 7 Oct 1857; John Parker, bm; m 7 Oct 1857 by John Freeman, J. P.

McDaniel, Jesse & Rebecah Philips, 29 Jun 1837; Ambrose Roach, bm.

McDaniel, Jesse & Elicabeth Edwards, 10 Jan 1858; M. Wilkerson, bm; m 10 Jan 1858 by M. Wilkerson.

McDaniel, Jethro & Lusinda Flinn, 5 Jan 1854; Jas. Crawford, bm.

McDaniel, John & Mary Sperling, 4 Jun 1816; William McKinney, bm.

McDaniel, John L. & Mary E. Edwards, 23 May 1860; A. J. Scoggin, bm; m 24 May 1860 by John Edwards, Elder.

McDaniel, Joseph R. & Elizabeth Cooper, 22 Oct 1850; C. L. Henson, bm.

McDaniel, Lewis & Nancy Womach, 30 Jan 1861; John B. Womick, bm; m 30 Jan 1861 by J. H. Carpenter, J. P.

McDaniel, Moses & Malinda Scoggin, 15 Mar 1829; Joseph Scoggen, bm.

McDaniel, Reuben & Patsey Lea, 22 Sept 1823; George McDaniel, bm.

McDaniel, Sampson & Leanner G. S. Womack, 14 Apr 1826; Alanson Padgett, bm.

McDaniel, Spencer R. & Sarah C. Baxter, 18 Dec 1850; J. A. Carpenter, bm.

McDaniel, Thomas & Sarah Walker, 7 Jan 1825; John Walker, bm.

McDaniel, Willis E. & Mary Beam, 30 Sept 1852; Martin Beam, bm; m 30 Sept 1852 by Wm. Harrill, M. G.

McDaniell, Godfrey & Catharine Walker, 23 Oct 1847; David Walker, bm.

McDanil, James & Elizabeth Matthes, 7 May 1799; J. Riggs, bm.

McDanil, Moses W. & Elizabeth McBrayar, 28 Feb 1861; James Rhodes, m 28 Mar 1861.

McDonald, Joseph & Penny Alphard, 15 Dec 1789; James McDonald, bm.

McDonald, Lewis & Martha Roach, 17 Dec 1855; Berry P. Hardin, bm; m 25 Dec 1855 by Edward Toms, J. P.

McDonald, William & Rachael Ellis, 14 Mar 1823; Everett Parsons, bm.

McDonold, John & Sarah Cockram, 6 Jan 1804; Henry Denens, bm.

McDow, David & Elizabeth Earls, 10 Jan 1805; Natha Earls, bm.

McDowell, Andrew & Harriet Lyles, 25 Sept 1837; John H. Wilkins, bm.

McDowell, John & Mary Mansfield Lewis, 23 Oct 1810; Isaac Craton, bm.

McDowell, Jos. & Louisa Twitty, 7 Dec 1841; Jos. W. Calloway, bm.

McEntir, James & Providence Arthur, 23 Sept 1830; Charles L. H. Schieffelin, bm.

McEntire, A. G. & Elender Walles, 15 Sept 1839; Bartlett Henson, bm.

McEntire, Aron & Susannah Bennick, 4 Jun 1833; William Covington, bm.

McEntire, Bird & Elizabeth Snider, ____ 1807; William Covington, Aaron McEntire, bm.

McEntire, Champion & Sarah Waters, 10 Sept 1831; Aaron Waters, bm.

McEntire, Joseph W. & Caroline Burnet, 5 Feb 1844; J. W. Green, bm.

McEntire, Josiah & Martha J. Horde, 7 Feb 1839; Wm. Covington, bm.

McEntire, Prier & Jamima Lattimore, 3 Jan 1828; William McEntire, bm.

McEntire, William & Polley Wilkinson, 23 Feb 1823; James Nowlin, bm.

McFadden, John & Synthea Taylor, 14 Oct 1824; Jas. O. Terrell, bm.

McFadin, Alexander & Mary Twity, 22 Feb 1785; Anthony Dicky, bm.

McFarland, A. D. & Nancy Towerey, 25 Sept 1851; Elisha Waters, bm; m 28 Sept 1851 by Thomas E. Davis, M. G.

McFarland, Alfred & Nancy Gettys, 21 Apr 1829; John Price, bm.

McFarland, Alfred & Luraner Stewart, 4 Oct 1832; William Stewart, bm.

McFarland, Aron D. & Letty Hunt, 29 Sept 1840; L. B. Bryan, bm.

McFarland, Daniel C. & Winney Price, 30 Sept 1852; Robert L. Price, bm; m 30 Sept 1852 by R. T. Price, J. P.

McFarland, George & Rebeca Carson, 28 Feb 1825; Daniel McFarland, bm.

McFarland, James & Isabella Gattis, 18 Oct 1809; W. McFarland, bm.

McFarland, James & Susanna Taylor, 21 Oct 1835; William H. Taylor, bm.

McFarland, James K. & Darcus Deviney, 29 Apr 1857; Jno. A. McFarland, bm; m 19 Apr 1857 by Wm. G. Mode, J. P.

McFarland, James S. & Martha P. Devinny, 2 Jan 1866; John E. McFarland, bm.

McFarland, John & Mary Devany, 16 Mar 1804; Aaron Devey, bm.

McFarland, John & Margaret C. McFarland, 11 Jan 1845; A. D. McFarland, bm.

McFarland, John E. & Hannah Swezey, 3 Jan 1852; L. D. Allen, bm.

McFarland, Robert & Mary T. Abrams, 9 Sept 1839; Joseph Green, bm.

McFarland, Samuel & Elizabeth W. Carson, 29 Sept 1846; A. G. Logan, bm.

McFarland, William & Rebecca Ann Johnson, 28 May 1851; Wiley Johnson, bm; m 28 May 1851 by John McFarland, J. P.

McFarland, William G. & Anna McFarland, 8 Feb 1838; John McFarland, bm.

McGahhey, James & S. M. Weast, 8 Nov 1854; M. G. Weast, bm.

McGaughe, Josiah & Delila Deen, 26 Feb 1823; Richard Deen, bm.

McGaughey, James Withrow & Elizabeth Megahey, 11 Dec 1816; John Easely, bm.

McGaughey, Jeremiah & Jane Smith, 15 Sept 1795; Daniel MCGauhey, bm.

McGaughey, Joseph & Martha Dunlap, 13 Mar 1819; James McGauhhey, bm.

McGaughey, William & Mimy Patterson, 3 Aug 1792; George Watson, bm.

McGaughy, James & Elizabeth Burnett, 24 Oct 1812; Joseph Allen, bm.

McGaughy, Lenoyr & Peggy Burnitt, 30 Sept 1820; Henry Burnett, bm.

McGaughy, Robt. & Ruth Burnitt, 23 Jan 1797; Lewis Burnett, bm.

McGaughy, Thomas & Polly Burnett, 20 Dec 1803; William Burnett, bm.

McGauhey, Daniel & Martha Parker, 13 Jan 1849; John Moore, bm.

McGinty, Henry E. & Nancy Wallis, 29 Dec 1840; A. G. McEntire, bm.

McGinty, James & Martha Wallis, 3 Aug 1845; A. G. McEntire, bm.

McGinnis, Andrew & Lucinda Smith, 28 Nov 1833; Jacob Smith, bm.

McGinnis, Christopher H. & Malinda Moore, 21 Apr 1820; Samuel F. Cutler, bm.

McGlamry, Jesse & Nancy Roper, 17 Sept 1789; William Queen, David Roper Jr., bm.

McGroves, William & Nancy Baldridge, 8 Dec 1823; John Baldridge, bm.

McGuinn, Alexander & Margaret Thompson, 12 Apr 1810; John W. Allen, bm.

McGuire, Westley & Margaret Carson, 24 Oct 1837; Ansel J. Hardin, bm.

McHan, Alanson & Catharine Morris, 16 Jul 1841; J. H. Alley Jr., bm.

McHan, Daniel & Rebecca Wells, 14 Apr 1845; T. Davis, bm.

McHan, Henry & Elizabeth Wells, 26 Nov 1845; Daniel McHan, bm.

McHan, James Jr. & Rebecca Davis, 18 Nov 1834; Toliver Davis, bm.

McHan, Jemes & Milly Hicks, 2 Dec 1821; Micheal Tanner, bm.

McHan, Jemes & Anna Wood, 10 Jun 1830.

McHan, John & Anna Morrow, 18 Sept 1844; L. B. Carmichall, bm.

McHan, Lewis & Nancy McGowan, 22 Dec 1822; Garland Dickerson, bm.

McHan, Thomas & Eda Bowman, 6 Jan 1819; Alanson McHan, bm.

McHann, Alson & Polly Bowman, 11 Dec 1818; Thomas McHann, bm.

McHann, Hezekiah & Adaline Wells, 20 Jan 1851; Jeremiah Mchann, bm.

McHann, John & Polly Colbreth, 11 Dec 1818; Thoms McHann, bm.

McIntire, Josiah & Luvina Proctor, 18 Jun 1818; William Botts, bm.

McKelvy, Thomas O. & Martha Blanton, 26 Jan 1860; Joab Willkie, bm; m 2 Feb 1860 by Jacob Willkie.

Mackey, David & Sally Potts, 29 Oct 1788; Henry Lewis, bm.

McKibben, Marcus A. & M. A. Herndon, 11 Jan 1842; W. A. Gamewell, bm.

McKinney, Henry & Mary Robbins, 18 Mar 1788; William Robbins, bm.

McKinney, James & Elizabeth Horn, 30 Aug 1840; Wm. H. McKinney, bm.

McKinney, John M. & Martha Daniel, 15 Nov 1834; William G. Daniel, bm.

McKinney, Miller & Mary C. Camp, 2 Sept 1844; David D. Lollar, bm.

McKinney, Simeon & Lethe McKinney, 10 Apr 1838; William H. McKinney, bm.

McKinney, Thomas & Mary A. Ford, 22 Sept 1853; Wm. H. Miller, bm; m 22 Sept 1853 by Campbell Smith.

McKinney, W. A. & Biddy S. McDaniel, 4 Oct 1860; G. W> Lookadoo, bm; m 4 Oct 1860 by D. Ponnell.

McKinney, William & Betey Dugger, 12 Aug 1817; J. Callihan, Willis McKinney, bm.

McKinney, William Jr. & Dianna Wilson, 4 Oct 1830; William H. McKinney, bm.

McKinney, Wm. A. & Louisa Camp, 10 Oct 1849; C. L. Henson, bm.

McKinny, Burnice & Milly Jones, 22 Aug 1807; John Jones, bm.

McKinny, George & Martha Miller, 20 Mar 1797; James Miller Jr., bm.

McKinny, James M. & Jane McKinney, 18 Nov 1824; Jonathan H. McKinney, bm.

McKinny, Jason & Mary Moreland, 18 Aug 1835; James L. Wilkins, bm.

McLure, Alaxander & Sarah Lockey, 13 Feb 1850.

McMahan, Barnard & Elisabeth Wadkins, 5 Apr 1855; B. R. Doggett, bm; m 5 Apr 1855 by Wm. Harrill, M. G.

McMahan, James & Mary Lee, 21 Dec 1824; Richard Allen, bm.

McMahan, James & Ann McHan, 2 Dec 1860; G. E. Blanton, bm; m 8 Jan 1860 by W. S. Hill, J. P.

McMerrell, John & Jane Mitchel, 26 Jan 1860; W. W. Elliott, bm; m 26 Jan 1860 by J. Gilkey, J. P.

McMillen, Andrew L. & Providence Hannon, 14 Nov 1829; Langley B. Camp, bm.

McMillin, William & Sarah Littlejohn, 22 Sept 1805; Peter Hunter, bm.

McMorey, William & Ginsa Gilmore, 3 Apr 1811; Abram Irvine, bm.

McMullen, David & Mary Paris, 24 May 1792; Lewis Martin, bm.

McMullin, John & Polley Weathers, 13 Feb 1823; John Proctor, bm.

McMurray, Columbus C. & Happy Arledge, 23 Mar 1852; John Jackson, bm; m 23 Mar 1852 by Luke Waldrop, J. P.

McMurry, John & Peggy Smith, 26 May 1811; James McMory, John Collins, bm.

McMurry, Samuel & Betsey Williams, 1 Mar 1823; David Thompson, bm.

McMurty, Samuel & _____, 25 Jan 1797.

McNair, John & Betsey McRonneles, 5 Sept 1816; Hugh McReynolds, bm.

McNease, Henry & Rachael Gesling, 9 Jun 1786; Charles Gasling, bm.

McNeely, John & Ruth Simons, 26 Mar 1816; Thomas McNeilly, Edward Cook, bm.

Macom, John & Annah Woodward, 25 Oct 1791; Daniel Laiswell, bm.

McPherson, James & Narcissa Lyles, 20 Jul 1816; Jonas Liles, bm.

McReynolds, Hugh & Peggy White, _____; Thos. White, Joseph Reynolds, bm.

McReynolds, Joseph & Sarah Wilson, 13 Dec 1803; Thos. White, John Barber, bm.

McSwain, Benjamin & Rebakah Smith, 10 May 1810; Reuben Hamrick, James McSwain, bm.

McSwain, David & Lucy McSwain, 2 Feb 1833; James McSwain, bm.

McSwain, William & Sally Bostick, 7 Jan 1812; Chesley Bostick, bm.

McSwain, William Jr. & Sarah McSwain, 13 Nov 1833; William McSwain, bm.

McSwain, William Sr. & Nancy Bridges, 16 Apr 1811; Thomas Davis, bm.

McTire, Achebel & Sarah White, 11 Jan 1808; Ellickander McTire, bm.

Macom, John & Annah Woodward, 25 Oct 1791; Daniel Laiswell, bm.

Mafarlin, John & Peggy Queen, 14 Apr 1791; John Logan, bm.

Magaugh, John & Polly Clark, __ May 1808.

Magness, Benjamin & Nancy Walker, 10 Jul 1808; Jno. Harrill, bm.

Magness, Benjamin & Adaline Sweesey, 14 Jan 1847; James Weer, bm.

Magness, Jacob & Edith Webb, 21 Aug 1806; Bangamin Magness, bm.

Magness, Joseph & Esther Beam, 19 Dec 1827; Robert Magness, bm.

Magness, William & Sally Hamrick, 29 Jan 1818; Jacob Magnes, Charles Talton(?), bm.

Malone, John & Gracy Eaves, 12 Sept 1800; Robinson Freeman, bm.

Manar, William & Nancy Mode, 25 Oct 1832; William S. Blacke, bm.

Maning, T. W. & H. Z. Morrow, 4 Apr 1866; H. F. Morrow, bm; m 4 Apr 1866 by Wm. Harrill.

Manor, Craten & Rebecah Walker, 9 Mar 1861; John Guffey, bm; m 9 Mar 1861 by Jas. M. Spratt.

Marlow, Elisha & Rody Debord, 5 Jul 1817; George Debord, bm.

Marlow, Elisha & Elizabeth Robinson, 7 Jan 1862; Starling Hudgins, bm; m 7 Jan 1862 by C. L. Harris, J. P.

Marlow, James & Betheny M. Freeman, 1 Feb 1817; William Adair, bm.

Marlow, Robert & M. A. Searcy, 29 Mar 1844; Jonathan Nanney, bm.

Marlow, Thomas & Patsey Williams, 18 Oct 1792; John Sorrels Jr., bm.

Marlow, Thomas & Rachel Whitaker, 30 May 1844; A. B. Moore, bm.

Marshal, Jesse & Nancy Campbell, 20 Aug 1839; George W. Guffey, bm; m 21 Aug 1839 by Hugh Watson, J. P.

Marshal, Wm. & Nancy McDaniel, 20 Jul 1848.

Marshall, Benjamin & Elizabeth Guffy, 22 Jan 1801; Jas. Porter, bm.

Marshall, John A. & Mary Thompson, 11 Oct 1843; Reubin Grist, bm.

Marshall, William & Mary M. McDaniel, 23 Feb 1854; John Clements, bm; m 23 Feb 1854 by John Freeman, J. P.

Martin, A. C. & Mary Sweezy, 14 May 1863; D. M. Price, bm.

Martin, A. M. & Susanah Latimore, 31 Jan 1839; D. D. Harrill, bm.

Martin, Abraham & Betsy S. Weatherford, 27 Feb 1820; John Martin, Geo. Cabaniss, bm.

Martin, Adam & Polly Baber, 31 Oct 1807; Saml. Young, bm.

Martin, Asa & Sally Painter, 14 Jun 1806; Jacob Fisher, bm.

Martin, Henry & Susannah Ferrell, 1 May 1818; Jonathan Curtis, bm.

Martin, James & Elizabeth Gold, 27 Dec 1832; Daniel Gold, bm.

Martin, Jesse & Sally Wilson, 20 Mar 1795; William Battle, bm.

Martin, Joseph H. & Affa B. Sursey, 30 Sept 1843; M. E. Goode, bm.

Martin, Pinckney & Lucinda Hughs, m 7 May 1865 by Wm. J. Willkie.

Martin, Reuben & Cary Pool, 1 Mar 1819; Thos. Garner, bm.

Martin, Samuel & Rachal Bland, 28 Jan 1833; William Bland, bm.

Martin, Thomas & Alley Williams, 20 Oct 1822; Daniel Grigg, bm.

Martin, Thomas & Polley Gold, 16 Dec 1824; Daniel Gold, bm.

Martin, William & Fanny Morris, 12 Apr 1803; Hodge Raburn, bm.

Martin, William & Elizabeth R. Grigg, 18 Feb 1823; Young Brizendine, bm.

Martin, William & Jane Hall, 28 Dec 1865; J. E. Carter, bm; m 31 Dec 1865 by Wm. J. Willkie, M. G.

Mashburn, Drury & Tempy Morgan, 10 Jan 1842; Abner Morgan, bm.

Mason, Jeramiah P. & Martha Mason, 12 Oct 1840; William Mason, bm.

Massie, Thos. G. & Delia E. Twitty, 17 Apr 1851; D. J. Twitty, bm.

Matheney, John & Elizabeth Hambrick, 18 Jan 1828; George Champion, bm.

Mathews, Daniel & _____, ___ 1799; Jas. Blackwell, bm.

Mathews, James & Crecy Colbert, 12 Jul 1839; Thomas Crews, bm.

RUTHERFORD COUNTY MARRIAGES 1779-1868

Mathews, John & Martha J. Mitchell, 17 Dec 1866; Edmund Foster, bm; m 20 Dec 1866 by E. L. Taylor, M. G.

Mathis, George & Emly Walker, 3 Mar 1861; Edmond Foster, bm; m 3 Mar 1861 by Robt. G. Twitty, J. P.

Maxfield, Andrew & Elizabeth Green, 19 Mar 1824; Amos Green, bm.

Mayes, Stephen & Vienna Green, 20 Oct 1826; Royley Blanton, bm.

Mayes, Stith & Tobitha Morrow, 13 Jan 1820; James Morrow, bm.

Mayfield, Isham & Mary Soward, 23 May 1783; Robert Newton, bm.

Mayfield, Nathaniel & Sally Gear, 22 May 1802; Robert Newton, bm.

Mayfield, Nathanl. & Kiziah Liles, 4 Mar 1805; Jas. Liles, bm.

Mayfield, Robert & Genny Grise, 5 Sept 1827; Thomas Smart, bm.

Mayhu, Wm. & Viny Luquire, 22 May 1797; John Tucker, bm.

Mayse, James F. & Adaline Padgett, 15 Jun 1835; James Blanton, bm.

Medly, William & Sarah Durham, 13 Oct 1795; Henry Durham, bm.

Melton, A. & Martha Melton, 3 Mar 1859; P. Mooney, bm; m 3 Mar 1859 by B. E. Rollins, M. G.

Melton, A. J. & Scyntha Upton, 20 sept 1859; M. O. Dickerson, bm; m by Jesse S. Nelson.

Melton, Abner G. & Nancy Fortune, _____; Cornelius Melton, bm.

Melton, Andrew J. & Huldah Melton, 3 Feb 1841; Reuben M. Proctor, bm.

Melton, Barnabas & Sarah M. Long, 28 Nov 1854; Andrew M. Long, bm; m 1 Dec 1854 by John Freeman, J. P.

Melton, Bengemon & Sarah Felpeck, 1 Sept 1865; John Davis, bm; m 7 Sept 1865 by John Davis, J. P.

Melton, Benjamin J. & Nancey Melton, 21 May 1844; Jesse R. Melton, bm.

Melton, Bird M. & Rachel A. Walker, 5 Aug 1847; J. P. Street, bm.

Melton, Burton J. & Lucinda Walker, 7 Jun 1843; Samuel Melton, bm.

Melton, Daniel & Narcissa Luquire, 23 Apr 1842; J. J. Melton, bm.

Melton, Daniel Jr. & Catharine Eaves, 27 Oct 1836; John Collens, bm.

Melton, Daniel T. & Eliza Howser, 12 Aug 1860; Eli Whisnant, bm.

Melton, Dreury & Polly Parris, 18 Sept 1828; James W. Carson, bm.

Melton, E. D. & Martha Blankinship, 17 Feb 1857; P. N. Long, bm.

Melton, Elisha & Rachael Melton, 20 Sept 1825; Jesse R. Wells, bm.

Melton, Gilford & Tempy Filbeck, 3 Mar 1856; Robert R. Filbeck, bm; m 8 May 1856 by A. Harrill, J. P.

Melton, Henry & Mirah Daves, 11 Jan 1838; Andrew J. Melton, bm.

Melton, Hiram & Sophia Gowing, 15 Oct 1827; James M. Erwin, Thomas Lyles, bm.

Melton, Isaiah W. & Lurena Melton, 3 Oct 1853; A. J. Wells, bm.

Melton, J. J. & Caroline McMurrey, 12 Dec 1846; Alfred Weer, bm.

Melton, J. W. & Nancy Melton, 20 May 1866; A. W. Melton, bm; m 20 May 1866 by B. E. Rollins.

Melton, James H. & Jane Biggerstaff, 19 Jan 1833; Aaron Biggerstaff Jr., bm.

Melton, James H. & Susanna Walker, 26 Dec 1836; Jesse R. Wells, bm.

Melton, Jefferson & Margaret L. Moore, 5 Oct 1852; Wm. Moore, bm.

Melton, Jesse & Mary Melton, 8 Dec 1814; Reuben Melton, Elisha Melton, bm.

Melton, Jesse & Susanna Mooney, 5 Feb 1851; J. R. Pendergrass, bm.

Melton, John & Elisabeth Melton, 14 May 180-; Joshua Melton, bm.

Melton, John & Elizabeth Melton, 24 Jul 1815; Charles Allen, bm.

Melton, John & Rebecca Kenipe, 7 Mar 1829; William Proctor, bm.

Melton, John M. & Lurany Deck, 19 Mar 1826; Pleasant Fortune, bm.

Melton, John W. & Charlotte Byars, 5 Mar 1833; Elias Padget, bm.

Melton, Joseph & Pollyan Blankenship, 6 Nov 1855; G. W. Deck, bm; m 6 Nov 1855 by B. E. Rollins.

Melton, Jos. & Jane Biggerstaff, 16 Feb 1860; Draper Toney, bm; m 16 Feb 1860 by John Freeman, J. P.

Melton, Joseph C. & Clary W. Smiley, 17 Sept 1849; William Whitesides, bm.

Melton, Joshua & Sarah Melton, 11 Jan 1804; Joseph Green, bm.

Melton, Joshua & Polly C. Wells, 4 Dec 1826; Alfred B. Melton, bm.

Melton, Lenoir & Martha Huckaby, 30 Jul 1834; Samuel Melton, bm.

Melton, Lindsey F. & Sarah Fortune, 3 Mar 1826; Williamson Fortune, bm.

Melton, Reuben & Nancy Green, 16 Sept 1850; Burton J. Melton, bm.

Melton, Richard S. & Lettice Melton, 14 Jul 1831; Nathan Melton, bm.

Melton, Samuel & Peggy Davis, 17 Jan 1816; Henry Norvell, bm.

Melton, Samuel & Jane Hardin, 2 Aug 1850; John T. green, bm.

Melton, Silas & Peggy McCurry, 19 Apr 1804; Wm McFarland, bm.

Melton, Silas & Rincy Apley, 2 Mar 1853; Felix W. Deviney, bm; m 2 Mar 1853 by Wm. G. Mode, J. P.

Melton, Silas R. & Margaret Moore, 6 Dec 1812; James Moore, bm.

Melton, Spencer & Rosannah Whitesides, 6 Jun 1831; Isaac Whiteside, bm.

Melton, Spencer & Isabella Lively, 9 Jan 1840; Daniel Melton, bm.

Melton, Squire & Mary C. Smart, 8 Nov 1845; Elijah Crow, bm.

Melton, Stephen & Nancy Tarry, 1 Jan 1850; Adolphus Mooney, bm.

Melton, William & Elizabeth Liveley, 8 Feb 1840; Squir Melton, bm.

Menis, John & Franke Drake, _____; John Troop, bm.

Menteith, G. W. & E. A. Guffy, 16 May 1866; J. R. Cochran, bm.

Menteith, J. C. & A. D. Cochran, 1 Jan 1866; J. B. Eaves, bm.

Menteith, John & Isabela Guffey, 28 Oct 1840; Wm. Menteith, bm.

Menteith, William Jr. & Rachel Clemmons, 30 Nov 1836; George W. Guffey, bm; m 1 Dec 1836 by Hugh Watson, J. P.

Metcalf, Allen D. & Emaline Wood, 4 Oct 1849; Quincy S. Metcalf, bm.

Metcalf, Bradley & Nancy McGuire, 9 Apr 1822; Henry D. Metcalf, bm.

Metcalf, Danza & Mary Bradly, 1 Sept 1792.

Metcalf, Isaac & Margaret Hampton, 3 Dec 1781; Warner Metcalf, bm.

Metcalf, Preston & Mary Brown, 6 Aug 1852; M. O. Dickerson, bm; m 8 Aug 1852 by T. B. Justice, M. G.

Metcalf, Preston & Charlotte Pope, 1 Jan 1857; William Bradley, bm.

Metcalf, W. B. & Iztha Brown, 5 Aug 1849; J. B. Webb, bm.

Metcalf, William D. & Catharine Morriss, 25 Jan 1814; James A. Irwin, bm.

Metcalf, Williams & Elmina Allen, 11 Feb 1835; Neelley McGuire, bm.

Miers, David & Falliby Mills, 13 Dec 1797; Richd. Yeildling, bm.

Michael, James M. & Rosannah Wall, 14 Jan 1866; W. S. Padgett, bm; m 24 Jan 1866 by Wm. Harrill.

Michael, P. E. & Elisabeth A. Kestler, 26 Oct 1843; David Michael, bm.

Michal, G. W. & Martha M. McDowell, 25 Jun 1861; M. O. Dickerson, bm.

Michail, Davied & Elizabeth Smart, 26 Oct 1846; John H. Carpenter, bm.

Mickle, Jeremiah & Abigal Welch, 15 Apr 1801; George Welch, bm.

Millard, James & Clary King, _____; Joseph Millard, Jno. Crawford, bm.

Millard, Joseph & Susanah Bigam, 7 May 1850; George B. Ford, bm.

Millard, Lafayette & Millie Owens, 11 Mar 1865; John Flin, Wm. L. Jones, bm; m 11 Mar 1855 by Henry Culbreath.

Miller, Alexander & Fany Pates, 7 Mar 1793; John Miller, bm.

Miller, Andrew & Elizabeth Parish, 4 Jan 1820; Joseph M. Black, bm.

RUTHERFORD COUNTY MARRIAGES 1779-1868

Miller, Aspesio E. & Nancy Jane Harriss, 20 Dec 1842; Jos. M. Miller, bm.

Miller, David & Mary K. Miller, 18 Nov 1824; Isaac Craton, bm.

Miller, David B. & Mary Matilda Erwin, 13 Jan 1827; Thoe F. Birchett, bm.

Miller, Frank D. & Esther Depriest, 25 Apr 1854; W. A. E. Roberts, bm.

Miller, George W. & Rody Randle, 2 Jan 1833; Charles Bird, bm.

Miller, H. M. & Elizabeth Brisco, 16 Mar 1858; Drury Dobbins, bm.

Miller, Humphrey P. & Mary Harris, 23 Jan 1851; B. A. Baber, bm.

Miller, James M. & Frances Booker, 27 Jul 1841; Daniel Michal, bm.

Miller, James V. & Meriah R. Hannon, 15 May 1821; Willliam S. Mills, bm.

Miller, Jerome & Martha Maria S. S. Hord, 21 Oct 1830.

Miller, John & Susana Twitty, 15 May 1783; Andw. Hampton, bm.

Miller, John & Jane Smith, 22 May 1789; Robert Smith, bm.

Miller, Joseph & Sally Jones, 19 Aug 1829; Sims Harris, bm.

Miller, K. B. & Mary McAfee, 27 Jul 1848; D. J. Twitty, bm.

Miller, N. W. & Elizabeth Jane Toms, 31 Aug 1861; Jas. A. Miller, bm; m 5 Sept 1861 by T. B. Justice.

Miller, Thomas & Charlotte Montague, 11 May 1814; Jos. M. Black, bm.

Miller, Thomas & Polly Mayfield, 18 Dec 1821; Carter Allen, bm.

Mills, Adolphus & Amanda Mills, 28 Jan 1841; John M. Jones, bm.

Mills, Ambroes & Mrs. Nancy Jones, 1 Feb 1824; D. Dickey, bm.

Mills, George J. & Ann E. Mills, 19 Oct 1865; A. R. Bryan, bm; m 19 Oct 1865 by Nl. Shotwell, M. G.

Mills, Ladson A. & Jane Hamilton, 17 May 1845; Walter Duffy, bm.

Mills, Otis P. & Rachel Carson, 28 Nov 1833; Thomas Dews Jr., bm.

Mills, Peter P. & Susanna Crowder, 30 Sept 1849; Joseph C. Waldrop, bm.

Mills, W. B. & Sarah A. N. Blanton, 12 Nov 1850; James Helms, bm.

Mills, William & Winny Coward, 22 Mar 1823; Noah Mills, bm.

Mills, Wm. & Nancy Garret, 16 Apr 1846; Noah Mills, bm.

Mills, William E. & Eliza Bryan, 10 Nov 1842; D. J. Twitty, bm.

Mills, Willis L. & Lorena or Laura McMury, 8 Jan 1843; Rhd. Whiteside, bm.

Millwood, James C. & Viana Mode, 19 Jan 1867; A. Mode, bm; m 24 Jan 1867 by J. B. Wilson, J. P.

Millwood, Morgan & Siller McEntire, 19 Dec 1866; A. Mode, bm; m 20 Dec 1866 by H. B. Wilson, J. P.

Mince, John B. & Jane Canada, 19 May 1836; Randolph Grant Jr., bm.

Mints, Robert & Mary Ann Green, 15 Aug 1828; Major R. Alexander, bm.

Mitcalf, Davis & Margret Williams, 6 Oct 1840; Jonathan Williams, bm.

Mitchel, Andrew & Jane Miller, 12 Jan 1791; Sam Carpenter, bm.

Mitchel, J. W. & Julia Ann Ballard, 3 Oct 1859; William Church, bm; m 4 Oct 1859 by Wm. Rucker, J. P.

Mitchel, Joseph & Peggy McMurry, 23 June 1815; _____, bm.

Mitchell, Elbert & Elizabeth Caroline Coston, 12 Nov 1821; William Coston, bm.

Mitchell, H. G. & Mary M. Daniel, 22 Oct 1866; C. Burnett, bm; m 25 Oct 1866 by H. M. Miller, J. P.

Mitchell, T. E. & Salley McFadden, 22 Sept 1866; H. G. Mitchell, bm.

Mitchell, W. A. & Lou Bradly, 4 Dec 1866; H. C. Davis, bm.

Mitchil, George & Elinor (Nelly) Bates, 1 Nov 1797.

Mocaboy, Matthew & Darcus Lee, 20 Dec 1815; Wm. Lee, bm.

Mode, Able H. & Rachel Deviney, 10 Mar 1861; J. T. Mode, bm; m 10 Mar 1861.

Mode, Isaiah W. & Evaline Wallis, 31 Oct 1844; Chretian Dalton, bm.

Mode, J. T. & Sarah C. Gambol, 26 Dec 1865; Jos. G. Fortune, bm.

Mode, James M. & H. D. Melton, 6 Jul 1865; J. J. Grayson, bm; m 6 Jul 1865 by B. E. Rollins.

Mode, James W. & Nancy G. McFarland, 27 Apr 1851; A. J. Deviney, bm; m 27 Apr 1851 by Wm. G. Mode, J. P.

Mode, James W. & Nancy Mooney, 19 Apr 1858; John S. Hill, bm.

Mode, John W. & Frances Norrel, 29 Jul 1841; Wm. J. Walker, bm.

Mode, Joseph T. & Sarah Hunt, 24 Aug 1862; J. T. Mode, bm; m 24 Aug 1862 by Wm. G. Mode, J. P.

Mode, Martin & Mary Upchurch, 27 Jan 1851; Andrew Mode, bm.

Mode, Samuel & Agniss Wilson, 30 Jan 1840; Joseph Causner, bm.

Mode, Williams & Sarah Parker, 29 Jan 1801; Andrew PArker, bm.

Mode, William G. & Winnifred Crow, 4 Nov 1827; William Gamble, bm.

Mode, William G. & Winnifred Crow, 7 Nov 1837; Absalom Waters, bm.

Moffitt, W. P. & Rhody C. Grant, 11 Mar 1866; S. B. Grant, bm; m 11 Mar 1866 by J. W. Morgan, J. P.

Money, Jacob & Faney Crowder, 7 Jan 1817; Benjamin Newton, bm.

Monie, Henry & Esther Laswell, 30 Jul 1807; Danl. Laswell, bm.

Monney, George & Mary Mooney, 30 Jun 1825; Solomon Young, bm.

RUTHERFORD COUNTY MARRIAGES 1779-1868

Mony, Gorge & Jene Coykendawl, 19 Jan 1797; Joseph Carpenter, bm.

Mood, Isaac & Anny White, 3 May 1808; John Hardcastle, bm.

Moode, William Junr. & Mary Proctor, 20 Nov 1825; John Proctor, bm.

Moodey, John S. & Nancy Hamrick, 6 Mar 1839; James Morrow, bm.

Mooney, Adolphus & Martha R. Beaty, 17 Aug 1858; Jos. H. Martin, bm; m 17 Aug 1858 by Wm. G. Mode.

Mooney, Alfred B. & Elizabeth Bowden, 5 Jan 1837; Peter Finger, bm.

Mooney, Christa & Ollive Hague, 16 Jan 1812; Frederick T. Alley, bm.

Mooney, Daniel & Hannah McSwain, 30 Apr 1807; H. W. Kerr, bm.

Mooney, David & Catharine Davis, 24 Dec 1838; Isaac V. Davis, bm.

Mooney, Felix & Betty Toney, 7 Feb 1828; Solomon Mooney, bm.

Mooney, Jacob & Polly Thogmorton, 29 Jan 1825; Asa Mooney, bm.

Mooney, James T. & Malinda Ronie, 16 Jan 1840; David Mooney, bm.

Mooney, James W. & Sarah B. Early, 23 Nov 1865; Wm. G. Price, bm; m 23 Nov 1865 by Wm. G. Mode, J. P.

Mooney, Jonathan & Milley Taylor, 26 Jan 1815; Joseph Taylor, R. H. Taylor, bm.

Mooney, Jonathan & Methena McCurry, 24 Sept 1833; James M. McCurry, bm.

Mooney, Jonathan & M. A. Michael, 24 Sept 1866; A. Mooney, bm; m 25 Sept 1866 by Wm. Harrrill, Elder.

Mooney, Michael & Rachel Waters, 4 Jan 1843; Elijah Waters, bm.

Mooney, P. M. & Beck Ann Huntsinger, 8 Jan 1855; Draper Toney, bm; m 8 Jan 1855 by B. E. Rollins, M. G.

Mooney, Peter & Charlott Green, 9 Sept 1803; John Donner, bm.

Mooney, Peter & Sarah Broom, 7 Sept 1830; Bartlet Crowder, bm.

Mooney, Peter & Delpa Melton, 24 Dec 1847; Jas. Melton, bm.

Mooney, Valentine & Mary A. E. Barry, 2 Aug 1832; John B. Miller, bm.

Mooney, Wm. A. & Sarah L. Camp, 19 May 1846; D. J. Twitty, bm.

Moony, Alfred B. & Elizabeth Bowden, 8 Mar 1837; Joseph J. Scoggin, bm.

Moony, Daneil & Nelly McNeasse, 15 Sept 1786; Jonathan Moony, bm.

Moony, George & Jane Long, 30 Apr 1847; John L. Taylor, bm.

Moony, Isaac & Caren Harrison, 13 Mar 1845; N. D. Carrier, bm.

Moor, Balis & Anna Spurlin, 26 Nov 1824; William Weathers, bm.

Moor, S. J. & Marianna Melton, 1 Jan 1856; J. L. Edwards, bm; m 7 Jan 1856 by A. Harrill, J. P.

Moor, Thomas & Sarah Rogers, 4 Mar 1797; Enoch Hamrick, bm.

Moor, Thomas P. & Elizabeth Huggins, 8 Feb 1828; Hiram Clark, bm.

Moor, Tilenius & Nancy S. Cochran, 18 Jul 1831; John Moore, bm.

Moore, William & Mary French, 24 Apr 1781; James Hamilton, bm.

Moore, Alfred B. & Luvina Marlow, 30 Oct 1839; John Baxter Sr., bm.

Moore, Caleb A. & Jamimah Logan, 27 Oct 1830; T. F. Birchett, bm.

Moore, Daniel & Nancy Padget, 15 Dec 1849; John Goforth, bm.

Moore, Farmer & Betsey Mathews, 3 Jun 1807; John Moore, bm.

Moore, Francis & Poley Griggg, 26 Dec 1815; John Moore, Richard Moore, bm.

Moore, Francis & Nancy Bostick, 18 Dec 1855; Geroge S. Harrill, bm; m 18 Dec 1855 by Wm. Harrill.

Moore, Francis & Mrs. Catherine McBryer, m 29 Mar 1866 by A. W. Harill, J. P.

Moore, Frederick A. & Mary Elvira Black, 10 Mar 1834; James M. Walker, bm.

Moore, Goerge & Mary Roberts, 8 Jan 1813; Thomas Roberts, J. M. Roberts, bm.

Moore, George W. & Martha Green, 6 Apr 1860; Eleazor McArthur, bm; m 6 Apr 1860 by Wm. Harrill, M. G.

Moore, Jackson & Sarah Coxey, 24 Feb 1847; Joseph Fready, bm.

Moore, James & Mrs. Betsa McSwain, 17 __ 1811; John Moore, bm.

Moore, James G. & Marry Goode, 28 Feb 1839; William A. Baber, bm.

Moore, John & Martha Coventon, 11 MAr 1800; Anthony Enlore, bm.

Moore, John & Selina Flack, 12 Dec 1825; Charles Lewis Jr., bm.

Moore, John & Katharine Watson, 9 Jan 1826; Hiram Clark, bm.

Moore, John & Sarah Magaha, 17 Dec 1847; John H. Carpenter, bm.

Moore, John & Selah Webb, 23 Jul 1851; Martin P. Harrill, bm; m 23 Jul 1851 by Wm. Harrill, M. G.

Moore, John Jr. & Mary Mathes, 24 Oct 1805; John Moore Sr., bm.

Moore, John Junr & _____, 13 Oct 1816; John Person, bm.

Moore, Jonathan & Sarah Paterson, 7 Mar 1807; John Moore, John Fondren, bm.

Moore, Morris R. & Sarah Morris, 7 Aug 1846; M. White, bm.

Moore, Ransom J. & Nancy Gosea, 24 Feb 1824; Stephen Jones, bm.

Moore, Richard & Mattey Patterson, 8 Jun 1803; S. Harrill, John Moore, bm.

Moore, Samuel & Anna Depriest, 30 Nov 1814; Henry Norvell, bm.

Moore, Thomas & Elizabeth Bostwick, 22 Aug 1842; John T. Baber, bm.

Moore, Thomas & Milly Ann Morrow, 7 Aug 1858; A. P. Moore, bm; m 9 Aug 1858 by W. A. Tanner.

Moore, William Jr. & Grizzy Flack, 19 Feb 1831; John Moore Jr., bm.

Moore, Wilson & Katy Sorrels, 7 Jan 1822; James Sorrels, bm.

Moore, Z. P. & Viney Foster, 1 Jun 1860; J. A. Carpenter, bm; m 5 Jun 1860 by W. H. Bostic.

Moorehead, David & Sarah Fortune, 23 Feb 1823; William Fortune, bm.

Moorehead, William & Betsy Fortune, 1 Aug 1830; William Guffey, bm.

Moorhead, Elias & Sally Fortune, 6 Aug 1824; Jonathan B. Wilson, bm.

Moorhead, Enoch J. & Martha Guffey, 28 Sept 1840; James C. Moos, bm.

Moorhead, James & Ahney Thacker, 17 Aug 1804; Richard Fortune, bm.

Moorhead, John F. & Mary Yelton, 22 Jan 1840; Henry Yelton, bm.

Moorland, William & Mary McIntier, 3 Aug 1800; James McEntire, bm.

More, John Jr. & Anna Davis, 21 Oct 1830; John Murray, bm.

More, Perry & Kizeah Coxey, 14 Feb 1850; Jos. Frady, bm.

Morehead, Enoch B. & Cynthia Weeks, 30 MAr 1846; Alxr. Weeks, bm.

Morehead, John & Nancy L. Cochran, 5 Dec 1864; John F. Morhead, bm; m 6 Dec 1865 by D. S. McCurry, J. P.

Morehead, John F. & Nancy Melton Fortune, 1 Dec 1835; William Morehead, bm.

Morehead, John F. & Martha Gettis, 9 Jul 1847; James A. Gettys, bm.

Morehead, Wm. & Faithy M. Freeman, 14 Apr 1842; A. B. Freeman, bm.

Moreland, John & Polly Lee, 3 Jan 1822; Larkin Lee, bm.

Morgain, Jessey & Martha An Walker, 2 Jul 1854; Luis Price, bm; m 2 Jul 1854 by H. Padgett, J. P.

Morgan, A. W. & Mary S. Nanney, ____ 18--; M. W. Morgan, bm; m 17 May 1860 by J. W. Morgan, J. P.

Morgan, Daniel & Catharine Cochran, 26 Nov 1851; Wm. H. Miller, bm.

Morgan, Davis & Damaris Koone, 13 Feb 1833; Jacob Michal, bm.

Morgan, James & Peggy Grant, 17 Dec 1802; Alexr. Grant, bm.

Morgan, James & Rebecca C. Nanny, 26 Apr 1866; E. Morgan, bm.

Morgan, Jesse & Polly Grant, 1 Dec 1809; Permenter Morgan, bm.

Morgan, Jethro & Julia Ann Koon, 9 Dec 1858; E. P. Morgan, bm; m 20 Dec 1858 by J. W. Morgan, J. P.

Morgan, John & Eliz. Richardson, 25 Apr 1799; James Kilpatrick, bm.

Morgan, John & Lurana Battle, __ Feb 1804; John Moore, bm.

Morgan, John & Elvira Callehan, 6 Jul 1835; Solomon W. Davis, bm.

Morgan, John P. & Amarriettea Ownby, 5 Jan 1846; Daniel Morgan, bm.

Morgan, Jones H. & Rebecca Morgan, 5 Jan 1836; Jonathan Morgan, bm.

Morgan, Jordan & Lucy Davis, 30 Mar 1813; John Morgan, bm.

Morgan, Lewis R. & Gracy Morgan, 2 Oct 1839; Jonathan Morgan, bm.

Morgan, Moses & Martha Ledbetter, 26 Sept 1839; James W. Carson, bm.

Morgan, Moses W. & Altha Wilkerson, 11 Feb 1850; J. Ledbetter, bm.

Morgan, Porter O. & Alsira Nanny, 8 Jun 1852; Meron Koone, bm; m 8 Jun 1852 by T. B. Justice, M. G.

Morgan, Posey H. & Sarah Queen or Quinn, 17 Nov 1846; U. W. Morgan, bm.

Morgan, Stephen & Gracey Morgan, 5 Jan 1842; W. H. Miller, bm.

Morgan, Wm. & Martha Jane Brisco, 14 Mar 1861; J. V. Jay, bm; m 17 Mar 1861 by E. Morgan.

Morgan, Wilson & Rebecca Morgan, 26 Sept 1836; Permenter Morgan, bm.

Moris, Churchwell & Catharine Miller, 17 Dec 1850; A. Hamby, bm.

Moris, Elijah & Nancy Allen, 16 Mar 1811l; Willis Allen, bm.

Moriss, Micajah & Sally Moore, 2 Feb 1790; Rd. Daugherty, bm.

Morland, Thomas & Elizebeth Addams, _____; Sam Hamrick, William Putman, bm.

Morris, Ans. D. R. & Lcuinda McClean, 31 Jan 1822; Thomas Morris, bm.

Morris, Churchwel & Nancy Richardson, 12 Nov 1832; Robt. G. Twitty, bm.

Morris, Churchwell & Elizabeth Gray, 12 Mar 1827; James O. Terrell, bm.

Morris, Decator & Penelope Edwards, 11 Mar 1853; James M. Garett, bm.

Morris, Goerge & Mary Dickey, 30 Jan 1805; Anthony Dickey, bm.

Morris, Isaac & Charity Patton, 29 Feb 1829l; Philip Humphrey, bm.

Morris, J. A. & Phebe Atkins, 19 Nov 1857; A. Mooney, bm; m 19 Nov 1857 by G. Hamilton, M. G.

Morris, James & Elisabeth Grant, 8 Jan 1783; Jno. Henson, bm.

Morris, James & Elizabeth Garrett, 20 Aug 1818.

Morris, James B. & M. A. Gaither, 26 Dec 1859; L. F. Churchill, bm; m 31 Dec 1859 by Nl. Shotwell, M. G.

Morris, John & Isabella Sweany, __ Oct 1805; John Bryant, bm.

Morris, Jno. & Elizabeth Driskill, 29 Dec 1820; Thomas Morris, bm.

Morris, John & Jane McKinney, 2 Nov 1830; Charles Simmons, bm.

Morris, John & Nanicy Wilkison, 4 Dec 1832; Noah Davis, bm.

Morris, Noah & Mary Lynch, 21 Dec 1866; John Cannier(?), bm. (C. H.)

Morris, Sanders & Martha Richardson, 19 Jan 1839; William Richardson, bm.

Morris, Thomas & Catharine Dicky, 22 Sept 1795; Thomas Hunter, bm.

Morris, Thomas Jr. & Mary Baxter, 28 Dec 1836; Churchwell Moris Jr., bm.

Morris, Thos. H. & Elizabeth Foster, 10 Sept 1844; Thomas E. Jefferson, bm.

Morrison, Andrew & Elizabeth Adaline Wilson, 23 Sept 1835; John Watson, bm; m 24 Sept 1835 by Hugh Watson, J. P.

Morrison, Daniel & Mary Green, 4 Oct 1821; Richard Sercy, bm.

Morrison, G. H. & Lora A. Spratt, 21 Feb 1866; Wm. P. Watson, bm; m 21 Feb 1866 by B. W. Andrews, J. P.

Morrison, James & Rachael Patton, 21 Jan 1823; Elijah Pattun Jr., bm.

Morrison, Jesse & Mary Elliott, 1 Jul 1839; J. D. Justice, bm.

Morrison, Joseph & Dorothy Whitesides, 1 Nov 1842; Isaac Whiteside, bm.

Morrison, Robert P. & Charity E. Andrews, 7 Nov 1832; Patrick A. Watson, bm.

Morrison, Thomas & Elizabeth Robinson, 2 Jan 1829; William J. Long, bm.

Morrow, Alfred & Nancy McMaham, 31 Dec 1821; James McMahan, bm.

Morrow, James & Elizabeth Suttle, 7 Jun 1796; John Morrow, bm.

Morrow, James Jr. & Nancy M. Greeman, 16 Jan 1831; Stith Mayes, bm.

Morrow, James V. & Mary Padget, 11 Nov 1859.

Morrow, Jesse & Polly Holland, 30 Oct 1799; William Morrow, bm.

Morrow, John F. & Sarah Stedman, 27 Dec 1849; Rufus G. Morrow, bm.

Morrow, Marcus & Mary Bowman, 23 Mar 1837; Alfred Morrow, bm.

Morrow, Nevils H. & Mary Jane Wilson, 25 Sept 1852; James V. Morrow, bm; m 26 Sept 1852 by Edward Toms, J. P.

Morrow, Thomas & Didamy Johns, 20 Sept 1845; Zack Johns, bm.

Morrow, William & Sarah Doggett, 3 Jan 1835; Stith Mayes, bm.

Morrow, Willis G. & Nancy Bridges, 1 Mar 1843; M. S. Morrow, bm.

Mosely, David & Emerillas Butler, 18 Mar 1852; James P. Mosely, bm; m 18 Mar 1852 by W. A. Tanner, J. P.

Mosely, Jas. P. & Nancy Good, 9 Oct 1854; Andrew Hudlow,bm; m 9 Oct 1854 by Wm. Harrill, M. G.

Moss, A. C. & Elizabeth Melton, 24 Nov 1845; W. B. Andrews, bm.

Moss, Howel & Sarah McEntire, 23 Feb 1796; Benga Wilkirson, Thomas White, bm.

Moss, James & Catren McDonnald, 9 Jan 1798; Benjm. Wilkison, bm.

Moss, Milton & Susanna Crow, 30 Mar 1852; Eli Whisnant, bm.

Mosteller, George & Elizabeth Miller, 26 Feb 1799; Joseph Carpenter (signed Joseph Zimmerman), bm.

Mull, Peter & Barbere Carpenter, 23 Feb 1789; Ligt. Williams, bm.

Mullins, Daniel Coleman & Didamy Lily, _____; James Lyles, bm.

Mullins, Robert W. & Elizabeth Crowder, 22 Feb 1822; Frederick Grigg, bm.

Mullins, William & _____, 13 Mar 1801 or 1802; Britten Liles, bm.

Mullins, William & Nancy Cockerham, 30 Dec 1820; Richard Richardson, bm.

Murphey, William A. B. & Temperance Ledbetter, 1 Aug 1833; Thomas Ledbetter, bm.

Murphy, James M. & Anna Dalton, 15 Dec 1806; Asa Bowman, bm.

Murray, Andrew J. & M. Kilpatrick, 2 Jul 1842; M. H. Kilpatrick, bm.

Murray, James W. & Elizabeth Whiteside, 1 Feb 1859; John W. Murray, bm; m 3 Feb 1859; m 3 Feb 1859 by J. M. Chitwood, J. P.

Murray, John & Mary Balden or Baldwin, 28 Sept 1813; Anthony Stone, bm.

Murray, Lemuel & Catharine Rutherford, 13 Nov 1839; Jos. M'Dowell, bm.

Murray, William & Polly West, 10 Mar 1821; John Jones, John Lambey, bm.

Murray Wm. D. & Elizabeth Jenkins, 25 Dec 1846; James W. Murray, bm.

Murray, William Davis & Elisabeth Beaty, _____; J. H. Alley, bm.

Murry, John A. & Nancy Huntsinger, 14 Mar 1859; L. F. Philips, bm; m 24 Mar 1859 by James W. Murray, J. P.

Murry, Thos. R. & Lillian Wood, 9 Aug 1849; R. F. Hamilton, bm.

Musick, Ephraim & Agniss Mcmillin, 12 Oct 1791; David McMillin, bm.

Musick, Jonathan & _____, 15 Dec 1802; James Young, bm.

Nailer, Joshua & Eliz. Barnett, 14 Feb 1798; Jesse Richardson, bm.

Nailler, Joshua & Mourning Harril, 10 Sept 1799; Perygreen Magness, bm.

Nalin, James R. & Nancy Cochram, 30 Jan 1838; Manos H. Dawson, bm.

Nalon, Henry C. & Lorena Johnson, 12 Oct 1865; James Nalon, D. T. Searsey, bm; m 12 Oct 1865 by T. H. W. Whiteside, J. P.

Naney, Cebern & Alvira Koone, 16 Nov 1852; John C. Keeter, bm; m 17 Nov 1852 by T. B. Justice, M. G.

Nanney, Amy Harriss, 16 Dec 1805; Daniel Haris, bm.

Nanney, Andrew & Nancey Stott, 24 Oct 1838; Madison, Koone, bm.

Nanney, D. D. & Naoma Koon, 24 Feb 1866; Barnet Hill, bm; m 27 Feb 1866 by Washington Haynes, M. G.

Nanney, Edmond & Sabirah Whiticar, 9 Feb 1821; Thomas Whiticar, bm.

Nanney, George & Arminey Largen, 13 Nov 1859; Joseph G. Nanney, bm; m 13 Nov 1859 by J. Gilkey, J. P.

Nanney, Henry & R. E. Keeter, 31 Dec 1857; John M. Keeter, bm.

Nanney, James H. & Lewesey J. Nanney, 29 Apr 1856; Joseph G. Nanney, bm; m 19 Apr 1856 by J. Gilkey, J. P.

Nanney, John & A. E. Keeter, 10 Nov 1859; John M. Keeter, bm; m 10 Nov 1859 by J. Gilkey, J. P.

Nanney, Jonathan & Esther Marlow, 2 Feb 1842; Thomas Nanny, bm.

Nanney, Joseph G. & Armentey Largen, 3 Nov 1859; George Naney, bm; m 3 Nov 1859 by J. Gilkey, J. P.

Nanney, Jourdan & Martha Loften, 6 Mar 1845; Thomas Nanney, bm.

Nanney, Randall & Caty Gear, 13 Apr 1824; Walter B. Rutherford, bm.

Nanney, Randol & Rebeceh B. Largin, 6 Dec 1851; Martin Harris, bm; m 7 Nov (sic) 1851 by T. B. Justice.

Nanney, Thomas & Polly Flack, 17 Oct 1824; John Geer, bm.

Nanney, Thomas & Almira(?) Koon, 15 Aug 1840; A. Mchan, bm.

Nanny, Amos & Tempe Wilkerson, 13 Dec 1847; Andrew Peet, bm.

Nanny, James & Sally Hill, 16 Oct 1816; Jos. Hunter, bm.

Nanny, John & Sarah Harrel, 17 Aug 1843; John Arwood, bm.

Nanny, Nicholas & Polley Revis, 4 Sept 1816; Morgan Reavis, bm.

Nanny, Nicholas & Nancy L. Keeter, 4 Nov 1860; T. W. Hawkins, bm; m 4 Nov 1860 by T. G. Hawkins.

Nanny, Royal & Marey Hambrick, 12 Sept 1844; Avington Hills, bm.

Nanny, Samuel & Catharine Laughter, 11 Aug 1837; Lewis Hill, bm.

Nanny, Shadrack & Polly Wheler, 11 Jan 1804; Isarel Robertson, bm.

Nanny, Wm. & Jane Sorrels, 17 Sept 1857; J. P. Sorrels, bm.

Nany, Isaiah & H. D. Hill, 7 Nov 1864; Harvey C. Hollifield, bm; m 10 Nov 1864 by T. P. Sorrels, J. P.

Nany, James & Mary Camp, 12 Nov 1828; Guilford Eaves, bm.

Neal, David D. & Mary Blanton, 10 Jan 1864; A. J. Scoggin, bm; m 10 Jan 1864 by Nathan Scoggin, J. P.

Neal, J. G. & R. E. Weaver, 8 Oct 1866; John L. Weaver, bm; m 9 Oct 1866 by G. W. Ivy, bm.

Neal, Joab & Barbary Jordan, 26 Oct 1832; Joel Cloud, bm.

Neal, Moses & Avy Fowler, 1 May 1811; Charles M'Clain, bm.

Neal, Stephen N. & Mary E. Harris, 9 Nov 1854; M. B. Neal, bm; m 9 Nov 1854 by J. H. Carpenter, J. P.

Neall, Charles & Jane Henson, 16 May 1793; John Thomas, bm.

Neel, Payton & Rebeca McMillian, 12 Aug 1800; Andrew Hamilton, bm.

Neely, Robert & Sarah Russel, 23 Apr 1822; Joseph Stinson, bm.

Neighbors, Charles & Nancy Elems, 2 Feb 1819; Berry Jones, bm.

Nelon, John & Mary Dalton, 22 Aug 1835; Manos H. Dawson, bm.

Nelon, Thomas & Harriet Malissa Cochran, 1 Jan 1839; Moses Morgan, bm.

Nelson, Anson B. & Mahala C. Waldrop, 6 Jun 1837; John Gray Bynum, bm.

Nelson, Bherimon & Mary Humphris, 22 Mar 1791; Robt. Potter, bm.

Nesbitt, James & Narcissa Bird, 16 Jul 1823; Ambrose Mills, bm.

Newman, David & Sophronia Williams, 24 Sept 1851; Alson McMurry, bm.

Newman, John & Jane Thompson, 2 Feb 1845; Richard Morris, bm.

Newman, William & Delilah Allison, 27 Aug 1815; Thomas Denton, bm.

Newman, Wm. & Elizabeth C. Garret, 25 Mar 1841; John Ellison, bm.

Newman, Willis & Mary Foster, m 20 Sept 1851 by Samuel Stone, J. P.

Newton, George & Matty Rucker, 5 Feb 1814; Ebenezer Newton, bm.

Newton, John & Nancy Casky, _____ 1809; William Newton, Andrew Taylor, bm.

Newton, Robert & Frances Soward, 6 Dec 1782; Jonathan Hampton, bm.

Newton, Robert & Sarah Robertson, 31 Dec 1817; F. F. Alley, bm.

Nichols, Jonathan A. & Rebecca Parker, 13 Aug 1866; P. B. Morgan, bm; m 13 Aug 1866 by J. W. Morgan, J. P.

Nichols, Wm. A. & Mary Clingman, 19 Jul 1855; H. E. Sloan, bm; m 19 Jul 1855 by R. P. Franks.

Niell, Thomas & Jency Ray, 25 May 1819; J. H. Alley, bm.

Niely, William & Nancy Crosby, 10 Apr 1809; Jacob Covell, bm.

Nix, Andrew M. & Margaret Tanner, 26 Nov 1831; Andrew Tanner, bm.

Nix, Aron & Margaret C. L. Grant, 11 Dec 1834; Samuel H. Nix, bm.

Nix, George W. & Lucinda Smith, 1 Jan 1835; John Rich, bm.

Nix, John & Martha Long, 11 Oct 1791; Alexander McGaughy, bm.

Nix, John & Conny Wadkins, 18 Oct 1808; William Flack, bm.

Nix, Joseph & Nancy Welch, 18 Dec 1827; John Mason, bm.

Nix, Robert A. & Hannah Hill, 5 Apr 1832; C. Andrew Moore, bm.

Nix, Samuel & Mary L. Clark, 23 Jan 1840; Thomas Morris, bm.

Nix, William & Jane Anderson, __ Dec 1796; James Erwin, bm.

Nix, Wm. F. & E. P. Wells, 5 Jan 1867; William J. Willkie, bm.

Nixon, John & Milly Dycus, 14 Apr 1807; Robert Nixon, bm.

Nixon, John & Elizebeth Nunally, 15 Nov 1809; Larkin Dycus, bm.

Noblitt, William & Polly Jackson, 22 Aug 1811; Moses Noblitt, bm.

Nodine, J. C. & Martha Foster, 17 Oct 1852; J. J. G. VAughan, bm; m 17 Oct 1852 by J. M. Hamilton, J. P.

Nodine, Nathaniel & Florabell Vaughn, 20 Sept 1851; J. J. G. Vaughan, bm; m 21 Sept 1851 by Henry Culbreath, M. G.

Norman, George & Polly Figgins, 10 Jan 1831; David Hamrick, bm.

Norman, Thomas & Sally Willis, 15 Jul 1819; John Norman, bm.

Norman, Wm. & Mary Nunley, 8 Oct 1859; M. Hall, bm; m 9 Oct 1859 by C. Livingston, M. G.

Norvell, Henry & Mary Melton, 27 Jan 1816; Samuel Melton, bm.

Norvell, Spencer P. & Martha Harrison, 2 Apr 1836; James Gettys, bm.

Norvelle, W. E. & Mary Ann Biggerstaff, 9 Dec 1861; W. E. Walker, bm; m 12 Dec 1861 by P. G. Washburn, J. P.

Norvill, J. S. & Sarah E. Buff, 3 Aug 1860; M. O. Dickerson, bm; m 23 Aug 1850 by John Freeman, J. P.

Norvill, John S. & Jane K. Long, 3 Aug 1849; Wm. G. Roberts, bm.

Norvill, M. E. & Nancy Price, 8 Mar 1855; J. W. Price, bm.

Norvill, M. E. & Nancy Earls, 24 Jul 1860; B. W. Baber, bm; m 24 Jul 1860 by John Freeman, J. P.

Norvill, Samuel & Nancy N. King, 18 Mar 1854; J. G. Early, bm.

Norvill, Wily & Fanny Cawhorn, 15 Apr 1819; Peter Freeman, bm.

Novell, Spencer & Cathrine Davis, 18 Jan 1818; Andrew Bell, bm.

Nowlen, Nelson & Susannah Elliott, 15 Aug 1828; Paschal T. Grigg, bm.

Nowlin, David & Luany Garner, 16 Mar 1797; Phillip Moore, bm.

Nowlin, David & Sealah Padgett, 17 Arp 1830; S. Christopher Gold, bm.

Nowlin, Hardon & Srah Crowder, ____; David Nowlin, William Garner, bm.

Nowlin, John & NancyPoston, 12 Nov 1831; David Gardner, bm.

Nowlin, Lewis & Sarah Whiteside, 4 Aug 1785; David Nowlin, Peter Woodward, bm.

Nowlin, Peter & Polley McIntire, 27 Apr 1819; David Nowlin, bm.

Nunally, Jeremiah & Janey Davis, 30 Mar 1809; Simon Davis, bm.

Nunely, Archebel & Rebackay Murfy, 18 Oct 1792; Abraham Clark, bm.

Odam Berry or Bowen, Berry & Susannah Odum, 30 Jan 1841; Wm. Cooper, bm.

O'Hanlan, Jas. Jr. & M. J. Alexander, 16 Nov 1855; R. L. Gilkey, bm; m 16 Nov 1855 by E. Rowley, M. G.

Oliver, James W. & Sealy Melton, _____ 181-; John Guffey, bm.

Oliver, John & Maryan Withrow, 15 Jul 1795; John Carson, bm.

Oneal, Richard & Nancy Grigg, 17 Jul 1828; James M. Allan, bm.

Orr, Robert & Leah Polk, __ Feb 1790; James Wilson, Saml Carpenter, bm.

Orsborn, Littleton S. & Rachel Sims, 5 Jul 1827; Littleton Sims, bm.

Otrey, Alexander & Thany Irvine, 27 Feb 1803; Absalom Otrey, bm.

Otry, Nelus & Nany Eaves, 9 Jun 1801; Jonathan Carpenter, bm.

Owenby, Ezekial & Nancy Alford, 21 Dec 1852; Ambrose Owenby, bm.

Owenby, Joshua & Milley Wheeler, 15 Jan 1823; John Hill, bm.

Owens, Albert A. & Catharine Williams, 15 Jan 1847; John Teal, bm.

Owens, Alfred & Betsy Owens, 18 Jan 1833; Joseph Hardin, bm.

Owens, Alfred B. & Mary Fortune, 16 Sept 1844; Amos Owens, bm.

Owens, Almon P. & Mary Jinkins, 1 Jan 1844; Amos Owens, bm.

Owens, Amos & Mary Sursey, 1 Jan 1844; A. P. Owens, bm.

Owens, Calvin & Candis Milliard, 20 Spet 1860; Henry Culbreath, bm; m 20 Sept 1860 by H. Culbreath.

Owens, David & Celia King, 11 Nov 1833; Joseph Robbins, Jr., bm.

Owens, David & Celia Putman, 17 Mar 1845; Wm. Cole, bm.

Owens, David & Mriah Covignton, 17 Apr 1850; George B. Fords, bm.

Owens, Gilford & Mary Grissle, 10 Dec 1859; Joseph A. Cole, bm; m 15 Dec 1859 by H. Culbreath, M. G.

Owens, Hampton & Lavina Burgess, m 21 Jun 1851 by Samuel Stone, J. P.

Owens, Isham & Frances Bridges, 18 Nov 1835; James Robbins, bm.

Owens, J. Willis & Louisa Blanton, 13 Dec 1863; Isham Owens, bm; m 13 Dec 8163 by J. B. McDaniel, J. P.

Owens, John & Polly Clinton, 9 Jan 1813; Robert Anderson, bm.

Owens, John & Martha N. Smith, 29 Dec 1856; Wm. Cole, bm; m 6 Jan 1857 by J. N. Covington, J. P.

Owens, John & Nancy Milwood, 28 Jul 1860; R. Depriest, bm; m 19 Jul 1860 by R. Depriest, J. P.

Owens, John Jr. & Peggy Owens, 2 Jul 1830; Alfred Owens, bm.

Owens, Joseph & Sealay Dayves, 25 Feb 1813; Thomas Owns, bm.

Owens, Joseph & Susanna Roach, 18 Jan 1849; John Owens, bm.

Owens, Ned & Eliza Scruggs, 8 Aug 1854; Lawson Philips, bm; m 8 Aug 1854 by J. H. Carpenter, J. P.

Owens, Solomon & Sarah Robbins, 29 Dec 1855; John Robbins, bm; m 30 Dec 1855 by A. Harrill, J. P.

Owens, Thomas & Elizabeth Depriest, 16 Aug 1843; Ramon Owens, bm.

Owens, William & Peggy Cole, 9 Sept 1807; John Cole, bm.

Owins, James & Prishy Waldrop, 29 Oct 1837; Edmund Waldrop, bm.

Owins, Jonas & Sarah Pagett, 7 Aug 1859; Peter A. Carpenter, bm; m 7 Aug 1859 by E. M. Carpenter, bm.

Owins, Thomas & Sophia Cline, 12 Apr 1825; Hennery Williamson, Luke Mullins, William Mullins, bm.

Ownbey, Ambrose & Elizabeth Hinson, 1 Jan 1793; James Ownbey, bm.

Ownbey, Arthur & Barbary Hill, 27 Jan 1795; James Ownbey, bm.

Ownbey, Porter & Martha Morgan, 23 Feb 1797; John Ownbey, bm.

Ownbey, Powel & Susannah Jackson, 19 Jan 1821; Harbard Hills, bm.

Ownbey, Powell Stamper & Elizabeth Ownbey, __ Nov 1798; John Ownbey, bm.

Ownbey, Robert & Matilda Ownbey, 18 Dec 1815; Rt. Hills, bm.

Ownbey, Thomas & Winny Shelton, 10 Dec 1799; James Ownbey, bm.

Ownbey, William & Sally Brown, 12 __ ____; James Ownbey, bm.

Ownby, Ephriem & Sarah Hunter, 10 Feb 1827; John Hunter, bm.

Ownby, John & Elizabeth Hill, 11 Mar 1805; Arthur Ownby, bm.

Ownby, John & M. Coon, 17 Feb 1812; George Coone, bm.

Ownby, Jonathan & Elizabeth Walkins, 23 Mar 1840; Ephriam Ownby, bm.

Ownby, Joseph & Nancy Watkins, 5 Mar 1836; William H. Walton, bm.

Ownby, Thomas & Mourning Hill, 10 Apr 1798; Robert Hills, bm.

Pace, Moses & Margaret Barclay, 4 Nov 1810; Burrel Pace, bm.

Pack, Alexander & Narcissa Waldrop, 4 Mar 1849; Malahi Newman, bm.

Pack, Jack & Sally Allison, 23 Aug 1810; John Allison, bm.

Pack, Jackson & Mahala Nelson, 14 Feb 1847; Lewis King, bm.

Pack, Jackson & Priscilla Smith, 13 Aug 1854; William K. Taber, bm.

Pack, Wm. & Mariler Thompson, 1 May 1853; David Newman, bm; m 1 May 1853 by J. M. Hamilton, J. P.

Padget, Abraham & Sary Dedmon, 13 Dec 1813; Mansfield Padgett, bm.

Padget, Hix & Carline Pentuff, 2 Aug 1860; George J. Bennick, bm; m 2 Aug 1850 by E. M. Carpenter.

Padget, Isaac & Fanny Davis, 4 Aug 1813; Isaac holifield, Edmmond Padgt, bm.

Padget, Wm & _____, ___ 1815; D. Lyles, bm.

Padgett, C. A. C. & Minerva Green, 15 Mar 1861; M. S. Padgett, bm; m 16 Mar 1861 by H. Harrill, J. P.

Padgett, Crayton & Amelia B. Collins, 15 Mar 1866; Wm. H. Harrill, bm; m 18 Mar 1866 by D. Ponnell.

Padgett, Edmund & Milley A. White, 23 Jun 1849; T. Webb, bm.

Padgett, Green B. & Catherine Cooper, 24 Oct 1845; Isaac Padgett, bm.

Padgett, Hampton & Mary T. Price, 31 Jan 1840; Mark D. Padgett, bm.

Padgett, J. B. & Louisa Colbert, 27 Aug 1860; Lewis McDonald, bm.

Padgett, Jacob Jr. & Rody Freeman, 7 Oct 1836; Jacob Padgett Sr., bm.

Padgett, Jerrel & Margaret Hill, 14 Jan 1845; Mark D. Padget, bm.

Padgett, John & Betsy Cockerham, 21 Jan 1809; Henry McKinney, Martin McCowess(?), bm.

Padgett, Mark D. & Emily Price, 23 Feb 1838; John Padgett, bm.

Padgett, Marvel S. & Sarah Michal, 22 Aug 1861; C. A. C. Padgett, bm; m 29 Aug 1861 By H. Harrill, J. P.

Padgett, Merida & Elizabeth Webb, 10 Aug 1849; James M. Tate, bm.

Padgett, Miles & Parthenia Lancester, 14 Aug 1853; Wm. D. Lancaster, bm.

Padgett, Nehemiah & Betsy Bridges, 3 Oct 1809; John Padgett, Jonathan Dobbins, bm.

Padgett, Pinckney & Mary Roach, 2 Jan 1860; T. Jefferson Downy, bm.

Padgett, William B. & Sarah Byars, 4 Mar 1840; Ausbun McGinnis, bm.

Page, A. M. & Mary Oliphant, 29 Nov 1853; John H. Gilkey, bm; m 29 Nov 1853 by Thomas E. Davis, M. G.

Pain, Columbus & Rebecca Pain, 27 Dec 1866; Noah Morris(?), bm. (C. H.)

Painter, Alfred & Martha Sutton, 11 Jan 1851; J. H. Carpenter, bm.

Painter, George & Sarah Pell, 10 Aug 1813; William Pell, bm.

Painter, George & Rebecca Freeman, 18 Aug 1824; Marvill Melton, bm.

Painter, Leonard & Lucy Smith, 22 Jun 1807; James Truelove, bm.

Painter, Michael & Nancy Upchurch, 4 Sept 1813; John Freeman, bm.

Painter, Ransom & Sarah Grant, 2 Sept 1838; Bowen Painter, bm.

Painter, William & Sarah Robbins, 15 May 1821; Middleton Sutton, bm.

Panter, Calvin & Eliza Padget, 14 Apr 1843; A. Padgett, bm.

Panter, Joel & Jane Stewart, 15 Nov 1848; H. H. Howser, bm.

Panter, Samuel & Elizebeth Swan, 21 Jul 1812; Miles Aster, bm.

Panter, Wm. & Anjaline C. Gee, 11 Mar 1847; Joseph Berry Snider, bm.

Panther, George & Polly Nanny, 26 Nov 1834; Charles Lewis, bm.

Parham, Litteton & Betsy Martin, 29 Oct 1810; William Parham, James Humphreys, bm.

Parker, Elijah & Letty Grayson, 22 Jun 1827; Archy Lane, bm.

Parker, Jethro & America Hunter, 3 Apr 1860; Alfred Hall, bm; m 4 Apr 1860 by J. W. Morgan, J. P.

Parker, John & Mrs. Peggy Towry, 16 Nov 1819; Jesse Ledford, bm.

Parker, Jordan & Elizabeth Crease, 21 Aug 1846; James Hey, bm.

Parker, Joseph & Rachael Black, 7 Feb 1824; John Parker, bm.

Parker, Parkerson J. & Prudence Wood, 30 Apr 1827; William Dedman, bm.

Parker, Thomas & Sary Abnathey, 22 Feb 1814; John Parker, bm.

Parker, Thomas & Nancy Wilkerson, 19 Mar 1839; Elijah Parker, bm.

Parks, Samuel & Pheby Cauldwell, 24 Jan 1794; William Mackey, bm.

Paro, William & Sally Reavis, 28 Oct 1829; Joel Wood, bm.

Parrack, Samuel & Polly Daren, 22 Feb 1816; Joseph Taylor, bm.

Parrick, Thomas & Peggy Short, 24 Jul 1806; Charles Short, bm.

Parris, Albert & Rebecca A. Wheeler, 9 Jun 1852; Obadiahr Cockerham, bm; m 9 Jun 1852 by Wm. Rucker, J. P.

Parrish, Nathaniel & Harriet Walker, 5 May 1819; Andrew Miller, bm.

Parsons, Leverett & Sophia Hill, 9 Dec 1823; Jeremiah Williams, bm.

Parten, John & Martha Hockens, 9 Dec 1860; Henry Nanny, bm; m 9 Dec 1860 by J. Gilkey, J. P.

Patrick, Thomas & Rebekah Nix, 11 Sept 1812; Wm. Nix, bm.

Patten, Elijah & Nancy Watson, 9 Feb 1819; Francis Morrison, bm.

Pattern, Robert & Eliza Mooney, 6 Jul 1815; James Pattern, Edwin Muni, bm.

Patterson, David & Ruthy Camp, 20 Mar 1825; Joshua Cmap, bm.

Patterson, Edward & Mildred Lewis, 11 May 1818; Chas. Lewis, bm.

Patterson, Hampton W. & ELizabeth More, 19 Dec 1826; John Patterson, bm.

Patterson, John & Mary Fauch, 14 Nov 1796; Samuel Bailey, bm.

Patterson, Robert & Peggy Nowlin, ____ 1809; David Nowlin Sr., bm.

Patterson, Samuel & Lilly Crowder, 17 Sept 1825; William Moore, bm.

Patterson, William & Sarah Grigg, 13 Oct 1813; John Moore, bm.

Payne, John & Sarah Hayden, 1 Jun 1838; Mitchell Hayden, bm.

Payne, Moses & Elizabeth Walker, 10 Sept 1827; Jonathan Walker, Thos. Payne, bm.

Pearson, Charles & Martha Bradly, 10 Nov 1793; Jno. Doile, bm.

Pearson, John & Peggy Grant, 24 Apr 1807; Elijah Dolton, bm.

Peeler, Joh H. & Margaret Lattimore, 23 Apr 1840; John Lattimore, bm.

Peeples, Lewis & Polly Patterson, dau. of David Patterson, 6 Nov 1813.

Peerson, John & Clarkey Ann Staton, 25 Aug 1840; James Egerton, bm.

Peerson, Joseph & Elizabeth Hullett, 15 Jul 1830; William W. Hullett, bm.

Peler, David & Elizabeth London, 12 Apr 1825; Henerey London, bm.

Pelham, A. & Martha M. McGehee, dau. of William McGehee, 20 Dec 1833; O. P. Mills, bm.

Pell, Jonathan & Pheby Beazel, 26 Jan 1790; Sherod Upchurch, bm.

Pell, William & Polly Smith, 2 Dec 1795; Js. Hampton, bm.

Pentiff, Robert & Drusilla Dicus, 12 Oct 1835; E. M. Carpenter, bm.

Pentuff, Michael & Susan Emaline Champion, ____ ____ 180--; Hix Padgett, bm; m 24 Oct 1860 by R. Depriest, J. P.

Pentuff, Ronny & Rebecca Rollins, 9 Sept 1858; Robert Pentuff, bm; m 12 Sept 1858 by B. E. Rollins.

Perkin, John & Nancy Robinson, 24 Dec 1792; Richd. Lewis, bm.

Pers, John & Thany Edwards, 18 Dec 1823; Sims Harris, bm.

Petillio, Millington & Mary Ledbetter, 24 Aug 1794; Elijah Green, bm.

Pettit, Elias & Mary Grogan, 23 Dec 1839; Thos. W. Grogan, bm.

Pettit, Henry & Anne Mooney, 10 Dec 1815; William Toney, bm.

Petty, Elijah & Sally Parker, 23 Jul 1850; M. Wilkerson, bm.

Philbeck, J. A. & Hulda Wells, m 5 Jul 1855 by R. P. Franks, M. G.

Philbeck, James & Amy Walker, 26 Feb 1849; John Filbeck, bm.

Philbeck, James P. & Sarah Ann Price, 18 Sept 1859; Wm. H. Philbeck, bm.

Philbeck, Phillip & Elisabeth Davis, 14 Nov 1819; William Davis, bm.

Philbeck, Richard & Eliza Womack, 18 May 1833; John Davis, bm.

Philbeck, Richard & Nancy Davis, 3 Dec 1842; William Davis, bm.

Philbeck, T. F. & ____, 12 Sep 1864; J. P. Philbeck, bm.

Philbeck, William & Rachel Edwards, 17 Nov 1814; Georg Philbeck, John Edwards, bm.

Philips, Drury & Susanah Hardin, 18 Feb 1845; William H. Hardin, bm.

Philips, Iredel B. & Jane Baxter, 8 Oct 1849; E. M. Carpenter, bm.

Philips, James Landrum & Mary S. Murray, 24 Jul 1852; James W. Murray, bm.

Philips, Lawsson & M. M. Hanes, 9 Feb 1854; J. P. Philips, bm; m 9 Feb 1854 by J. H. Carpenter, J. P.

Phillips, Hilmon & Nancy Webb, 9 Feb 1854; John D. Webb, bm; m 15 Feb 1854 by J. H. Carpenter, J. P.

Phillips, T. P. & Eliza Camp, 20 Mar 1866; James Wood, bm; m 17 Mar 1866 by J. M. Williams, M. G.

Pickering, John & Mary Ann Sloop, 2 Oct 1844; George H. Sloop, bm.

Pickit, William & Mary Denton, 15 Sept 1803; John Doyle, bm.

Piles, Leonard & Mary Bizenin, 1 Apr 1794; Joseph Carpenter (signed Joseph Zimmerman), bm.

Pinner, James P. & Susannah Moore, 16 Oct 1851; Ransom Pinner, bm; m 16 Oct 1851 by Wm. Harrill, M. G.

Pintuff, Barney & Rebecca Rollens, 9 Sept 1858.

Plummer, Bennett & Unity Workman, 8 Jan 1833; Martin Irvine, bm.

Plummer, Joseph & Sarah McMorry, 17 Dec 1796; Alexander Downey, bm.

Poindexter, Edward L. & Judith Baber, 13 Jun 1826; Robert Baber, bm.

Ponnell, Dove & Sally Whiticar, 13 Nov 1828; John Padgett, bm.

Ponnell, Martin & Cynthia Walker, 16 Oct 1831; Dove Ponnell, bm.

Poole, Laban P. & Letty S. Earle, 18 Jul 1812; E. Hannon, bm.

Poole, Miles & Mary Willson, 6 Jan 1820; Abraham Martin, bm.

Pope, Benjamin & Polly Johnston, 14 Apr 1828l; Emanuel Morton Carpenter, bm.

Pope, Jasper & Sarah Green, 13 Dec 1853; Benj. Pope, bm.

Pope, Joseph & Susanah Mooney, 13 Jul 1834; George Mooney, bm.

Pope, L. C. & Elviery Wells, 11 Sept 1854; Toliver Wallace, bm; m 11 Sept 1854 by Wm. Harrill, M. G.

Porter, Alexander & Elizabeth Chittim, 21 Jan 1795.

Porter, David & Rachele Black, 18 Jul 1791; Gavin Irvine, bm.

Porter, David & Patsey L. Anderson, 15 Jun 1804.

Porter, David H. & Salena Gay, 27 Nov 1825; Jas S. Wallis, bm.

Porter, J. M. & Mary Watson, 26 Mar 1844; Wm. A. Wallis, bm.

Porter, John & Rebecca Blackwell, 12 Sept 1825; Charles Blackwell, bm.

Porter, Nathanl. W. & Elizabeth Grove, 22 Dec 1808; John Vickers, bm.

Porter, Robert J. & Margaret Irvine, 23 Mar 1816; Elles Nalor, bm.

Porter, Samuel F. & Margaret Todd, 22 Oct 1839; Alfred B. Callahan, bm.

Porter, William & Margaret Baldridge, 20 Mar 1807; John Baldridge, bm.

Porter, Wm. A. & Minerva Daves, 17 Aug 1847; James Davis, bm.

Porter, William Colson & Hanner Porter Wallace, 21 Feb 1811; Nathaniel P. Wells, Robert Callahan, bm.

Portrum, Henry & N. M. Whiteside, 23 Jul 1863; T. R. Egerton, bm; m 23 Jul 1863 by W. H. Logan, M. G.

Poston, William & Nancy Love, 15 Aug 1825; Charles Love, John Fondren, bm.

Potter, Royal & Rebekah Reavis, 8 Mar 1793; Isham Reavis, bm.

Potter, Thomas & Ruth Moore, 8 Jul 1782; Jesse Novil, bm.

Powel, Abram & Mary Harden, 29 Aug 1811; James Linsey, James Harden, bm.

Powell, Ransom & Miriam Rowland, 2 Sept 1797; Thos Hunter, bm.

Powers, Thomas & Nelly Wiggins, 14 Aug 1807; Edward Dyhcus, bm.

Prater, Andrew & Mary Ann Nailer, 12 Jan 1828; Morris McCarthy, bm.

Prator, Amos & Althany Allin, 13 Jun 1815; Jos. M. Black, bm.

Presly, John & Mary Runnels, 11 Jan 1807; A. Mills, bm.

Prewit, William & Nancy Cook, 12 Jan 1835; John H. Swafford, bm.

Price, Adam & Adaline Harris, 14 Mar 1858; R. M. Price, bm; m 14 Mar 1858 by John Freeman, J. P.

Price, Bennet & Elizabeth Henderson, 5 Jun 1834; John H. Alley, bm.

Price, Drury D. & Luciler Ann Price, 9 Aug 1860; Luis Justice, bm; m 9 Aug 1860 by J. M. Chitwood, J. P.

Price, F. & Isabel Price, 9 Dec 1852; B. C. Fortune, bm; m 9 Dec 1852 by B. E. Rollins.

Price, F. L. & Elizabeth Wells, 26 Mar 1846; B. W. Baber, bm.

Price, Francis & Jinny Guffey, 22 Mar 1821; Terry Lively, bm.

Price, George & Polly Cook, 25 Oct 1804; David Davis, bm.

Price, Gillum & Mary Gates, ____ 180-; Richard Price, bm.

Price, Gillum & Artemary Wilson, 31 Dec 1835; William L. Price, bm.

Price, J. R. & J. S. Walker, 14 Aug 1861; A. M. Ledbeter, bm; m 14 Aug 1861.

Price, James & Barbary Carpenter, 15 Aug 1833; Lewis Price, bm.

Price, John & Jane Sims, 10 Oct 1811; Littleton Sims, bm.

Price, John W. & Anna Price, 12 Mar 1840; John S. Price, bm.

Price, Jos. G. & Drucillar Earls, 11 Nov 1858; Joseph Bracket, bm; m 11 Nov 1858 by John Freeman, J. P.

Price, Littleton & Emaline Fortune, 30 Jan 1843; Pleasant Fortune, bm.

Price, Martin G. & Jane B. Price, 1 Nov 1860; J. T. Mode, bm; m 1 Nov 1850 by Wm. G. Mode, J. P.

Price, Michael Mc. & Lurany Davis, 16 Dec 1842; Jo Crow, bm.

Price, Migamin J. & Louisa McFarland, 15 Jan 1852; Wm. G. Price, bm; m 15 Jan 1852 by Robt. T. Price, J. P.

Price, Oliver D. & H. C. Mode, 11 Dec 1866; J. C. Henson ,bm; m 18 Dec 1866 by K. J. McCrow, bm.

Price, Peter & Margaret A. Proctor, 9 Feb 1862; Drury D. Price, bm; m 9 Feb 1862 by John M. M. Price, J. P.

Price, Randolph Lewis & Sally Taylor, 21 Mar 1811; Abraham Crow, bm.

Price, Robert & Salla Willke, 24 Dec 1826; William L. Price, bm.

Price, Robert & Leanner Price, 18 Dec 1832; William L. Price, bm.

Price, Robert & Elisabeth Carpenter, 24 Jan 1839; David Whisnant, bm.

Price, Robert & Mary Oliver, 24 Jul 1851; J. M. Chitwood, bm; m 24 Jul 1851 by Robert T. Price, J. P.

Price, Spencer & Nancy Lively, 14 Dec 1825; Lewis Lively, bm.

Price, Thomas F. & Sarah Harrell, 15 May 1860; Wm. G. Price, bm; m 15 May 1860 by Wm. G. Mode, J. P.

Price, William & Elisabeth Hampton, 10 Dec 1783; Elias Alexander, bm.

Price, William & Polly Eaves, 15 Sept 1806; Abraham Hardin, bm.

Price, William & Nancy Gattys, 22 Dec 1831; Spencer Price, bm.

Price, William & Mary Elison, 25 Jul 1844; John Newman, bm.

Prichard, Joel & Malinda Tesnier, 2 Aug 1850; James Loveless, bm.

Prichard, Joshua & Nancy Jones, 20 Apr 1854; Neasbite Dimsdale, bm; m 20 Apr 1854 by Wm. Dimsdale, J. P.

Prince, Jos B. & Mary L. Lyles, 7 Oct 1851; Tyra Riding, bm.

Prince, William & Lidia Earle, 2 Apr 1808; Theron Earle, bm.

Procter, James & Rebekah Green, _____ 1808; Mayfield Crean, bm.

Proctor, John & Teresy White, 26 Feb 1826; Salley Moore, bm.

Proctor, Joseph M. & Elizabeth A. Jones, 17 Sept 1859; K. J. M. Grayson, bm; m 18 Sept 1859 by J. S. Grayson, J. P.

Proctor, Moses & Luvina White, 3 May 1818; Edman Hearn, bm.

Proctor, Ransom & Elizabeth McCurry, 10 Jan 1833; William Procter, bm.

Proctor Ransom & Mary Waters, 26 Feb 1850; A. C. Martin, bm.

Proctor, Reuben & Sarah Queen, 15 Jun 1820; Jonathan Waters, James Crow, bm.

Proctor, Thomas & Rebecca Horn, 13 Feb 1825; James Horn, bm.

Proctor, W. S. & Sarah Ann Pope, 26 Jan 1855; Jonathan Walker, bm.

Proctor, William & Jane Welch, 4 Jul 1789; Andrew Logan, bm.

Pulliam, Joseph & Sally Blankinship, 28 Feb 1839; John Blankinship, bm.

Pullum, John & Sarah Coxe, _____; George Flack, bm.

Purdon, John & Susanna Graham, 3 Feb 1782; Thomas McKeown, bm.

Purdon, John & Margaret Anderson, 28 Jul 1815.

Putman, David & Rosanah Sanders, 1 Mar 1832; O. G. Camp, bm.

Putman, Drury D. & Sarah Shake, 11 May 1837; Thomas Roberts, bm.

Putman, Elias & Nancy Roberts, 17 Dec 17956; Benjamin Putman, bm.

Putman, Elias & Nancy Wesson, 9 Jun 1831; David Hamrick, bm.

Putman, Elias & Mirah Hews, 31 Mar 1847; Iverson L. Roberts, bm.

Putman, John & Lucy Covington, 22 Dec 1808; Josiah Covington, bm.

Putman, Thomas Y. & Sarah J. Robbins, 23 Jan 1865; D. D. McDaniel, bm; m 26 Jan 1865 by D. D. McDaniel, J. P.

Putman, W. A. & Nancy An Wesson, 1 Feb 1866; D. B. Wesson, bm; m 2 Jan 1866 (sic) by G. W. Rollins.

Putman, William & Nancy Spurlin, 25 Oct 1840; Thomas Putman, bm.

Putman, Willson & Milly Coales, 22 Apr 1839; Francis A. Littlejohn, bm.

Putmon, Lias & Rachel Poastor, 13 Nov 1834; William Postor, bm.

Queen, George & Betsey Queen, 8 Nov 1818; Mariday Queen, bm.

Queen, Isaac & Ruth Hunt, 24 May 1832; Jos. G. Deveney, bm.

Queen, Marideth & Jene Wedan, 16 Feb 1797; Benjamin Newton, bm.

Queen, Richard & Margeret Snider, 27 Mar 1796; William WHite, Benjamin Wilkirson, bm.

Queen, Samuel & Dicey Rolls, 21 Feb 1788; William Queen, William Goinges, bm.

Queen, Timothy & Mrs. Sary White, 15 Aug 1793; Henery More, bm.

Queen, Wm. & Marian Hales, 27 Mar 1856; Charles Hales, bm; m 17 Mar 1856 by J. Gilkey, J. P.

Quin, John W. & Sarah Jane Young, 15 Dec 1863; J. V. Jay, bm.

Quin, Morrace & Unisa Liles, 26 Mar 1811; J. M. Roberts, James Rutherford, bm.

Quin, Morris & Inthy Roberts, 14 Feb 1837; Gabil Washburn, bm.

Raburn, Isaiah & Polly Humphreys, 23 Feb 1814; Hodge Roburn, bm.

Radford, John & Eliz. J. Hoyle, 15 Nov 1864; Peter Doggett, bm; m 15 Nov 1864 by T. P. Sorrells, J. P.

Radford, Joseph & Mary Sargent, 25 Apr 1832; Thomas B. Reid, bm; m by Hugh W. Watson, J. P.

Radford, Thomas & Sally Nanny, 13 Jun 1825; William Adair, bm.

Rainswaters, Gabril & Nancy Toney, 17 Jun 1829; Elijah Melton, bm.

Rainy, Stephen & Elizabeth McDaw, 20 May 1814; John McDow, bm.

Rallans, Thomas & Elizebeth Armstrong, 17 Apr 1792; Martin Armstrong, bm.

Ramsay, Simon & Sidney Hayes, 9 Jan 1832; Edward Buckner, bm.

Ramsey, Alexander & Agness Die, 23 Nov 1820; Anna Webber, John Die, bm.

Ramsey, David & Rebecca Hains, 22 Nov 1825; David Searcy, bm.

Ramsey, Henry & Margaret Flowers, 30 Sept 1860; James Thomas, bm; m 30 Sept 1860 by M. Wilkerson, J. P.

Ramsey, Logan & Mildred Searcy, __ Aug 1814; Richard Searcy, bm.

Ramsey, Samuel & Male Ann ____, 26 Nov 1793; Samuel Young, bm.

Randal, Thomas & Rachael Webb, 21 Oct 1824; Joseph Scoggins, bm.

Randall, Amos & Catharine Teal, 20 Apr 1831; William Teal, bm.

Randels, Gidon & Amey Cockrum, 25 __ 1798; Jesse Mills, bm.

Randol, Bluford & Kissiah Willis, 15 Jul 1819; David Willis, bm.

Randol, Thornton & Jane Owins, 18 Oct 1804; George Randol, bm.

Ray, J. H. & Mary L. Lynch, 28 Nov 1859; Norman Lynch, bm.

Ray, Nathan & Mary Koone, 27 Aug 1847; Dewalt Koone, bm.

Read, Olin & Elizan Youngblood, 1 Oct 1841; John Read, bm.

Read, Robert & Cloah Weaver, 7 Apr 1835; Moses Edwards, bm.

Reavis, Edward & Elizabeth Doyle, 1802-05; Jno. Doyle Jr., bm.

Reavis, John & Elizabeth Fowler, 28 Dec 1803; David Dickey, bm.

Reavis, William & Betsy Burge, 23 Sept 1816; Joseph Doyle, bm.

Rector, Joel & Polly Stice, 15 Apr 1814; Philip Stice, bm.

Reed, John & Elizabeth Smart, 15 Dec 1792; William Mitchel, bm.

RUTHERFORD COUNTY MARRIAGES 1779-1868

Reed, John & Milisa Woten, _____ 1836; Thomas F. Edwards, bm.

Reed, Pinkney & Intha E. Kilpatrick, 22 May 1832; Daniel Michal, bm.

Reed, William & Mary Clements, 16 Apr 1817; Preston Goforth, bm.

Reed, William & Elizabeth Marshal, 17 Oct 1863; B. F. Hicks, bm; m 18 Oct 1863 by T. B. Justice.

Reel, J. A. & E. D. Allen, 4 Jan 1845; John M. Alen, bm.

Reel, Joseph & Patsy Jones, 14 Jul 1835; Standerfer Jones, bm.

Reel, William & Sarah Allen, 23 Aug 1852; Daniel Reel, bm.

Reele, Danel & Nancey C. Hensley, 6 Aug 1850; James A. Hensley, bm.

Reevis, James & Mary Bagwell, 25 Nov 1812.

Reid, John Jr. & Nancy Logan, 19 Feb 1829; Joseph Reid, bm.

Reid, Joseph & Martha E. Weaver, 11 Sept 1861; J. M. Andrews, bm; m 11 Sept 1861 by A. R. Bennick.

Reid, Wm. K. & E. A. Church, 6 Jun 1859; E. Carrier, bm; m 7 Jun 18590 by A. Hamby, Elder.

Reinhardt, Daniel & Frances Hoyle, 25 Aug 1803; B. A. Ramsaur, bm.

Reinhardt, John J. & Charlotte Smith, 23 Oct 1840; W. H. Cabaniss, bm.

Reinhardt, Joseph A. & Drusilla Burge, 1 Jul 1846; Jesse J. Webb, bm.

Renels, Perygreen & Celia McEmore, 16 Sept 1790; Samuel Carpenter, bm.

Renn, Shadrach & Elizabeth Runnells, _____ 1789; E. Hannons, bm.

Rewker, Jessee & Abisha Reder, 14 Jun 1819; Joseph Wilson, bm.

Reynolds, Ellis & Sally Waller, 19 Mar 1830; Robert Turner, bm.

Reynolds, John & Caty Magness, 7 Jul 1810; Abner Womack, bm.

Reynols, William & Lurany Holland, 20 Dec 1817; Elijah Reynolds, bm.

Rice, Elijah & Catherine Adkins, _____; Benjamin Burns, bm.

Rich, David & Rhody Hains, 1 Sept 1817; Andrew Earley, bm.

Rich, John & Susanna Barlyhorn, 12 Sept 1799; Robt. Rich, bm.

Rich, John & Mary Hill, 10 Nov 1801; Hennery Hills, bm.

Rich, John & Rebecca Thompson, 8 Jan 1835; Hampton Patterson, bm.

Rich, Robert & Elizabeth Porter, 26 Mar 1822; Philip Fulks, bm.

Richardson, Charles Jr. & Polly Morrow, 6 Jan 1813.

Richardson, Hyram L. & Catharine Bowman, 28 May 1816; William D. Metcalf, bm.

Richardson, Jas. M. & Ann Bird, 2 Nov 1816; Silas Melton, bm.

Richardson, Joseph & Mary Barnett, 22 Dec 1824; James M. Erwin, bm.

Richardson, William & Polly Bowman, 11 Jan 1803; Charles Richardson, bm.

Ridings, Tyrey & Amarilus Prince, 22 Nov 1840; Aspasio Earle, bm.

Ridley, James N. & Catharine Queen, 28 Apr 1831; Hugh Watson, bm.

Ridley, Mathew & Nancy Feggins, 21 Dec 1802; Robert Hartin, Aaron Bridges, bm.

Ridley, William & Ann Mary Smith, 6 Jul 1802; Wilson Putman, bm.

Riggs, Timothy Jr. & Ann Welch, 14 Mar 1785; Timothy Riggs, Sr., bm.

Right, Benj. & Betsey Self, 8 Feb 1826; John Self, bm.

Rippy, James & Rebekah Frances, 11 Jun 1836; Frances Alexander, bm.

Roach, Ambrose & Elizabeth McDaniel, 6 Sept 1836; Silverster C. Collins, bm.

Roach, James & Elizabeth Raggsdale, 22 Sept 1813; Henry Conklin, John Good, bm.

Roach, Littleberry & Susannah Mays, 22 Mar 1823; John Roach, bm.

Roach, Newton & Mary ALlen, 30 Nov 1866; W. J. Roach, bm; m 4 Dec 1866 by Wm. J. Willkie.

Roach, Perry & Elizabeth Horn, 20 Mar 1860; Daniel Horn, bm; m 22 Mar 1860 by H. Culbreath, M. G.

Roache, John & Harriet Cole, 17 Sept 1829; Joseph Roache, bm.

Robbins, Elisha & Susan Taylor, 28 Jan 1858; J. A. Carpenter, bm; m 28 Jan 1858 by J. H. Carpenter, J. P.

Robbins, George W. & A. Butler, 2 Nov 1842; J. A. Carpenter, bm.

Robbins, Hezekiah & Cyntha Rollins, 11 May 1859; William A. Camp, bm.

Robbins, James & Dicey Owens, 30 Sept 1831; David Owens, bm.

Robbins, John Jr. & Mary Owens, 14 Jan 1861; James McMahan, bm; m 15 Jan 1861 by John M. M. Price, J. P.

Robbins, P. L. & Nancy M. Price, 26 Aug 1859; James P. Philbeck, bm.

Robbins, Philip & Louisa A. Lancaster, 5 Apr 1841; Newton Cole, bm.

Robbins, Philip & Alvira Martin, 25 Jan 1854; Jackson Robbins, bm; m 17 Jan 1854 by J. H. Carpenter, J. P.

Robbins, Thomas & Elizabeth Owens, 28 Jul 1855; Robert R. Philbeck, bm; m 29 Jul 1855 by A. Harrill, J. P.

Roberson, Alford & Jane Jolley, 8 Aug 1858; Drury Roberson, bm; m 8 Aug 1858 by J. A. Grant, J. P.

Roberson, Shade & Mary Coxy, m 27 Dec 1866 by W. H. Logan, M. G.

Roberson, Walton & Rosanah McMahan, 7 Feb 1843; John Watkins, bm.

Roberts, Abel H. & Harriett E. Hyder, 4 Oct 1837; Wright H. Wilson, bm.

Roberts, Iverson & Eunisah Putman, 19 Aug 1846; Elias Putman, bm.

Roberts, John & Margaret Quin, 9 Mar 1813; Josiah Roberts, Morris Quin, bm.

Roberts, John & Susan Clemments, 22 Aug 1837; Cornelius Clements, bm.

Roberts, Josiah & Mary Linsey, 1 Sept 1803; Morris Roberts, bm.

Roberts, Morris & Mary Linsey, 4 Feb 1804; James Linsey, William McSwain, bm.

Roberts, Richard Washington & Rachael H. Wells, 28 Mar 1827; Robert Wells, bm.

Roberts, Samuel & Elizabeth Hill, 4 Apr 1815; Philip Fulk, bm.

Roberts, W. A. E. & Jane Depriest, 16 Feb 1850; J. V. Jay, bm.

Roberts, William & Eliza McEntire, 3 Jul 1830; Joseph Hardin, bm.

Robertson, Drury & Jain Harris, 7 Dec 1833; John Robertson, bm.

Robertson, Drury & Lizebeth Hill, 30 Jul 1840; David Williams, bm.

Robertson, G. B. & Rebecca Dobbins, 3 Oct 1859; Nehemiah Dobbins, bm; m 8 Oct 1859 by W. M. MacSwane, bm.

Robertson, George & Hannah Smith, 11 Feb 1822; Israel Robertson, bm.

Robertson, Ichabudy & Mirah Nanney, 14 Dec 1846.

Robertson, J. H. & Didema Haney, 29 Mar 1847; Newton Cole, bm.

Robertson, J. Hampton & Mary M. Biggerstaff, 24 Sept 1860; R. H. Biggerstaff, bm; m 27 Sept 1860 by B. E. Rollins.

Robertson, James & Isabella M. Long, 4 Jan 1832; James F. Long, bm.

Robertson, John & Ann Harris, 10 Mar 1834; Drury Robertson, bm.

Robertson, John & Mary Kizer, 29 Jan 1857; Thomas Robertson, bm; m 30 Jan 1857 by John Koone, C. L. M.

Robertson, John W. & Rebecca Davis, 25 Aug 1838; Isaac Padgett, bm.

Robertson, Mathew & Rutha M. Kizar, 30 Jul 1855; D. D. Kizer, bm; m 31 Jul 1855 by Bailey Bruce, G. M.

Robertson, Smith & Sarah Rogers, 4 Jun 1860; R. J. Downey, bm; m 4 Jun 1860 by W. H. Bertie, J. P.

Robertson, Smith R. & Selia McCluer, 28 Dec 1846; J. L. Terrell, bm.

Robertson, Thomas & Margret Smart, 7 Apr 1783; John Walker, bm.

Robertson, Wm. J. & Milly Ann Barefield, 15 Feb 1860; Charles Webb, bm; m 15 Feb 1860 by J. H. Carpenter, J. P.

Robinson, Luke & Drusilla Green, 1 Nov 1805; John Robinson, bm.

Robinson, Luke & Judith Burge, 16 Nov 1817; Joseph Green, bm.

Robinson, Thomas & Mary Lewis, 20 Jul 1797; John Robinson, bm.

Robinson, Thomas & Nancy Wheeler, 23 Apr 1816; John Hill, bm.

Robinson, William & Catharine Carrick, 7 Jan 1793.

Robison, George W. & Vianah Padgett, 29 Jun 1848; Miles Padgett, bm.

Robison, J. W. & M. C. Joley, 29 Jan 1863; Wm. J. Robertson, bm; m 29 Jan 1863 by Wm. Devenport, J. P.

Roch, James & Matilda Philips, 25 Nov 1834; John Padgett Sr., bm.

Roddy, Ephraim & Hariot H. Earle, 25 Jan 1817; Aspasio Earle, bm.

Rodgers, Harriss & Sarah Davis, 5 Jul 1834; Isaac Rogers, bm.

Rodgers, John H. & Mary Green, 17 Dec 1867; Morgan R. Lovelace, bm; m 17 Dec 1867 by B. B. Byers, J. P.

Roe, Doctor & Intha Fowler, 4 Feb 1847; Ransom Ponder, bm.

Rogers, Isaac & Elizabeth Burns, 31 Dec 1822; Joseph Brady, bm.

Rogers, Jesse & Elizabeth Burns, 9 Dec 1843; C. R. Blanton, bm.

Rogers, John & Leurany Burns, 6 Mar 1829; John Burns, bm.

Rogers, Nathaniel & Charlott Westbrooks, 23 Dec 1820; John Rogers, bm.

Rogers, William & Delilah Brooks, 29 Mar 1838; John Rogers, bm.

Rogers, Wm. & Milly N. B. Downey, 6 Feb 1861; Allen Rogers, bm; m 7 Feb 1861 by Wm. Harrill, Elder.

Rollins, B. E. & Mary Melton, 9 aug 1852; John Freeman, Ellen R. Carrier, bm.

Rollins, D. D. & Nancy Robins, 7 Jan 1845; J. E. Rollins, bm.

Rollins, D. O. & Louisa Davis, 17 Jan 1861; A. D. Rollins, bm; m 29 Jan 1861 by G. W. Rollins, Elder.

Rollins, Daniel & Rebeccah Fowler, 6 Nov 1818; George Rollins, bm.

Rollins, George W. & Malinda Jinkins, 7 Mar 1854; Benjamin Jinkins, bm; m 7 Jan 1854 by Wm. Harrill, J. P.

Rooker, George W. & Sarah Ann Canipe, 22 Apr 1852; Eli Whisnant, bm.

Rooker, William & Levina Lynch, 13 Sept 1824; William Taber, bm.

Rooker, William Jr. & Hettey McGlamrey, 2 Mar 1816; Wm Rooker Sr., bm.

Rooper, David Jr. & Sarah Frances, 25 Feb 1788; Charles Rooper, James Rooper, bm.

Ross, James & Polly Owins, 14 Apr 1803; Jno. Carson, bm.

Ross, John & Sarah Tanner, 21 Jun 1837; George W. Tanner, bm.

Ross, Martin & Artimincy Melton, 14 Jul 1828; Hiram Melton, bm.

Ross, Moses & Mary Spurling, 8 Sept 1808; Andrew Taylor, bm.

Rowley, Erastus Jr. & Martha L. Morris, 14 Sept 1841; Milton Rowley, bm.

Rucker, Mordecai & Susanna Allen, _____; Thomas Hall, bm.

Ruff, Daniels & Delila Hill, 15 Apr 1836; Arey Hill, bm.

Runnels, Stephen & Frances Renn, 27 Mar 1793; John McLean, bm.

Runyan, Jeremiah & Tabitha Collins, 15 Jul 1829; David Hamrick, bm.

Runyan, Reuben H. & Margaret S. Gibbins, 3 Sept 1835; Jeremiah Runyan, bm.

Russel, George & Roda Reavis, 23 Feb 1791; Edward Reavis, bm.

Russel, William & Nancy Reavis, 12 May 1816; Morgan Reavis, bm.

Russell, Abner & Polley Keltor, 10 Feb 1802; Mosses Russell, bm.

Russell, Davis & Rachael Bagwell, 7 Oct 1815; William Russell, bm.

Russell, J. D. & Sarah C. Davis, 23 Dec 1865; L. P. Erwin, bm; m 28 Dec 1865 by G. W. Rollins.

Rutherford, William & Martha C. Carson, 16 Sept 1851; A. B. Gilkey, bm; m 16 Sept 1851 by Thomas E. Davis, M. G.

Rutledge, James & Ann Cherry, 18 Oct 1808; Robt. Finley, bm.

Sales, Robertson J. & Martha Marlow, 24 Mar 1855; B. G. Haynes, bm; m 19 Mar 1855 by T. B. Justice.

Salor, Abraham & Elisabeth Love, 8 Aug 1785; William Ashly, bm.

Sanders, Ruben & Mary Blackwell, 11 Jan 1831; Ambrose Mills, bm.

Sanders, Sollomon & _____, 10 Dec 1813; Andrew Parker, bm.

Sarratt, Gilbert & Charlett L. Irvine, 31 Aug 1837; Charles H. Ellis, bm.

Scearcy, James & Martha Dickey, 3 Dec 1826; Moses Dickey, bm.

Schneider, M. J. & L. T. Bechtler, 26 Dec 1855; Chas. E. Bechtler, bm; m 26 Dec 1855 by Erastus Rowley, M. G.

Schroebel, John & Sally Wells, 14 Aug 1822; Humphrey Wells, bm.

Schroebel, Thomas & Saleter Moore, 9 Sept 1845; Spencer Eaves, bm.

Scoggan, Joseph & S. A. Wilson, 1 Mar 1860; R. K. Wilson, bm;l m 1 __ 1860 by B. E. Rollins.

Scoggin, James O. & Malinda McGwire, 22 Feb 1834; Joseph Jay, bm.

Scoggin, James W. & P. M. Hawkins, 28 Dec 1865; A. J. Scoggin, bm; m 28 Dec 1865 by N. Scoggin, J. P.

Scoggin, John N. & Nancy Weathers, 24 Jan 1848; D. D. Lollar, bm.

Scoggin, Lewis & _____, 30 Dec 1822; Richmond Webb, bm.

Scoggin, Oliver & Mary Ann Richardson, 21 Jun 1837; Joseph J. Scoggin, bm.

Scoggin, Richard & Mary C. Doggett, 15 Apr 1845; William Warren, bm.

Scoggins, Charles & Sally Dye, 28 Mar 1810; Abner Womack, bm.

Scoggins, Ezequel & Caty Fortener, 1 Jul 1820; John Bradley, bm.

Scoggins, Jackson & Sarah Scoggins, 13 Sept 1841; William Whitaker, bm.

Scoggins, Jesse & Mary M. Cochram, 15 Oct 1849; H. Deaton Cocherhan, bm.

Scoggins, John L. & Sarah H. Robertson, 3 Apr 1864; William Scoggin, bm; m 5 Apr 1864 by N. Scoggin, J. P.

Scoggins, Joseph Jay & Elvira Scoggins, 15 Aug 1836; Marcus O. Dickerson, bm.

Scoggins, Nathan & Nancy Walker, 17 Oct 1849; Jackson Scoggins, bm.

Scogin, Burgis & Polly Webb, 2 Oct 1807; Elias Webb, bm.

Scogin, Ezekle & Rebecah Taylor, 22 Jan 1807; Larkin Dycus, bm.

Scogin, Harronton & Elizabeth Headleston, 11 Jun 1833; Wm. Thompson, bm.

Scott, James & Nancy Montague, 6 May 1803; Robert Finley, bm.

Scott, Joseph & Sarah Meglamery, 30 Jun 1785; Jessey Mcglamery, William Bracket, John Shadocks, bm.

Scott, Moses & Lucinda Green, 7 Apr 1828; Robert G. Twitty, bm.

Scott, Patrick & Ailsy Hampton, 17 Dec 1791; Jas. Scott, bm.

Scott, William & Mary K. Corruth, 20 Oct 1820; Geroge M. Logan, bm.

Scott, Wm. & Nancy Lee, 16 Sept 1847; Albert Steadman, bm.

Scroggins, Ezekiel & Rebecca Taylor, 17 Jan 1807; Jo. Jay, bm.

Scruggs, A. D. & T. F. Bland, 28 Dec 1865; Daniel Scruggs, bm; m 28 Dec 1865 by J. H. Carpenter, J. P.

Scruggs, C. S. W. & M. S. Camp, 24 Dec 1849; C. J. Webb, bm.

Scruggs, David & Viena Hawkins, 23 Feb 1842; John Bridges, bm.

Scruggs, Jesse M. & Nancy Allen, 6 Feb 1845; E. D. Hawkins, bm.

Scruggs, Lorenzo & Polly Ann Tate, 3 Aug 1860; David Scruggs, bm; m 9 Aug 1860 by D. Ponnell.

Scruggs, Richard & Irvinzena Hawkins, 7 Feb 1838; J. M. Webb, bm.

Scruggs, Stoball & Phereby Davis, 1 Aug 1817; David Webb, bm.

Scrugs, Ellia & Elizabeth Kennedy, 3 Oct 1832; Achilles Durham, bm.

Searcey, John & Sally Ledbetter, 17 Oct 1825; David Searcy, bm.

Searcey, John D. & Matilda Flinn, 16 Sept 1837; J. B. Sloan, bm.

Searcy Henry & Susanah Laughter, 22 Jul 1848; James Brown, bm.

Searcy, Hiram & Anna Debord, 3 Jan 1824; David Searcy, bm.

Searcy, John & Mary Ingle, 4 Sept 1823; Elijah Searcy, bm.

RUTHERFORD COUNTY MARRIAGES 1779-1868

Searcy, John & Sarah Harriss, 17 Nov 1832; Richard Ledbetter, Jr., bm.

Searcy, Marion A. & Martha Jones, 28 May 1860; S. D. Searcy, bm; m 19 Jun 1860 by Wm. Devenport, J. P.

Searcy, Paul F. & Elizabeth E. Dalton, 19 Dec 1859; Jeremiah Shitle, bm; m 21 Dec 1859 by J. H. Whiteside.

Searcy, Robert & Mary Ledbetter, 20 Jul 1830; Amos Green, bm.

Searcy, Saml D. & Jane Gibbs, 15 Nov 1852; D. W. Brown, bm; m 18 Nov 1852 by T. B. Justice, M. G.

Searcy, Thomas & Milley Dickey, 13 Jul 1825; Elijah Searcy, bm.

Searcy, William & Frances Dalton, 19 Oct 1790; Thomas Morriss, bm.

Searcy, William B. & Martha Flinn, 20 Oct 1832; Paul Flynn, bm.

Searsey, Adam Hampton & Tinsey Nanny, 29 Mar 1851; John W. Norvill, bm; m 30 Mar 1851 by T. B. Justice.

Searsey, David & Betsey Spivy, 12 Jan 1804; Richard Searsey, bm.

Searsey, Robert & Polly Spivey, 13 Oct 1802; John Dalton, bm.

Searsy, David & Anna Ownby, 4 Oct 1821; Robert Hills, bm.

Searsy, Elijah & Rebecca An Pack, 25 Sept 1845; Riley Dimsdale, bm.

Sebastian, Edmund & Mary P. Ledbetter, 24 Jan 1829; Jonathan Ledbetter, bm.

Sebastian, Edmund & Mary Ann Whitesides, 12 Apr 1837; William H. Miller, bm.

Selby, Joseph & Maryan Moore, 2 Jun 1850; Peter A. Carpenter, bm.

Self, Ligaah & Poley Bumgarner, 20 Oct 1807; Edward Towney, Nathanl White, bm.

Sellers, Elijah & Polly Campbell, 17 Apr 1809; Robt. Campbell, bm.

Sellers, Jacob & Anna Scott, 29 Jul 1800; Isac Selers, bm.

Sellers, John & Polly McGaughy, 13 Apr 1820; Jno. Clarke, bm.

Sercy, David & Jesten Dalton, 23 Jul 1801; John Dalton, bm.

Settle, Benjamin & Ann Lee, 3 Jan 1799; Geo. Settle, bm.

Settle, Isaac Jr. & Anny Craigg, 8 May 1812; Bush Settle, bm.

Settle, Wm. & Jean Terrell, 21 Oct ____; Bushard Settle, bm.

Settles, Joseph & Mrs. Ann Crawford, 11 Dec 1809; John Elm, bm.

Shannon, James & Bekey Commins, 16 Jul 1801; William McDaniel, Daniel McDaniel, bm.

Shaw, Bazzel & Susana Snider, 25 Jan 1809; Saml. Crawford, bm.

Shaw, Charles & Peggy Suttles, 4 Feb 1809; Bassil Shaw, bm.

Sheegog, Richard & Pegga Moore, 9 Jan 1821; Andly Hamilton, bm.

Shehan, James & Sarah Camp, 16 Apr 1854; Wm. Camp, bm.

Shehan, John & Rebecah Simmons, 28 Sept 1852; A. J. Hamilton, bm; m 28 Sept 1852 by J. M. Hamilton, J. P.

Shehan, T. W. & Julia Waren, 10 Apr 1861; James Waren, bm; m 11 Apr 1861 by H. Culbreath.

Shehane, Wm. & Sarah Jones, 19 Feb 1854; David Owens, bm; m 19 Feb 1854 by J. M. Hamilton, J. P.

Shelly, James F. & Mary Callihan, 16 Dec 1845; John Upchurch, bm.

Shemwell, William & Elizabeth Banter, 5 Jan 1836; Michael B. Freeman, bm.

Shepherd, James & Elisabeth Hill, 11 Sept 1788; John Lattimore, Jesse McGlamry, bm.

Sherly, Thomas & Betsey Deering, 7 Jun 1798; William Metcalf, bm.

Sherrell, Bedford & Elizabeth P. Harriss, 22 Nov 1837; James P. Foster, bm.

Sherry, John & Winney Horton, 10 Feb 1800; Edwin Horton, bm.

Shields, A. M. & H. L. Jones, 18 May 1859; Willie Green, bm; m 19 May 1859 by B. E. Rollins, M. G.

Shitle, E. A. & Elizabeth Padgett, 26 Feb 1866; Geo. Efler, bm; m 1 Mar 1866 byt J. R. Bowman, M. G.

Shitle, J. & Malisa Nailan, 23 Dec 1858; J. J. Bradley, bm; m 30 Dec 1858 by Wm. H. Logan, M. G.

Shop, David & Sarah Smith, 10 Sept 1846; A. J. Gilkey, bm.

Short, ____ & Ruelly Bracket, 14 Jul 1790; Sam Carpenter, bm.

Short, Abner & Rachel C. Short, 19 Jul 1863; J. T. Mode, bm; m 19 Jul 1863 by Wm. G. Mode, J. P.

Short, Daniel & Rebecca Smith, 3 Apr 1856; Benjaman Panther, bm; m 3 Apr 1856 by Wm. G. Mode, J. P.

Short, Joseph & Winney Goin, 23 Nov 1854; Andrew Hamilton, bm; m 23 Nov 1854 by Wm. G. Mode, J. P.

Short, W. H. & Susanah Queen, 14 Sept 1865; Aaron Devney, bm; m 14 Sept 1865 by A. Hunt, M. G.

Shotwell, Alexander H. & Jane Eliza McEntire, 3 Jul 1861; L. F. Churchill, bm; m 3 Jul 1861 by Nl. Shotwell, M. G.

Shuford, Jacob R. & Mrs. Malinda Tombs, 22 Jul 1845; D. J. Twitty, bm.

Shuford, Thomas R. & Esther Irvin, 12 Sept 1840; Wm. Twitty, bm.

Sieds, Henery & Barbara Whitlock, 26 Aug 1799; Joseph Carpenter, bm.

Sills, Jesse & Sally Taylor, 22 Nov 1831; Felix W. Deviney, bm.

Sills, John & Caroline Eaves, 16 Jun 1848; A. G. McEntire, bm.

Sills, Joseph & Melvinah Black, 10 Dec 1865; W. G. hicks, Martin Hicks, bm; m 10 Dec 1865 by A. Hunt, M. G.

Silva, Squire & Minerva Carpenter, 29 Apr 1835; Reuben Hill, bm.

Simmons, Charles & Didamia McKinney, 1 Feb 1807; Jesse Richardson, bm.

Simmons, Edward & Nancy Erwin, 22 Nov 1827; Richard L. Erwin, bm.

Simmons, Elisha & Mary Lowry, 30 Nov 1812; Edward Good, bm.

Simmons, James & Elizabeth J. Ramsour, 5 Feb 1831; Thomas Dews Jr., bm.

Simmons, James G. & Mirah Camp, 15 May 1849; B. T. Blanton, bm.

Simmons, John & Sarah Melton, 18 Apr 1848; J. V. Jay, bm.

Simmons, Moses & Mary Lewis, 18 Sept 1811; Chas. Lewis, bm.

Simmons, Squire S. & Elizebeth An Eskridge, 18 Aug 1840; Wm. L. Eskridge, bm.

Simons, James & Sally Lee Porter, 10 Apr 1827; Robert S. Porter, Beryman H. Durham, bm.

Simons, Joshua & Sally Lewis, 13 Sept 1813; Moses Simmons, bm.

Sims, Andrew H. & Mrs. Nancy Queen, 1 Mar 1831; Josiah Jones, bm.

Sims, James & Ibba or Obba Watson, 8 Mar 1819; William Morrison, bm.

Sims, James & Hannah Olavine McCurry, 7 Aug 1854; D. T. Melton, bm; m 8 Aug 1854 by James Baber.

Sims, Littleton & Hannah Mitchel, 31 Dec 1792; Robert Young, bm.

Sims, Littleton & Rachel Reid, 7 Dec 1827; Littleton S. Osburn, bm.

Sims, William R. & Sarah Ann Betts, 7 Jan 1835; Littleton S. Osborn, bm.

Sirret, William & Susannah Dobbins, 2 Jul 1812; James Dobbins, John Bridges, bm.

Sisk, John & Nancy Daves, 21 Apr 1859; A. J. Melton, bm; m by J. S. Grayson, J. P.

Sisk, Martin & Omey Allen, 16 Dec 1842; J. O. Crow, bm.

Sisk, Oliver & Jane Walker, 30 Nov 1858; John Watts, bm.

Sisk, Wm. & J. L. Burch, 15 Dec 1859; John Davis, bm; m 15 Dec 1859 by J. H. Grant, J. P.

Sison, Richard & Lucy Franklin, 3 Oct 1814; Timothy Hany, Francis Haney, bm.

Skipper, T. B. & Judy Ann Green, 17 Jul 1850; M. Wilkerson, bm.

Slade, Thomas L. & Susan Kenndy, 8 Mar 1830; W. Slade, bm.

Slagle, David & Judy Wadkins, 18 Feb 1824; John Nix, bm.

Sloan, John Jr. & Melinda Caruth, 14 Jul 1803; A. Carruth, bm.

Sloop, James C. & Levina Purkins, 30 May 1843; Daniel Michal, bm.

Sloop, John & Elizabeth Stott, 28 Oct 1844; H. W. Patterson, bm.

Smally, George & Jane Fleming, 20 Oct 1813; Wm. Fleming, bm.

Smart, Cornelius C. & Lurany Smiley, 13 Nov 1856; Elijah M. Huthens, bm; m 13 Nov 1856 by James M. Spratt, J. P.

Smart, D. P. & Priscilla Harrill, 14 Oct 1864; John Smart, bm; m 16 Oct 1864 by J. B. McDaniel, J. P.

Smart, Henry K. & Ann M. Guffy, 15 Dec 1853; B. W. Freeman, bm; m 15 Dec 1853 by John Freeman, J. P.

Smart, Hiram & Cidney B. Carson, 13 Mar 1822; John Carson, bm.

Smart, James & Nancy Scott, 8 Mar 1794; Lewis Tomerton Jr., bm.

Smart, John & Cereny Melton, 19 Dec 1835; Wm E. Mills, bm.

Smart, Joseph & Elizabeth Logan, 30 Apr 1809; William McBrayer, bm.

Smart, Joseph D. & Mary Ann Jones, 7 Aug 1846; Benjamin Brooks, bm.

Smart, L. H. & Emealy Warlick, m 6 Sept 1855 by James M. Spratt, J. P.

Smart, Reuben & Margaret Melton, 28 Dec 1833; Thomas Smart, bm.

Smart, Thomas & Rutha Heddlestone, 8 Nov 1788; James Guffey, bm.

Smart, Thomas & Peggy McDow, 15 Oct 1808; Joseph Smart, bm.

Smart, Thomas & Elizabeth Baldridge, 28 SEpt 1811; John Baldridge, bm.

Smart, Thomas & Peggy Flemming, 4 Feb 1822; James Huddleton, bm.

Smart, William & Peggy Clemmens, 5 Feb 1822; Joseph Clements, bm.

Smart, Wm. & Mary L. Hollifield, 10 Sept 1849; John Smart, bm.

Smart, William Jr. & Deida Burns, 9 Apr 1838; Thomas Smart, bm.

Smart, Wm. R. & Dida Burns, 28 Nov 1846; Drury Burns, bm.

Smart, Wm. R. & Margaret M. Melton, 17 May 1851; W. A. Tanner, bm.

Smawley, Joseph & Margaret Williams, 5 Nov 1850; John C. Halleburton, bm.

Smethers, Garnett & Susanna Dolton, 19 Feb 1788; William Balad, bm.

Smiley, Henry & Catharine Hutchens, 23 Jan 1845; Jesse Smily, bm.

Smiley, Jesse & Sarah Freeman, 14 Nov 1812; Dugger Freeman, bm.

Smiley, Jesse Madison & Anna Brindle, 3 Dec 1842; Jesse Smiley, bm.

Smith, C. D. & Sarah A. Vickers, 25 Jan 1848; J. M. Vickers, bm.

Smith, Clator & Mary Harrill, 5 Sept 1815; Charles Smith, James Bridges, bm.

Smith, D. L. & Naoma Ashworth, 2 Jan 1860; T. H. W. Whitesides, bm; m 2 Jan 1859 (sic) by James H. Whitesides, J. P.

Smith, D. M. & Margret Good, 23 Nov 1859; Willis Green, bm; m 24 Nov 1859 by T. B. Justice, M. G.

Smith, Daniel & Milly Hill, 30 Sept 1809; Charles Hill, bm.

Smith, E. M. & Rebecca C. Hunter, 8 Dec 1863; C. Burnett, bm; m 8 Dec 1863 by T. B. Justice.

Smith, Edmon & Mary Moorlan, 19 Sept 1797; John Roberts, bm.

Smith, Franklin & Lucinda Johnson, 10 Feb 1848; Wille M. Peele, bm.

Smith, Franklin & Jane Keeter, 2 Jul 1857; J. M. Keeter, bm; m 2 Jul 1857 by C. F. Townsend, J. P.

Smith, G. W. & Mary Hardin, 12 Nov 1859; Drury Dobbins, bm; m 13 Nov 1859 by Robert Poston.

Smith, George & Narcisser Keeter, 12 Dec 1850; John C. Keeter, bm.

Smith, Geo. & Linda Crook, 5 Jul 1855; Elbert Keeter, bm; m 5 Jul 1855 by John Koone.

Smith, Harmon & Rachel Waggoner, 10 Dec 1821; John Moreland, bm.

Smith, Hugh & Betsey Walker, 18 Jan 1805.

Smith, J. & Margaret Pack, 22 Dec 1846; A. Mills, bm.

Smith, J. W. & Sarah Spurlin, 21 Sept 1849; M. O. Dickerson, bm.

Smith, Jacob & Sarah Harden, 6 Sept 1796; Francis Beatey, bm.

Smith, Jacob & Nancy Haney, 12 Sept 1825; Ephraim Padget, bm.

Smith, Jacob & Emaine Win, 4 Aug 1854; John G. Smith, bm.

Smith, James & Nancy Cloud, 9 Apr 1809; G. M. Logan, bm.

Smith, James & Caroline Toney, 15 Jun 1820; Aaron Toney, bm.

Smith, James & Nancy Tomison, 17 Mar 1823; Israel Robertson, bm.

Smith, James & Sophia Foster, 20 May 1849; John Johnes(?), bm.

Smith, James J. & Polly M. Humphries, 22 Apr 1840; Thomas Smith, bm.

Smith, Joel & Winny Moss, 30 Mar 1807; John Willson, bm.

Smith, Joel & Liddia Braddy, 9 Dec 1812; Daniel Smith, Benjamin Davis, bm.

Smith, Joel & Lucinda Dobbinss, 16 Aug 1827; Jacob Smith, bm.

Smith, Joel & Easther Earby, 10 Aug 1830; Isham Blankinship, bm.

Smith, John & Rhoda Simmons, 16 Sept 1807; Wm. Smith, bm.

Smith, John & Elizabeth Haney, 31 Dec 1832; Ephraim Padget, bm.

Smith, John & Adaline Haynes, 26 Jul 1847; Joel Smith, bm.

Smith, John & Jane Geer, 7 Oct 1848; John H. Justis, bm.

Smith, John & Susan Keeter, 16 Nov 1856; Henry Nanny, bm; m 16 Nov 1856 by J. Gilkey, J. P.

Smith, John W. & Drisilla Butler, 13 Apr 1848; A. Durham, bm.

Smith, Joseph & Sally Johnson, ____; Robt. ___hran, bm.

Smith, Laban & Mira Head, 1 Feb 1832; John J. Williams, bm.

Smith, Lewis & Mary Wekel, 25 Oct 1791; George Painter, bm.

Smith, Mathew R. & Juely Roberson, 14 Feb 1843; Geo. W. Nix, bm.

Smith, Mines & Sarah Salmon, 5 Feb 1856; William Salmon, bm; m 5 Feb 1856 by J. A. Grant, J. P.

Smith, Oliver & Zilla Ledbetter, 29 Jan 1853; J. L. Ward, bm; m 3 Feb 1855 by M. Wilkerson, J. P.

Smith, Richard & Margaret Wood, 13 Feb 1839; John Tomberlin, bm.

Smith, Robert & Elizabeth Roberson, 16 Oct 1789; Walter Carson, bm.

Smith, Robert & Mary Griggs, 22 Nov 1804; John Roberts, bm.

Smith, Robert & Lucinda Pack, 8 Jun 1848; G. H. Wilkins, bm.

Smith, Samuel & Polly Wilson, 17 May 1832; Jas. Ward, Jr., bm.

Smith, Tarlton & Sally Robbins, 13 Apr 1798; Dan. Maddin, bm.

Smith, Thomas & Sarah Gray, 11 Jul 1839; Micajah Hall, bm.

Smith, Walton & Catharine Wilkie, 23 Feb 1835; Jacob Smith, bm.

Smith, William & Hannah Cole, 17 Mar 1789; David Cole, bm.

Smith, Wm & Mrs. Rachel Lademouer, 29 Sept 1793; Thomas Storkton, bm.

Smith, William & Narcissa Scoggin, 4 Apr 1844; R. Scoggin, bm.

Smith, William & Mary A. Prather, 19 Sept 1850; Wm. C. Prather, bm.

Smith, William & Susanah Hicks, 29 Dec 1866; J. G. C. Deviney, bm; m 19 Dec 1866 by A. Hunt.

Smith, William Jr. & Betsy Byars, 13 Nov 1827; Noah Sullins, bm.

Smith, William B. & Elender Hoyle, 7 Feb 1850; Gabriel Revels, bm.

Smith, William J. & Elsabeth Moris, 9 Jan 1820; David Allen, Henry Burnett, bm.

Smith, William S. & Sarah Burge, 3 Feb 1803; Other Smith, David Burge, bm.

Smith, Woody B. & Elizabeth Johnston, 17 Jun 1827; James M. Arthur, bm.

Smith, Zachery & Rachel Humphreys, 10 Jan 1838; Isaac Harris, bm.

Smith, Zechariah & Elizabeth Harris, 21 Mar 1822; Benjamin Keeter, bm.

Snider, George & Nancey Cooper, 4 Oct 1796; John Cooper, William Mayohu, bm.

Snider, J. B. & Nancy McMahan, 11 Nov 1852; James A. Stedman, bm; m 11 Nov 1851 by Alanson Padgett, M. G.

Snowden, Thomas & Barzilla Pruit, 23 Dec 1849; William Splawn, bm.

Sorrels, Henry R. & Martha L. Jones, 30 May 1859; James H. Sorrels, bm; m 30 May 1859 by W. A. Tanner.

Sorrels, Israel & Mary Whitaker, 16 Apr 1832; Thomas Green, bm.

Sorrels, J. C. & Emly Lewis, 14 Dec 1866; Amos Hamrick, bm; m 16 Dec 1866 by W. H. Logan, Elder.

Sorrels, J. P. & Eliza J. Wallace, 30 Sept 1858; L. F. Sorrels, bm; m 30 Sept 1858 by T. B. Justice.

Sorrels, James & Matilda Hunter, 22 Jan 1822; Wilson Moore, bm.

Sorrels, John & Prissilla Debord, 14 Jan 1818; Wm. Hunter, bm.

Sorrels, Walter & Rebekah Bates, 4 Jul 1796; Wilam Mitchel, bm.

Sorrels, Walter & Nancy Hill, 28 May 1799; Zadock Hills, bm.

Sorrels, Walter & Marey Bankston, 28 Sept 1844; J. C. Gilkey, bm.

Spake, G. W. & Emeline Watkins, 18 Jan 1867; George Spake, bm; m 24 Jan 1867 by B. Bonner, M. G.

Spann, James & Mary Bird, 2 Jun 1828; Anthony Dickey, bm.

Spann, William & Hanna Flack, 6 Apr 1796; James Morris, bm.

Spann, William Jr. & Matilda Picket, 25 Nov 1827; Isaac Craton, bm.

Spark, Calvin J. & Dulceney Culbreth, 3 Feb 1842; R. Champion, bm.

Sparks, C. L. & E. A. Watson, 29 Oct 1866; A. H. Bradley, bm.

Sparks, J. L. & M. A. Mince, 14 Apr 1859; Andrew Owens, bm.

Sparks, Lewis M. & Sarah Bridges, 28 Nov 1837; John Bridges, bm.

Sparks, W. A. & Martha L. Bedford, 29 Aug 1866; M. L. Wells, bm; m 6i Sept 1866 by B. B. Byers, J. P.

Sperlin, Jonathan & Rebecca Smith, 8 Feb 1835; Gabrel Butts, bm.

Spicer, Clabourn & Jane Graham, 20 Mar 1851; Eli Arledge, bm.

Spicer, James & Martha Barfield, 2 Sept 1837; Aaron W. Whiteside, bm.

Splaawn, Stephen D. & Arminta C. Lancater, 2 Jul 1839; Philip Robbins Jr., bm.

Splawn, Nathan & Susannah McDaniel, 24 Jul 1829; Reuben McDaniel, bm.

Splawn, William & Susannah Cole, 8 Mar 1841; Philip Robbins, bm.

Splawn, Wm. & Jane Waldroup, 31 Dec 1850; Ransom Ponds, bm.

Splawn, William Jr. & Jane Waldroup, 8 Jun 1840; William Splawn Sr., bm.

Sprat, William & Mary Sterling, 26 Jul 1819; Wm. A. Bell, bm.

Spratt, A. A. & Martha Cochran, 9 Jan 1865; B. R. Morrison, bm.

Spratt, Andrew & Elizabeth E. Guffey, 29 Mar 1838; George M. Reid, bm.

Spratt, James M. & Jane Erwin, 17 Sept 1849; James W. Alley, bm.

Spratt, S. L. & S. J. Andrews, 29 Jul 1861; J. R. Cochran, bm; m 30 Jul 1861 by Jas. M. Spratt.

Spruel, John & Elisabeth Jones, 9 Oct 1794; Joseph Grayson, bm.

Spurlin, Clater & Malinda Edards, 6 Mar 1840; John B. Miller, bm.

Spurlin, Hicks & Debby C. Bankston, 17 Sept 1819; Ricahrd Scogin, Andrew Bankston, bm.

Spurlin, Isaac & Jane Weaver, 4 Aug 1832; David Hamrick, bm.

Spurlin, Isaac J. & Belinda Lookadoo, 7 Mar 1844; Jesse Lookadoo, bm.

Spurlin, Mathew & Nancy Smith, 18 Feb 1821; Street Harrill, Alexander Bealey, bm.

Spurlin, W. S. & Nancy Melton, 25 Dec 1863; C. W. Spurlin, bm; m 26 Dec 1863 by D. Ponnell.

Stafford, Nimrod & Sarah Wallis, 23 Oct 1832; Joseph S. Wallis, bm.

Stafford, R. E. & Sarah Cochran, 19 Mar 1866; John A. Morrison, bm; m 22 Mar 1866 by B. W. Andrews, J. P.

Stafford, Robert T. & Polly Hutchins, 13 Jul 1828; Alexander Hill, bm.

Stafford, Stephen L. & Lucinda Long, 28 Dec 1836; James T. Long, bm.

Stallings, Samuel & Margret Lackey, 18 Dec 1834; William Wray, bm.

Staten, Reuben & Katy Laughter, 23 Jul 1824; Joel Wood, bm.

Staton, Anderson & Sally Tart, 23 Dec 1822; Elias McFadin, bm.

Staton, James & Mrs. Jane Staten, 18 May 1825; Jonathan Tart, bm.

Staton, John W. & Mary Thompson, 6 Jan 1818; Jos Cloud, bm.

Staton, Samuel & Mary Rhodes, 13 May 1828; Anderson R. Staton, bm.

Stedman, James A. & Martha Culbreath, 29 Apr 1836; Edward Culbreath, bm.

Steedman, Townson W. & Hanah Hunt, 14 Dec 1853; A. C. Martin, bm; m 14 Dec 1853 by Wm. G. Mode, J. P.

Steel, Abraham & Francis Taylor, 5 Jan 1801; Joshua Taylor, bm.

Steel, Abraham & Nancy Alfred, 1 Nov 1820; James Bradly, bm.

Steel, John & Nancy Brown, 9 Apr 1797.

Steel, Robt. J. & Polly Parish, 1 Jul 1816; Ch. Daniel, bm.

Stein, G. H. & M. L. Hayden, 19 Oct 1861; Thos. C. Smith, bm; m 22 Oct 1861 by A. Hamby, Elder.

Stenett, Dabner & Betsey Owens, 8 Jul 1809; John Owens, bm.

Stephens, Wm. H. & Nancy Sorrels, 8 Sept 1844; T. F. Edwards, bm.

Sterlin, John & Elizabeth Marshell, 17 Sept 179-; James Thompson, George Watson, bm.

Stevens, Thomas B. & Sally Polly, 20 Mar 1827; Aaron D. McFarland, bm.

Stewart, Aaron & Rachel Bracket, _____; R. Gilkey, clk, wit.

Stewart, John H. & Elizabeth Ann Diviny, 8 Sept 1961; K. J. McCrow, bm; m 8 Sept 1861 by Wm. G. Mode, J. P.

Stice, Charles & Peggy Nettles, 17 Feb 1807; Philip Stice, bm.

Stice, Wiliam & Polly Nittles, 18 Jul 1818; Charles Stice, bm.

Stockton, Davis & Malinda Callihan, 13 Sept 1830; Samuel Wallis, bm.

Stokes, John & Jane Dowdle, 13 Feb 1843; J. E. Perkins, bm.

Stoner, Henry & Elizabeth Wilson, 13 Apr 1799; William Willson, Thomas Thompson, bm.

Stoner, John & Reachel Collins, ___; Micajah Cornwell, John McEntire, bm.

Stot, A. H. & Catharine Green, 13 Dec 1842; Noah Whiteside, bm.

Stott, William E. & Elizabeth Wesson, 12 Oct 1798; J. Miller, Thos. ___, bm.

Stover, John & Sally Waller, 1 Jun 1816; Jacob Stover, bm.

Street, John & Elizabeth Smith, 25 Nov 1848; David Walker, bm.

Street, Noah W. & Elizabeth Walker, 14 Nov 1831; Jesse Richson Walker, bm.

Street, William & Rachael Murry, 22 Mar 1841; J. Malton, bm.

Street, William F. & C. A. Ensley, 30 Jan 1864; Jesse R. Street, bm; m 4 Feb 1864 by Jas. M. Spratt, J. P.

Strickland, Julius & Cathrine Hesters, 24 Feb 1817; Isaac Craton, bm.

Stroud, James & Any Morgan, 20 Feb 1840; Abner Morgan, bm.

Stroud, Thomas & Marry Evens, 22 May 1818; Elijah Reynold, bm.

Stuart, William & Betsey Deviney, 29 Jan 1811; Robert Deviny, bm.

Sturd, Aaran & Rachel Bracket, 19 Jun 1853; Jab. Panther, bm; m 19 Jun 1853 by Wm. G. Mode, J. P.

Sullins, A. W. & Susen Hannon, 24 Oct 1847; Jos. C. Daniel, bm.

Sullins, Jesse & Katharine Eaves, 27 Jan 1825; Guilford Eaves, bm.

Sullins, Josiah & Nancy Davis, 27 Mar 1823; John Flinn, bm.

Sullins, Noah & Milly Byars, 8 Nov 1827; Bartlet Hale, bm.

Sullivan, J. M. & S. C. Padgett, 8 Aug 1866; J. B. Eaves, bm; m 9 Aug 1866 by G. M. Webb.

Summers, James M. & Catharine Kerr, 20 Dec 1861; John Shinn, bm; m 20 Dec 1861 by Wm. Devenport.

Surcy, Anderson & Jane Williams, 26 Jan 1867; Wilely Whitesides, bm; m 31 Jan 1867 by Wm. Flinn, J. P.

Surcy, Wm. & Martha Huggins, 10 Jan 1866; Geo. Hall, bm; m 11 Jan 1866 by T. H. W. Whiteside, J. P.

Suttle, Benjamin F. & Sarah Baxter, 19 Sept 1821; Lewis Camp, bm.

Suttle, George & Franky Taylor, 17 Jun 1830; George Purden Hay, bm.

Suttle, Isaac & Cintha Laughter, 28 Nov 1839; Jonathan Ownby, bm.

Suttle, James W. & Catharine Moore, 7 Jun 1859; Elias Carrier, bm; m 9 Jun 1859 by Wm. Harrill, Elder.

Suttle, John & Susana Hargess, 12 Feb 1808; Bushrod Suttle, bm.

Suttle, John M. & Charlotte M. Miller, 9 Nov 1853; George M. Suttle, bm.

Suttle, John R. & Jane Young, 7 Sept 1836; Thomas McKinney, bm.

Suttle, Joseph & Mary W. McKennie, 1 Apr 1823; Alfred McKiney, bm.

Suttle, Joseph & Mary Ann Smith, 5 Mar 1846; John Smith, bm.

Suttle, Joseph & Eliza Camp, 20 May 1856; John P. Eaves, bm.

Suttle, Robert & Charity Shaw, 30 Jan 1809; Mark Suttle, bm.

Suttle, Robert & Jane Smith, 22 Jun 1861; A. W. Harril, bm; m 23 Jun 1861 by C. Burnett, J. P.

Suttle, W. B. & Marey King, 4 Nov 1858; L. P. McBrayer, bm.

Suttles, Evan & Linda Johnson, 30 Jan 1840; Hiram Dunkin, bm.

Suttles, J. H. & Mary C. Hicks, 10 Jun 1864; Joseph Sills, bm; m 12 Jun 1864 by A. Hunt, M. G.

Suttles, William & Tempey McDaniel, m 1 Sept 1867 by J. W. Morgan, J. P.

Sutton, Coalby & Milly Sutton, 25 Jan 1805; James Sutton, bm.

Sutton, Edmond & Rebecca Grizzle, 30 Dec 1824; Aaron Butler, bm.

Sutton, Elias R. & Mary J. Henson, 6 Dec 1856; J. G. Henson, bm; m 6 Dec 1856 by Jas. H. Carpenter, J. P.

Sutton, James & Elender Johnson, 2 Aug 1841; Issac Suttles, bm.

Sutton, John & Mary Hinson, 6 May 1793.

Sutton, John Jr. & Elizabeth Craigg, 7 Aug 1815; William Sutton, bm.

Sutton, Marvill & Sally Davis, 20 Feb 1829; William Sutton Jr., bm.

Sutton, Middlton & Easter Painter, 27 Apr 1821; Noah Hampton, bm.

Sutton, Powell & Rhoda Taylor, 11 Nov 1823; Edmund Sutton, bm.

Sutton, Robert & Polly Sutton, 9 Jan 1812; Drury King, bm.

Sutton, William & Nancey King, 1 Oct 1807; Abraham Whilmoth, bm.

Sutton, William & Mary Doggett, 11 Jan 1821; Robt. Sutton, bm.

Sutton, William & Polly Adkins, 23 Apr 1829; Marvill Sutton, bm.

Swafford, John H. & Edy Prewitt, 12 Jan 1835; William Swafford, bm.

Swafford, Joseph W. & Susanah Pruit, 1 Mar 1839; John B. Garner, bm.

Swafford, William & Elizabeth Hyles, 2 Oct 1800; John Sides, bm.

Swanson, W. B. & Eliza J. Cornwell, 28 May 1849; J. W. Hampton, bm.

Sweadon, Robert & Rebkah Covington, 28 Feb 1792; Jas. Crawford, bm.

Sweany, Daniel & Jane McClure, 13 Apr 1787; James Gray, bm.

Sweesy, J. B. & Sinthy Earls, 25 Jan 1859; J. W. Sweezy, bm; m 25 Jan 1859 by John Freeman.

Sweezy, Elijah & Afa Chitwood, 23 Jun 1818; James Chitwood, bm.

Sweezy, J. W. & Margaret A. Gettys, 11 Aug 1860; Joseph P. Green, bm; m 15 Aug 1860 by G. W. Rollins, Elder.

Sweezy, James H. & Jinsey B. Calton, 29 Oct 1839; John Sweezy, bm.

Sweezy, John M. & Liddy Williams, 10 Jan 1854; G. W. Deck, bm.

Sweezy, William G. & Nancy Norville, 22 Apr 1844; T. B. Calton, bm.

Swezey, Alfred H. & Nancy P. Horten, 3 Aug 1852; Spencer Eaves, bm.

Swezey, John & Shusanah Lyles, 21 Nov 180-; Jas. Withrow, bm.

Swink, John & Mary Smith, 17 Sept 1795; William Qeen, Joseph Culin, bm.

Taber, William & Mira Taylor, 13 Nov 1826; William Scott, bm.

Tabor, John & Mary Allen, 14 Jul 1797.

Tabor, John Jr. & Agness Justice, 16 Apr 1788; John Tabor Sr., bm.

Tabor, Jonathan & Elizabeth Hix, 12 Sept 1791; John Tabor, bm.

Tailor, John & Susanna Vickory, 12 Oct 1795; John Wilson, bm.

Taner, William A. & Nancy But, 28 Jan 1836; Charles Blanton, bm.

Tanner, Andrew & Susan Depriest, 29 Oct 1831; Isham Wood, bm.

Tanner, Daniel & Elizabeth Ross, 3 Apr 1793; Michl. Tanner, bm.

Tanner, George & Elizabeth Wood, 7 Apr 1821; Daniel Tanner, bm.

Tanner, George W. & Martha Carpenter, 5 Nov 1838; Jacob D. Carpenter, bm.

Tanner, James & Elizabeth Hudlow, 1 Oct 1832; James V. Jay, bm.

Tanner, Mickael & Catharine Braddy, 20 Oct 1821; George S. Williams, bm.

Tart, Jonathan & Milinda Morris, 27 Mar 1828; Thomas Morris, bm.

Tate, Asa & Milly Ann Carpenter, 24 Dec 1839; John G. Lee, bm.

Tate, David & Nancy Blanton, 22 Oct 1802; Robert McClanon, bm.

Tate, David & Jane Neal, 6 May 1841; J. H. Carpenter, bm.

Tate, Henry P. & Susanah Logan, 1 Sept 1838; James Jolley, bm.

Tate, James M. & Elizabeth Goode, 3 May 1837; M. R. Alexander, bm.

Tate, Jesse & Naney Scruggs, 29 Oct 1835; William Kandey, Robert Scruggs, bm.

Tate, Thomas & Sarah Jane Jolly, 24 Oct 1865; M. O. Dickerson, bm; m 25 Oct 1865 by D. Ponnell, M. G.

Tayler, William & Nancy Carter, 21 Nov 1840; Jesse Sills, bm.

Taylor, Charles & Elizabeth Potts, 5 May 1788.

Taylor, David M. & Almina Halford, 11 May 1865; J. L. Williams, bm.

Taylor, Elias L. & Harriet P. Edwards, 16 Feb 1841; J. McEntire, bm.

Taylor, James & Patsy Ballard, 29 Oct 1852; Dilliad Crawford, bm; m 4 Nov 1852 by Alanson Padgett, M. G.

Taylor, James & Sarah Martin, 4 Jan 1857; Jackson Robbins, bm; m 4 Jan 1857 by J. H. Carpenter, J. P.

Taylor, James L. & Eliza E. Kilpatrick, 12 Feb 1835; Martin Beam, bm.

Taylor, James M. & Sallie A. McKinny, 11 Oct 1865; J. L. Rucker, bm; m 12 Oct 1865 by A. Hamby, Elder.

Taylor, Jason J. & Jane Elizabeth McFadden, 7 Jun 1860; Henry M. Miller, bm; m 21 Jun 1860 by A. Hamby, Elder.

Taylor, Jeremh. & Eliza King, 17 Sept 1798.

Taylor, Jesse & Sarah Henson, 13 Jan 1812.

Taylor, John & Peggy Early, 25 Nov 1806; Robert Taylor, bm.

Taylor, John H. & Susan Flinn, m 9 Oct 1859 by Wm. Harrill, M. G.

Taylor, Joseph & Elizabeth Hunt, 25 Jul 1816; Green Crow, bm.

Taylor, Joseph & Rhoda Elliott, 25 Dec 1838; Charles Dunkin, bm.

Taylor, Lewis & Wincey Collins, 24 Apr 1799; Isaac Cloud, bm.

Taylor, McEntire & Betsey Sutton 8 Aug 1825; Powell Sutton, bm.

Taylor, Miller E. & Mary Keeter, 25 Mar 1832; John Bradly, bm.

Taylor, O. P., son of Joshua Taylor, & Martha Good, daughter of James Good, 12 Oct 1867; m 17 Oct 1867 by E. L. Tagler, M. G. (C. H.)

Taylor, Robert & Martha Patterson, 13 Aug 1801; Stephen Willis, bm.

Taylor, Robert L. & E. A. Whiteside, 8 Aug 1863; M. H. Kilpatrick, bm.

Taylor, Wm. & Martha McCurry, 12 Nov 1857; John A. McFarland, bm; m 12 Nov 1857 by Wm. G. Mode, J. P.

Taylor, Wm. K. & Marry Payne, 15 Feb 1837; Nathaniel Payne, bm.

Taylor, Williamson W. & Sarah Twitty, 19 Jan 1852; Wm. L. Griffin, bm; m 23 Jan 1852 by A. Hamby, M. G.

Teal, John & Elizabeth Davis, 9 Nov 1829; George Davis, bm.

Teal, John & Dicy Owen, 10 May 1841; Archibald Cady, bm.

Teal, Samuel & Polly Wilkerson, 11 Jan 1819; William Depreast, bm.

Teal, W. & J. Elizabeth Moony, 3 Jan 1867; P. A. Parden, bm; m 3 Jan 1866 (sic) by G. W. Rollins.

Teal, William & Mary Wilkerson, 14 Nov 1831; Amos Randall, bm.

Terrell, Buffon D. & Martha McFaddin, 12 Oct 1830; John Baber, bm.

Terrell, James & ____, 17 Jul 1803; Benjn. Hawkins, Frances Alexander, bm.

Terrell, James O. & Ermyna R. Kilpatrick, 25 Jan 1829; Arthur Erwin, bm.

Teseniear, J. A. & R. C. Brooks, 11 Sept 1865; B. N. R. Glover, bm; m 12 Sept 1865 by John McFarland, J. P.

Tesenyear, Nickolas & Elizabeth Blanton, 10 Oct 1863; A. Harrill, bm; m 11 Oct 1863 by R. Depriest.

Tessenner, David & Sarah Brooks, 17 Nov 1846; N. Tessenner, bm.

Tessennier, Jos. & Cindrilla Brooks, 19 Nov 1846; Drury Green, bm.

Tessenyear, Nicholas & Lucy Lawson, 26 Jan 1825; Anderson Womack, bm.

Tessenyear, William & Rhoda Green, 7 Oct 1834; Nicholas Tesssenyar, bm.

Thogmorton, Reubin & Theby Clark, 25 Aug 1828; Benjamin Clark, bm.

Thomas, Aaron & Sarah Silvy, 29 Dec 1797; William Silvey, bm.

Thomas, George & Fannier Fortenberry, 7 Mar 1822; John Baber, bm.

Thomas, James & Mary Morris, 8 Oct 1793; John Buyers, bm.

Thomas, James & Polly Johnson, 29 Jul 1812; Edward Cook, bm.

Thomas, James & Sarah Wilson, 25 Aug 1860; Jonthan Dalton, bm; m 25 Aug 1860 by M. Wilkerson, J. P.

Thomas, James H. & Polly Miry Bradley, 6 Aug 1859; Noah Jolly, bm; m 6 Aug 1859 by J. W. Morgan, J. P.

Thomas, Joseph & Valentine Jenkins, 29 Dec 1784.

Thomas, Peter & Patsey Stice, 20 Nov 1820; Philip Stice, bm.

Thomas, Samuel & Rachel Hampton, 22 Jul 1794; Benjamin Hampton, bm.

Thomas, Thomas & Hanah March, 10 Jun 1819; Aaron Thomas, bm.

Thomason, William & Willey Smith, 20 May 1820; John Whitaker, bm.

Thompson, Butler & Mary Jones, 21 Dec 1845; L. B. Bryan, bm.

Thompson, Edward & _____ Sorrels, 19 Feb 1791; Richd. Beales, bm.

Thompson, Gideon & Nancy Nix, _____.

Thompson, Gideon & Mary Green, 9 Dec 1840; Jackson King, bm.

Thompson, Hosa H. & Rebeca Colbart, 18 Apr 1847; James Culbreath, bm.

Thompson, John & Elizabeth Culbreath, 15 Jan 1844; Joab Willkie, bm.

Thompson, Martin & Katharine Waldrop, 14 Jun 1823; Edmond Waldrop, bm.

Thompson, Nelson & Rosannah Fletcher, 9 Feb 1821; Josiah Sullins, bm.

Thompson, Robert & Matilda Lankford, 17 Oct 1813; Alexr. Carruth, bm.

Thompson, Samuel & Jane Wilmoth, 23 Jan 1818; Jehaida Thompson, bm.

Thompson, Thomas & Philadelpia Willson, 29 Jan 1789; John Reed Thompson, William Lusk, bm.

Thompson, Wm. & Mrs. Nancy Henderson, 17 May 1818; G. M. Logan, bm.

Thompson, William & Polly Dalton, 11 May 1823; Robert McAfee, bm.

Thompson, William & Elizabethg Dicus, 11 Aug 1826; Robert K. Wilson, bm.

Thompson, William N. & Irene Atkin, 21 Oct 1866; J. L. S. McCurry, bm; m 21 Oct 1866 by J. S. Grayson.

Thomson, Peter & Hanna Riggs, 21 Jan 1794; Reuben Riggs, bm.

Thomson, Richard & Polly Hopson, 8 Nov 1802.

Thomson, Solomon & Rachel Dalton, 8 Sept 1849; R. O. Ledbetter, bm.

Thornbury, Peter & Nancy Earwood, 26 Dec 1837; Robert Jones Jr., bm.

Throgmorton, Diabray & Agness Clarke, 26 Feb 1828l Benjamin Clark, bm.

Tillinghast, Jno. H. & Sarah J. Wilkins, 17 Oct 1865; T. B. Twitty, bm.

Tilton, N. H. & Mary Morres, 25 Apr 1845; Thos. Egerton, bm.

Timmons, William & Hanc Culen, 18 Dec 1794; Joseph Cullin, bm.

Tissennear, Alfred & Missiner Turner, 23 Apr 1865; Elias Albright, bm. (C. H.)

Todd, John & Mary Baxter, 21 Sept 1825; Thomas Baxter, bm.

Tomberlin, Benjamin & Mary Ann McHann, 21 Dec 1833; James Grant, bm.

Tomberlin, Edmon & Jane Smart, 5 Sept 1791; Joseph Patterson, bm.

Tomberlin, Freeman & Nancy Mullins, 26 Feb 1791; Chalres Grant, bm.

Tomberlin, George & Nancy McHan, 6 Jul 1845; John Tomberlin, bm.

Tomberlin, George J. & Mary Haynes, 14 Jan 1859; Irvin Humpherys, bm.

Tomberlin, John & Mary A. Carson, 5 Jan 1859; Wm. L. Ensley, bm; m 6 Jan 1859 by Jas. M. Spratt.

Tomberlin, S. M. & Nancy Hill, 22 Dec 1865; J. H. Tomberlin, bm; m 25 Dec 1865 by W. H. Logan, Elder.

Tomberlin, William & Francis Scott, 24 Dec 1829; Geo. Washington Hill, bm.

Tombolin, Andrew & Polly Keeter, 27 Feb 1834; Samuel White, bm.

Tombolin, John & Elizabeth Hampton, 23 Dec 1820; Elias Upchurch, bm.

Tomerlin, Freeman & Rhoda Daugherty, 6 Dec 1796; William Ballard, bm.

Tomerlin, Lewis & Jane Driskal, ____ 1795; John Guffy, bm.

Toms, Edward & Sarah Baber, 25 Nov 1834; James Goode, bm.

Toms, Edward & Jane Kerr, 26 Nov 1844; Thomas Kerr, bm.

Toms, Rodney & Malena Webb, 6 Jan 1842; Edward Toms, bm.

Toms, Thomas & Minerva Taylor, 7 Aug 1844; James Goode, bm.

Toms, William & Purmila Toms, 27 May 1822; William Baxter, bm.

Toms, William & Jane Carson, 11 Feb 1839; James Goode, bm.

Toney, Abraham & Martha Jenkins, 12 May 1840; Joshua Toney, bm.

Toney, Albert & Elizabeth Horten, 14 Feb 1853; Draper Toney, bm.

Toney, Benjm. B. & C. M. Marlow, 20 Dec 1845; Merion Koone, bm.

Toney, Draper & Cecil D. Murry, 29 Oct 1849; Samuel L. Whiteside, bm.

Toney, Draper & Hulday L. Lookadoo, 21 May 1857; G. W. Freeman, bm; m 27 May 1857 by B. E. Rollins.

Toney, F. M. & Sarah D. McFarland, 20 Sept 1853; W. H. Gettys, bm; m 21 Sept 1853 by John Freeman, J. P.

Toney, G. W. & Mary Gettys, 31 Jan 1846; W. H. Gettys, bm.

Toney, G. W. & Jane Green, 8 Nov 1860; C. H. Yelton, bm.

Toney, Henry A. & Ailsey Sweezy, 12 Feb 1838; Samuel Biggerstaff, bm.

Toney, James & Margaret L. McCurry, 3 Apr 1838; Samuel Biggerstaff, bm.

Toney, Jefferson & Masse E. Murry, 6 Jan 1851; S. L. Whiteside, bm.

Toney, John P. & Manday Biggerstaff, 4 Apr 1857; Drpaer Toney, bm; m 9 Apr 1857 by John Freeman, J. P.

Toney, Joshua & Mary Mooney, 8 Nov 1829; Solomon Mooney, bm.

Toney, Thomas & Jane Rogers, 15 Jan 1818; Aaron Toney, George Dimsdale, bm.

Toney, Thomas D. & Parasade Lookadoo, 5 Feb 1865; S. P. Biggerstaff, bm; m 5 Feb 1865 by J. W. Murray.

Toney, William & Jane Benson, 15 Jan 1803.

Tony, Garret & Jincy Conner, 10 Apr 1821; John Bradly, bm.

Torrance, E. B. & E. B. Wells, 18 Jan 1840; T. M. Hardin, bm.

Towery, Martin S. & Inthy T. Early, 20 Sept 1853; John D. McCurry, bm; m 20 Sept 1863 by Williamson Fortune, J. P.

Townsend, C. F. & Martha L. Cochran, 24 Feb 1852; Elias Carrier, bm.

Towrey, Levy & Elisabeth Taylor, 13 Feb 1823; Adam Towrey, bm.

Towry, A. H. & Mary Price, 20 Aug 1866; John Deveny, bm; m 20 Aug 1866 by A. Hunt, M. G.

Towry, George & Catharine Bedford, 13 Apr 1818; Adam Towry, bm.

Towry, Isaac & Rebecky Brinkle, 22 Nov 1836; Henry Brandal, bm.

Treadwell, Temmons L. & Eliza Allison, _____ 1826; Hugh Quin, bm.

Trexler, Adam & Evaline M. Bennick, 3 Nov 1851; A. C. McEntire, bm.

Trout, George W. & Willey Doggett, 14 Jan 1830; Buffon D. Terrell, bm.

Truelove, James & Katharine Painter, 18 Feb 1804; George Painter, bm.

Turner, Elias & Marray Wils, _____ 1802; Edward Dikins, Andrew Hyles, bm.

Turner, Elijah & Francis Moore, 11 Feb 1846; Wm. Wilkins, bm.

Turner, Samuel Jr. & Patiance Edwards, 18 Dec 1801; Matthathas Turner, Samuel Turner Sr., bm.

Turpin, Obediah & Jane McDow, 8 Dec 1794; Thos. Camp, bm.

Twigs, Timothy & Joicy Wilass, 8 Apr 1793; William Qeen, bm.

Twitty, Allen & Martha Miller, 27 Feb 1787; Nathan Gooch, bm.

Twitty, Jackson & Eliza Gross, m 14 Feb 1867 by V. Micheal.

Twitty, Jackson & Eliza Gross, 14 Feb 1867; Wm S. Guthrie, bm; m 8 March 1867 by John Davis, J. P. (C. H.)

Twitty, John R. & Elizabeth Wilken, 9 Nov 1819; Wm. Graham, bm.

Twitty, Lafayette & Clarisa A. Mitchell, 16 May 1853; A. Hamby bm.

Twitty, Robert G. & Mary W. Logan, 12 Jun 1832; O. B. Irvine, bm.

Twitty, Russel & Polly Mills, 3 Nov 1790.

Twitty, W. L. & Sarah D. Miller, 31 Dec 1861; Jas. A. Miller, bm; m 31 Dec 1861 by Nl. Shotwell, M. G.

Twitty, Wade (colored) & Betty Miller, 1 Nov 1866; J. W. Clarke, bm.

Umphis, J. Philip & Rebecca Parrish, 15 Mar 1859; A. B. Bradley, bm; m 15 Mar 1859 by James H. Whiteside, J. P.

Upchurch, Adam & Betsy Freeman, 17 Apr 1824; John Freeman, bm.

Upchurch, Daniel & Adaline Egerton, 4 Jan 1861; Josep Upchurch, bm; m 6 Jan 1861 by T. G. Hawkins, J. P.

Upchurch, Elias & Anne Campbell, 14 Feb 1821; John Tomberlin, bm.

Upchurch, James & Nancy Bradly, 29 Dec 1804; Joseph Upchurch, bm.

Upchurch, Josep & Mary Moode, 4 Jan 1861; Daniel upchurch, bm; m 10 Jan 1861 by T. G. Hawkins, J. P.

Upchurch, Jos. & Patsy Bradly, 21 Jul 1804; Abram McKinny, bm.

Upchurch, Sherwood & Elizabeth Tomberlinson, 21 Oct 1790; George C. Poindexter, bm.

Upchurch, Sherwood & Polly Pell, 2 Jan 1804.

Upchurch, William & A. M. Harden, 24 Dec 1858; Wm. L. Davis, bm; m 24 Dec 1858 by B. E. Rollins.

Uptergrove, William & Nancy McMurry, 8 Apr 1799; James McMurry, bm.

Upton, Boyed & Margaret Jonson, 10 Sept 1856; William Sisk, bm; m 10 Sept 1856 by J. N. Biggerstaff, J. P.

Upton, E. & J. E. Whisanant, 4 Oct 1865; E. D. Melton, bm.

Upton, Edward & Susanah Blankenship, 26 Dec 1860; F. Y. Hicks, bm; m 26 Dec 1860 by B. E. Rollins, M. G.

Upton, Thomas & Rueth Hambee, 20 Aug 1789; Wm. Queen, Wm. Monroe, bm.

Upton, Thos. E. & Nancy Morris, 16 Sept 1830; Albert F. Forney, bm.

Vance, Davis & Nancy Davis, 16 Jan 1786; John Walker, bm.

Vance, Mathew & Sally Grant, 9 Feb 1821; David Hill, bm.

Vandeford, George & Marged Francis, 22 Sept 1796; Joseph Francis, bm.

Vanhoose, John & Elizabeth Goodwin, 8 Oct 1799; Britain Liles, bm.

Vanzant, Abram & Hanner Blackburn, 13 Jan 1795; Frs. Riggs, bm.

Vanzant, Isaac & Mary Smith, _____ 1802; Abram Vanzant, John Harrill, bm.

Vanzant, James & Sally Upgrove, 10 Mar 1802.

Vanzant, Lewis & Elizabeth Hunt, 29 Dec 1828; Alfred McFarland, bm.

Varner, Henry & Christian Enloe, 8 May 1799; D. Dickey, bm.

Vernon, H. F. & L. Blackwell, 29 Feb 1844; J. B. Miller, bm.

Vess, A. L. & Cyntha Conner, m 1 Jan 1867 by Wm. Flinn, J. P.

Vess, Josiah & Zelia Early, 27 Apr 1846; J. R. Early, bm.

Vest, Andrew L. & Linna Holferd, 14 May 1789; R. O. Ledbetter, bm.

Vickers, J. M. & Catharine Smith, 21 Dec 1848; Jas. W. Allen, bm.

Vickers, James Burton & Isabella Malinda Long, 29 Nov 1860; Franklin Long, bm; m 13 Dec 1860 by Jas. M. Spratt.

Vickers, Thomas J. & Nancy L. Guffy, 29 Sept 1860; Francis M. Long, bm; m 4 Oct 1860 by Jas. M. Spratt, bm.

Vickers, Wesley & Letty Melton, 27 Dec 1854; J. W. Hampton, bm; m 28 Dec 1854 by B. E. Rollins, M, G.

Vickers, William B. & Martha L. Long, 29 Aug 1860; J. L. Wallace, bm; m 29 Aug 1860 by John Freeman, J. P.

Vigors, Elijah & Mary Allen, 1 Oct 1828; John Whiteaker, bm.

Vinsant Garret & Margrett Smith, 11 Jul 1782; Jacob Vanzant, bm.

Wade, H. R. & Cynthia Foreman, 1 Jan 1845; J. B. Jones, bm.

Wadkins, Isah & Poley Searcy, 10 May 1813; Lyddall Watkins, bm.

Waggoner, Isaac & Nancy Smith, 21 Dec 1815; William Smith, bm.

Waldrop, Caswell & Rachel Bagwell, 14 Jan 1835; Ambrose Mills, bm.

Waldrop, Edmund & Mary Ann Waldrop, 23 Oct 1840; Samuel Wilkins, bm.

Waldrop, Johnson & Mary Cockerham, 29 Sept 1842; James Morris, bm.

Waldrop, Jonathan & Martha Lavitta Dickey, 9 Aug 1830; Chruchwell Moris, bm.

Waldrop, Robert & Nancy McClarking, 4 Nov 1800; Joseph Waldrop, bm.

Waldrop, Robt. S. & Elizabeth Edwards, 25 Oct 1854; J. C. Waldrop, bm; m 25 Oct 1854 by J. M. Hamilton, J. P.

Waldrop, Samuel & Mary Coward, 19 Nov 1840; Thomas Egerton, bm.

Waldrop, Zachariah & Hester McClerkin, 8 Oct 1808; Thos. Littlejohn, bm.

Walker, Asahel Mc. & Rhoda Wilson, 17 Nov 1844; Josephus Gibbs, bm.

Walker, Chesley B. & Nancy McDaniel, 8 Jan 1857; Wm. Davis, bm; m 13 Jan 1856 (sic) by G. W. Rollins, M. G.

Walker, Danl. & Sarah Moony, 15 Jan 1797; David Mooney, bm.

Walker, David & Elizabeth Eakins, 12 Mar 1817; Jos. Bowen, bm.

Walker, David & Nancy Street, 8 Dec 1826; Thomas McDaniel, bm.

Walker, David & Mrs. Mary Randal, 11 Jun 1865.

Walker, David D. & E. C. Lynch, 24 Mar 1861; A. K. Lynch, bm; m 24 Mar 1861 by Wm. Davenport.

Walker, Davidson & Martha Scoggin, 14 Feb 1859; J. W. Walker, bm; m 16 Feb 1859 by G. W. Rollins.

Walker, Elias M. & Isebella Walker, 18 Apr 1844; John S. Walker, J. B. Jones, bm.

Walker, Elnathan G. & Nancy Wilson, 30 Oct 1849; John Freeman, bm.

Walker, Geo. W. S. & Mirah E. Lollar, 26 Mar 1849; Wm. A. Gray, bm.

Walker, J. & L. A. Resenear, 17 Jan 1866; J. Mode, bm.

Walker, J. B. G. & Julia Morris, 22 Feb 1860; Joseph A. Goode, bm; m 22 Feb 1860 by J. V. Jay, J. P.

Walker, J. D. & Harriet Blackwell, 27 Sept 1863; M. O. Dickerson, bm; m 6 Oct 1853 by Alanson Padgett, M. G.

Walker, J. L. & Isabella C. Smart, 1 Sept 1861; W. D. Hutchins, bm; m 1 Sept 1861 by J. Norvill, J. P.

Walker, J. W. & Elizabeth Wilson, 2 Mar 1849; William Davis, bm.

Walker, Jacob & Lilea Miller, 6 Nov 1795; Wm. Buckingham, bm.

Walker, James & Mary Powell, 8 Jul 1818; N. Hampton, bm.

Walker, James H. & Drucilla Price, 3 Jan 1867; John R. PRice, bm; m 3 Jan 1867 by Mijamin Price, J. P.

Walker, James S. & Rebecca Johnston, 21 Sept 1831; Thomas S. Long, bm.

Walker, Jeremiah & Sarah Hill, 19 Nov 1832; Thomas McDaniel, bm.

Walker, Jeremiah Jr. & Sarah Mode, 9 Sept 1833; William Manor, bm; m 12 Sept 1833 by Hugh Watson, J. P.

Walker, Jesse R. Jr. & Rachel Fawbush, 22 Jan 1857; J. P. Eaves, bm; m 22 Jan 1857 by W. A. Tanner, J. P.

Walker, Jessee & Menime Whitacer, 24 Dec 1818; William Walker, Abraham Whaitacer, bm.

Walker, Joel & Angeliley Wall, 22 Jan 1831; Charles Lewis Sr., bm.

Walker, John or Covington, Josiah & Mary Morgan, 21 Feb 1785; Josiah Covington, bm.

Walker, John & Anne Forbus, 22 Oct 1819; David Forbus, bm.

Walker, John & Ann Mooney, 24 Sept 1859; W. S. Proctor, bm; m 25 Sept 1859 by J. S. Grayson, J. P.

Walker, John Jr. & Sarah Allen, 24 Oct 1834; Jeremiah Walker Jr., bm; m __ Oct 1834 by Hugh Watson, J. P.

Walker, John R. & Sarah D. Wood, 9 Dec 1861; Wm. E. Walker, bm; m 15 Dec 1861 by B. E. Rollins.

Walker, John W. & _____, ___ 18--; Wm. Ellison, bm.

Walker, John W. & Nancy McKinney, 10 Mar 1826; Jacob Walker, bm.

Walker, Johnathan & Levina Biggerstaff, 6 Feb 1862; John Walker, bm; m 6 Feb 1862 by W. J. Norvill.

Walker, Jonathan & Nancy E. Shelly, 28 Nov 1845; David Walker, bm.

Walker, Jonathan & Nancy Towery, 4 Dec 1859; W. J. Norvill, bm; m 4 Dec 1859 by W. J. Norvill, J. P.

Walker, Joshua & Elisabeth Hunt, 28 Nov 1844; John Walker, bm.

Walker, Liews Adams & Julana Wall, 16 Mar 1861; Joel Walker, bm; m 19 Mar 1861 by William McSwain, M. G.

Walker, Lyman & Nancy Alexander, 9 Jun 1832; O. B. Irvine, bm.

Walker, Martin & Drusy Webb, 8 Dec 1825; Joel Walker, bm.

Walker, Noah E. & Sarah J. Lancaster, 18 Oct 1859; D. D. Walker, bm; m 18 Oct 1859 by T. B. Justice.

Walker, O. P. & Martha M. Suttle, 21 Feb 1847; Martin Walker, bm.

Walker, Thaddeus & Nancy Byars, 16 Mar 1795; Samuel Broadway, bm.

Walker, Thaddeus & Mary E. Harrill, 27 Sept 1856; Joel Walker, bm; m 30 Sept 1856 by G. W. Rollins.

Walker, Thomas & Nelly Colwell, 28 Dec 1786; Jonathn Pell, bm.

Walker, Thomas Jr. & Nancy Biggerstaff, 10 Apr 1830; Colsbury Dycus, bm.

Walker, W. S. & Nancy J. Price, 9 Apr 1861; R. M. Price, bm; m 9 Apr 1861 by G. W. Rollins, Elder.

Walker, William & Nancy Driskill, 12 Dec 1804; Saml. Anderson, bm.

Walker, Wm. & Isabella Guffey, 24 May 1842; Wm Guffey, bm.

Walker, Wm. & Celia Wall, 1 Jan 1849; T. M. Walker, bm.

Walker, Wm. E. & J. E. Harris, ____ 1865; E. S. Goode, bm.

Wall, Amos & Temperance Randle, 19 Jan 1825; Jacob Michal, bm.

Wall, George & Margaret McFaden, 11 Dec 1794; David Dickey, bm.

Wall, J. N. & Margret E. Gillispia, 6 Jan 1866; T. M. Walker, bm; m 18 Jan 1866 by D. Ponnell.

Wall, Jepptha A. & Elizabeth Goode, 7 Oct 1841; Willis Wall, bm.

Wall, John H. & Malinda Padgett, 9 Mar 1840; William B. Padgett, bm.

Wall, Kinchen & Mahaley Whitecar, 9 Sept 182-; Willis Wall, bm.

Wall, R. H. & T. E. Huntly, 21 Aug 1865; J. M. Michael, bm; m 6 Aug 1865 (sic) by A. W. Harill, J. P.

Wall, Willis & Arrany Padget, 12 Sept 1830; John Padget, bm.

Wallace, A. K. & Nancy A. Clements, 28 Dec 1847; H. C. Watson, bm.

Wallace, A. K. & Candis Johnston, 24 May 1858; Wm. F. Wilson, bm; m 25 May 1858 by Jas. M. Spratt, J. P.

Wallace, F. L. & M. Elisabeth Carson, 3 Sept 1865; D. S. McCurry, bm; m 3 Sept 1865 by Wm. J. Willkie.

Wallace, H. B. & M. S. Johnson, 20 Oct 1845; H. E. McGintry, bm.

Wallace, J. L. & M. J. Stacy, 1 Feb 1860; E. B. Freeman, bm; m 1 Feb 1860 by John Freeman, J. P.

Wallace, James & Patsy Eaves, 7 Mar 1808; Wm. Mullins, bm.

Wallace, L. A. & Harriet A. Andrews, 6 Oct 1858; J. D. Justice, bm; m 7 Oct 1858 by T. B. Justice.

Wallace, Toliver & Nancy Dycus, 26 Sept 1833; William A. Tanner, bm.

Wallace, W. L. & Ann L. Roberds, 27 Dec 1865; W. B. Dobbins, bm.

Wallace, W. W. & J. N. Rutherford, 1 Nov 1842; Wm. Ray, bm.

Wallace, Waid & M. L. Dobbins, 28 Dec 1865; Wm. J. Willkie, bm.

Wallace, William O. & Adaline Wilson, 21 Dec 1836; Nimrod S. Stafford, bm.

Wallace, Wm. W. & Nancy M. Watson, 18 Sept 1849; B. W. Andrews, bm.

Waller, J. Adam & Elizabeth Moreland, 14 Nov 1846.

Waller, John H. & Rachael Braddy, 27 Sept 1821; John Baber, bm.

Wallis, Joseph Sira & Bathsaba Hall, 30 Nov 1820; James Hill, bm.

Wallis, Nathaniel P. & Marian Tomerlen, 11 Oct 1860; John A. Justis, bm; m 11 Oct 1860 by J. Gilkey, J. P.

Wallis, Oliver & Cathorine Odier, 16 Nov ___; Nathaniel Wallis, bm.

Wallis, Robert A. & Martha Brown, 15 Mar 1854; R. L. Bilkey, bm; m 15 Mar 1854 by A. Hamby, M. G.

Wallis, Samuel & Mary Cherry, 24 Feb 1818; Nathl. Wallis, bm.

Wallis, Wm & Esther Cherry, 1 Sept 1825; John Cherry, bm.

Wallis, William O. & Nancy Brackett, 8 Jul 1832; Thos. M. Bratton, bm.

Ward, A. B. & Elizabeth Price, 10 Apr 1844; James Egerton, bm.

Ward, Frederic Jr. & Keizah Ward, 11 Dec 1837; Harriss Elliott, bm.

Ward, James & Patsey Ledbetter, 21 Mar 1814; Zadoc Harris, bm.

Ward, James & Marthay Elmes, 1 Oct 1821; John Goodbread, bm.

Ward, Johnston L. & Patience Williams, 27 May 1837; Augustus Williams, bm.

Ward, Richard & Mary Ledbetter, 14 Sept 1840; J. Goodbread, bm.

Ware, Robert & Hariet Fortune, 4 Feb 1834; Thos. Fortune, bm.

Warren, Elijah & Anna Crane, 4 Apr 1850; G. Dickerson, bm.

Warren, H. M. & Martha Harvy, 31 Aug 1865; Joseph Suttle, bm; m 31 Aug 1865 by Wm. Harrill.

Warren, John & Polly Milliard, 22 Apr 1824; John Shearor, bm.

Warrin, Robert & Sary Randol, 18 Sept 1836; John Border, bm.

Wasburn, Reubin & Sarah Scoggin, 7 Oct 1808; Gilbird Harel, bm.

Washburn, Benjamin & Delpha Filbeck, 6 Nov 1825; Phillip Filbeck, bm.

Washburn, Thomas & Ann Eseridge, 22 May 1807; John Reynolds, bm.

Wassom, Jacob & Sally Johns, 3 Nov 1815; David Liles, bm.

Wassom, Jonas & Catharine Weaver, 1 Jan 1816; R. K. Wilson, bm.

Wateres, W. & A. McDannel, 26 Apr 1860; John Odom, bm; m 24 Apr 1860 (sic) by B. E. Rollins.

Waters, Aaron D. & Elisabeth Hunt, 8 Jul 1831; Champeon Mctire, bm.

Waters, Elisha & Nancy M. Hail, 3 Nov 1853; M. O. Mooney, bm; m 3 Nov 1853 by Wm. G. Mode.

Waters, James & Sarah Mooney, 27 Apr 1836; David Mooney, bm.

Waters, John O. & Sarah A. Fortune, 26 Dec 1865; J. G. Fortune, bm.

Waters, Jonathan & Sarah Morehead, 23 Nov 1808; Alexander Moorhead, bm.

Waters, Jonathan & Betsy Hutchins, 2 Dec 1819; John Waters, bm.

Waters, Powhattan B. & Pamela J. Waters 7 Jul 1831; Robert G. Twitty, bm.

Waters, Thomas & Olive E. Tailor, 29 Dec 1841; N. Dan J. Moody, bm.

Waters, Wm. & Elizabeth Lookado, 7 Jan 1845; John Hutchins, bm.

Watkins, Alfred Mc. & Maryan Suttles, 3 Aug 1842; Geo. W. Baxter, bm.

Watkins, Ambrose & Elizabeth Thompson, 4 Apr 1804; Andrew Herron, bm.

Watkins, Ambrose & Viney Robertson, 2 Oct 1839; William Pullam, bm.

Watkins, John & July An Butler, 9 Jun 1858; B. McMahan, bm; m 10 Jun 1858 by Wm. Harrill, M. G.

Watkins, Philip Jr. & Ann E. Harris, 26 Sept 1855; K. C. Watkins, bm.

Watkins, Stephen & Lithy Stewman, 7 Jan 1809; Thomas McGuire, bm.

Watson, Adam & Caty or Katharine Hughs, 25 Jun 1788; John Hughs, bm.

Watson, Alexander & Cynthia Bradly, 4 Feb 1808.

Watson, Daniel & Nancy Goforth, 17 Feb 1834; John E. Gofotth, bm; m 20 Feb 1834 by Hugh Watson, J. P.

Watson, David & Isble Hughs, 19 Sept 1792; James Ross, bm.

Watson, Elijah P. & Catharine Morrison, 8 Mar 1837; Joseph Morrison, bm.

Watson, G. P. & C. E. Erwin, 18 Mar 1861; W. M. Erwin, bm; m 21 Mar 1861 by Nl. Shotwell, M. G.

Watson, George & Polly Miller, 7 Jan 1793; James Finly, bm.

Watson, Hugh & Catharine Andrews, 30 Dec 1790; John Andrews, bm.

Watson, Hugh & Margaret Watson, 16 Dec 1817; Daniel Watson, bm.

Watson, Hugha & Jinsey Long, 31 Jan 1814; Jas. W. Carson, bm.

Watson, J. C. & Frances Alexander, 2 Sept 1858; G. P. Watson, bm; m 2 Sept 1858 by Jas. M. Spratt, J. P.

Watson, Jas W. & Nancy L. Mode, 10 Sept 1866; G. R. Guffey, bm; m 12 Sept 1866 by Nl. Shotwell, M. G.

Watson, John & Jane Smart, 30 Dec 1785; George Mitchel, bm.

Watson, John A. & Ruth Porter, 14 Sept 1840; Wm. P. Porter, bm.

Watson, P. W. & Mary E. McFarland, 19 Mar 1850; T. J. Long, bm.

Watson, S. A. & S. E. Largin, 20 Dec 1865; G. B. Guffey, bm; m 21 Dec 1865 by Nl. Shotwell.

Watson, W. P. & Emily S. Gettys, 19 Mar 1866; R. W. Logan, bm; m 29 Mar 1866 by Nl. Shotwell, M. G.

Watson, William & Jane Hix, 23 Feb 1814; John Guffey, bm.

Watters, D. H. & Frances H. Baty, 2 Sept 1866; J. O. Watters, bm; m 2 Sept 1866 by B. E. Rollins.

Watters, John & Rachel Deviny, 16 Feb 1804; Wm. McFarland, bm.

Watts, John & Elisabeth Bomgarner, 6 Sept 1800; Daniel Workman, bm.

Weast, Adam & Sophia Fortune, 13 Mar 1826; Marvell Melton, bm.

Weast, Jacob L. & Susan Dykes, 6 May 1848; Wm. G. Robertson, bm.

Weast, Joseph H. & Elizabeth Jane Weeks, 12 Jan 1853; William S. Robertson, bm.

Weast, Marvel & Sarah L. Deck, 27 May 1855; J. M. Mode, bm; m 27 May 1855 by John Freeman, J. P.

Weast, Wm. B. & Malinda Jane Rollins, 2 May 1852; James W. East, bm; m 2 MAy 1852 by John Freeman, J. P.

Weathers, Willis & Elizabeth Webb, 23 Nov 1824; Mansfield Padgett, James Lyles, bm.

Weathers, Willis & Drucilla Black, 26 Apr 1856; W. B. McEntire, bm; m 27 Apr 1856 by John Koone.

Weaver, Adam & Heather Depriest, 24 Dec 1850; James Baber, bm.

Weaver, Francis A. & Mahuldah H. Williams, 22 Oct 1839; John H. Alley Jr., bm.

Weaver, H. & P. L. Grason, 2 Feb 1860; John Odom, bm; m 2 Feb 1860 by R. E. Rollins.

Weaver, John & Biddy Crowder, 11 Apr 1861; M. S. McCurry, bm; m 14 Apr 1861 by James W. Murray.

Weaver, Joseph & Elizabeth Gaye, 28 Jan 1792; Shade Green, bm.

Weaver, Thomas & Ellin Earley, 9 Nov 1866; J. W. Naney, bm.

Weaver, William & Olley Melton, 13 Sept 1855; J. Melton, bm; m 13 Sept 1855 by B. E. Rollins.

Webb, Achilis & Maria Dobbins, 27 Dec 1854; Albert Tate, bm; m 27 Dec 1854 by J. H. Carpenter, J. P.

Webb, Chambers & Eliza Leek, 10 Jul 1833; Martin Walker, bm.

Webb, Charles C. & Mary Tate, 19 Nov 1845; B. H. Padgett, bm.

Webb, Clinton & _____ Robinson, _____; John Robinson, bm.

Webb, Daniel & Francis Harrill, 6 Jul 1815; Micajah Davis, bm.

Webb, David & Patey McMerrey, 22 Feb 1831; John McNeley, bm.

Webb, George M. & P. J. Blanton, 16 Apr 1851; B. S. Blanton, bm.

Webb, Gilbert & May Suttle, 27 Jun 1861; Joseph Harmon, bm; m 27 Jun 1861 by Wm. Harrill, Elder.

Webb, Henry & Jane Harrill, 3 Apr 1850; C. J. Webb, bm.

Webb, Hiram & Sarah Hollifield, 9 Mar 1812; Daniel Webb, Isaac Holifield, bm.

Webb, James & Sarrah Blanton, 23 May 1824; Obediah Blanton, Alfred Webb, bm.

Webb, James & Malinda Depriest, 6 Jan 1834; Edward Toms,bm.

Webb, James & Zilla Bradley 9 Aug 1855; J. N. Scoggin, bm; m 23 Aug 1855 by J. W. Morgan, J. P.

Webb, James P. & Malinda H. Whiteside, 22 Nov 1849; W. L. Hampton, bm.

Webb, Jeremiah & Sarah Copland, 19 Jan 1809; D. McBrayer, bm.

Webb, Jeremiah & Cinderilla Allen, 19 Dec 1838; Robert King, bm.

Webb, Jess J. & Jane Butler, 3 Jan 1861; P. D. Carpenter, bm; m 3 Jan 1861 by J. H. Carpenter, J. P.

Webb, Jesse & Mary Burge, 12 Oct 1842; John Burge, bm.

Webb, John & Nancy Padgett, 2 Feb 1837; Ransom Hawkins, bm.

Webb, John D. & Luraney Padgett, 26 Nov 1844.

Webb, John M. & Nancy Hampton, 3 May 1849; W. L. Hampton, bm.

Webb, K. Lewis & Sarah Haynes, 21 Jan 1845; Daniel Webb, bm.

Webb, Lewis & Elizabeth Waters, 12 Jun 1827; John Haney, bm.

Webb, Noah & Polly Waggoner, 20 Dec 1823; Richmond Webb, bm.

Webb, P. P. & C. A. Jackson, 23 Sept 1865; J. C. Webb, bm; m 28 Sept 1865 by G. W. Rollins.

Webb, Ransome & Ivy Smith, 11 Jan 1858; John Hider, John J. Bradley, bm; m 13 Jan 1858 by W. A. Tanner.

Webb, Robert & Margaret Roach, 30 Apr 1824; Joseph Roach, bm.

Webb, Sherrod A. & Drucilla Haney, 9 Feb 1854; John D. Webb, bm.

Weber, A. C. & Mary Harton, 22 Apr 1851; T. J. Harton, bm; m 23 Apr 1851 by P. F. Kistler, M. G.

Weber, John & Hannah Philips, 11 Mar 1840; John Callihan, bm.

Weber, Solomon & Sarah Humpries, 2 Jan 1812; Benjamin Ellis, bm.

Webster, J. A. & M. E. Harris, 14 Jun 1858; Joseph H. Harris, bm.

Webster, Thomas & Polly McGwin, 17 Apr 1822; George Jones, bm.

Weeaks, Benjamin & Hanner Allen, 15 Jul 1800; Charles Allin, bm.

Weeks, A. Robert & Emily Wilson, 16 Oct 1854; Joseph H. Weast, bm; m 18 Oct 1854 by B. E. Rollins, M. G.

Weeks, Andrew & Drusilla Deck, 1 Feb 1849; Lawson Deck, bm.

Weeks, Archabel & Elizabeth Depriest, 17 May 1809; Rbt. Smith, bm.

Weeks, Noah & Martha McBrayer, 12 Aug 1831; Robert Magness, bm.

Weeks, Theophilus & Winney Johnston, 4 Oct 1813; Benj. Johnston, bm.

Weost, Jacob & Maery Yenwood, 2 Dec 1794; Daniel Wartman, bm.

Weir, Anonymous & Mary Ann Harrill, 3 Feb 1847; Alfred Weir, bm.

Weir, James & Sarah Covington, 18 Oct 1825; Jno. Harrill, bm.

Welch, Cornelius & Sally Cansellor, 9 Mar 1819; Thomas Hicks, bm.

Welch, David Alexander & Milly Melton, 9 Sept 1799; Joseph Green, application for license.

Welch, Geo. & Eliza. Summerhill, 7 Nov 1808; Jno Summerhill, bm.

Welch, James & Mary Sims, 26 Mar 1783; Wm Walker, bm.

Welch, John & ____ Anderson, __ Nov 1794; Wm Nix, bm.

Wells, A. J. & Rebecca J. Melton, 19 May 1853; Isaah W. Melton, bm.

Wells, J. R. & Margret S. Bridges, 17 Sept 1866; John W. Wells, bm.

Wells, James & Lucy Upchurch, 15 Dec 1817; Elias Upchurch, bm.

Wells, Jesse & Patsey Melton, 8 Nov 1825; John Wells, bm.

Wells, Jessee R. & Mrs. Martha L. Walker, m 5 Sept 1865 by G. W. Rollins.

Wells, John & Malinda Neeley, 11 Sept 1826; James W. Carson, bm.

Wells, John & Sarah C. Baber, 3 Jan 1859; M. L. Wells, bm; m 6 Jan 1859 by G. W. Rollins, M. G.

Wells, John K. & Mary Y. Carson, 18 Dec 1832; Roebrt W. Harris, bm.

Wells, M. L., son of Jno. Wells, & Sintha Eliza Bedford, m 5 Dec 1867 by B. B. Byers, J. P.

Wells, Marcus, son of John Wells decd., & Mary Webb, dau. Jessee Webb, decd., m 22 Aug 1867 by G. M. Webb.

Wells, Noah & Elizabeth Goode, 19 Jul 1805; Jo. Jay, bm.

Wells, Osborne & Lydia Padgett, 21 Sept 1830; Jesse R. Wells, bm.

Wells, Richard & Elender Groves, 5 Dec 1850; Saml. Melton, bm.

Wells, Samuel M. & Drusilla Melton, 16 Dec 1824; Elias Padgett, Wm. Melton, bm.

Wells, Thomas P. & Pegga Hoyle, 9 Sept 1822; John Hoyle, bm.

Wells, Tolaver & Providence Culbreath, 22 Apr 1852; Daniel McHan, bm; m 22 Apr 1852 by Wm. Harrill, M. G.

Wells, William & Jane Elms, 11 May 1828; John A. Long, bm.

Welmon, William & Mrs. Rebeccah Weathers, 7 Nov 1816; Willis Weathers, bm.

Welsh, John & Sarah Meson, 28 May 1791; Gavn Irvin, bm.

West, Edmon & Sidia Humphreys, 1 Jan 1841; Wm. Umptres, bm.

West, John & Betsey Upton, 29 Oct 1804; Thomas Upton ,bm.

Westbrook, Howel F. & Mary Canady, 11 May 1835; William Baxter Jun., bm.

Westmoorland, John & Margaret Jackson, 6 Jul 1825; Josiah Sullins, bm.

Wever, Benjamin & Elisabeth Lequire, 9 Sept 1802; Martin Roberts, bm.

Wharey, George & Mrs. Marey Taylor, 16 Sept 1794; Thos. Wharey, bm.

Wheatly, J. B. & Adaline Metcalf, 7 Mar 1854; J. H. Gilkey, bm; m 10 Mar 1854 by Wm. Rucker, J. P.

Wheeler, Green & Rachael Hopkins, 25 Aug 1819; Andrew Hudloe, bm.

Wheeler, Green & Polly Humphreys, 13 Sept 1829; Andrew Early, bm.

Wheeler, Marke & Sally Peterson, 2 Dec 1822; Green Wheeler, bm.

Wheeler, Saml. & Elizabeth Garret, 15 Nov 1792; Ben Laughter, bm.

Whisenant, Henry & Rebecca Beheler, 16 Jul 1836; Samuel G. Porter, bm.

Whisnant, Absalom & Aneliza Thomson, 10 Nov 1831; Thomas Parker, bm.

Whisnant, Eli & Mary Melton, 19 Nov 1851; Adolphus Mooney, bm.

Whisnant, Isaac S. & Jane Deal, 4 Jun 1854; Ephraim Whisnant, bm; m 4 Jun 1854 by Wm. G. Mode, J. P.

Whitaker, R. D. & Eunice Walker, 9 Dec 1861; D. Ponnel, bm.

Whitaker, T., son of John Whitaker, & N. E. Wall, dau. of W. Wall, m 20 Nov 1867 by D. Ponnell.

Whitaker, William & Martha Mayse, 10 Jan 1831; Elijah Walker, bm.

White, Alfred & Alvira Grant, 10 Apr 1843; Andrew Tomerlin, bm.

White, Allen & Mary Moss, 26 Dec 1822; Thomas Wilkinson, bm.

White, Bartlett C. & Arta L. Brooks, 9 Dec 1839; B. Washburn, bm.

White, David & Ollive Proctor, _____; Lewis Ledford, bm.

White, David & Nancy Proctor, 6 Oct 1814; Auguston White, bm.

White, George & Nancy Dobbins, 9 May 1824; Ald Durham, John Padgett, bm.

White, Henry & Sarah Moss, 3 Mar 1798; John Martin, bm.

White, James & Polley English, 1 Jul 1817; John Hardcastle, bm.

White, Jeremiah & Catrine White, 8 Feb 1798; Benjm. Wilkison, bm.

White, Jeremiah & Nancy R. Green, 1 Jul 1852; David White, bm.

White, Jno. & Pattsey Orman, _____; Thos. White, John Barber, bm.

White, John & Barbary Thompson, __ Apr 1840; Jordan Beam, bm.

White, John A. & Sarah Camp, 18 Dec 1827; William Camp, bm.

White, John R. & Mira McGagha, 23 Oct 1837; Moses White, bm.

White, Lewis & Sary Dicus, 15 Feb 1843; G. B. Dycus, bm.

White, Moman & Sarah Baxter, 17 Feb 1830; George W. Baber, bm.

White, Richard & Mary Ann Wood, 20 Nov 1846; William _____, bm.

White, Robert G. & Ester Orman, _____; Thos. White, John Barber, bm.

White, Samuel & Lucinda Keeter, 10 Mar 1828; Joseph Harmon, bm.

White, Thomas & Elisabeth Morris, 5 Jan 1796; Benjamon Wilkeson, bm.

White, Thomas & Eliza Short, 17 Apr 1864; William Gamble, bm; m 17 Apr 1864 by K. J. McCrow.

White, William & Polley Plummer, 3 Oct 1811; John Hardcastle, bm.

White, William & Mary Ann Sorrels, 24 Feb 1862; F. D. Wood, bm; m 27 Feb 1862 by J. Gilkey, J. P.

Whiteker, J. H. & Rebecca Melton, 29 Sept 1859; M. O. Dickerson, bm.

Whiteker, John & Rebecca Fleming, 27 Oct 1819; James Edwards, bm.

Whitesid, J. L. & Nancy Ledbetter, 8 Feb 1863; John Ledbetter, bm; m 8 Feb 1863 by J. L. Taylor, J. P.

Whiteside, A. W. & Priscilla Flack, 20 Dec 1858; W. L. Higgins, bm; m 23 Dec 1858 by J. L. Taylor, J. P.

Whiteside, Davis & Rebecca L. Murry, 8 Aug 1866; J. H. Whiteside, bm.

Whiteside, DeLayfaett & Nancy Hampton, 10 Jan 1847; C. J. Webb, bm.

Whiteside, Jacob & Jane H. Smart, 21 Aug 1832; Spencer Blankenship, bm.

Whiteside, James H. & Jane Linch, 17 Aug 1840; A. W. Whiteside, bm.

Whiteside, James H. & Minerva Egerton, 9 Mar 1846; T. H. W. Whiteside, bm.

Whiteside, James M. & U. E. Whiteside, 18 Nov 1857; W. C. Whitesides, bm; m 18 Nov 1857 by T. B. Justice, M. G.

Whiteside, John & Sarah Whiteside, 23 Oct 1788; Thos. Whiteside, Adam Whiteside, bm.

Whiteside, John & Sarah Blankenship, 24 Feb 1831; James Long, bm.

Whiteside, John Jr. & Rhoda Williams, 24 Dec 1831; William Whiteside, bm.

Whiteside, Jonathan & Nancy Lewis, 22 Jan 1824; Charles Lewis Sr., bm.

Whiteside, Jonathan L. & Mary Logan, 29 Aug 1849; J. M. Webb, bm.

Whiteside, Joseph G. & Louisa Rhodes, 11 Nov 1831; Robt. G. Twitty, bm.

Whiteside, Joseph U. & Mary M. Edwards, 18 Jun 1829; Charles Lewis Jr., bm.

Whiteside, Noah & Malinda Linch, 29 Mar 1827; Thomas Whiteside, bm.

Whiteside, Noah & Adaline Whietside, 22 Nov 1849; G. J. Webb, bm.

Whiteside, Richard & Sarah Edgerton, 6 Oct 1842; Thos. Egerton, bm.

Whiteside, Samuel L. & Nancy N. Gettys, 20 Jan 1851; W. H. Gettys, bm.

Whiteside, Thomas & Jensey Flack, 14 Jul 1834; Amos Green, bm.

Whiteside, Thomas H. W. & Catharine E. Lynch, 26 May 1840; Francis A. Littlejohn, bm.

Whiteside, William & Elizabeth Brindle, 6 Dec 1842; Solomon Lettimore, bm.

Whiteside, Wm. F. & Elizabeth Grayson, 16 May 1796; Johnston Dickey, bm.

Whitesides, Jonathan U. & L. King, 19 Dec 1815; Matthew Devent, bm.

Whitesides, Joseph U. & Rhody Ledbetter, 22 Dec 1857; J. R. Ledbetter, bm; m 22 Dec 1857 by J. W. Morgan, J. P.

Whitesides, Whittenton & Elizabeth Lewis, _____ 182-; Charles Lewis, bm.

Whitesides, William & R. M. Smiley, 17 Nov 1847; Elsey W. Smiley, bm.

Whitesides, Wm & Elizabeth Malisa Edgerton, 19 Oct 1852; B. H. Egerton, bm; m 21 Nov 1852 by Luke Waldrop, J. P.

Whitmire, W. H. & Fannie Hamby, 1 Feb 1866; C. Burnett, bm; m 1 FEb 1866 by Daniel May.

Whitsides, William & Sarah Ledbetter, 26 Sept 1853; J. K. Lynch, bm; m 27 Sept 1853 by Bailey Bruce, M. G.

Whitten, Alfred & Caroline M. Prince, 12 Sept 1825; William Prince, bm.

Whitten, Silas R. & Elonor K. Earle, 27 Oct 1815; Wm. Prince, bm.

Wigins, William & Polley Haney, 23 Dec 1829; Drury Dobbins, bm.

Wilcox, John & Eliza Rowland, 19 May 1801; Chas. Lewis, bm.

Wiley, John W. & Elizabeth Washbern, 6 May 1849; C. E. Green, bm.

Wilis, Thomas & Susanana Miller, 4 Feb 1796; Wiliam Wilis, bm.

Wilkenson, John & Susanah Moore, 23 Jun 1796; Benjan. Wilkenson, James White, bm.

Wilkerson, Jethro & Poley Morgan, 14 Nov 1814; Permenter Morgan, bm.

Wilkerson, M. A. & Elmira Koon, 5 Mar 1866; J. W. Crawford, bm; m 8 Mar 1866 by J. W. Morgan, J. P.

Wilkerson, Moses & Rebecca Hall, 31 Oct 1848; M. Wilkerson Sr., bm.

Wilkie, Oliver & Jane Brooks, 18 Sept 1861; James B. Willkie, bm; m 19 Sept 1861 by Henry Culbreath, M. G.

Wilkins, Charles & Lucy Morriss, 7 Dec 1802; Richd. Wilkins, Jos. Haskew, bm.

Wilkins, Henderson & Marget Allen, 18 Sept 1834; William Allen, bm.

Wilkins, Hezekiah & Sarah Eskridgee, 24 Oct 1829; Reuben Wilkins, bm.

Wilkins, James T. & Mary M. Gray, 12 Mar 1860; J. H. McKinney, bm; m 15 Mar 1860 by J. S. Ervin.

Wilkins, John & Fanney Blanton, 15 Aug 1804; Wm. Blanton, Rubin Blanton, bm.

Wilkins, John H. & Mrs. Mildred C. Bowin, 12 Sept 1837; Robt. G. Twitty, bm.

Wilkins, Josiah & _____, 27 Dec 1832; Zechariah Wilkins, bm.

Wilkins, R. D. & E. Twitty, 21 Feb 1848; K. B. Miller, bm.

Wilkins, Richd & Nancy Hambrick, 14 Jun 1803; James Bridgis, bm.

Wilkins, Samuel & Jane Morris, 4 Jan 1848; W. H. Miller, bm.

Wilkins, Thomas & Nancy L. Harris, 15 Sept 1840; Samuel Wilkins, bm.

Wilkins, William & Jane Camp, 20 Apr 1826; John S. Ford, bm.

Wilkins, Zechariah & Belariah Hill, 20 Dec 1825; Daniel Hill, bm.

Wilkinson, Jesse & Melinda Elliott, 21 Aug 1832; Micajah Hall, bm.

Wilkinson, John V. & Emily A. Wood, 14 Feb 1857; J. P. Eaves, bm; m 15 Feb 1867 by T. B. Justice, M. G.

Wilkirson, John & Milly Ledbetter, 24 Dec 1866; Wm. Hamilton, bm; m 29 Dec 1866 by J. W. Morgan, J. P.

Wilkisson, William & Rebecca Davis, _____; Benjamine Wilkisson, bm.

Willfong, Peter & Susana Hill, 9 Apr 1796; Joh Hoyle, bm.

Williams, Alfred & Sarah Franklin, 14 Jul 1853; Burten Franklin, bm; m 14 Jul 1853 by R. T. Price, J. P.

Williams, Alin L. & Mry L. Price, 28 Mar 1864; J. T. Mode, bm; m 28 Mar 1864 by Wm. G. Mode, J. P.

Williams, Alston & Elviry Rogers, 1 Apr 1852; Goven Williams, bm; m 1 Apr 1852 by Wm. Harrill, M. G.

Williams, Andrew & Susanah Allen, 16 Jan 1819; Leroy Williams, bm.

Williams, Augustin & Sarah Ledbetter, 10 Jul 1837; William Elliott, bm.

Williams, Burton & Elizabeth Mashburne, 18 Dec 1827; James Richardson, bm.

Williams, Charles S. & Mira Matilda Cockerhan, 22 Jan 1857; M. Wilkerson, bm.; m 11 Jan 1857 by M. Wilkerson, J. P.

Williams, Daniel & Arty Callehan, 18 Jun 1827; David Williams, bm.

Williams, Eli H. & Elizabeth Adkins, 23 Aug 1824; Harvey Carrier, bm.

Williams, George R. & Peggy Melton, 26 May 1831; Thomas Hawkins, bm.

Williams, George S. & Nancy Hampton, 13 Apr 1822; Thoe F. Birchett, bm.

Williams, Govan & Barbary Rogers, 18 Mar 1852; Hughey Webb, bm; m 18 Mar 1852 by Wm. Harrill, M. G.

Williams, Jacob & Barbara Dobson, 23 Dec 1797; Richd. Yelding, bm.

Williams, James & E. M. McGiness, 10 Sept 1856; Noah Byas, bm.

Williams, Jeremiah & Oliva Hill, 2 Dec 1822; Leverett Parsons, bm.

Williams, Jerimaiah & Katharine Mitcalf, 2 Feb 1826; WilliamD. Metcalf, bm.

Williams, John & Sarah Pruitt, 8 Oct 1808; William Pruitt, bm.

Williams, John & Mary Panter, 12 Oct 1819; Robert Sutton, bm.

Williams, John & Minerva Owens, 17 Aug 1846; William Davis, bm.

Williams, John L. & Harriet A. Keeter, 31 Oct 1862; J. A. W. Keeter, bm; m 2 Nov 1862 by T. B. Justice, b.m

Williams, John W. & Sally Webb, 17 Jan 1828; George Williams, bm.

Williams, Jonathan & Sally Lankford, _____; Hinto Hill, Wm. Dimsdale, bm.

Williams, Jonathan & Rhody Elliot, 17 Mar 1803; William Elliot, bm.

Williams, Jonathan Jr. & Elender Whiteside, 17 Nov 1850; James O. Williams, bm.

Williams, Jones O. & Elizabeth Whitesides, 9 Mar 1842; John Elms, bm.

Williams, Lewis & Katharine Smart, 25 Dec 1804; Bartlet Eaves, bm.

Williams, Lewis & Winiford Green, 5 Nov 1818; David Blackwell, bm.

Williams, Norman & Nancy Ledbetter, 16 Jul 1825; Jonathan Ledbetter, bm.

Williams, Philip & Jane Walker, 25 May 1792; Thomas Rowland, bm.

Williams, Pulaski B. & Easter Ann Hannon, 20 Oct 1840; J. J. Herndon, bm.

Williams, R. J. & M. O. Goode, 24 May 1857; D. W. Geer, bm; m 24 May 1857 by T. B. Justice.

Williams, Samuel & Eleanor Williams, 31 Aug 1866; J. B. Carpenter, bm; m 6 Sept 1866 by W. H. Logan.

Williams, Samuel H. & Lucy Harris, 28 Dec 1819; Jonathan Williams, bm.

Williams, Thomas & Katherine Potts, 9 Aug 1785.

Williams, Thomas & Syreany Blackwell, 5 May 1827; James Young, bm.

Williams, Thomas & Mahala Thomason, 26 Jul 1832; William Adair, bm.

Williams, Thomas & Polly Elms, 19 Oct 1814; Nancy Elms, bm.

Williams, Turner & Sarah Williams, 25 Mar 1830; George Williams, bm.

Williams, Walter & Milly Green, 25 Dec 1821; Elijah Searcy, bm.

Williams, William & Polley Welman, 14 Sept 1820; Bannister Grigg, bm.

Williams, William & Nancy Johnston, 19 Dec 1832; Lewis Johnston, bm.

Williams, Wm. & Hannah Roach, 1 Aug 1855; W. E. Allen, bm.

Williams, Wm. R. & Sarah Gilliam, 31 Dec 1843; Thos. Ledbetter, bm.

Williams, William R. & Levina J. Garret, 24 Feb 1850; James M. Garrett, bm.

Williamson, Bauldy & Nancy Browder, 24 Aug 1817; Joseph G. Williamson, bm.

Willis, Benjamin & Ane Galis, 27 Jun 1793; Benjn. Beaver, bm.

Willis, James & Easter Wilson, 8 Nov 1827; David Willis, bm.

Willis, John & Peggey Calton, 25 Jan 181-; David Hoyle, bm.

Willis, John & Ann Jonston, m 2 Jul 1812.

Willis, Stephen Jr. & Martha Wharey, 3 Sept 1782; Stephen Willis Senr., bm.

Willkie, James B. & Miranda Collins, 5 Dec 1835; Walton Smith, bm.

Willkie, Joab & Sally Jay, 10 Mar 1824; Ad. Christopher, bm.

Willkie, W. J. & Delila McBrayer, 25 Jan 1859; E. McArthur, bm; m 25 Jan 1859 by Wm. Harrill, M. G.

Willkie, Wm J. & Margaret Read, 16 Mar 1854; A. B. Gilkey, bm; m 16 Mar 1854 by J. Gilkey, J. P.

Willkie, Wm. M. & Minervy Walker, 14 Nov 1835; Wm. C. Blanton, bm.

Willson, James & Alley H _____, 28 Aug 1864; J. L. Williams, bm; m 28 Aug 1864 by Wm. Devenport.

Wilmoth, Gabriel & Salley Dogged, 11 Dec 1807; John Wadkins, bm.

Wilson, A. E. & Mary C. Edwards, 31 Oct 1866; Joseph Scoggin, bm; m 1 Oct 1866 (sic) by G. W. Rollins.

Wilson, Anderson & Isabella Pack, 1 Aug 1841; Joseph Suttle, bm.

Wilson, Bartley & Martha Crow, 15 Jun 1820; John Crow, bm.

Wilson, Charles & Betsey Holifield, _____; Isaac Holifield, Edmund Padgett, bm.

Wilson, Daniel & Betsey Smith, 9 Dec 1821; Leonard Painter, bm.

Wilson, G. B. & Leaner Wammack, 8 Nov 1865; N. W. Wamick, bm.

Wilson, Green & Sally Davis, 5 Mar 1827; John T. Ford, bm.

Wilson, H. B. & Mary A. Williams, 27 Feb 1854; W. B. Wilson, bm; m 2 Mar 1854 by G. W. Rollins.

RUTHERFORD COUNTY MARRIAGES 1779-1868

Wilson, Hartwell & Nancy Gear, 6 Oct 1807; John Battle, bm.

Wilson, J. J. & M. N. Flin, m 27 Sept 1866 by W. H. Logan, M. G.

Wilson, J. T. & Martha Conner, 28 Feb 1866; Anderson Wilson, bm; m 1 Mar 1866 by W H. Logan, Elder.

Wilson, James & Lucy Wilkerson, 3 Dec 1834; William Wilkerson, bm.

Wilson, Jas. & _____; 20 Jan 1842; Jas Suttle, bm.

Wilson, John & Lydia Suttles, 28 Oct 1831; George Suttle, bm.

Wilson, John C. & Celia Norvell, 26 Sept 1844; Samuel McCure, bm.

Wilson, John U. & Elizebeth Green, 20 Dec 1832; Thomas Wilson, bm.

Wilson, John U. & Melinda Bridges, 21 Jan 1836; Ephraim Bridges, bm.

Wilson, Orvile M. & Sarah M. Bagwell, 26 Feb 1829; Morgan Reavis, bm.

Wilson, Philip D., son of Thos. Wilson, & D. J. Melton, dau. of L. F. Melton, m 18 May 1867 by G. M. Webb.

Wilson, R. K. & Dulcie A. Goforth, ____ 18--; A. E. Wilson, bm; m 1 Aug 1861 by Wm. Harrill.

Wilson, Ransom & Elizabeth Blankinship, 19 Nov 1819; Alexander Ervin, bm.

Wilson, Richard & Biddy S. McDaniel, 16 Nov 1855; R. R. Wilson, bm; m 20 Nov 1855 by John Edwards, Elder.

Wilson, Robert & Sally Harrell, 21 Oct 1826; T. F. Birchett, bm.

Wilson, Roburt & Betsey Haney, 26 Feb 1807; Jesse Richardson, bm.

Wilson, S. A. & A. C. Blanton, 3 Sept 1863; Samuel Harrill, bm; m 3 Sept 1863 by G. W. Rollins, Elder.

Wilson, W. G. & Mary Flinn, 5 Feb 1859; P. F. Searcy, bm; m 6 Feb 1869 by M. Wilkerson, J. P.

Wilson, William & Nance Haney, 21 Mar 1803; Gilbird Harrall, bm.

Wilson, William & Delilah Crowder, 8 Jul 1819; Robert Crowder, bm.

Wilson, William & Sarah Elvira Freeman, 30 Sept 1826; Meredeth Freeman, bm.

Wilson, William & Malenda McKinney, 29 Dec 1826; William H. McKinney, bm.

Wilson, William & Cynthia Cowherd, 31 Oct 1837; Joel J. Harriss, bm.

Wilson, William & Sarah Green, 22 Jan 1853; Jeremiah Webb, bm.

Wilson, William F. & Marthy J. Stafford, 4 Jan 1853; Jesse Lane, bm; m 4 Jan 1853 by John Freeman, J. P.

Wilson, Wm. G. & Angeline Wells, 12 Oct 1848; Robert H. Wilson, bm.

Wilson, Wright H. & Clarissa Roberts, 7 Dec 1835; John H. Wilkins, bm.

Winkles, William & Lucinda Largent, 6 Sept 1832; Thos L. McEntire, Tho. T. Patton, Saml. Hillman, bm.

- 164 -

RUTHERFORD COUNTY MARRIAGES 1779-1868

Winters, Mitchel & Elizabeth Moore, 17 Jan 1809; Josiah Roberts, Hardy Hardin, bm.

Wise, Benjamin & E. Gaultny, 11 Aug 1789; Charles Richardson, bm.

Wiseaman, Wm. D. & Victoria L. Durham, 12 Mar 1859; Plato Durham, bm.

Withrow, James & Margaret Atherington, 3 Oct 1818; Jno. Carson, bm.

Withrow, James Junr & Rixa Wells, 8 Oct 1822; James Withrow Sr., bm.

Withrow, John & Polly Atherington, 22 Jan 1798; Jno. Carson, bm.

Withrow, John Jr. & Kathraine Logan, 4 Mar 1829; James Withrow Jr., bm.

Withrow, T. J. & Priscilla Harrill, 20 Oct 1865; W. P. Withrow, bm; m 22 Oct 1865 by G. W. Rollins.

Withrow, W. P. & S. K. Sweezey, 16 Nov 1865; J. H. Withrow, bm; m 29 Nov 1865.

Wolf, Jacob & Nancey Thompson, 14 Dec 1825; Aron McEntire, Thomas Dedmon, bm.

Womack, David & Esther Tanner, 4 Oct 1809; Philip Wood, bm.

Womack, Gasaway & Martha Parker, 17 Dec 1838; Abraham Womack, bm.

Womack, John & Elizebeth Bridges, 28 Feb 1867; J. Womack, bm.

Womack, Jonas & Sally Melton, 14 Sept 1852; Gilford Melton, bm.

Womack, Jos. & Easter Lee, 16 Jan 1855; L. P. Erwin, bm.

Womack, Thomas M. & Elizabeth Pollard, 5 Feb 1834; Saml. G. Wootton, bm.

Womake, Willis & Phebe Green, 5 Sept 1831; Henry Green, bm.

Womick, A. B. & M. P. McDaniel, 20 Aug 1855; J. Young, bm.

Womick, A. B. & Jane McDaniel, 15 Jan 1867; John Kanedy, bm.

Womick, Noah W. & Sallie D. McDaniel, 15 Aug 1865; Andy McDaniel, bm; m 19 Sept 8165 by M. McMahan, M. G.

Wood, F. D. & Salina A. Lynch, 4 Apr 1866; H. H. Mitchell, bm; m 5 Apr 1866 by A. Hamby, Elder.

Wood, Henry S. & Susana Watkins, 12 Apr 1837; William Wood, bm.

Wood, Isham & Esther Head, 7 Feb 1827; Henry Keeter, bm.

Wood, Isham & Drusilla McGwire, 19 Nov 1836; Isham Head, bm.

Wood, Nelson & Lavinia Waldrop, 11 Nov 1833; William Richardson, bm.

Wood, Richard & Mary (Polly) Hullet, 11 Jan 1803; Dennis Carrll, bm.

Wood, William & Martha Tanner, 22 Jun 1818; Thomas McDaniel, bm.

Wood, William & Lucy Tomberlin, 28 Sept 1849.

Woodward, Isaac & Irena Suttle, 24 Jul 1830; Nathan Hamrick, bm.

Worley, Obadiah & Rebecca Coward, 13 Jun 1821; James Coward, bm.

Worley, Silas & Judia Lankford, 29 Sept 1801; Lewis Taylor, bm.

Worlley, Pleasant & Lucy Neal, 10 Dec 1810; Thomas Worlley, bm.

Worlly, Thomas & Rachel Blackwell, 22 Oct 1811; Benjamin Fowler, bm.

Wortman, Daniel & Susanah Shoup, 26 Aug 1808; Lewis Bumgarner, bm.

Wortman, Henry & Marget Hoyl, 2 Feb 1809; Daniel Wartman, bm.

Wragg, James & Mary McClure, 14 Jan 1818; Arthur McCluer, bm.

Wright, J. A. & Eliza Harrill, m 18 Aug 1857 by H. Harrill, J. P.

Wright, Jesse & Cela Bridges, 29 Jan 1849; Wm. Right, bm.

Wright, Jesse & Sarah Pope, 8 Jan 1867; Daniel Lovelace, bm.

Wright, William & Elesebeth Wolf, 18 Apr 1808; John Foutch, bm.

Write, John & Elisebeth Parot, 23 Aug 1802; Richard Bostick, bm.

Wylie, James Jun & Rosana Hopper, 9 May 1833; Benjamin Ellis, bm.

Wylie, Samuel & Rachel Hopper, 19 Aug 1834; James Hamrick, bm.

Yarborough, George & Judith McCombs, 16 Jul 1825; William McCombs, Sheldrake McCombs, bm.

Yarbrey, Jessee & Lucinda Pagett, 17 Dec 1840; Joel Smith, bm.

Yealding, Richard & Milly Mills, 5 Nov 1788; William Henry, bm.

Yearby, Andrew & Nancy Harris, 1 Oct 1817; William Fleming, bm.

Yearby, James & Frances Wise, 22 Dec 1814; Robt. Newton, bm.

Yelton, Charles & Letty Lane, 18 Dec 1844; William Lane, David Walker, bm.

Yelton, Fra M. & Har C. Toney, 11 Jan 1855; Dra Toney, bm; m 11 Jan 1855 by B. E. Rollins, M. G.

Yelton, Henry & Rebecca B. Robertson, 10 May 1842; Wm. Roberts, bm.

Yelton, J. W. & Lisa McCurry, 20 Mar 1866; W. J. Toney, bm; m 20 Mar 1866 by Henry A. Toney, J. P.

Yelton, Jacob & Susanna Davis, 14 Mar 1836; Joshua Earles, bm.

Yelton, James & Mary Canup, 29 Mar 1827; Moses White, bm.

Yelton, John & Polly Deck, 30 Aug 1806; Richard Fortune, bm.

Yelton, John & Ferreby Constant, 16 Sept 1826; William Harrison, bm.

Yelton, John & Martha Hutchins, 6 Feb 1845; Henry Smiley, bm.

Yelton, Leonard & Rebecca Fortune, 10 May 1836; Joshua Earles Jr., bm.

Yelton, Wm. J. & Easter L. Toney, 9 Mar 1856; Leonard Yelton, bm.

York, Abner & Sally Alviry Norville, 24 Sept 1818; Sam Norvell, bm.

York, Andrew W. & Nancy York, 19 Jun 1817; John York, bm.

York, John & Rachel Lee, 25 Jan 1805; D. Lyles, bm.

Young, Asa & Nelly Laughter, 14 Jun 1830; Martin Young, bm.

Young, G. W. & Margaret Lorance, 26 Feb 1859; M. O. Dickerson, bm; m 28 Feb 1859 by John Edward, Eld.

Young, Griffin & Rebeca Scott, 6 Apr 1809; Andw. Young, bm.

Young, Henry & Lavina Nanny Martin, 29 Dec 1831; William Self, bm.

Young, James & Elizabeth Bowman, 11 Feb 1802; James Kilpatrick, bm.

Young, James L. & Elvira Laughter, 13 Jul 1831; Ambrose Mills, bm.

Young, James Madison & Susanna Hicks, 5 Nov 1838; Allen Taber, bm.

Young, John & Mary Sides, 1 Jan 1799; Jesse Kuykendall, bm.

Young, Martin & Debora Deboard, 29 Jan 1828; John Hall, bm.

Young, Marvil W. & Emily A. Allen, 10 Aug 1851; J. E. A. Waldrop, bm; m 10 Aug 1851 by Luke Waldrop, J. P.

Young, Nathan & Sarah A. Logan, 10 May 1855; G. W. Jobe, bm; m by T. E. Davis.

Young, Paul H. & Penelope E. Mills, 13 Aug 1830; John Mills Jr., bm.

Youngblood, Harvey & Lucinda Right, 14 May 1859; Toliver Hays, bm; m 19 May 1859 by J. L. Taylor, J. P.

Zimmerman-- see Carpenter.

Zitter Coonrod & Elizabeth Walbert, 1 Aug 1791; Christopher Walbert, bm.

Baber (cont.)
  Matilda 4
  Milley Ann 8
  Polly 102
  Robert 18, 122
  Sarah 147
  Sarah C. 157
  Sinthy 91
  W. A. 4
  William A. 109
  Wm. 18, 94
Bagwell, Catharine 44
  Cinthia 90
  G. H. 88
  Mary 91, 127
  Mira 47
  Nancy A. 5
  Narcissa 85
  Rachael 131
  Rachel 150
  S. H. 5, 25, 44
  Sarah M. 164
  Wm. O. 26, 30, 41, 74,
    80
Bailey, Bettsey 81
  Emsey 35
  Hiram 35
  John 5
  Lewis 37
  Phebe 50
  Samuel 68, 79, 81, 84,
    120
  Sarah 80
Baily, John 77
  Samuel 5, 41
Baits, Cyntha 20
Baker, Baxter 76
  Elizabeth 19
  Nelly 76
  Treecy 8
Balad, William 136
Balden, Mary 113
Baldridge, Elizabeth 136
  John 5, 99, 123, 136
  John (Jr.) 5
  Joseph McK. 9
  Margaret 123
  Nancy 3, 99
  William 5
Baldwin, Mary 113
Ballard, Eliza 57
  Julia Ann 107
  Patsy 144
  Polly 5
  Samul 87
  Susanah 34
  William 30, 34, 36,
    147
Balton, Priscilla J. 54
Baly, Jonathan 5
Banard, Martin 26
Bankston, A. 6
  Andrew 140
  Debby C. 140
  Marey 139
Banter, Elizabeth 134
Banther, Barbary U. F.
    60
  Elizabeth 14
  Eve 14
  Georg J. 14
  Jane 57
Barber, John 48, 101,
    159
Barclay, Margaret 118
Barefield, Milly Ann 129
Barfield, Martha 139
Barlyhorn, Susanna 127

Barnett, Eliz. 113
  Mary 128
  William 72
  Wm. 6
Barr, Maryan 72
Barry, Mary A. E. 108
Bartell, O. 85
Bartlett, Matilda 46
Barton, Eliga (Sr.) 6
Bates, E. M. 59
  Elinor 107
  Elizabeth 40, 79
  Humphrey 6
  Nelly 107
  Rebecca 33
  Rebekah 139
  Sarah 41
  Sousan M. 44
  William 21
Battle, Ann 43
  John 164
  Lurana 110
  William 102
Baty, Frances H. 155
Bauldrige, M. 2
Baxter, Alfred W. 96
  Caroline 70
  Catharine 8
  Esther 37
  G. W. 6, 64
  Geo. W. 154
  James 6, 27
  Jane 122
  John 82
  John (Jr.) 9
  John (Sr.) 109
  Joseph 6, 8, 27
  Margaret 27
  Mary 112, 146
  Patsey 89
  Sarah 142, 159
  Sarah C. 27, 97
  Thomas 7, 146
  William 147
  William (Jr.) 22, 158
Baxtger, Jane 39
Baxton, Nancy C. 8
Bea, David 52
Beales, Richd. 146
Bealey, Alexander 140
Beam, Abi 63
  Amelia R. 37
  Anna 42
  Biddy 29
  David 2
  Elizebeth 76
  Esther 101
  J. O. 40
  J. W. 15
  Jordan 159
  Louisa 76
  M. A. 40
  Martin 12, 29, 37, 40,
    97, 144
  Mary 97
  Priscilla C. 40
  Rebekah 48
  Salley 52
  Sarah R. 55
Beann, Hannah 31
Bear, Christian 7
Beatey, Francis 94, 137
  Wallace 7
  Y. F. 76
Beaty, Abel 72
  Elisabeth 113
  Martha R. 108
Beaver(?), Benj. 27

Beaver, Benjn. 163
Beazel, Pheby 121
Bechtler, Chas. E. 131
  L. T. 131
Bedford, Catharine 148
  Elizabeth 16
  J. H. 21
  James 72, 87
  Jonas 83
  Martha 15
  Martha L. 139
  Mary Ann 40
  Nancy 15, 89
  Sarah 49
  Sintha Eliza 157
  Unicey 29
Bedix, Leah M. 85
Been, Marten 1
  Mary 1
Beheler, Rebecca 158
Bell, Andrew 60, 116
  Catharine B. 4
  James 8, 79
  Wm. A. 139
Benard, Martin 8
Benit, M. C. 89
Bennett, John 91
  Maria J. 91
Bennick, A. R. 85, 127
  Evaline M. 148
  George E. M. 1
  George J. 119
  Sarah A. L. 1
  Susannah 97
Benson, Jane 147
Benton, Jesse H. 31
Berry, Elizabeth 88
  Juda 45
Bertie, W. H. 19, 129
Betts, Sarah Ann 135
Bias, L. Chefus 13
  Shefus 75
  Thos. 87
Biddey, Nancy 31
Bigam, Susanah 105
Bigerstaf, Aron 8
Bigerstaff, Sarah 16
Biggerstaff, Aaron 76
  Aaron (Jr.) 104
  Betsey 32
  Biddy 76
  F. W. 72
  J. N. 12, 76, 149
  Jane 71, 104
  John W. 8
  Joseph 8
  Levina 151
  Luranah 75
  Manday 147
  Mary Ann 116
  Mary M. 129
  Nancy 152
  Noah 16
  R. H. 129
  Ransom P. 8, 76
  S. P. 147
  Samuel 147
Bigham, Charlotte 19
  Clarissa 11
Bilkey, R. L. 153
Bill, Rebecca 45
Birchett, Lucy M. 78
  T. F. 34, 109, 164
  Theo F. 7, 42, 106
  Theo. F. 78
  Theodorick F. 12
  Thoe F. 162
Bird, Balding 85

Bird (cont.)
Charles 9, 106
Charlotte 28
George 78
Mary 139
Narcissa 115
Talitha 85
Birdges, Sarah 93
Birk, Ann 127
Bishop, W. A. 71
Bizenin, Mary 122
Black, Caroline 39
Drucilla 155
Elizabeth 27
Hugh 86
Jesse R. 9
John 27, 73
Jos. M. 106, 123
Joseph M. 105
Margaret Nancy 77
Margart 39
Mary Elvira 109
Melvinah 134
Rachael 120
Rachel 19
Rachele 122
W. W. 75
William 21
Blackburn, Hanner 149
Blacke, William S. 101
Blackwel, Joseph 89
Blackwell, Charles 123
David 35, 162
Elizabeth 69
Harriet 151
Jas. 102
Jonathan 69
L. 149
Mary 131
Polly 9
Rachel 166
Rebecca 123
Syreany 162
Blakinship, Elizabeth
164
Blan, Martha Ann 65
Bland, C. T. 45
Elizebeth C. 27
Martha 52
Nancy 50
Rachal 102
T. F. 132
William 27, 102
Blankenship, Elizabeth
73
Elzira E. 71
M. L. 10
Mourning 85
Nancy 31
Peggy 38
Pollyan 104
Sarah 160
Spencer 159
Susanah 149
W. W. 80
Blankinship, Barnett 85
Elizabeth 31
Frances 69
Isham 137
John 2, 79, 125
Martha 103
Maryann 79
Nancy 2
Polly 65
Sally 125
Blanton, A. C. 164
A. J. 11
Anna 79

Blanton (cont.)
Arthur 11
B. S. 156
B. T. 135
Betsy 76
Burwell 76
Charles 61, 143
Elizabeth 145
Fanney 161
Franklin 55
G. E. 48, 100
George 11
Herod 95
J. H. 4, 64
James 11, 12, 103
Jas. 11
Jeremiah 11, 38, 40
John 80
Josiah 11, 12
Julian 37
Louisa 117
Lucinda 17
Martha 99
Mary 35, 114
Mary Malinda 33
N. E. 56
Nancy 144
Nancy M. 25
Nercissa 31
Obediah 156
P. J. 156
Pamela 90
Priscilla 18
Riley 11
Royley 11, 103
Rubin 161
S. F. 11
Sally 74
Sarah A. N. 106
Sarrah 156
Susanna 64
Tempy 40
Thos J. 10
W. G. 64
William (Sr.) 11
Wm. 9, 15, 161
Wm. C. 163
Wm. J. 96
Block, Rochig 96
Boheelar, Trisa 3
Bohela, Lucinda 27
Bohelar, Trissa 4
Boheler, Nancy 73
Rebecker 12
Bolton, Eliza 12
Elizabeth 7
John 7
Mary 56
Boman, Martha 44
Bomar, John 12
Bomgarner, Elisabeth 155
Bomgartner, Mary 24
Bonner, B. 139
Booker, Frances 106
Border, John 153
Borders, Emeline 26
John 26, 50
Bordes, John 15
Bostic, W. H. 68, 110
Bostick, Chesley 101
Cinda 91
G. T. 56
Geo T. 22
Martha 79
Mary 70
Nancy 64, 109
P. 22
Reubin 12

Bostick (cont.)
Richard 12, 166
Sally 101
Susannah 22
Tempy 96
Wm. 5
Bostwick, Elizabeth 109
Botts, William 99
Bowan, Edda 30
Mary F. 3
Bowden, Elizabeth 108
Bowen, Berry 117
Jos. 150
Lethe 35
Lewis (Jr.) 35
Bowers, Richard 34
Bowin, Mildred C. (Mrs.)
161
Bowman, A. 79
Asa 113
Catharine 127
Eda 99
Eli 44
Elizabeth 31, 167
J. B. 88
J. R. 24, 25, 49, 134
John 85
Louisa 85
Mary 44, 112
Nancy 40
Polly 99, 128
W. 44
Boyle, Reachell 65
Bracket, Joseph 124
Mary 37
Rachel 141
Ruelly 134
Thomas 47
William 132
Brackett, Frances 40
Nancy 153
Braddy, Catharine 143
Dolly 63
Jesse 63
Liddia 137
Margaret 93
Rachael 153
Braden, (?) 2
Bradley, A. 19
A. B. 80, 148
A. H. 139
Absalom 20
Amanda 14
Anny 41
Arminty 87
Betsy 74
Coalman 14, 88
Edward 14
Elizabeth 88
Frances 17
G. W. 14, 89
George 13
Henry 12
J. H. 83
J. J. 14, 17, 75, 83, 134
James Holland 13
Jane 19, 49
John 13, 14, 51, 53, 132
John J. 156
Jones 2, 6, 14, 42, 63, 88
Joseph 31
Lemman 5
Lucy 61
Lucy E. 3
M. P. 14

Burns (cont.)
Levy 19
Nancy 11
Sarah 11
Burton, A. W. 72
J. Melton 39
But, Nancy 143
Butler, A. 128
Aaron 142
Drisilia 138
Elizabeth 84
Emerillas 112
Frances 63
James D. 11
John 156
July An 154
Martha 26
Susan 63
Thomas 19
Wm. 27
Butner, Polly 48
Buttler, Elizebeth 36
Butts, Gabrel 139
Buyers, John 145
Byar, Abraham 7
Byars, Betsy 138
Charlotte 104
Eliz. 83
Elizabeth 7
James 7
Joseph 37
Milly 141
Nancy 152
Sarah 119
Byas, L. C. 13
Noah 162
Byers, B. B. 7, 15, 54,
55, 88, 130, 139,
157
Hannah 77
S. Burel 15
Bynum, John Gray 115
Byrd, James 17
Byrns, John 35
CHitwood, James 18
CRowder, Jarrel 29
Cabaniss, Geo. 102
James W. 22
W. H. 127
William H. 41
Cabines, Hester A. 18
Cady, Archibald 145
Cagdill, Fredrick 20
Cagle, Luvina 77
Callahan, A. B. 14, 58,
81, 83
Alfred B. 14, 123
Elisebeth A. 81
Elizabeth 65
J. H. 56
John H. 20
Luciller 83
Robert 123
Sarah 33
Callehan, Arty 162
Elvira 111
Callihan, Drury 20
Harriet 51
J. 100
John 20, 21, 80, 156
Malinda 141
Mary 79, 134
Newfany A. 79
Rhoda 80
Sally 21
Calloway, Jos. W. 45, 97
Joseph W. 68
Caloway, James 58

Calton, Dicy R. 47
Jinsey B. 143
Peggey 163
T. B. 143
Camp, Decdamia 68
Eliza 55, 122, 142
Geo. 20
George C. 1
Intha 77
James 51
Jane 2, 161
John 79
Joshua 57, 120
Julia B. 43
Langley B. 100
Lewis 142
Louisa 100
Lucy O. 7
M. S. 132
Mary 114
Mary C. 100
Mirah 135
Nancy E. 3
O. G. 125
Ruthy 120
Sarah 134, 159
Sarah L. 108
Sophia W. 45
St. Jno. 52
Stephen 3, 21
Susan A. 16
Terrell L. 21, 62
Thomas 70
Thos 70
Thos. 148
William 81, 159
William A. 128
Wm 21
Wm. 134
Campbell, A. B. 39
Anne 149
Caroline 1
Elizabeth 47
Nancy 58, 102
Polly 133
Robt. 21, 133
Canada, Jane 107
Canady, Mary 158
Canceller, Cay 23
Cancellor, John 21
Canipe, Nancey 9
Sarah Ann 130
Cannier(?), John 112
Cansellor, Sally 157
Cansiler, Julee 34
Cansler, Elisabeth 79
Canterell, Mary 85
Cantrell, Abraham 37
Cantrill, Abraham 92
Canup, Mary 166
Capel, Thomas 39
Carbender, Saml. 71
Samuel 73, 81
Carbenter, Samuel 69
Carbo, Harriet 15
Margaret 74
Carkews, Joseph 73
Carmichall, L. B. 99
Carn, M. D. 30
Carouth, Ruth 30
Carpeenter, P. A. 66
Carpenter, (?) 167
Barbary 124
Barbere 113
E. M. 3, 8, 22, 35,
36, 56, 95, 118,
119, 121, 122
Elisabeth 124

Carpenter (cont.)
Elizabeth 6
Emanuel M. 47, 79
Emanuel Morton 122
Fanny 96
J. A. 4, 32, 97, 110,
128
J. B. 89, 162
J. D. 22
J. H. 6, 12, 36, 49,
51, 52, 53, 68, 71,
78, 82, 95, 96, 97,
115, 118, 119, 122,
128, 129, 132, 144,
155, 156
J. L. 53
Jacob D. 143
James 70
Jas. H. 64, 142
John H. 9, 105, 109
Jonathan 117
Joseph 13, 22, 108,
113, 122, 134
K. T. 51
Kinchin 4
Manda C. 47
Margaret C. 63
Martha 143
Marthia Jane 22
Milly 36
Milly Ann 143
Minerva 135
Nancey 82
P. A. 80
P. D. 156
Peter A. 118, 133
Pheobe 18
Polly 39, 47
Ruthe 75
Sam 107, 134
Saml 117
Samuel 45, 69, 87, 127
Sary 87
Wm. 22
Carrell, John 26
Carrer, Harvy 30
Carrick, Catharine 130
Carrier, E. 23, 24, 45,
46, 71, 127
E. C. 45
E. R. 42
Elias 46, 142, 148
Ellen R. 130
H. D. 61
Harvey 162
Harvy 14, 33, 35
Jos B. 2
N. C. 108
Carrll, Dennis 165
Carruth, A. 135
Alexander 6, 22, 30
Alexr. 146
Elizabeth 62
Carson, Barbary 41
C. P. 58
Catharine 37
Cidney B. 136
Danl. 29
Dorias 96
Elisabeth 152
Elizabeth W. 98
Felix 23
Isabell C. 87
Isabella C. 9
James W. 24, 33, 49,
71, 103, 111, 157
Jane 23, 147
Janes W. 21

173

Conner (cont.)
Sarah A. 30
Susan 8
Wm. 29
Connor, Isaac 26
Constant, Edward 27
Ferreby 166
Consten, John 77
Cook, Edward 79, 101,
145
Elizabeth 62
Esther 83
Hanney 79
Hugh B. 19
Isam 27
James 33
Nancy 123
Polly 123
William 27
Cooke, Jas. 91
Cooksey, Elizabeth 82
Cool, Caty 26
Coon, M. 118
Coone, George 118
Ruth 10
Cooper, Catherine 119
Catty 67
Elizabeth 83, 97
John 138
Nancey 138
Saphirona 49
Wm 12
Wm. 83, 117
Wm. D. 50
Coopper, Martha 69
Copely, Ann 89
Copland, Sarah 156
Corbet, H. M. 25
Cornwall, John 48
Cornwell, Eliza J. 143
Micajah 141
Cornwiell, John 20
Corruth, Mary 6
Mary K. 132
Corson, Sarah 68
Corthron, Becky 92
Coston, Elizabeth
Caroline 107
William 107
Coulter, Alexander 80
Covel, Nancy 3
Covell, Jacob 115
Coventon, Martha 109
Patsey 28
Covignton, Mriah 117
Covington, A. J. 70
Anna 4
Drusilla 66, 84
J. N. 54, 117
Josiah 125, 151
Lucy 125
Mary 36
Nancy 75
Rebkah 143
Richard 28, 56
Richard (Sr.) 55
Sarah 157
Sussana 28
William 28, 55, 97
Wm. 98
Cowan, James L. 50
Sousan 8
Susanah 89
Coward, Cynthia E. 12
Elihue 28
Eliz. D. 77
James 25, 28, 166
Mary 150

Coward (cont.)
Rebecca 166
S. M. 94
Sarah 25
Winny 106
Cowder, Nancy 62
Cowen, H. 92
Cowherd, Cynthia 164
Coxe, Franklin 23
Sarah 125
Coxey, Amy 53
Ann 46
Kizeah 110
Mary 46
Sarah 13, 109
Coxsay, Osborn 28
Coxsey, Abigail 83
Absalom 3, 65
Coxsy, William 46
Coxy, Mary 128
Coykendawl, Jene 108
Crafford, Mary 80
Craigg, Anny 133
Elizabeth 142
Crain, Mofield 28
Crane, Anna 153
Craton, Elizabeth B. 28
Isaac 4, 31, 92, 97,
106, 139, 141
Crawford, A. W. 53
Ann (Mrs.) 133
D. L. 59
Dilliad 144
Emily 44
Emily Matilda 53
Francis 80
J. W. 161
Jas. 97, 143
Jno. 105
John 29, 89
Liddy 40
Polly 26
Saml. 133
Samuel 8, 29
Crean, Mayfield 124
Crease, Elizabeth 120
Crews, Joseph 32
Thomas 102
Cristmas, Catharine 17
Crook, Linda 137
Susannah 77
Crooks, Andr. 22
Milley A. C. 67
Polly 87
Sally 94
Crosby, Nancy 115
Cross, Elizabeth 25, 49
Crow, Abraham 124
Elijah 105
Gray 29
Green 144
Huldah L. 96
J. O. 135
James 125
James O. 74
Jasper L. 48
Jo 124
John 163
Martha 163
Susanna 113
Winnifred 107
Crowder, Bartlet 108
Bedy 40
Biddy 155
Catharine 49
Cynthia 33
Delilah 164
Elizabeth 113

Crowder (cont.)
Faney 107
James 31
Jarrel 29
John 7, 21
Lilly 121
Lisey 42
Polly 57
Rebeckka 88
Robert 164
Sally 63
Sarah 21
Srah 116
Susanna 106
William 63
Wm. 29
Cruise, Frances 1
Cud, Anna 82
Cufonton, Thos 62
Culbrath, William M. 55
Culbreath, Cathrine 3
Daniel 30
Edward 140
Elizabeth 146
H. 13, 30, 37, 57, 84,
88, 117, 128, 134
Henry 13, 19, 25, 27,
30, 75, 88, 105,
116, 117, 161
J. T. 35
James 30, 54, 146
John 69
Leathea Sofronia 55
Lorenzo D. 57
Martha 140
Providence 158
Rebecca 54
W. M. 7
William M. 30
Culbreth, Dulceney 139
Culen, Hanc 146
Culin, Joseph 143
Cullin, Joseph 146
Currier, H. D. 61
Curtis, Jonathan 102
Cutler, Samuel F. 99
Cysart, Nancy C. 72
Dalton, A. A. 32
Anna 113
Chretian 107
Elijah 2, 81
Elisebeth 5
Elizabeth 89
Elizabeth E. 133
Frances 133
Intha 89
James A. 30
James P. 30
Jesten 133
John 5, 95, 133
John C. 32
Jonthan 145
Malinda 26
Mary 115
Mary M. 79
Nancy 30
Polly 146
Rachel 146
Rhodey 32
Sally 46
Sarah 68, 74
Susan 32
Susanah 86
Susen 26
T. J. 70
Thomas 30
William 89
Daniel, Ann 54

175

Grant (cont.)
Sarah 119
Thomas 17, 53
William 53
Grason, Elizebeth 74
P. C. 73
P. L. 155
Graves, Eliza 23
Gray, Ann 95
Catharine 77
D. J. 54
David 45, 77
Elizabeth 111
George (Jr.) 61
Isabella 77
James 19, 44, 53, 143
James L. 77
Jane F. 4
John W. 2
Katharine 2
Lavinia 89
Mary M. 161
Sarah 138
Wm. A. 150
Grayson, B. G. 74
Elizabeth 45, 160
J. C. 17, 18, 82, 93
J. J. 107
J. S. 124, 135, 146,
151
Jno. M. 57, 81
Joseph 140
Joseph C. 53
K. J. M. 96, 124
Letty 120
Louisa 73
Polley 75
Rachel 31
Sally 34
Sarey M. 76
Wm. 90
Gready, Joseph 109
Greanhill, J. E. 64
Greeman, Lucy 67
Nancy M. 112
Green, Amos 82, 103,
133, 160
Artildia 43
B. 80
Bary 54
Benjamin 55
C. E. 27, 160
Catharine 141
Charlott 108
Cornelius 5
Dicy 5
Drury 72, 145
Drusilla 129
Drusy 19
Elijah 121
Elizabeth 30, 61, 93,
103
Elizebeth 164
Fanny 46
George 55
Green L. 56
H. B. 54
Harriat 54
Henrey 54
Henry 54, 165
Isaac 24
Isaiah 8
J. W. 98
James 18, 66, 80
Jane 147
John T. 104
Jonas 55
Jos P. 31, 32

Green (cont.)
Jos. 21
Joseph 18, 72, 98,
104, 129, 157
Joseph P. 143
Judy Ann 135
Leah 18
Lewis 56, 93
Lucinda 132
Margaret S. 55
Martha 109
Marthean 13
Mary 46, 55, 96, 112,
130, 146
Mary Ann 107
Mary J. 93
Maryan 16
Milly 54, 163
Minerva 119
Nancy 104
Nancy R. 159
Nann 18
Nelly 93
Nicy 92
O. C. 1
Patsy 56
Phebe 165
Polly 18, 93
Rachel 17, 30
Rebecca 65
Rebeckey 55
Rebekah 124
Rhoda 145
Rhody 17
S. D. 53
Sally 18, 69
Sarah 52, 122, 164
Sarah A. 70
Shade 155
Shadrach 54, 55
Susan 38
Susannah 19
Thomas 6, 10, 54, 55,
139
Thomas (Jr.) 24
Verzilla 41
Vienna 103
Viney 34
William 24, 36, 55, 62
William H. 52, 56
William Y. 29, 94
Willie 134
Willis 136
Winiford 162
Wm. 7, 54
Wm. H. 56, 62
Greenle, James H. 57
Greenway, Eliza A. 1
Greenwood, Hugh 57
Gregg, C. 95
Grice, Esther 20
Grifes, James 72
Griffin, Greenberry 57
Maryan 55
Matilda 30
Peggy 14
Polly 5, 51
Susana 53
Wm. L. 145
Grigg, Bannister 163
Burell 29
Burrel 8
Daniel 102
Elizabeth 89
Elizabeth R. 102
Febee 29
Federick 79
Frederick 113

Grigg (cont.)
Jain 78
Jesse 29
Nancy 117
Paschal T. 52, 116
Prissy 79
Sarah 121
Griggg, Poley 109
Griggs, Mary 138
Polly 59
Sarah 26
Griple, Sally 25
Grise, Genny 103
Grisle, Julyan 30
Grissle, Mary 117
Grist, Fanny 81
Reubin 102
Grizzle, Betsy 28
Rebecca 142
Temp. 68
Grogan, Mary 121
Thos. W. 121
Grose, Catherine 74
Philip H. 13
Priscilla 7
Gross, Eliza 148
Grove, Elizabeth 123
Groves, Cynthia 42
Elender 158
Jesse M. 58
Jincy 2
Malinda 58
Mira M. 3
Gualtney, John 83
Patsey 83
Gualtny, E. 165
Guffey, Eli 39
Elizabeth 89
Elizabeth E. 140
Fanny 58
G. B. 155
G. R. 154
George W. 59, 102, 105
Isabela 105
Isabella 86, 152
James 136
Jinny 123
John 21, 50, 58, 59,
86, 101, 117, 155
John S. 89
Martha 110
Mary J. 21
Mira M. 25
Nancy 20
Nancy M. 21
Polly 21
William 110
Wm 152
Guffy, Alvira 96
Ann M. 136
E. A. 105
Elizabeth 102
Jane R. 44
John 44, 59, 147
John R. 59
Martha M. 23
Mary Ann 95
Nancy L. 149
Sarrah 3
Sucky 36
Susanna 36
Guin, Henry 18
Gulin, George 81
Guthrie, Francis 37
Wm S. 148
Guttry, John 59
Gweltenney, John 19
Hadelston, David 19

Headleston (cont.)
132
Headlow, (?) 69
Hearn, Edman 125
Heddlestone, David 39
Rutha 136
Helms, James 106
Hembree, Abraham 67
Davis 67
Delilah 67
Hemphill, Margaret A. 44
Sarah E. 17
T. P. 17
Hemrick, Sealey 68
Henderson, Elizabeth 123
Irvin 87
Jane 84
Jeffferson 68
Mereney 79
Nancy (Mrs.) 146
Wm. 86
Hendrick, George 68
Nancy 88
Henry, William 166
Henseley, Mary 25
Hensley, Elizabeth J. 85
James 1
James A. 68, 127
Nancey C. 127
Nancy 66
Henson, Bartlett 97
C. L. 97, 100
Fanny 84
J. C. 68, 124
J. G. 142
James 68
Jane 115
Jno. 111
Mary 16
Mary H. 142
Philip 16
Phillip 64
Phillip (Sr.) 68
Sarah 144
T. G. 15
Herndon, Geo. 20
J. J. 162
John J. 23
M. A. 99
Wm. 9
Herron, Andrew 154
Heslep, Celia 48
Thomas 9, 48
Hester, James 69
Hesters, Cathrine 141
Hews, Mirah 125
Hey, James 120
Heyden, Narcissa 30
Hicks, B. F. 127
Bery 37
D. E. 43
Edith (Mrs.) 37
F. Y. 149
Hazzael 4
Martin 134
Mary C. 142
Milly 99
Susanah 138
Susanna 167
Thomas 157
W. G. 134
Wm 71
Wm. 16
Hider, John 156
Nancy 51
Polly 90
Susanna 90
Higgins, William 69

Hill, Alexander 70, 140
Arey 131
Asaph 70
Avington 78
Barbary 118
Barnet 113
Belariah 161
Charles 10, 70, 85,
90, 137
Charlotte 2
Daniel 161
David 69, 70, 149
Delila 131
Elisabeth 90, 134
Elizabeth 47, 118, 129
Geo. Washington 147
H. D. 114
Hannah 115
Hinto 162
Isaac 4
James 153
John 70, 117, 130
John S. 107
Lewis 114
Lizebeth 129
Louisa 59
Margaret 39, 90, 93,
119
Margret 65
Mary 70, 127
Milly 137
Mourning 118
Nancy 87, 139, 147
Oliva 162
Prisilla 82
Rachel 41, 60, 69
Reuben 135
Reubin 69
Rutha 39
Sally 2, 114
Sarah 151
Sophia 120
Stanhope 69
Susana 161
Susanna 27
W. 69
W. S. 100
William 70
Zilphia 88
Hilles, Sarah 20
Hilliard, Jesse 93
Hillman, Saml. 164
Hills, Avington 90, 114
Elizira 87
Harbard 118
Hennery 127
James 70, 71
John 30, 71
Mary 30
Olive 80
Prisila 86
Rob. 70
Robert 70, 118, 133
Rt. 118
Zadock 71, 139
Hilton, Winifred 76
Hines, Kindred 71
Mahala H. 6
Hinson, Elizabeth 118
Jane L. 46
Mary 142
Hip, Evaline 43
Hix, Elizabeth 143
Jane 155
John 71
Polly 38
Hobson, Nevill 93
Hockens, Martha 120

Hogan, William 16
Hoge, Salley 87
Hoges, Elizabeth 87
Hogin, Elizabeth 87
Nathaniel 87
Hogus, Jesse 7
Hoilifield, Mary L. 136
Hoke, Wm. J. 84
Holferd, Linna 149
Holford, Arminta 29
Holifield, Betsey 163
Cynthia 93
Isaac 119, 156, 163
Nolon 71
Holland, Lurany 127
Nercissa 62
Polly 112
Susannah 59
Theresa 13
Hollifield, A. P. 72, 93
H. C. 93
Harvey C. 114
Ransom 32
Sarah 156
Holyfield, Jane 78
Hopkins, Rachael 158
Hopper, B. T. 71
Diannah 27
Feriba 52
H. H. 51
Mary 52
Noah 51, 64
Rachel 166
Rosana 166
Hoppor, William 41
Hopson, Ann 93
Polly 146
Hord, John 21
Martha Maria S. S. 106
Mary Ann T. 21
Richd. T. 72
Susannah 20
Horde, Martha J. 98
Horn, Bettsey 73
Daniel 128
Elizabeth 100, 128
James 125
Jesy 73
Lydda 48
Rebecca 125
Sarah J. 37
Horne, Nancy 81
Horney, Wm. W. 73
Horse, Barbra 7
Horten, Elizabeth 147
Nancy P. 143
Horton, Edwin 72, 134
Elizabeth 36
Margaret 15
Nancy 7, 55
Paton 7
Rosey 36
Sarah 6, 39
Terrel 15
William 72
Winney 134
Houge, Rebecah 10
Houser, Caroline
Elizabeth 65
Sarah 53
Howard, Margaret 81
Howel, Thomas 73
Hower, H. H. 10
Howlett, Elisha 16
Howser, Eliza 103
H. H. 53, 73, 120
Sarah 73
Hoyl, Marget 166

184

Hoyl (cont.)
  Soln. 93
Hoyle, Benjamin 42
  David 163
  Elender 138
  Eliz. J. 126
  Frances 127
  Henry 93
  Joh 161
  John 158
  Pegga 158
Hoyles, Henry 73
Hraden, Hosea 12
Huchins, Mary 59
Huckabay, John 73
Huckaby, Lavina 16
  Martha 104
Huddelston, A. F. 39
Huddlestone, Agnis 73
  David 73
  Jean 73
  John 73
  Littuce 73
  Sarah 6
Huddleton, James 136
  Jane 21
Hudging, Wm. 74
Hudgins, N. P. 74
  Starling 101
Hudgs, Nimrod P. 74
Hudleston, James 21
Hudloe, Andrew 158
Hudlow, Andrew 33, 54,
  112
  Barbary 51
  Elizabeth 143
  Sarah 4
Huffmaster, Henrietta
  Augusta 94
Hufstedler, Wm. 42
Huggins, Elizabeth 109
  Martha 142
  Robert 3
Hughes, C. E. 96
  Elizabeth 95
  Malinda 37
  Minerva 81
  Nancy 46
Hughey, Hanah 34
Hughlen, Mary 8
Hughs, Benjamin 74
  Caty 154
  Isble 154
  John 154
  Katharine 154
  Lucinda 11, 102
  Sandford 11
Hullet, Elizabeth 56
  Mary 165
  Polly 165
Hullett, Elizabeth 121
  William W. 121
Humphres, John 74
Humphrey, Bryson 11
  Philip 111
Humphreys, Irvin 146
  James 120
  Jas. 90
  Malinda 14
  Mary 86
  Philip 64
  Polly 126, 158
  Precilla 65
  Rachel 138
  Sidia 158
Humphries, James 41
  Polly M. 137
Humphris, Arrana 95

Humphris (cont.)
  James 74
  Mary 115
Humphrys, Bannon 95
  James 14
Humpries, Sarah 157
Hunsinger, Adam 51
  Thomas 57
Hunt, A. 10, 34, 69, 74,
  134, 138, 142, 148
  A. (Rev.) 27
  Adam 59
  Cathrine 34
  Elisabeth 151, 154
  Eliza 10
  Elizabeth 144, 149
  Hanah 140
  Letty 98
  Lucinda 10
  Polly 81
  Rebecca 53
  Rebecca C. 48
  Ruth 125
  Sarah 34, 107
  Sinthy 29
  W. A. 74
  William 7, 74
  Wm. 50
Hunter, America 120
  Charlote 29
  Cynthia 6
  E. C. 47
  John 118
  Jonathan 69
  Jos. 114
  Joseph 23, 37, 69
  Martha 2
  Mary 61
  Matilda 139
  Nancy E. 67
  Peter 100
  Polly 29
  Rebecca C. 137
  Robert 78
  Sam. 29
  Saml. 29, 75
  Samuel 75
  Sarah 118
  Susan L. 86
  Thomas 112
  Thos 123
  W. 10
  William 10
  Wm. 139
Huntley, Joseph B. 19
  Miles W. 75
Huntly, T. E. 152
Huntsinger, Beck Ann 108
  John 75
  Nancy 113
  Parozade 92
Hurt, Betsey 86
  Polly 18
Hurtt, Joseph 18
Hutchens, Catharine 136
  Sarah 39
  Thos. 75
Hutchins, Betsy 154
  Elijah M. 75
  Intha 60
  Is. 76
  John 76, 154
  Martha 166
  Mary E. 58
  Moses 48
  Patsy 38
  Polly 140
  Sally 48, 70

Hutchins (cont.)
  W. D. 151
  Wm. D. 15, 73
Huthens, Elijah M. 136
Huton, Moses 80
Hutson, Moses 75
Hyde, Benjm. 5
Hyder, Amos L. 25
  Benjamin 76
  Benjamin (Jr.) 51
  Benjn. D. 76
  Catharine L. 85
  Catharine W. 78
  Harriett E. 129
  Maryan 25
Hyles, Andrew 148
  Elizabeth 143
Ingle, Mary 132
Irvin, A. C. 76
  Abram C. 42
  Esther 134
  Gavn 158
Irvine, A. W. 55
  Abram 22, 100
  Charlett L. 131
  Gavin 122
  Hanner 63
  Isaac J. 63
  John 17
  Margaret 70, 123
  Martin 76, 122
  O. B. 148, 151
  Thany 117
Irwin, James A. 105
  Mary 42
Isaacs, M. J. 83
Isbell, Lettice 31
Ives, George 78
Ivester, George 77
Ivy, G. W. 114
Jackson, Amos 24, 77
  Anna 24
  C. A. 156
  Elizabeth Elizer 35
  Jacob 35
  James 48, 82
  John 100
  Lucinda 77
  Margaret 158
  Mary Ann 87
  Nancy A. 42
  Patsey 75
  Patty 78
  Polly 116
  Soloman 77
  Susannah 118
  Syntha 82
Jaen, Sary 42
James, William 52
Jane, Frances Ellener 30
  Thom 30
Janes, Elizabeth 5, 86
  Fanny 44
  Jane 22
  Nancy 21
  Sally 33
  Thomas 33
  Thos. 22
Jarrel, Susan 75
Jarrell, Adam 59
  Mary 59
  Milton 77
Jay, J. V. 111, 126,
  129, 135, 150
  James V. 76, 143
  Jo. 132, 157
  Joseph 131
  Sally 163

Kelley (cont.)
Hanah 60
Henry 83
John 49
Zilphy 41
Kelly, A. J. 83
Henry 83
Polly 85
Keltor, Polley 131
Kenady, Catharine 72
Martha 51
Kenipe, Rebecca 104
Kenndy, Susan 135
Kennedy, Elizabeth 132
Kerr, Catharine 27, 90, 141
Clmmon 46
Eveline 85
H. W. 108
Henry M. 92
Jane 147
Lavina 89
Mary J. L. 94
Thomas 147
William K. 25
Kestler, Elisabeth A. 105
Ketter, Elizabeth 59
Keyel, John 13
Kilbern, Mary 8
Kilbreath, John 56
Kilkey, J. 20, 34, 82, 120
Killpartrick, Mary E. 13
Killpatrick, Cinthia G. 48
Dora C. 71
Kilpatrick, Eliza E. 144
Elvira M. 21
Ermyna R. 145
Hugh 84, 91
Intha E. 127
J. W. 21
James 48, 110, 167
Jane 91
Jane A. 34
Katharine W. 34
M. 113
M. H. 113, 144
Madison H. 34
Martha J. 60
Permealia 95
Polly 36
King, Barnabas 37, 40
Barnbas 22
Barney 8, 57
Catharine 94
Celia 117
Clary 105
Danniel 45
Dicy 9
Drury 142
Eliza 144
Henry 84
Jackson 146
Jane 94
Johnson S. 9
Jonas 85
Jonathan 27
L. 160
Lewis 118
Marey 142
Martha 35
Martha Ann 42
Martha B. 64
Mary 7
Nancey 142
Nancy 85

King (cont.)
Nancy N. 116
Noah 84
Rachel 57
Robert 156
Samuel 20
Samuel (Sr.) 85
Sarah 24
Kinley, Polly 86
Kirtien, Polly 85
Kistler, P. F. 93, 156
Paul F. 61, 64
Sarah 85
Kits, Elizabeth 21
Kizar, Rutha M. 129
Kizer, D. D. 129
Mary 129
Sarah 69, 76
Knipe, Jacob 21
Koon, Almira(?) 114
Elmira 161
Julia Ann 110
Mary 20
Naoma 113
Koone, Alvira 113
D. 44, 65, 70, 82
Damaris 110
Daniel D. 83
Dewalt 126
G. W. 85
Huldah 83
John 12, 59, 70, 85, 86, 129, 137, 155
Madison 113
Mary 126
Merion 147
Meron 111
William 57
Kuikendall, Rebekah 73
Kuykendall, James 76
Jesse 167
Lackett, Minerva 57
Lackey, James 86
Margret 140
Lademor, Prudence (Mrs.) 24
Lademouer, Rachel (Mrs.) 138
Lago, Jane 44
Laiswell, Daniel 101
Lambey, John 113
Lancaster, Louisa A. 128
Mary E. 41
Sarah J. 152
Wm. D. 119
Lancater, Arminta C. 139
Lancester, Parthenia 119
Land, Nancy 21
Lands, Mary 65
Lane, Archy 120
Jesse 86, 164
Letty 166
Peter 86
William 166
Lankford, John 22, 90
Judia 166
Matilda 146
Nathan 22
Patsey 45
Sally 90, 162
Sibey 22
Susanna 22
Lansing, Jane C. 55
Largant, Noah 86
Largen, Armentey 114
Arminey 114
Mary 75
Largent, George D. 75

Largent (cont.)
Lucinda 164
Sarah 13
Largin, Rebeceh B. 114
S. E. 155
Lashley, Elizabeth 74
Laswell, Danl. 107
Esther 107
Latimore, Jemima 81
Rachel 74
Susanah 102
Lattamore, Rachel 73
Lattimore, Francis 24
Jamima 98
John 73, 121, 134
Margaret 121
Thomas 24
Laughter, Ben 158
Catharine 114
Cintha 142
Elvira 167
Jemima 84
Katy 140
Nancy 52
Nelly 167
Samel 87
Samuel 44
Susanah 132
Wiley 52
Lawrence, Edith E. 23
Lawson, Lucy 145
Lea, Joseph 87
Patsey 97
Leadbetter, Easther 93
Ledbeter, A. M. 123
Ledbetter, Andrew 65
B. 88
Isaac (Jr.) 13
J. 111
J. R. 160
Jain 13
Jane 14
Jo. 88
John 41, 159
Johnston 65
Jonathan 60, 133, 162
Jonson 87
M. U. 88
Martha 111
Mary 121, 133, 153
Mary P. 133
Middy 13
Milly 161
N. H. 28
Nancy 159, 162
Patsey 153
Polly 65
R. O. 30, 89, 146, 149
Rebecca 42
Rhoda 160
Richard 88
Richard (Jr.) 133
Salinda 24
Sally 132
Sarah 160, 161
Tabitha 77
Temperance 113
Tempy 64
Tempy Malinda 5
Thomas 113
Thos. 163
Zilla 138
Ledford, Ca.Rah 54
Daniel H. 88
Ephraim 27
J. A. 68
Jesse 120
Lawson H. 88

Long (cont.)
  William 58, 73, 91, 92
  William (Cpt.) 10
  William J. 112
Lookado, Elizabeth 154
  George 92
Lookadoo, A. W. 58
  Belinda 140
  G. W. 100
  Gorge 92
  Henry 92
  Hulday L. 147
  Jesse 92, 140
  Jesse J. 92
  John 92
  Julia A. 88
  Parasade 147
  Wiley 22
Loqure, John 43
Lorance, Margaret 167
Love, Ann 61
  Charity 68
  Charles 68, 92, 123
  Elisabeth 131
  James 28, 75
  Nancy 123
Lovelace, D. 54
  Daniel 166
  G. L. 93
  J. S. 16
  James 92
  Malena 56
  Margaret 93
  Morgan R. 130
Loveles, Green 55
Loveless, D. 55
  James 124
  William 56
Lovelis, Eliz. 13
Lovies, James 93
Lovles, William 54
Loweless, Elizabeth 55
Lowrance, M. S. 93
Lowrey, Elizabeth 75
Lowry, Mary 135
Luallen, Ruth 21
Lucas, John 93
Lucket, Saml. 88
  Sarah 88
Luckett, Saml. 87
Luckydoo, Rachel 59
Lunsford, Dinsey 2
Luntesford, Sarah 29
Luquire, Mira 31
  Narcissa 103
  Viny 103
Lusk, William 146
Lyles, Adaline 10
  D. 45, 119, 167
  Elizabeth 42
  Harriet 97
  James 113, 155
  Mary L. 124
  Narcissa 101
  Shusanah 143
  Thomas 104
Lynch, A. A. 2
  A. K. 150
  Catharine E. 160
  E. C. 150
  E. M. 94
  Edison 84
  Elizabeth 34
  Evelina 85
  Eveline 6
  J. K. 94, 160
  Laxton 84
  Levina 130

Lynch (cont.)
  Malena 84
  Martha M. 84
  Mary 112
  Mary Amanda 84
  Mary L. 126
  Norman 93, 126
  Salina A. 165
  Sarah Ann 64
  W. M. 34
M'Callon, James 37
M'Clain, Charles 114
M'Dowell, Jos. 113
M'Gahey, Jos. 17
MCGauhey, Daniel 98
MGlamry, Jes 43
MacSwane, W. M. 129
Mackey, William 120
Maddin, Dan. 138
Maddox, Elizabeth Cox 87
Madeson, Jas. 74
Madison, Elizabeth 57
Magaha, Sarah 109
Maghe, Wm. 43
Magnes, Jacob 4, 101
Magness, Bangamin 101
  Caty 127
  Eliza 94
  Perygreen 113
  Robert 54, 101, 157
  Sarah 51
Mahrick, Sally 101
Malton, J. 141
Maneth, Marget 73
Manor, William 151
Mantieth, Sarah 73
Maraw, William 84
March, Hanah 145
Marloe, Patsy 10
Marlow, Almira M. 53
  C. M. 147
  Delpha 70
  Esther 114
  James 47, 53
  Jas. 47
  John 75
  Lucy 75
  Luvina 109
  Martha 131
  Melley 10
  R. F. 57
Marshal, Elizabeth 127
Marshall, Emily 21
  Rhue 58
Marshe, Nancy 86
Marshell, Elizabeth 141
Martail, Elizabeth 13
Martias, Benjamin 58
Martin, A. C. 125, 140
  Abraham 122
  Alice 48
  Alvira 128
  Betsy 120
  Carey J. 84
  John 4, 20, 102, 159
  John B. 43
  Jos. H. 108
  Lavina Nanny 167
  Lewis 87, 100
  Nancy 57
  Patey 20
  Sarah 144
  Thomas 30, 63
Martindale, Nelly 33
Mase, Dolley 11
Mashburne, Elizabeth 161
Mason, John 115
  Martha 102

Mason (cont.)
  Thos. 65
  William 102
Mathes, Mary 109
Mathews, Betsey 109
Matthes, Elizabeth 97
Matthews, Mary 72
Maxwell, William 3
May, Daniel 39, 66, 82,
    83, 89, 95, 160
Mayes, Stephen 16
  Stith 11, 60, 112
Mayfield, Polly 106
Mayhue, Viney 1
Mayhute, Wm. 1
Mayohu, William 138
Mays, Nancy 16
  Sarah 15
  Susannah 128
Mayse, Martha 158
Mc--, John 7
McAfee, Mary 106
  Robert 30, 146
  Robt. 93
  Susan M. 57
McArthur, E. 163
  Eleazor 109
  L. Elizabeth 64
  M. L. 50
  Walter 50
  Walter S. 94
McBrayar, Elizabeth 97
  Levisa 64
McBrayer, Amelia 41
  D. 15, 156
  Delila 163
  J. W. 9
  James 94
  L. N. 36
  L. P. 142
  Margaret 70
  Martha 157
  Rebakah 7
  William 136
  Wm. 95
McBrayor, Mary 81
McBrier, Leaher 64
McBryar, Samuel 95
McBryer, Catherine
    (Mrs.) 109
McCann, John 95
McCarthy, Morris 123
McClain, E. 20
  Eliza 5
  Rebekah 20
  Robert 7, 46
McClan, Robert 26
McClanon, Robert 144
McClarking, Nancy 150
McClean, Lcuinda 111
McClerkin, Hester 150
McCluer, Arthur 24, 36,
    37, 73, 84, 166
  Isaac D. 91
  John 36, 95
  Milly 95
  Richard 81
  Selia 129
McClure, Arthur 95
  Betsy 19
  Caroline 63
  Jane 19, 45, 143
  Margt. 37
  Mary 166
  Mary J. 35
McCollom, Polly 77
McCombs, (?) (Maj.) 41
  Betsey (Mrs.) 41

McCombs (cont.)
Judith 166
Sarah 64
Sheldrake 166
William 166
McCowess(?), Martin 119
McCraw, Bitha 70
Polley 74
McCraws, Beyard 96
McCrow, E. J. 28
K. J. 10, 29, 48, 124,
141, 159
McCure, Samuel 164
McCurry(?), Silas 96
McCurry, Christina 53
Cynthia 65
D. L. 58
D. S. 110, 152
Elizabeth 125
Hannah Olavine 135
J. L. S. 146
James M. 108
Jas. M. 88, 96
John 67, 96
John D. 148
Joseph 57, 73
Lewis 77
Lisa 166
M. S. 73, 155
Mareny 88
Margaret L. 147
Martha 144
Methena 108
Patsy 29
Peggy 104
Smith 96
W. A. 53
W. S. 31
McCury, Jos. 85
McDade, Rody 54
McDaniel, Andrew 22
Andy 165
Biddy S. 100, 164
D. D. 15, 125
Daniel 78, 96, 133
Dicey 69
Elicabeth 18
Elizabeth 19, 128
George 97
Hanah 64
J. B. 26, 27, 32, 40,
55, 56, 77, 88, 117,
136
James M. 61
James T. 45
Jane 165
Jason 71
John 81
John L. 40
Joseph R. 22
Julia Ann 92
Lydia 15
M. C. 15
M. P. 165
Mary 35
Mary M. 102
Moses 30
Nancy 102, 150
Nancy C. 71
Reuben 19, 96, 139
Sallie D. 165
Sally 81
Samson 96
Sarah 11, 96
Sarah M. 55
Susanah 40
Susannah 139
Tempey 142

McDaniel (cont.)
Thomas 150, 151, 165
William 133
McDanil, J. R. 49
McDannel, A. 154
McDanniel, Reuben 88
McDannil, William 66
McDaw, Elizabeth 126
McDonald, James 97
Lewis 119
McDonel, Jane 62
McDonnald, Catren 113
McDow, Elizabeth 37
Jane 148
John 126
Peggy 136
McDowel, Mirah 31
McDowell, M. A. 48
Martha M. 105
McEmore, Celia 127
McEntire, A. C. 148
A. G. 38, 70, 99, 134
Aaron 28, 55
Aron 165
Arthur 95
Drusilla 95
Drusy 12
Dulcena 18
Eliza 129
J. 27, 144
J. Y. 61
James 41, 110
Jane Eliza 134
Jno. 67
John 56, 141
Laura 69
Martha A. 48
Martha Jane 67
Mary A. 27
Rhoda 95
Roda 28
Samuel 12
Sarah 112
Sarah A. 1
Siller 106
Thomas L. 54
Thos L. 164
W. B. 34, 155
William 98
Wm. 28, 95
McFadden, Jane Elizabeth
144
Margarett 14
Salley 107
McFaddin, Martha 145
Susannah 5
McFaden, Margaret 152
McFadin, Alexander 8
Elias 140
McFarland, A. D. 98
Aaron D. 141
Alfred 149
Anna 98
Daniel 98
Eliza E. 49
James 23
Jno. 7
Jno. (Dr.) 6
Jno. A. 98
John 34, 56, 98, 145
John A. 49, 144
John E. 77, 98
Louisa 124
Margaret C. 98
Martha R. 23
Mary 23
Mary E. 155
Nancy G. 107

McFarland (cont.)
Rachael 34
Rebecca 23
Sarah D. 147
W. 98
Wm 104
Wm. 155
McGagha, Mira 159
McGahey, Rebecca 35
McGahhey, James 22
McGain, Polly 20
Thomas 20
McGaughy, Agnis 76
Alexander 115
Marget 17
Polly 3, 133
Rachel 77
McGauhey, Daniel 98
McGauhhey, James 98
McGaukey, Daniel 8
McGee, Mashew 53
McGehee, Martha M. 121
William 121
McGhey, Polly 22
McGiness, E. M. 162
McGinnis, Ausbun 119
McGintry, H. E. 152
McGlamrey, Hettey 130
McGlamry, Jesse 13, 134
McGowan, Nancy 99
McGowin, Polly 96
McGuin, Michael 8
McGuire, Nancy 105
Neelley 105
Sarah 67
Thomas 154
Westley 68
McGwin, Polly 157
McGwinn, Sarah M. 17
McGwire, Drusilla 165
Malinda 131
McHan, Alanson 99
Ann 100
Catharine 12
Daniel 99, 158
John 61
Nancy 146
McHann, Casea 31
Mary 14
Mary Ann 146
Mary M. 33
Thomas 99
Thoms 99
McIntier, Mary 110
McIntire, Alaxander 1
Polley 116
Rachel 28
Susaah 1
McKay, Jarusha 70
McKennie, Mary W. 142
McKeown, James 67
Thomas 125
McKiney, Alfred 142
McKinney, Alfred 51
Didamia 135
Elizabeth 14, 21
Henry 119
J. H. 161
Jane 100, 111
John (Jr.) 9
Jonathan H. 100
Leathy 55
Letha 100
Malenda 164
Nancy 151
Rebecca 17
Susanah 80
Thomas 142

McKinney (cont.)
W. A. 92
William 80, 97
William H. 72, 100, 164
Willis 100
Wm. H. 100
McKinny, Abram 149
Polly 81
Sallie A. 144
McKown, Jane 67
McLure, John 62
Talatha 62
McMaham, James 112
Nancy 112
McMahan, B. 16, 19, 36, 68, 154
Barnard 51
James 4, 63, 128
M. 165
Mary 68
Nancy 138
Rosanah 128
McMellion, Margaret 61
McMerrey, Patey 156
McMillian, Rebeca 115
McMillin, David 113
Elizabeth 36
Robt. 36
McMinn, Mary 78
McMorry, Sarah 122
McMory, Catherin C. 11
James 100
John 11, 26, 36
McMubry, Ann 63
McMurrey, Caroline 104
McMurry, Alzira 77
Anson 115
C. C. 77
Catherine 26
James 149
Jane 5
Nancy 149
Peggy 107
Samuel 77
McMury, Alston 13
Laura 106
Lorena 106
McNease, Nelly 108
McNeilly, Thomas 101
McNeley, John 156
McOme, Andess 19
McRenolds, Joseph 50
McReynolds, Ann 50
Hugh 100
James 50
Joseph 50
Robert 50
McRonneles, Betsey 100
McSwain, Betsa (Mrs.) 109
D. D. 93
George 16
Hannah 108
James 101
Lucy 101
Mary 16
Richard 61
Sarah 101
Susannah 61
William 101, 129, 151
Wm. 49, 60
McSwaine, Mary 60
McTire, Ellickander 101
McTyre, Martha 34
McWhirter, Milton 46
McWilliams, Mira 77
Mcglamery, Jessey 132

Mchan, A. 114
Mchann, Jeremiah 99
Mcmillin, Agniss 113
Mctire, Allick 28
Champeon 154
Mecom, J. R. 25
Medcalf, Elizebeth 94
Megahey, Elizebeth 98
Meggs, John 86
Meglamery, Sarah 132
Mellan, John 4
Melone, Mary 18
Melton, A. J. 135
A. W. 104
Alfred B. 104
Andrew J. 104
Artimincy 130
Barnabas 25
Burton J. 104
Cereny 136
Clara O. 92
Cornelius 103
D. F. 28
D. J. 164
D. S. 65
D. T. 135
Daniel 53, 93, 105
Daniel T. 10
David 39
Delpa 108
Drusilla 72, 158
E. D. 149
E. J. 87
Elijah 9, 126
Elisabeth 104
Elisha 104
Elizabeth 39, 45, 56, 81, 104, 112
Gilford 165
H. D. 107
Hiram 130
Huldah 103
Isaah W. 157
J. 155
J. H. 96
J. J. 103
J. S. 31
Jane 2
Jas. 108
Jerrel 45
Jesse R. 103
John 19
Joshua 104
Julian 57
L. F. 164
Lettice 104
Lettice J. 53
Lettuce W. 40
Letty 150
Lindsey F. 39, 45
Lucy M. 3
Lurena 104
Margaret 136
Margaret M. 136
Marguet 39
Marianna 108
Martha 103
Marvel 11
Marvell 155
Marvill 47, 119
Mary 104, 116, 130, 158
Mary L. 53
Milly 157
Minerva 39
Mirrah G. 11
Nancy 103, 104, 140
Nathan 104

Melton (cont.)
Olley 155
Patsey 157
Peggy 162
Polly 53
Rachael 103
Rebecca 159
Rebecca J. 157
Reuben 93, 104
Rhoda 54
S. A. 43
Sally 38, 54, 165
Saml. 158
Samuel 103, 104, 116
Sarah 104, 135
Sarah J. 73
Sarah L. 45
Sealy 117
Silas 127
Silas R. 45
Squir 105
Squire 96
Susan 29
Wm. 158
Menteeth, William (Jr.) 58
Menteith, Jane 58
Wm. 105
Meson, Sarah 158
Metcalf, Adaline 158
Catharine 96
Catharine E. 61
Elmina 49
Henry D. 105
Isabella 76
Louisa A. 76
Martha J. 94
Martha M. 76
Mary Jane 76
Polly 84
Quincy S. 105
W. Barton 14
W. D. 33
Warner 105
William 84, 134
William D. 36, 127, 162
Wm. 76
Metcalfe, Cynthia 14
Milley 30
Mical, Jacob 65
Michael, David 105
Francis 73
J. M. 152
M. A. 108
V. 148
Vincen 93
Vinson 85
Michal, Daniel 7, 31, 43, 106, 127, 135
Jacob 28, 70, 77, 110, 152
Jerry 47
Mary 33
Sarah 119
Sarah E. 6
Michel, Fanny 64
Miler, Sarah 38
Miles, Jasock 13
Millard, Joseph 105
Miller, Andrew 1, 120
Ann Elizabeth 9
Betty 148
Catharine 111
Charlotte M. 142
David 19
Elizabeth 43, 113
Elizabeth B. 28

Miller (cont.)
Esther 16
George W. 88
H. A. 7
H. M. 1, 107
Henry M. 63, 144
J. 36, 141
J. B. 149
James 31, 42, 71, 89
James (Jr.) 100
Jane 107
Jas. A. 106, 148
John 8, 105
John B. 108, 140
Jos. M. 106
Joseph B. 9
K. B. 161
Lilea 151
Martha 100, 148
Mary 1
Mary K. 106
Nancy 4
Polly 154
Sarah 9
Sarah D. 148
Susan 93
Susanana 160
W. H. 5, 9, 48, 111,
  161
William H. 133
Wm. H. 100, 110
Wm. J. T. 52
Milliard, Betsy Jane 57
Candis 117
Clarissa 84
Mary 57
Polly 153
Milligan, Mary 13
Mills, A. 123, 137
Amanda 106
Ambrose 43, 48, 76,
  85, 115, 131, 150,
  167
Ann E. 106
Elizabeth 33
Evaline 20
Falliby 105
Harriet 21
Jane 84
Jesse 126
John (Jr.) 167
L. A. 66
Margaret C. 23
Marvel 77
Milly 43, 166
Mourning 89
Nancy 2, 9
Noah 106
O. P. 121
Otis P. 24
Penelope E. 167
Polly 148
William E. 33
Willliam S. 106
Wm E. 136
Wm. S. 20
Milton, Letty 29
Pheby 90
Milwood, Nancy 117
Mince, M. A. 139
Minor, Margaret 19
Mitcalf, Betsy 36
Katharine 162
Mitchall, Rachael 6
Mitchel, Algey 77
Cathrin 52
Elizabeth 58
George 155

Mitchel (cont.)
Hannah 135
Jane 6, 100
Jane Almira 71
Jas. 58
Thaney 52
Wilam 139
William 126
Mitchell, Caldona A. 66
Clarisa A. 148
Ellet 74
H. G. 107
H. H. 51, 165
Martha J. 103
Narcissus L. 95
Parthena B. 50
Sarah R. 92
Mitchy, George 6
Mittchieford, Wm. 48
Moade, James 31
Moblitt, M. C. 53
Mode, A. 106
Andrew 107
G. 34
H. C. 124
J. 150
J. M. 155
J. T. 34, 64, 87, 88,
  107, 124, 134, 161
J. W. 91
Martha A. 49
Nancy 101
Nancy L. 154
Sarah 151
Seley 31
Viana 106
Wm. G. 15, 33, 59, 64,
  73, 74, 75, 81, 88,
  96, 98, 104, 107,
  108, 124, 134, 140,
  141, 144, 154, 158,
  161
Moffitt, W. P. 67
Monroe, Ann 24
Wm. 149
Montague, Charlotte 106
Nancy 132
Providence 4
Moode, Mary 149
Moody, N. Dan J. 154
Mooney, A. 76, 108, 111
Adolphus 105, 158
Alfred B. 85
Ann 151
Anna 22
Anne 121
Asa 108
Catharine 7
Chrysly 61
David 108, 150, 154
Drusilla 69
Eliza 120
Elizabeth 77
Frances 96
Geo. 96
George 10, 122
Jo. 9
Levina 39
M. O. 78, 154
Mary 8, 107, 147
Nancy 107
P. 103
Peter 18, 40
Sarah 15, 154
Solomon 108, 147
Susanah 122
Susanna 104
Wm. A. 61

Moony, Alfred B. 48
Elizabeth 145
Jonathan 108
Sarah 150
Moore, A. B. 102
A. P. 110
Acky 49
Acmy 74
Adline 93
Alfred B. 74
C. Andrew 115
Caleb A. 10, 41, 64,
  75
Catharine 142
Christina 72
Christy 37
Cintha 81
Delilah 43
Dicey 26
Elisha 90
Elizabeth 24, 63, 165
Francis 12, 148
Frankey 53
George M. 55
Jackson 93
James 19, 104
Jane 23
Jemima 92
Jno. 71
John 6, 10, 23, 40,
  44, 99, 109, 110,
  121
John (Jr.) 110
John (Sr.) 109
Judith 56
M. A. 33
M. R. 27
Malinda 99
Margaret 72, 104
Margaret L. 104
Martha 7
Marthy C. 80
Mary 50
Mary A. 23
Mary E. 83
Mary M. 64
Maryan 133
Matilda 23
Miranna 50
Nancy 66, 79
Nanney 41
Pegga 133
Peggy 56
Phillip 66, 116
Polly 6, 34, 56
Rachel 90
Rebecca 38
Richard 109
Ruth 123
Saleter 131
Salley 124
Sally 24, 54, 111
Sam. 28
Sarah 78
Susanah 160
Susannah 122
Thos. 95
William 121
Wilson 139
Wm. 104
Moorehead, Eliza 58
John 92
Mary Ann 92
Moorhead, Alexander 154
Enoch C. 20
Mary Ann 24
Moorlan, Mary 137
Moos, James C. 110

Parker (cont.)
Sally 121
Sarah 107
Thomas 158
Parkes, Thos. 94
Thos. L. 50
Parks, Benjn. 91
Nancy 35
Parot, Elisebeth 166
Parris, Polly 103
Parrish, Rebecca 148
Parsons, Everett 97
Leverett 162
Parten, Mirey 72
Paterson, Sarah 109
Pates, Fany 105
Patten, A. L. 3
Charity E.. 6
Mary M. 34
Pattern, James 120
Patterson, Betsey 10, 81
David 89, 121
Eunice 57
H. W. 2, 39, 77, 135
Hampton 127
John 120
Joseph 146
Marget 9
Martha 144
Mattey 109
Mimy 99
Nancy 89
Polly 30, 121
Robert 9, 57, 81
Salley 57
William 10
Patton, Charity 111
Elijah 24
Harriet 6
Margaret M. 7
Nancy Ann 78
Rachael 112
Tho. T. 164
Pattun, Elijah (Jr.) 112
Payne, Lewis 34
Marry 145
Nathaniel 145
Thos. 121
Pearson, Rebecca 95
Peele, Wille M. 137
Peeler, Andrew 91
Elizabeth 91
Henry 42
Maryan 91
Peet, Andrew 114
Pell, Jonathn 152
Mira 82
Polly 149
Sarah 119
William 82, 84, 119
Pendergrass, J. R. 104
Pentuff, Carline 119
Nancey A. 8
Robert 121
Perkins, Elisa 4
Eliza 86
J. E. 4, 141
John E. 86
Perkson, Malinda C. 38
Person, John 109
Peterson, Sally·158
Petters, Channy 50
Pettit, Henry 69
Petty, John T. 57
Joseph 84
William L. 57
Philbeck, Delila 59
Drusey 69

Philbeck (cont.)
Elizebeth 54
Georg 122
George 54, 59
J. P. 122
James P. 128
Polly 32
Richard 32
Robert R. 128
Wm. H. 121
Philips, Hannah 156
Hilmon 95
J. P. 122
Jane 6
L. F. 113
Lawson 118
Martha Jane 51
Matilda 130
Rebecah 97
Sampson 70, 71
Stephen 33
Temperance 70
Phillips, D. D. 63
Maryann 86
Philps, Angelina 64
Picket, Matilda 139
William 33
Pinner, Ransom 122
Pintuff, Elmina 8
Planton, George 74
Plummer, Polley 159
Poap, Lercresa 59
Poastor, Rachel 125
Poindexter, George C.
149
Polk, Lean 117
Pollard, Elizabeth 165
Polly, Sally 141
Ponder, George W. 96
Ransom 130
Ponds, Ransom 139
Ponnel, D. 2, 158
Ponnell, D. 11, 29, 38,
50, 61, 71, 92, 100,
119, 132, 140, 144,
152, 158
Dove 122
M. 15
Ponter, Eave 33
George 33
Pool, Anna 7
Cary 102
Diadamy 72
Dicy 68
Fanney 88
Pope, Benj. 122
Benjamin 79, 80
Caroline 80
Charlotte 105
L. C. 9, 21
Lydia 9
Nancy 47
Sarah 166
Sarah Ann 125
Porter, Alexander 9
Ann 47
Elasebeth 83
Elizabeth 127
Jas. 102
Malinda 81
Margaret 19
Polly 43
Robert S. 135
Ruth 155
Sally 42
Sally Lee 135
Samuel G. 158
Sophia 74

Porter (cont.)
W. P. 82
Wm. P. 155
Poston, Nancy 116
Robert 137
Postor, William 125
Potiet, Margaret 68
Potter, Robt. 115
Potts, Elizabeth 144
Katherine 162
Sally 99
Powel, Malissa 44
Powell, Huldah 90
Joseph W. 75
Mary 151
Milly 71
Prater, Thomas 43
Prather, Mary A. 138
Nelly 76
Wm. C. 138
Prator, Ann 40
Thomas 40
Preston, Lewis 76
Prewett, Jamimah 17
Prewitt, Edy 143
Price, Anna 124
D. M. 102
Drucilla 151
Drury D. 124
Eliza 29
Elizabeth 86, 153
Emily 119
Esther 61
Frederick F. 90
Isabel 123
J. M. M. 53
J. W. 116
Jane B. 124
John 82, 98
John (Jr.) 49
John M. M. 124, 128
John R. 151
John S. 124
Leanan 4
Leanner 124
Letty 8
Lewis 124
Luciler Ann 123
Luis 110
Mary 23, 148
Mary B. 12
Mary T. 119
Mijamin 58, 93, 151
Mry L. 161
Nancy 116
Nancy J. 152
Nancy M. 128
Olivine M. 12
R. M. 123, 152
R. T. 46, 98, 161
Richard 123
Robert 46
Robert L. 98
Robert T. 124
Robt. T. 124
S. E. 58
Sabra 72
Sally 31, 32
Sampson 29
Sarah Ann 121
Sarah L. 64
Spencer 124
Starling 18
Tabitha 49
William L. 123, 124
Winney 98
Wm. G. 49, 108, 124
Pricne, John H. 17

Scott (cont.)
William 86, 143
Scruggs, Danial A. 60
Daniel 132
David 132
Eliza 118
Elizabeth 80
Jesse 15
Margaret 71
Naney 144
Pruddy 83
Rebecca 38
Robert 83, 144
Sally 66
Sarah J. 60
Tempia 36
Scrugs, Deademia 15
Elizabeth 35
Mary A. 80
Rosannar 9
Searcy, D. T. 16
David 126, 132
Elijah 132, 133, 163
Hiram 33, 55
John D. 44
Lucinda 74
Lusinda 73
M. A. 101
Martha 25
Martha E. 66
Mary 52
Mildred 126
Milley 46
P. F. 164
Paul F. 42
Poley 150
Richard 126
Robert (Jr.) 88
S. D. 133
S. U. 94
Searsey, D. T. 113
Malinda 74
Richard 133
Sebastian, Edmond 94
Seffus, Salley 7
Selah, Sarah 24
Selers, Isac 133
Self, Betsey 128
Eliah 20
John 128
William 167
Sellers, Isaac 60
Polly 60
Sarah 25
Seratt, Polly 45
Sercy, Richard 112
Settle, Bush 133
Bushard 133
Geo. 133
Seward, Caty 47
Jane 48
Shadocks, John 132
Shagog, Richard 50
Shake, Sarah 125
Shamwell, Dicey 92
Mary 47
Nancy 47
Shanon, Elizabeth 66
Shaw, Bassil 133
Charity 142
Shean, Elizabeth 33
Shearor, John 153
Sheaves, Jas. 11
Sheehen, Sarah 46
Sheets, Wm. C. 48
Shehan, James 75
Mary A. 75
Shelly, Nancy E. 151

Shelton, Anne 87
Joel 87
Winny 118
Shemwell, N. E. 4
Shinn, John 141
Shipman, Elizabeth 18
Jacob 18
Shipp, W. M. 31
Shitle, C. E. 8
J. 14
Jeremiah 133
Shitles, Elisa 39
Short, Charles 120
Eliza 159
John 6
Peggy 120
Rachel C. 134
Shotwell, F. A. 90
N. 3, 20
N. (Rev.) 24
Nl. 42, 61, 81, 106,
111, 134, 148, 154,
155
Nl. (Rev.) 42
Shoup, Susanah 166
Shroud, Sarah 6
Shuemaker, Landy 36
Sides, John 143
Mary 167
Sills, Jesse 144
Joseph 142
Silvers, Sidney 81
Silvey, William 145
Silvy, Sarah 145
Simmons, Betsay 7
Bradley 85
Charles 111
E. J. 20
John 11
M. F. 43
M. L. 69
M. W. 20
Mary A. 78
Mary M. L. 73
Mildred M. 76
Moses 32, 73, 135
Nancey 15
Phebe 90
Rebecah 134
Rhoda 137
Squire 7
Simons, Ruth 101
Sims, Elizabeth 25
Jane 124
Littleton 25, 117, 124
Mary 157
Rachel 9, 117
Sarah A. 9
Susan C. 92
Singeltary, Nancey 33
Singletary, James 27
Singleton, Nancy 56
Sisk, Mary 81
William 149
Sism, Nancy 46
Slade, W. 135
William 27
Sloan, H. E. 115
J. B. 28, 132
Sloop, George H. 122
Mary Ann 122
Smart(?), Moses 51
Smart, Betsey 16
Cornelius C. 76
Deide 19
Elizabeth 76, 105, 126
H. K. 23, 58
Isabella C. 151

Smart (cont.)
Izabella 59
James 59
Jane 92, 146, 155
Jane H. 159
John 136
Jos. 16, 49
Joseph 16, 136
Katharine 162
Margaret 9, 16
Margret 129
Martha 16
Mary 1
Mary C. 105
Mary E. 86
Polly 49, 56
THomas 19
Thomas 103, 136
William 58, 59
Smat, William 26
Smawley, J. B. 5
Smelly, Clary 45
Smiley, Clary W. 104
Eliza 92
Elsey W. 160
Henry 166
Jesse 65, 136
Lurany 136
M. 75
Martha Ann 76
Mary 92
R. M. 160
Smily, Jesse 136
Smith, A. 69
Adaline 30
Ann Mary 128
Anna 71
B. 93
Betsey 163
C. 21
Campbell 30, 48
Caroline J. 20
Catharine 149
Charles 136
Charlotte 127
Daniel 41, 137
Edmon 26
Edy 21
Eliz. 77
Elizabeth 15, 82, 141
Hanah 20
Hannah 129
Ivy 156
Jacob 62, 99, 137, 138
Jain 71
James 17, 82
James (Maj.) 39
James J. 46
Jane 98, 106, 142
Jinsy 26
Jo. 71
Joel 35, 62, 137, 166
John 71, 142
John G. 137
Julia 65
Laben 60
Leonra S. D. 38
Lucinda 78, 99, 115
Lucy 119
M. 65
Malvina 18
Margrett 150
Maria L. 41
Martha N. 117
Mary 143, 149
Mary A. 35
Mary Ann 142
Melinda 62

Smith (cont.)
Minimia 71
Minor W. 37
N. S. 83
Nancy 46, 54, 140, 150
Nancy T. 18
Other 138
Peggy 100
Polly 25, 121
Priscilla 118
Rachel 82
Rbt. 157
Rebakah 101
Rebecca 134, 139
Robert 80, 106
Sarah 134
Susannah 18
Thomas 137
Thos. C. 140
Tolliver 46, 50
Walton 163
Willey 145
William 38, 71, 150
Wm. 42, 137
Snider, Elizabeth 97
Joseph Berry 120
Margeret 125
Susana 133
Snowden, Susanna 51
Somers, J. N. 20
Sorrells, Rebecca 6
T. P. 126
Sorrels, (?) 146
Ama 56
Elizabeth 28
Elizebeth 21
J. P. 114
James 75, 110
James H. 139
Jane 114
John (Jr.) 102
Katy 110
L. F. 139
Lusinda 82
Malinda 82
Margaret 48
Mary Ann 159
Nancy 141
Olive 12
T. P. 4, 10, 46, 67,
71, 82, 83, 114
Walter 48
Wm. W. 12
South, Tabitha 73
Souther, Sally 50
Soward, Frances 115
Mary 103
Spake, George 139
Spann, William 43
Sparks, Alpha 37
Calvin J. 43
MAry E. 94
Mary A. 32
Spawn, Wm. 40
Sperling, Mary 97
Spicer, Deliah 82
Mary 87
Nancy 48
Sarah 55
Spivey, Polly 133
Spivy, Betsey 133
Splaun, Sebary 68
Splawn, William 139
William (Sr.) 139
Spratt, James M. 2, 21,
74, 86, 136
Jas. M. 2, 42, 43, 44,
57, 58, 59, 75, 86,

Spratt (cont.)
101, 140, 141, 146,
149, 152, 154
Lora A. 112
Springfield, Katy 84
Sprouce, Margaret 79
Mary 94
Wm. 79
Sprulin, Drusilla 3
Isaac 3
Spurlin, Anna 108
C. W. 140
Jesse 68
Martha L. 7
Nancy 125
Sarah 137
Susanah 80
Wesley S. 55
Spurling, Mary 130
Stacy, Henrietta L. 91
M. J. 152
Osborne 1
Stafford, Belinda 91
Lavina 50
Marthy J. 164
Nimrod S. 153
Nimrod T. 20
Stephen L. 91
Standford, Mary 36
Stanley, Nancy 77
Starkes, Sarah 6
Staten, Catharine 84
Jane (Mrs.) 140
Mary 81
Staton, Anderson R. 140
Clarkey Ann 121
Steadman, Albert 132
Stedman, James A. 138
Sarah 112
Stephens, H. L. 8
Stepp, Rebecker 84
Sterling, Mary 139
Stewart, Jane 120
Luraner 98
William 98
Stewman, Lithy 154
Stice, Charles 141
Elizebeth 42
Patsey 145
Philip 126, 141, 145
Phillip 62
Polly 126
S. 81
Susanah 75
Still, Eave 77
Elizabeth 86
Stinnit, Kissy 8
Stinson, Joseph 115
Stockton, Davis 38, 63
Stogden, Susannah 57
Stogdon, Sophiah 78
Stokes, Frances T. 6
William 6
Stone, Anthony 113
Sally 59
Samuel 24, 115, 117
Storkton, Thomas 138
Stot, Marey 60
Stott, Elizabeth 135
H. E. 40
Louisa E. 70
Nancey 113
Stover, Jacob 141
Street, Anthony 45
Cinthia 45
J. P. 103
Jesse R. 141
Jinsy 29

Street (cont.)
Leviney 69
Margaret 28
Nancy 150
Rachel 45
Stricling, M. J. 68
Stumon, Jinney 16
Sullings, Salley 83
Sullins, J. 38
Jesse 7, 39
Josiah 89, 146, 158
Noah 42, 138
Z. 15
Za. 83
Zachariah 66
Summerhill, Eliza. 157
Jno 157
Summy, Peter 45
Sumner, James 29
Surcey, Sary 74
Sursey, Affa B. 102
Martha 88
Mary 117
Nancy 13
Suttelles, Nancy 22
Suttin, Cynthia 29
Suttle, Buchrod 142
Bushrod 84
Catharine 13
Catharine M. 64
Easther 64
Elizabeth 112
George 66, 164
George M. 142
Irena 165
James W. 64
Jane 12
Jas 164
Jos. 64
Joseph 96, 153, 163
Judieth 22
Mark 142
Martha M. 152
May 156
Nancy 7
Sarah 64
Urcillah 64
Suttles, Isaac 142
J. H. 41
Lydia 164
M. E. 45
Maryan 154
Nassy 77
Peggy 133
Sarah 84
Susan 83
Sutton, Betsey 144
Edmund 142
Elias R. 68
Eliza 68
Elizabeth 57
James 38, 142
Jas. 79
Martha 119
Marvel 36
Marvill 143
Mary 25
Matilda 9
Middleton 68, 120
Milly 142
Mirah 38
Polly 142
Powell 144
Robert 85, 162
Robt. 143
William 38, 84, 142
William (Jr.) 142
Swafford, James 24

199

Truelove, Betsey 47
James 119
Tubbs, Elisabeth 5
Tucker, John 103
Tunnel, Catherine 27
Turner, Matthathas 148
Missiner 146
Robert 127
Samuel (Sr.) 148
Turpin, Salley Richards
46
Thomas 46
Twitty, Allen 65
Bellanah 55
D. J. 41, 102, 106,
108, 134
Delia E. 102
E. 161
Louisa 97
Margaret A. 20
Mary 24
Mildred 12
Robert G. 25, 52, 94,
132, 154
Robt. G. 46, 103, 111,
160, 161
Sarah 145
Susana 106
Susanna 52
T. B. 146
Toliver 93
W. 26
W. L. 45
William 12, 71
Wm. 134
Wm. L. 20
Twity, Mary 98
Tyas, Sarah 50
Tyler, Anney 1
Polly 7
Umptres, Wm. 158
Underwood, Joseph 6
Upchurch, Adam 19
Daniel 149
Elias 54, 147, 157
J. S. 95
John 134
Josep 148
Joseph 149
Lucy 157
Mary 107
Mildred 19
Nancy 63, 119
Sarah 75
Sherod 121
Sherrod 61
Upgrove, Sally 149
Upton, Betsey 158
Daniel 79
E. R. 64
Elizabeth 13
Mary 70
Rebecca 96
Sarah 81
Scyntha 103
Thomas 70, 158
Usery, Lively 25
VAughan, J. J. G. 116
Vance, S. C. 10
Vanhoose, Lucy 47
Vansant, Lewis 53
Vanzant, Abram 149
Jacob 150
James 53
Rachel 53
Vassey, Charity 64
Prusia 78
Vassy, Mary 78

Vaughan, J. J. G. 116
Vaughn, Elizabeth 14
Florabell 116
Vermilion, Betsey 46
Vess, Belinda 13
Josiah 39
Vickers, Amanda 21
Harriet 135
J. M. 136
James B. 91
John 77, 123
Louisa 8
Margret 61
Mary 66
Sarah A. 136
Terrissa 58
Vickory, Susanna 143
WHite, William 125
WIlkinson, Polley 98
WIlliams, Ligt. 113
WIllkie, Joseph C. 94
Sarah 52
Wadkins, Betsey 48
Conny 115
Elisabeth 100
Elizabeth 36, 83
Elzira 47
Joel 83
John 163
Judy 135
Polly 87
Temperance 4
Wadlington, Delila 65
Waggoner, Nancy 21
Polly 156
Rachel 137
Walbert, Christopher 167
Elizabeth 167
Waldrop, Edmond 146
Edmund 118
J. C. 150
J. E. A. 167
Jechonias 83
Joseph 150
Joseph C. 17, 84, 106
Katharine 146
Lavinia 165
Luke 1, 17, 82, 100,
160, 167
M. R. 33
Mahala C. 115
Mary Ann 150
Narcissa 118
Prishy 118
Rebeca 4
T. D. 4
Waldrope, Margit 83
Waldroup, Jane 139
Walker, Amy 121
Anna 59
Betsey 137
C. B. 31
C. S. 61
Catharine 97
Cynthia 122
D. D. 152
David 97, 141, 151,
166
Dulcena 83
Elijah 34, 158
Elizabeth 24, 121, 141
Emly 103
Eunice 158
F. 50
Felix 14
Harriet 120
Isebella 150
J. B. 29

Walker (cont.)
J. R. (Jr.) 45
J. S. 123
J. W. 150
Jacob 151
James L. 79
James M. 109
Jane 47, 135, 162
Jeremiah (Jr.) 151
Jesse Richson 141
Joel 151, 152
John 6, 28, 41, 97,
129, 149, 151
John S. 150
Jonathan 3, 24, 121,
125
Joseph 9, 22
L. J. (Mrs.) 16
Lorin 90
Lucinda 103
Lucrecy 79
Malinda 52
Margery 37
Martha 29, 73
Martha An 110
Martha L. (Mrs.) 157
Martin 2, 25, 49, 152,
155
Mary 29
Mary A. 94
Mary J. 10
Mary M. 12
Minervy 163
N. E. 41, 94
Nancy 61, 101, 132
Nancy C. 35
Nancy Mc. (Mrs.) 66
Rachel A. 103
Rebecah 101
S. A. 72
Sally 5, 38
Sarah 33, 97
Susanna 104
Susannah 30
T. M. 152
Thd. 34
Thomas 5, 8
Thos. 8
Ursilla 40
Usely 34
W. E. 116
Wiley S. 10
William 6, 43, 69, 151
Winney 14
Wm 157
Wm. E. 51, 151
Wm. J. 107
Walkins, Elizabeth 118
Nancy 74
Wall, A. C. 16, 17
Angeliley 151
Celia 152
Druzilla 35
Easter 71
Julana 151
L. H. 17
N. E. 158
Rosannah 105
W. 158
Willis 152
Wm. 51
Wallace, A. K. 25, 60
Eliza J. 139
Hanner Porter 123
Harbert 56
J. L. 47, 91, 150
M. A. 35
Quintina A. 82